Ensuring Minority
Success in
Corporate Management

PLENUM STUDIES IN WORK AND INDUSTRY

Series Editors:
Ivar Berg, *University of Pennsylvania, Philadelphia, Pennsylvania*
and Arne L. Kalleberg, *University of North Carolina, Chapel Hill, North Carolina*

WORK AND INDUSTRY
Structures, Markets, and Processes
Arne L. Kalleberg and Ivar Berg

ENSURING MINORITY SUCCESS IN CORPORATE MANAGEMENT
Edited by Donna E. Thompson and Nancy DiTomaso

INDUSTRIES, FIRMS, AND JOBS
Sociological and Economic Approaches
Edited by George Farkas and Paula England

MATERNAL EMPLOYMENT AND CHILDREN'S DEVELOPMENT
Longitudinal Research
Edited by Adele Eskeles Gottfried and Allan W. Gottfried

WORKERS, MANAGERS, AND TECHNOLOGICAL CHANGE
Emerging Patterns of Labor Relations
Edited by Daniel B. Cornfield

Ensuring Minority Success in Corporate Management

Edited by

Donna E. Thompson

and

Nancy DiTomaso

Rutgers Graduate School of Management
Newark, New Jersey

Plenum Press • New York and London

Library of Congress Cataloging in Publication Data

Ensuring minority success in corporate management / edited by Donna E. Thompson
and Nancy DiTomaso.
    p.   cm.—(Plenum studies in work and industry)
    Proceedings of a symposium sponsored by Rutgers Graduate School of Manage-
ment.
    Bibliography: p.
    Includes index.
    ISBN 0-306-42944-6
    1. Minority executives—United States—Congresses. I. Thompson, Donna E. II.
DiTomaso, Nancy. III. Series: Rutgers University. Graduate School of Management.
HD38.25.U6E57   1988   88-19683
658.4'09'089—dc19   CIP

© 1988 Plenum Press, New York
A Division of Plenum Publishing Corporation
233 Spring Street, New York, N.Y. 10013

Printed in the United States of America

To Jack, Lauren, and Ryan
and to Tom and Jessica

Contributors

Antonio Acevedo, Vice President, Bankers Trust Co., New York, New York

Robert N. Beck, Executive Vice President, Corporate Human Resources, Bank of America, San Francisco, California

David H. Blake, Dean, Rutgers Graduate School of Management, Newark, New Jersey

Ernest D. Chu, Vice President and Chief Financial Officer, HABER, Inc., Towaco, New Jersey

David R. Clare, President, Johnson & Johnson, New Brunswick, New Jersey

Wilbert S. Crump, Director, Equal Employment Opportunity, Allied Signal Inc., Morristown, New Jersey

George Davis, Department of English, Rutgers, The State University of New Jersey, Newark, New Jersey

Nancy DiTomaso, Rutgers Graduate School of Management, Newark, New Jersey

Elizabeth P. Dixon, Manager, Corporate Equal Opportunity Policy, AT&T, Basking Ridge, New Jersey

Horace B. Edwards, Secretary of Transportation, State of Kansas, Topeka, Kansas

John P. Fernandez, Division Manager, Human Resource Forecasting and Planning, AT&T, Basking Ridge, New Jersey

David L. Ford, Jr., School of Management, The University of Texas at Dallas, Richardson, Texas

Robert A. Hofstader, Manager, Education and Development Unit, Exxon Research and Engineering Company, Florham Park, New Jersey

William F. Holmes, Vice President and Manager, Equal Opportunity Programs, Bank of America, San Francisco, California

Ming Hsu, Director, New Jersey State Division of International Trade, Newark, New Jersey

International Business Machines Corporation, Armonk, New York

Lois M. Jackson, Manager, External Affairs, IBM World Trade Americas Group, International Business Machines Corporation, North Tarrytown, New York

John L. Jones, Director, Personnel, Americas Operations, Xerox Corporation, Stamford, Connecticut

Gail Judge, Vice President, Personnel, McNeil Pharmaceutical (a Johnson & Johnson company), Springhouse, Pennsylvania

Rosabeth Moss Kanter, Class of 1960 Professor of Business Administration, Harvard Business School, Boston, Massachusetts

Serafin U. Mariel, President, New York National Bank, Bronx, New York

Nancy L. Merritt, Senior Associate, de RECAT & Associates, Inc., San Jose, California (formerly with Bank of America, San Francisco, California)

Hector Juan Montes, Vice President, Matthews and Wright, Inc., New York, New York

James H. Scott, Treasurer, Amherst College, Amherst, Massachusetts

Shelley A. Smith, Department of Sociology, University of South Carolina, Columbia, South Carolina

Seymour Spilerman, Department of Sociology, Columbia University, New York, New York

Roy Stewart, Manager, Equal Opportunity/Affirmative Action, AT&T, Basking Ridge, New Jersey

Arthur Strohmer, Director, Human Resources, Merck & Co., Inc., Rahway, New Jersey

William Stubblefield, Hilton Head Island, South Carolina

Donna E. Thompson, Rutgers Graduate School of Management, Newark, New Jersey

Marta Tienda, Department of Sociology, University of Chicago, Chicago, Illinois

Mutsuo Yasumura, Senior Vice President, Cato Yasumura Behaeghel, Inc. (a fully owned subsidiary of Young and Rubicam), New York, New York

Foreword

To be a corporate executive in America is to achieve a universally recognized measure of personal and professional success. The high income, privilege, prestige, and authority enjoyed by most corporate executives all attest to "making it." That is why the advancement of racial and ethnic minorities into the executive suite is one of the key barometers of the nation's progress toward full equality of opportunity.

But the quest for equal opportunity in corporate management has been difficult and frustrating. Black, Hispanic, and Asian men and women are rarely found among those who run or significantly influence the direction of American corporations. The wide gap between the expectation and the reality is a continuing topic of interest to business leaders and racial and ethnic minorities, as well as to scholars of the business scene. This book edited by Thompson and DiTomaso contributes significantly to our understanding of this problem, and, most importantly, provides useful guidelines on what to do about it.

Interest in the diversity of corporate management comes at a time of unprecedented challenge to United States success in the world economy. American business must now compete against aggressive producers and financiers in Western Europe and Japan. More competition also has emerged from some of the rapidly developing countries in Latin America and the Pacific Rim. Our ability to design, manufacture, sell, and export goods and services in a global marketplace will increasingly determine our standard of living and prominence on the world stage.

The quality of human resources is a key element in the nation's ability to meet the global economic challenge. Success will require the development and use of the nation's best talent. We cannot afford to exclude any segment of the population and expect to prevail against our global competitors.

Equal employment opportunity (EEO) was not high on the nation's agenda until a quarter century ago when President John F. Kennedy issued an executive order that required companies holding government contracts to pursue affirmative action in their employee selection and promotion practices. The scope of EEO enforcement was widened considerably when Congress adopted Title VII of the Civil Rights Act of 1964, which created the Equal

Employment Opportunity Commission. Further strengthening of enforcement measures occurred during the past two decades through both executive and congressional actions.

But throughout the period of heightened interest in equal job opportunity, most of the attention was focused on entry-level blue and white collar occupations. To be sure, corporate management opportunities were not excluded from interest, but relatively few administrative complaints or court actions focused on middle management, and almost none on senior executive positions. Although few minorities were in management jobs, the enforcement emphasis focused elsewhere.

Even so, since the 1960s, there has been a marked change in the career goals of minority group students. Today, business administration is the dominant field of interest among black and Hispanic college students; 25 years ago, education and social sciences occupied that position. Increasing numbers of minority students have enrolled in Masters of Business Administration programs, in hopes of pursuing careers in professional management. The vanguard of the new minority-management elite has now entered corporate America, and is poised for the next step toward executive leadership.

And herein lies the problem. Because so few racial and ethnic minorities have broken through the ranks of middle management into senior executive positions, many have become frustrated, and some disgusted, with the corporate world. Black and Hispanic managers, in particular, believe they are being treated differently because of race, and many despair of ever reaching the executive suite. The experience of the vanguard minority managers has led some to abandon the quest for upward mobility and to seek better opportunities in entrepreneurship. Their experiences also influence the aspirations of younger minorities now completing their education in business studies, and looking ahead to careers in corporate management.

In short, the small number of racial minority executives who have moved into senior positions has raised serious questions about the fairness of corporate leaders and the competence of minority managers. A few have received attention in recent years as senior executives and even CEOs of major corporations: Jerry Williams at A. M. International, Barry Rand at Xerox, Richard Zoizueta at Coca-Cola; and Gerald Tsai at Primerica. But these men (there are no minority women in such positions) are extraordinary exceptions to the rule that corporate leadership in America is still a white, male preserve.

Earlier this year, *Black Enterprise* magazine identified 25 black senior executives of major Fortune 500 companies. A similar listing of Hispanic and Asian corporate executives would be difficult; no racial or ethnic minority group is represented in such positions in a percentage even remotely comparable to its presence in the total labor force.

It is easy to say that if the top executives of American corporations wanted minorities in the executive suite, they need only say the word, and it would happen. But as Thompson and DiTomaso and their contributors explain so clearly, that response to the problem is much too facile and glib. Some senior executives genuinely believe they have made a commitment to minority managerial advancement and are surprised, and often frustrated by the lack of progress. On the other hand some minority managers recognize the highly competitive and personalized process of advancement, and are determined to stick it out and try to beat the system.

It is important to understand clearly the problem of minority executive advancement if an effective solution can be found. As stated in the old Talsnudis proverb: "If you don't know where you're going, any road will take you there."

The beginning of wisdom may be to recognize that the status of racial and ethnic minorities in private corporations is closely bound up with the status of minorities in society as a whole. There is an unwritten, unspoken set of assumptions among white Americans about minorities that necessarily affects perceptions, attitudes, and behavior when it comes to evaluating minority-group talent and selecting minority-group managers for responsible and demanding assignments. Such perspectives and attitudes, often unconscious, but always learned at an early age, affect the opportunity spectrum for racial and ethnic minorities at all levels of development, from schooling to work experience. We do not live in a color-blind society although many aspire to that goal.

As a faculty member of the Wharton School, University of Pennsylvania, I met some of the young black MBAs who are now in corporate management. Some were the first in their family to receive a college education, and most chose business graduate studies after deciding not to pursue law, medicine, journalism, and other professions. Most came from families in which there was no one else experienced in corporate management, and had little, if any, knowledge of what to expect once they entered corporate life.

This is a transitional phenomenon in the widening career horizons of black and other minority professionals. One hopes that minorities will continue to obtain quality academic preparation for careers in business and management. As the general status of minorities in society improves, so, undoubtedly, will their presence in the executive suite.

But more can be done to manage the problem, and that is the message of this book. Thompson and DiTomaso begin with a major thesis: that a clear definition and better understanding of the problem of minority advancement will lead to the identification of organizational changes that will result in greater progress in the future. Through careful scholarship and dispassionate analysis, the book probes the vision of each major actor in the drama—employers and minority group managers. By sharing the perspectives of each—often sharply different on the nature and cause of the problem—it illuminates the often frustrating clash of interests that retards more rapid advancement of minorities into senior-level corporate positions. Thompson and DiTomaso suggest that all the actors must work harder to solve the upgrading problem, and can do so with more purpose and effectiveness if they direct their efforts toward organizational as well as attitudinal change. Time alone will not solve the problem, but perhaps time and skilled management can. If American corporate leaders cannot manage multiethnic diversity and take effective measures to use the best talents of all segments of the population, then what hope is there for business success in an increasingly diverse global environment? That is both the challenge and the opportunity presented in this book.

Bernard E. Anderson

Philadelphia

Preface

The premise on which this volume is based is that discrimination is a cost not only to those who are excluded but also to those who do the excluding. Therefore, ensuring minority success in corporate management is a goal that should be adopted by top managers of all corporations for their own benefit as well as for the benefit of society and of minority managers themselves. We are presenting a positive message: Our companies, our society, and the people within will be able to make better products, more innovative and creative decisions, and develop more satisfying work environments if all people who have a contribution to make are involved in a meaningful way. In a complex world, more information, more points of view, more ideas and reservations are better than fewer, and in an interdependent world, the more people who buy into a process, the more likely it will succeed. It is for these reasons that any excluded groups should be given opportunities to reach for and gain the highest levels of corporate management, to join the predominant world of white, Anglo males who currently make most of the decisions for the lives of others.

Not all of the messages are positive, however. We know the potential social costs of continued exclusion from the good things of life. We miss out on the potential benefits of change, and we accept substantial risks for maintaining the status quo. We read about it everywhere, and many experienced it in the United States in the 1960s. In fact, we heard the stories so often that many of us have become inured to them, or even more so, have denied that problems still remain (see Kluegel, 1985). So it is difficult in the face of what continues to be an extremely emotional and controversial set of issues to offer much that is new.

We want this volume to help break the dual cycle of minority pessimism and majority indifference by focusing on what has been done, and what can and should be done, rather than on what has not been done. Most of us think we know the problems—whether accurately or not—so the next step is problem solving. This is the organizing principle for this book.

The idea for this volume and much of the material grew out of the planning for a conference that was sponsored by Rutgers Graduate School of

Management and held on September 24–25, 1984. The conference was designed to facilitate communication between academic and corporate communities regarding the circumstances for minorities in management careers. In a preconference planning meeting with corporate executives, the message was clear: Tell us something we do not already know, show us what will work, do not just tell us again that there is a problem. This is what we set out to do, and from all accounts, succeeded. The conference combined the knowledge of nationally recognized speakers, the advantage of corporate case studies, the real-life experiences of minority managers, and the learning process of panel discussions, and the potential for action from group recommendations. All were focused on finding solutions.

The conference would not have been possible without the support of a number of people and organizations. Sponsoring a conference was made possible when Fred H. Hoag, Jr., was loaned to Rutgers Graduate School of Management from the IBM Corporation, as part of their Executive Loan Program. In consultation with Dean David H. Blake, a decision to hold a conference was made. Fred worked closely with the editors of this volume in planning the conference. Others on the faculty and staff of Rutgers Graduate School of Management also took part in the conference and its preparation. We want to thank them for their assistance: Robert Schlosser, Director of the Professional Accounting Program; Alfreda P. Robinson, Assistant Dean, Admissions; Hal P. Eastman, Chair, Organization Management Area; Elaine Frazier, Manager, Placement; Oscar Figueroa, President, Rutgers Minority Investment Corporation; Patricia Johnson, Director, Rutgers University Technical Assistance Program; Elizabeth R. Cohen, Assistant Dean, External Relations; Adele Weiss, Administrator, Student Services; Richard D. Marshall, Professor; and Joan Orner, Secretary.

In addition to the substantial financial support from IBM in both loaning Fred Hoag to the school and providing resources for developing the conference and the research associated with it, other corporations also provided resources to make the conference possible: Allied-Signal, Inc., AT&T, Burger King (Newark), The Coca-Cola Company, Exxon Corporation, Johnson & Johnson, Nabisco Brands, Inc., New York National Bank, Pfizer, Inc., Prudential Insurance Company of America, Public Service Electric & Gas Company, Sea-Land Corporation, and Xerox Corporation. Along with these, over 60 companies sent participants to the conference, which was limited to a total participation of 160 persons.

Students of Rutgers Graduate School of Management also played a large role in doing the legwork before and during the conference. There are too many of them to name, but several received job offers as a result of contacts made in the process of putting the conference together. Although time and space were limited, if we had it to do over again, we would have made students an even more integral part of the proceedings.

Also because of time and space limits, we could include on the program only a few of the executives, corporations, and academics whom we would like to have participated. In this volume, we tried to make up for that loss by adding to the original conference proceedings. In the process of making contacts and soliciting additional material for the book, we were made aware of similar efforts by others to the end of ensuring minority success.

We want to acknowledge especially the work of the American Association of Collegiate Schools of Business (AACSB), the major accrediting body for business schools, Action Committee on Upward Mobility of Minorities, a group created by the AACSB Program to Increase Minorities in Business (PIMIB) Task Force. The program is no longer in existence, but during its functioning it was helpful in our efforts to develop this book. The purpose of the committee was to formulate strategies to increase minority representation in all management levels of the business community. The committee included representatives from corporations, academic institutions, and other organizations that have been active toward this end. Funding for the committee came from corporations and foundations. We especially want to thank Robert N. Beck, Executive Vice President, and Nancy L. Merritt, former Vice President, of Bank of America, who carried out staff responsibilities for the PIMIB committee. They have shared with us the materials that they gathered from various corporations on current policies and procedures and the summaries of their own problem-solving discussions from the PIMIB Task Force, and we, in turn, shared with them the results of our research and materials from this volume.

As part of the conference planning, the editors of this volume, along with Dean David H. Blake, undertook to do a survey of major corporations on the current status of minority managers in their companies, along with their programs and policies in regard to advancing minority managers in management careers. This research was also funded by the money provided from IBM Corporation. Preliminary results from the survey were included in the conference, and final results are included here. We want to acknowledge as well the work of Martin Selzer in the preparation and analysis of data for the survey.

Although many provided financial resources or time, some in addition shared aspects of themselves. For academics, writing is a way of life, but for many corporate executives it is not so familiar a process. For corporations, putting things in writing often means making policy statements and that often involves many levels of approval before pieces can be released. We are, therefore, especially grateful to the corporate executives and the companies who were willing to take the extra effort to include their material in this volume. They did so because they felt it would help others in the collective process of ensuring minority success. We also thank the academic authors who contributed the results of their research.

One of the contributions we feel this book makes is the unique blend of academic and managerial content and of research-based and practice-based recommendations. Although the academic and research-based material may be faulted for not drawing out practical implications, the managerial and practice-based material can be faulted for not being placed in the context of generalizable research findings. By including both in this volume we hope to bridge the gap which often exists between the academic and nonacademic worlds. Researchers live by canons of scientific procedure; corporate managers' views undergo revisions in accord with their empirical experiences in their particular settings.

Any volume such as this one is a product of many people and events, and despite all best intentions, it sometimes seems to take an inordinate amount of time. With all the coordination and separate duties to put a manuscript together with so many different authors in so many different organizations, it often seemed we would never get that last level of approval or finish the last section of writing. Fortunately, as authors and editors we had a good working relationship that served both as encouragement and an example of the stimulation and creativity of collective effort. Our contributions to the volume are equal. We decided on name order by tossing a coin.

REFERENCES

Kluegel, James R. 1985. If there isn't a problem, you don't need a solution. *American Behavioral Scientist* 28:761–784.

Contents

PART IV. FINDING SOLUTIONS: COMING TO GRIPS
WITH THE ISSUES

Chapter 10

**Making It in the Corporation: Retrospectives of Successful Minority
Managers** **173**

     James H. Scott, Amherst College

     Horace B. Edwards, State of Kansas

     Lois M. Jackson, IBM Corporation

     William Stubblefield, Hilton Head Island

     Serafin U. Mariel, New York National Bank

     Hector Juan Montes, Matthews and Wright, Inc.

     Antonio Acevedo, Bankers Trust Co.

Ensuring Minority
Success in
Corporate Management

I
Introduction

1

Minority Success in Corporate Management

Nancy DiTomaso and Donna E. Thompson

"Making it" has been the focus of the decade of the 1980s in the United States. Some argue that this is because of the rapid change of the two decades preceding the 1980s; others point out that it is because changes in the economic structure of the country have made this generation the first to face lower economic attainment than their parents. And, some say it is due to a deterioration in moral character. No matter what the reasons, though, the evidence is clear: The number of majors in business and other job-related fields in colleges has jumped from just over 20% in 1965–1966 to over 40% in 1980–1981 (National Center for Education Statistics, 1983–1984:118–119). The only job-related field that did not experience substantial increases in growth during this period is education: Instead, it declined by about half. The biggest increase and the most popular field at this time is, by far, business and management, with even engineering and computer science lagging far behind. Needless to say, the traditional arts and science fields have, in turn, experienced steady declines in enrollment since about 1970.

"Making it" means several things to this generation. Most of all, it means a secure and sizable income, and there are apparently two ways to get it. One is to start your own business, and many have. But to do so, one needs to have working capital. Thousands of small businesses fail each year, and a frequent cause is undercapitalization. A second way to make it in this generation is to move up the corporate ladder. Making it in a corporation, in fact, is often seen as a means to eventually owning one's own business. Making it in the corpo-

Nancy DiTomaso and Donna E. Thompson • Rutgers Graduate School of Management, Newark, New Jersey 07102.

rate world can mean, among other things, accumulating cash and know-how to do it on your own. This is the American dream of the 1980s.

The 1980s, however, are both an extension of and a departure from the 1960s and 1970s. The social revolution of the 1960s and economic revolution of the 1970s produced the peculiarity of the 1980s. The social revolution opened doors that had previously been closed to minorities (and women). The economic revolution, which brought first stagflation and then a massive restructuring of the economy, undermined the traditional rules of the game for making it at the same time that increasingly more people wanted to try. This brings us to the purpose of this book, namely to understand how minorities have fared in the drive to make it in corporate management.

The focus of this book is on minority success in management careers and not on minority-owned small businesses because even more so for minorities than for others, owning a small business is likely to be preceded by obtaining corporate success. Also, much has already been written about minority-owned businesses, beginning with the Nixon Administration's program on black capitalism and continuing with federal legislation that mandates that 10% of federal contract monies go to businesses owned by women and minorities. Much less has been written, however, about the road to success for minority managers within nonminority-owned corporations.

Of what has been written (see, e.g., America and Anderson, 1978; Davis and Watson, 1982; Dickens and Dickens, 1982; Fernandez, 1975; Jones and Schoen, 1977; Thompson, Steinberg, and Sharkey, 1976), most has been exclusively on black managers and from their perspective. (Fernandez, 1981, is the only prior work of which we are aware that compares black managers with other minorities.) In this book, we want to tell the rest of the story and to put it into context. We include not only the minority perspective on their success in corporate management but also the corporate perspective, and we compare different minority groups. We want to answer two basic questions:

1. Why have so few minorities been promoted and then succeeded in top management positions in major corporations?
2. How can corporations and schools of management improve the chances of their doing so in the future?

To answer these questions, we have organized the book around the four stages of problem solving: identifying the problem; gathering facts and information about critical issues, problems, and concerns; generating solutions; and developing plans of action. Clearly, there are many factors that contribute to the unequal outcomes for minority and majority managers in this country. We have chosen to concentrate on the dynamics of careers within corporations and understand what happens to minority managers compared to majority managers once they take their first jobs in management. As such, we will not explicitly discuss issues of education, socialization, and general preparation for the first job, except as these relate directly to the primary focus of the book.

I. MAKING IT IN THE MINORITY COMMUNITY

Minority successes in management positions in white-owned corporations is a relatively new concern within the minority community. Despite the emergence of a larger black middle class, for example, in the last several decades, the growth has, by and large, not come through movement up the corporate ladder. This is similarly true for Hispanics and to some extent, Asian-Americans. A very small, but growing, proportion of minorities are in administrative and management positions. Of those who are, the largest proportion are still in the public and nonprofit sectors. College-educated minorities have been more likely to pursue careers in the helping professions as nurses, teachers, social workers, ministers, undertakers, doctors, or lawyers than to seek business careers. Thus those minorities in the 1980s who want to make it in corporate management are at a distinct disadvantage because many have had limited exposure to careers in the white corporate world.

It is important, though, that we not give the wrong impression. There are minorities currently in business careers, and the numbers are increasing substantially in the post-civil-rights era. Among other things, equal employment opportunity legislation was passed following the riots of the 1960s, and consequent affirmative action programs have increased the numbers of minorities in management in nonminority businesses in the private sector (see, e.g., Smith & Welch, 1986, on black men). But, they are still disproportionately underrepresented compared to their proportions in the population at large.

Although blacks made up almost 12% of the population, they represented only 4.7% of the executive, administrative, and managerial workforce in 1980. Those whose origins are Hispanic (self-defined in the 1980 Census) are officially 6.5% of the population but only 2.8% of executive, administrative, and managerial employees. These figures include the public sector, where black and Spanish-origin employees made up 8.3% and 3.8%, respectively. Comparable figures for Asian-Americans are not reported separately, but other evidence suggests that they are overrepresented in professional jobs and underrepresented in top-level management jobs (Hirschman & Wong, 1984; also see Spilerman, Chapter 2, in this volume).

The prospects for the future do not seem to indicate a dramatic change in the proportion of minority managers. Blacks received only 4% of the master's degrees in business and management in 1980–1981, Hispanics 1½%, and Asians, approximately 3%. The situation for Hispanics and Asians, however, is apparently more likely to improve than that for blacks. Over the period between 1976–1977 to 1984–1985, the number of Hispanics enrolled in higher education increased 20.5%, the number of Asians 54.4%, but the number of blacks decreased by 19.2% (*Wall Street Journal*, September 23, 1986). In our study of minority managers in corporations reported elsewhere in this volume (Chapters 7 and 12), 94% of the companies in our sample reported less than 3% of their employees to be Oriental, 93% reported less than 12% black, and 95% reported less than 6% Hispanic—that is, less than their proportions in the population.

Even these figures may, however, overstate the progress of minority managers in corporate careers. As already noted, minority managers may be entrepreneurs in their own firms or work in minority-owned firms, many of which cater to minority markets. Further, minority managers in white-owned firms are not evenly distributed across all types of jobs and industries. They tend to be concentrated in staff—rather than line—positions, and often they deal with minority subordinates and minority issues in positions such as personnel, equal employment opportunity and affirmative action, corporate giving, and human or public relations. The few minority managers in line positions are more likely than not to deal with minority clients or customers: In sales or advertising, they specialize in minority markets, and in production-oriented jobs, they supervise minority workers.

Although many have decried the concentration of minority managers in staff jobs and jobs dealing with minority issues or clients as an indicator of bias, there is a double edge to the practice that should be noted. On the one hand, such jobs are clearly less powerful in corporations in the sense that they are less likely than line jobs to lead to top management positions. In this sense, placing minorities in such jobs does limit their opportunities for advancement. On the other hand, though. the practice can be seen as a means to opportunity. Because, as mentioned, many minority managers have neither family backgrounds nor educational training in business, it could be argued—and it has been in some circles—that these are the positions that provide the best fit for minority managers in the corporate world in the recent past (at least until a sizable number of minority managers have completed business school programs at the master's level). Furthermore, many of the minority managers now in corporations were recruited from the public or nonprofit sectors, and their backgrounds and training are likely to be in the social sciences or education and not in business. And, who better to deal with issues of equal opportunity and affirmative action than those who are most interested, namely minorities (and women); who better to oversee recruitment and hiring to ensure against discriminatory decisions than those who have claimed the need for protection; and who better to participate in decisions about corporate giving than those groups who feel they have been previously excluded from the benefits of the corporate world. Aside from any arguments about what is best or equitable in the assignment of minority managers in corporate jobs, corporations do not have as much latitude as some imply. Corporations required to have affirmative action plans are encouraged to place minority and female employees in monitoring and enforcement jobs for these programs (see the subsequent section on the legal requirements of employers).

Given the increase in the hiring of minority managers in major corporations over the last two decades, we would expect, and we find, that minorities are now entering middle management positions. But, they are still underrepresented at middle and almost nonexistent at top management levels. Only a few minority managers have reached the vice president level (middle or top management, depending on the company), and most of these are in human resources, especially in personnel and affirmative action or equal employment opportunity positions. Only in the banking industry do we find many minorities at the vice president level, but in banking the title is ambiguous in its meaning in that there are many more levels of vice presidents in banking and related fields than, for example, in manufacturing. In our study of corporations, only 10% to 15% (depending on whether staff or line positions) of the companies in our sample reported the highest level position for a minority manager in their firm to be at positions above vice president (group vice president, executive vice president, president, etc.), including divisions and subsidiaries, and only 30% to 40% (depending on whether staff or line) reported the highest level for a minority manager to be vice president or above. And, fully half of the companies in which the highest position of a minority manager in the firm was at the level of vice president or above indicated the position to be in banking or the international division of the company.

Thus the concern is that very few minorities are in top management positions in white-owned firms in the private sector. There are also very few minorities on the boards of directors of major corporations, and many of those who are on corporate boards are there as "social" rather than as "business" appointments.

Making it in the minority community, therefore, has only of late meant making it up the corporate ladder. For minorities, as for nonminorities, increasing numbers are planning careers in business. The chapters in this book are addressed toward understanding how success is attained for minority managers, so that the future may provide access, opportunity, and accomplishment.

II. UNDERSTANDING WHO IS A MINORITY

Because the civil rights movement of the 1960s was such a dramatic period for this country, the term *minority* has often been used synonymously since then for black. In fact, in the process of preparing this manuscript, many of our authors and contacts used the term *minority* when they clearly meant to refer only to blacks. Furthermore, in the context of the concern for the advancement of minority managers into top level positions, many used the terms *minority* or *black* but clearly meant to refer only to black males and not necessarily to black females. And, we have found in previous research on minority employment that some personnel directors tend to include within the minority category all foreign-born persons with dark skin, including, in many cases, Indians (from India) as black, Filipinos as Hispanic, Middle Easterners as Asian, and so on. Given that many immigrants to the United States from around the world are those with more education and occupational skills, it seems unreasonable to include them as a group in the same category as American-born minorities.

Thus there are at least three issues that we must consider to put the material in this book in proper context: (a) that all minorities are not the same; (b) that the problems of minority men are not the same as those of minority women; and (c) that not all minorities are disadvantaged. There is surely much more to be said on each of these issues than space permits here. The following discussion is just a reminder of the caution needed before generalizations can be made about the lessons to be learned regarding minority advancement in corporate management.

We have decided in this book to limit our focus primarily to blacks, Hispanics, and Asian-Americans. In most cases, we have restricted our focus further to U.S.-born persons from these three groups, although this was not really possible in some parts of the book (e.g., in our own study of corporations, we know that non-U.S.-born persons were defined by the companies as minorities in their responses to our questionnaire). We had assumed that the additional complexity of immigration would complicate the discussion of discrimination and disadvantage of minorities in management careers, but it became apparent in developing the book that there is no easy way to make this distinction. For Hispanics and Asians, immigrants constitute large portions of their members in the United States, but this is also true of blacks, many of whom came to the United States from the Caribbean Islands and other parts of the world. For each of the three minority groups, immigrants bring with them distinctly different problems and opportunities.

Before discussing some of the issues about the definition of a minority for each of the three groups included in this book, we need to clarify another issue: Our intent here is to deal with racial and ethnic minorities, whether male or female, and not the nonminority, female population. Because women as a group are a "protected class," as defined by legislation on equal employment opportunity and affirmative action, some people use the term *minority* to refer to all women, as well as to racial and ethnic minorities. In addition, some point to the evidence of disadvantage for women, particularly in the labor force, and conclude that they "should be" considered a minority because they are discriminated against and disadvantaged similarly to racial and ethnic minorities. Without necessarily taking a stand on this issue, we decided not to include nonminority women under the rubric of this book because we feel strongly that, despite whatever similarities may exist, there are enough differences in the circumstances for nonminority women from those of racial and ethnic minorities, both male and female, that we did not want to confuse our readers by trying to talk about them together. Further, there is a fair amount written about women in management (often limited in focus to nonminority women) and so little about racial and ethnic minorities in management that we felt we could make a greater contribution at this stage by addressing racial and ethnic minorities. At the same time, though, we want to be clear that we mean to include both male and female minority persons, and we recognize, as we discuss later, that problems for male minorities and female minorities are also often quite distinct.

A. Blacks

The black population in the United States includes both American-born blacks and those born in other parts of the world. Caribbean-born blacks, excluding recent immigrants from Haiti, tend to be better educated and occupationally skilled on average than American-born blacks (Jencks, 1985:744). Within the group of American-born blacks, distinctions are frequently made between those born in the rural South versus those born in the urban North. Traditionally, southern-born blacks were less well educated than northern-born blacks, both because of segregation and because of the poor quality of many southern schools. In recent years, this distinction may be less marked, both because of improvements in the South and because of a serious deterioration of school quality in the North. There are also important differences between inner-city blacks and those raised in suburbs and small towns. As the noted white flight in many northern cities of both residential and commercial property has left a declining tax base to support education and other city services, better-off blacks, too, have left for the suburbs.

In addition to these distinctions, it is important to remember that there has always been a black elite, in both the North and the South. Although small in proportion to the rest of the black population, it has made important contributions to black achievement in the United States. Further, there has always been a black middle class, populated by schoolteachers, postal workers, and others in the public and nonprofit sectors. With the growth of the civil rights movement and the expansion in general in the public sector following the baby boom, this sector of the black community has grown extensively.

Although we do not have empirical data on the family and educational backgrounds of the current population of black managers, it is safe to say that they do not represent a cross-section of the black community. More than likely they come from the black middle or working (blue collar) class, if not from the black upper class, and not from the worst-off segment of the black population. It is also more than likely that a disproportionate number of black managers come from families with heritage from the Caribbean islands.

Most black managers will acknowledge that they are in the positions they are in as a consequence of the civil rights movement, but many will feel that they have faced continued discrimination on the job. How this picture may change over the next several generations is not clear. Given the increased size of the black middle class, one might assume that an increasing proportion of black managers will enter the corporate world from family and educational backgrounds that are conducive to getting ahead in corporate careers. But, on the other hand, given the increased proportion of black, female-headed households and the poverty that is often a result, it may be that an increased proportion of the black population will be ill-prepared for corporate careers unless something is done to improve and ensure schooling for the black poor.

B. Hispanics

The Hispanic population in the United States is exceedingly diverse, such that it is impossible to draw generalizations that will fit the various Hispanic subpopulations. Hispanics have the highest level birth rate among minority groups, which, combined with the increasing immigration of Hispanics from other countries, makes it an ever larger proportion of the U.S. population.

Mexican-Americans, Chicanos, and Mexicans (legal and illegal) make up one large segment of the Hispanic population. Currently the largest segment of illegal immigrants to this country is from Mexico. In the West, Southwest, and increasingly, the Midwest, they make up a large and distinctive part of the population. On the East Coast, the largest proportion of the Hispanic population is Puerto Rican, whereas in the Southeast, primarily in Miami, the largest Hispanic population is Cuban. In addition, both in the West and the East, there are increasing numbers of Hispanics from Central and South America. Another group that may or may not define themselves as Hispanic, depending on the time period and other factors, are those whose parents originated in Spain.

Each of these segments of the Hispanic population has very different characteristics, problems, and opportunities. By and large, Spanish-Americans, like Italian-Americans, Irish-Americans, German-Americans, and so on, are not "Hispanic," in the sense of being a minority in this country. Rather, the families of many of these people have been in the United States for generations and have fully assimilated, although they may have maintained identification with both the language and culture of Spain. Most often, the referent when the term *Hispanic* is used to identify a minority group in this country is to those with heritages from Mexico, Puerto Rico, Cuba, or Central and South America. In some areas of the country, like Chicago, Hispanics refer to themselves as "Latino," purposely to differentiate themselves from the heritage with Spain.

As a former U.S. colony, the Puerto Rican population in the United States has unique status. Puerto Ricans are U.S. citizens, even if they were born on the island. The Puerto Rican population is a mixture of both black and Spanish populations, and thus skin color, as for blacks, is an issue among them. Some are very light skinned and think of themselves as "whites," whereas others are very darked skinned and are both black and Hispanic. As a means to avoid the color issue, many Puerto Ricans use the term "Anglo" rather than white when referring to non-Hispanics. (Of course, not all whites are Anglo-Saxon in ethnicity, so this is not a totally appropriate alternative.) A large proportion of the U.S. Puerto Rican population was born on the island and then immigrated to the United States in childhood, but a large proportion were also born in the United States. A major political issue that often separates Puerto Ricans from each other is support for or opposition to statehood for Puerto Rico.

Hispanics in the United States of Mexican heritage can be divided into three groups. Chicanos are those who were born in the United States but whose parents or grandparents are from Mexico. Mexican-Americans are immigrants to the United States who have become naturalized citizens. In addition, there is a large and increasing proportion of Mexican nationals in the United States, legally and otherwise. Some were recruited here during labor shortages in various parts of the U.S. economy, including steel mills in the Midwest and agricultural work in the West and Southwest. Both Chicanos and Mexican-Americans are U.S. citizens, whereas the others are not.

Many Hispanics from both Puerto Rican and those of Mexican heritage are treated as if they were illegal (or undocumented) aliens, whether or not they are, in fact, American citizens. With the increased numbers of the undocumented around the country, this has become an even greater problem for Hispanic citizens. Both Puerto Ricans and those of Mexican heritage are among the least educated of Hispanics and among the poorest. In both educational attainment and income, they lag behind blacks in this country. Thus, even though the proportion of Hispanics enrolled in higher education is increasing, whereas for blacks it is decreasing, Hispanics may still represent a smaller relative proportion of those with higher levels of education because they began from a lower base.

Another important segment of the Hispanic population is of Cuban heritage. There are at least two distinct groups in the United States: those who immigrated during and immediately following the Cuban revolution and those recent immigrants who left Cuba in what have been termed "boat lifts." The earlier immigrants are, on average, more highly educated and skilled, and have, in general, done well in the United States. Many were professionals or businesspeople in Cuba, and they brought their skills and resources with them when they came to the United States. The more recent immigrants do not have such advantages and have had a much more difficult time making it for that reason. Many, however, have settled in the Miami area and are protected in a sense by being in a largely Cuban area. Hispanic managers with Cuban heritage currently working in large corporations are most likely from families who immigrated to the United States earlier.

Another growing segment of the Hispanic population in the United States is from Central and South America. By virtue of being from so many different places, they primarily have in common that they are not Mexican, Puerto Rican, or Cuban. Beyond that, the differences are extensive, and it is impossible to make generalizations. Recent immigrants from Central America are largely poor and many undocumented. Those from South America may be from either privileged or disadvantaged backgrounds. Because legal immigration is restricted, it is likely that many are both illegal and poor.

C. Asian-Americans

The Asian and Asian-American populations are even more diverse, although overall they represent a small proportion of the U.S. population. Because of the distance and the ocean between the United States and Asia, there have been more constraints on Asian immigration, although less so now than prior to 1965 when there were specific quotas for Asian immigration to the United States. A large proportion of the U.S.-born Asian population comes from those whose families were recruited here at various times in the past when there were labor shortages. This is especially true of Chinese-Americans, but is also true of Japanese-Americans and others. Overall, though, a larger proportion of the Asian population in the United States are recent immigrants than is true for either blacks or Hispanics (perhaps at least until recently). In addition, the U.S. Asian population includes Koreans, Filipinos, Vietnamese, and those from many other countries and regions. Japanese-Americans made up the largest proportion of the Asian population until recently; Chinese-Americans are now almost as large in numbers as those from Japanese heritage. Those from other parts of Asia are also increasing in proportion. Some have argued that Asians are the fastest growing minority in the United States (Butterfield, 1986:18).

Asians and Asian-Americans as a group have higher educational levels and incomes than whites in the United States, even though they are underrepresented in corporate management careers. Some say this is because there is a tradition and cultural support within the Asian community for small business development or for training in the professions. For example, according to a recent article in *Fortune* (Ramirez, 1986), Asians and Asian-Americans are a "super" minority. They tend to outperform both whites and other minorities on most standardized tests and represent an increasingly large proportion of the student bodies at prestigious universities. Furthermore, Asians and Asian-Americans are overrepresented in the science and engineering fields that make them likely candidates for corporate careers. Yet Asians and Asian-Americans have not always felt that corporate careers were open to them. Instead, they have oriented themselves more toward the professions and entrepreneurship. This situation may be changing (e.g., Ramirez, 1986), but there still is a consciousness among Asians and Asian-Americans about discrimination of them due to their minority status.

The point of this discussion, limited as it is of necessity, is to note the many differences within the minority population and even within the "same" minority group. Related to this important point is that not all minority people are disadvantaged in the sense of facing discrimination in access to employment opportunities. Programs that are designed to assist the disadvantaged often benefit minority persons of privilege. And, programs that are aimed only at eliminating discrimination may not be able to identify all the ways in which it might occur, given the diversity and complexity of minority populations in the United States. At minimum, it is important to keep in mind the distinctions among race, ethnicity, and class because the issues that address each differ.

III. ISSUES FOR MINORITY WOMEN

Adding to the complexity is the importance of recognizing the differences in problems and opportunities for minority women compared to minority men. Depending on who is discussing it, the problems look greater or smaller. There have been charges in the past that minority women were preferred to minority men because they counted "twice" for affirmative action record-keeping. In addition, concern has been raised at various times that minority women were preferred because they are "less threatening" than minority men to the white men who dominate in positions of power and authority. We cannot settle these issues here because there are more factors that would need to be considered than space permits before conclusions could be drawn. At best, we can raise some of the issues that we should keep in mind.

Two issues stand out when we consider the problems—and opportunities—of minority women. First, in terms of occupational attainment and income, minority women look more like other women than they do like minority men. Minority women tend to be segregated into the same "women's jobs," which is true for women managers as well as for women in other occupations. In most studies of both occupational segregation and income, women managers fall behind men after a short period of time on the job (e.g., within 5 to 10 years). As for minority managers in general, minority women tend to be concentrated into some jobs more than others, most typically personnel, public relations, and in industries or occupations that are disproportionately female. We do not have firm evidence to suggest that minority women are more concentrated in their placements than minority men, but evidence for women in general suggests that this is likely to be the case. Such jobs typically have fewer ties to upper level jobs and less room for salary growth.

Despite what seems in general to be true for minority women compared to minority men, there is some evidence to suggest that minority women are favored in the labor market over minority men. Women in all race and ethnic categories, but especially black women of West Indian heritage and some Asian women, do better compared to white women with the same educational levels than do minority men in the same ethnic categories compared to white men of the same educational levels (see Jencks, 1985:744). That is, if one controls for ethnicity and education, minority women do *relatively* better than minority men compared to similarly situated whites, but in all cases, minority women still earn less than almost all minority and nonminority men.

Second, minority women, perhaps more so than for other women, face the prospect of being single more often than is true for minority men. The higher a woman moves up the corporate ladder, the more likely it is that she has never married and/or never had children. This is not true for males in top corporate positions. In addition, the demands of home and family (whether husband, children, or parents and other relatives) often place more demands on women than on men, thus making it more difficult for women to balance career and family than is true for men. The problems of finding marriage partners and balancing home life with careers is especially problematic for black women, much less so for Asian women, and in between for Hispanic women (see Smith and Tienda article in this volume, Chapter 3).

IV. THE LEGAL REQUIREMENTS OF EQUAL OPPORTUNITY AND AFFIRMATIVE ACTION

U.S. business is subject to two related, but distinct, requirements regarding nondiscriminatory employment: equal employment opportunity (EEO) legislation and affirmative action (AA) mandates. Equal opportunity legislation, which includes the Equal Pay Act of 1963 and Title VII of the Civil Rights Act of 1964, is administered by the Equal Employment Opportunity Commission (EEOC). The Equal Pay Act prohibits discrimination in salary and benefits between men and women working in the same establishments at jobs that are equal in terms of skill, effort, responsibility, and working conditions, although both merit and seniority considerations are legally permitted. Title VII of the Civil Rights Act prohibits discrimination based on race, sex, color, national origin, or religion and also has been interpreted as prohibiting sexual harassment. Title VII applies to all employers engaged in interstate commerce with 15 or more employees. The EEOC also administers the Age Discrimination Act of 1967. Related legal requirements are administered by the Office of Federal Contract Compliance Programs (OFCCP). OFCCP is responsible for enforcing Executive Order 11246 (applying to race, religion, color, and national origin) and Executive Order 11375 (applying to sex). These orders issued by President Lyndon Johnson apply to all federal contractors and subcontractors with contracts of $10,000 or more and require that "affirmative action" be taken with regard to women and minorities. In addition, for contractors with contracts of $50,000 or more and at least 50 employees, the affirmative action plans must be written and available for inspection if requested by OFCCP. OFCCP also administers the Rehabilitation Act of 1973, which covers the handicapped, and the Vietnam Era Veterans Readjustment Act of 1974. Both EEOC and OFCCP are part of the U.S. Department of Labor.

According to a 1977 study by the Business Roundtable, the costs to business of the equal employment opportunity legislation (including affirmative action requirements) are second only to legislation to protect the environment (*Cost of Government Regulations*, 1979). In other words, the costs are substantial. As is customary, legislation for EEO and AA has written guidelines that have been prepared by the enforcement agencies that detail what is considered by these agencies to be covered by the law. These regulations are very specific, very extensive, and binding. It is not within the purview of this book to outline all of the details of the laws requiring nondiscrimination in employment. That would take a book (or several) in itself. But to provide readers with a sense of what is involved for companies and also of some of the social, psychological, and political implications for employees, we want to discuss briefly the regulations for two of the most controversial aspects of the law: affirmative action and the guidelines for employee selection.

Executive Order 11246 not only prohibits discrimination against employees and applicants for employment but also requires that employers:

... must take affirmative action to insure that applicants are employed, and that employees are treated during employment, without regard to their race, religion, color or national origin (Code of Federal Regulations [CFR] 41, Ch. 60-50.2, 7-1-86 edition, p. 172).

The regulations go on to specify that such affirmative action must be taken in regard to each of the following, although it is not limited to these employment decisions: employment, upgrading, demotion or transfer, recruitment or recruitment advertising, layoff or termination, rates of pay or other forms of compensation, and selection for training, including apprenticeship (41 CFR Ch. 60-50.2:172). Each of these actions is then elaborated in more detail in terms of what the employer can do to ensure *both* nondiscrimination in decision making and equitable outcomes. It is the latter that has generated so much controversy. That is, affirmative action has been interpreted in the way the regulations have been written, not only to mean that employers must actively seek qualified minorities and women, but also that they are responsible and held accountable for finding and employing them.

The explicit focus on results and not just efforts are inherent in the definition given to affirmative action by the regulations:

An affirmative action program is a set of specific and result-oriented procedures to which a contractor commits itself to apply every good faith effort. The objective of those procedures plus such efforts is equal employment opportunity. Procedures without effort to make them work are meaningless; and effort, undirected by specific and meaningful procedures is inadequate. An acceptable affirmative action program must include an analysis of areas within which the contractor is deficient in the utilization of minority groups and women, and further, goals and timetables to which the contractor's good faith efforts must be directed to correct the deficiencies and, thus to achieve prompt and full utilization of minorities and women, at all levels and in all segments of its work force where deficiencies exist (41 CFR 60-2.10:113).

In addition to specifying what each of these steps entails, that is, the type of utilization studies that are considered acceptable and the level of specificity of goals and timetables, the regulations also discuss means for implementing all of these "good faith efforts" to the point of requiring such things as contact with specific community organizations that may have knowledge of potential candidates; formal briefing of community organization representatives on company premises; the inclusion of minorities and women on the personnel staff of the firm; permission for minority and women employees to participate in community activities (including career days, job fairs, etc.); recruitment at secondary schools, junior colleges, and "minority" schools; co-op programs; summer and work–study programs; training in motivation and skills for the unemployed; advertisement in the minority news media; and even that company publications must feature minorities in any pictures representing the work force.

The Office of Federal Contract Compliance reviews applications for all federal contracts for compliance with the regulations and also has a schedule of review of existing contractors. According to the regulations, all contractors must review their affirmative action plans annually, and they are subject to an OFCCP compliance review at OFCCP's discretion. OFCCP has a formula for determining which contractors will get reviewed, and priorities are established based on results, that is, the percentage of minorities (and women) in various job categories in the firm, compared with the industry and the relevant labor market. Contractors found in noncompliance are subject to penalties that may include back pay awards or even suspension from future federal contracts. Of course, most contractors take the necessary actions to comply, if they are found to be deficient, rather than incurring penalties.

The information for noncompliance often begins with mandated reports to EEOC that provide the information on the percentage of minorities and women in the work force of the company. These reports are shared with OFCCP. At the same time, EEOC handles complaints about discrimination and, under various regulations, has the option to bring suit. One of the most controversial aspects of EEOC reviews is their use of the "Uniform Guidelines on Employee Selection Procedures." These guidelines are relevant to any employer with 15 or more workers. They are used to evaluate the acceptability of screening devices used in hiring or promotion. There are two basic provisions to the uniform guidelines: (a) that any procedure having an "adverse impact" on the hiring, promotion, or other employment or membership opportunities of minorities (or women) will be considered to be discriminatory unless it is "validated" using the procedures outlined in the guidelines and (b) that employers must consider suitable alternative selection procedures and choose those that have the least adverse impact. Most of the guidelines explain the acceptable definitions and means of application for various types of statistical validities, as defined and used by professional psychologists. But the guidelines also include several provisions that have raised questions. One is the "four-fifths" rule, namely that any selection procedure for which the selection rate of minorities (or women) is less than 80% of that of nonminorities will be considered to have an adverse impact on the selection of minorities and therefore be considered discriminatory. Another provision requires that the employer validate any test found to have an adverse impact by use of the employees in the firm (rather than, for example, a sample of college students used for validation purposes by the developer of the test). Performing validation procedures, of course, also means maintaining extensive records on applicants, hires, promotions, and so on. It is a time-consuming and costly process, which requires training and expertise in the relevant methodological procedures. Even if an employer can validate a selection procedure, based on the requirements of the uniform guidelines, the "alternative procedures" provision is still operative.

Critics of two of the provisions of civil rights legislation, that is, the affirmative action requirement that goals and timetables be used as well as the use of the Uniform Guidelines on Employee Selection Procedures, have argued that both contribute to the introduction of "reverse discrimination" in employment decisions. That is, they argue that the implementation of the law has made it necessary for employers to hire minority employees only because of their race or ethnicity and irrespective of their qualifications, thereby actively discriminating against white applicants or employees. Employers have often been caught in the middle of such controversy because the implementation of these laws, like all others, is subject to court challenge, and there have been many—and costly—decisions rendered that make it difficult for employers to know how to act in such a way to avoid legal penalties. Some of the more celebrated cases have dealt with the legality of affirmative action plans that set aside a certain percentage of admissions, hires, or promotion slots for minorities or those that allow for the hiring (or promotion, etc.) of objectively lesser qualified minorities for the purposes of meeting the agreed-upon goals. It is additionally problematic for employers because the Supreme Court rulings on a series of affirmative action cases have rarely been clear-cut. Decisions have been based on such factors as whether the employer has a history of discrimination or whether the set asides are only intended to remedy "societal" discrimination; whether the employment decision is about hiring new employees or terminating old ones; and whether the persons receiving the benefits are the ones who themselves were victims of discrimination.

In the meantime, the Reagan administration has undertaken to change various provisions of civil rights legislation to make the paperwork for employers less "burdensome." In most cases, the administration has not been successful because of opposition not only from civil rights groups but also from employers themselves (Fisher, 1985). At an early point in the administration, new regulations for Executive Order 11246 were issued that raised the number of employees to 250 (from 50) and the contract amount to $1,000,000 (from $50,000). If they had been implemented, these regulations would have eliminated the requirement for written affirmative action plans for many employers. The regulations were strongly opposed, however, and, as a result, were postponed indefinitely. At a later date, the administration attempted to revise Executive Order 11246 to eliminate the language requiring specific "goals and timetables." These, too, were opposed, even by some members of the administration and have not, as of this writing, been successfully implemented. The administration has, however, cut the number of enforcement personnel in the various agencies, reduced the budgets, and replaced most of the key administrators. These actions, in and of themselves, have had an effect of reducing enforcement and causing concern among minority group members.

There are still many complicated and controversial issues surrounding the implementation of civil rights legislation. Given the results-oriented requirements of the regulations as they have been interpreted in past administrations, it is understandable that the primary concern for many employers is finding "qualified" applicants. At the same time, given what is perceived as a precariousness to the gains that minorities have made in the labor force and strong evidence that most whites oppose many of the steps that have been taken to provide legal remedies, especially affirmative action (Kluegel, 1985), it is not surprising that the primary concern for many minorities is that pressure continue to be brought to effect both equal opportunity and equal results.

V. TWO STORIES ABOUT MINORITY ADVANCEMENT IN MANAGEMENT CAREERS

In reading the literature and talking with people in corporations, one can easily sense that there are two stories about minority advancement in management. Readers of this volume need to be aware of the underlying assumptions that many make when this topic is discussed—and when it is avoided. One story is that as told by black managers (mostly black male managers) in the work that has been published. This story surely varies for other minority groups and for minority women, but the black male story will be described here because it is the most coherent and widely heard. The other story is that told by white managers. especially those at top levels, in their offices. In general, both stories are internally consistent, but they are also diametrically opposed to each other on many dimensions. In neither case, of course, are we claiming that these sentiments represent all black men or all white men. We are generalizing for the purpose of making a point.

Very briefly, the story told by black managers is that their inability to succeed to the top levels in nonminority corporations is due to discrimination in one form or another. They argue that they are just as well qualified as white managers because, after all, they say, they went to the same schools, received the same degrees, and have had the same employment experiences. And, they go on to say, that even if this were not true, it is irrelevant for top management positions because many white managers who have been promoted are not competent or have gotten their positions through politics and friendships, more than through merit. Along these lines, black managers also claim that after a certain level has been attained in a corporation (top of middle management and into top management) that all people are basically qualified and that the only discrimination between who makes it and who does not is politics and culture.

Black managers also argue that they will do better in politics once they have a wider network of other black managers, make connections that will favor them over others, and better information sources about the paths to take, the experiences to develop, and the relationships to foster. They argue that they will fare better when top management does become truly multicultural and, hence, when white managers come to accept the cultural differences that exist between blacks and whites (and among blacks) and/or come to see that the differences are not really as great as has often been assumed.

The story from top-level white managers is quite different. Although they will often not admit it in public, they argue that they cannot find enough qualified minority candidates, especially in the fields that are most critical to the development and growth of their businesses. They are especially concerned about the dearth of applicants in engineering and the sciences with good technical skills. They are much more likely to argue that minority managers (and they frequently mean black, male managers) have not gone to the same schools, have not received the same degrees, and in general, have not chosen the educational paths that would lead them into top corporate jobs.

Thus they feel that so many minorities end up in the human resources area because these jobs match their educational backgrounds and not because the company has pigeonholed minority managers as such. In general, white managers feel that minority managers have less adequate educational preparation, technical skills, and writing skills, and furthermore, when they talk frankly, they also feel that minority managers are less satisfied, and therefore, also less loyal, less willing to stick it out when the going gets tough, and more difficult to manage.

There is a general orientation from most white managers in most large companies to talk as if their companies were colorblind (see Fernandez article in this volume, Chapter 5). They say that they have tried most of the special programs that have been argued to be necessary for the success of minority managers and that these programs have either not helped, or have actually hurt, by creating differences that otherwise did not exist among people. Therefore, many companies have shifted back to a posture of arguing that there should be no special programs, that they will be religiously colorblind in their behavior in the future, and that they are already strongly committed to the success of minority managers. In some circles, there is (as noted by Kanter in Chapter 14) a certain impatience about even discussing the issue. They consider it a part of history, not part of the present (also see discussion by Kluegel, 1985).

Furthermore, white managers feel that their top managements are strongly committed to equal employment opportunity. if not affirmative action (see Fisher, 1985) and that if there are still problems in their companies, it is with middle, nonminority managers. But they do not consider this to be a major problem because they feel certain that middle level managers will take their cues from the top.

On one point both black managers and top-level white managers agree. That is that if companies make the development and success of minority managers part of the evaluation criteria for nonminority managers and part of the bottom line orientation for the company (i.e., part of the business plan), nonminority managers in the course of doing their jobs will find a way to make sure that minority managers get trained as necessary and that they succeed. (They do not all agree, however, that this should be done.)

In sum, there are really three issues that need to be addressed in any discussion of ensuring success for minority managers: (a) issues having to do with the policies and practices of organizations; (b) issues having to do with the relationship of minority managers to others, including peers, subordinates, and their own managers; and (c) issues having to do with the preparation or characteristics of minority managers themselves. The last topic is a very sensitive issue and the primary basis of difference in the formulation of the two stories described previously. Given that it is frequently mentioned in private, if not public, it seems important for the issue to be confronted. We need to be clear, however, that we do not think it has anything to do with inherent capacities or abilities, but if anything, to do with the structure of school systems and the availability of resources.

The problem-solving framework around which we have organized this book addresses each of these three levels: the individual, the interpersonal, and the organizational. In Part II of the book, we examine the current status of minorities in management through statistical analyses and interview material that together provide an overview of the facts as we know them. Facts, however, are often in the eye of the beholder, so in Part III, we examine the definition of the problem from the perspective of different actors: new job entrants, experienced managers and academics, and corporations. Part IV examines solutions from different perspectives. Successful minority managers discuss how they did it, whereas corporate representatives discuss what they consider to be successful programs or policies in their firms. We also provide an overview of corporate policies and programs. Finally, in Part V specific recommendations for action are made. Throughout the volume, the chapters provide background for a better understanding of why minority managers have not yet reached top management positions in the same proportions as nonminority managers, but the final goal of the book is to know what can be done to ensure their future success.

VI. REFERENCES

America, Richard F., and Bernard F. Anderson. 1978. *Moving ahead: Black managers in American business*. New York: McGraw-Hill.
Butterfield, Fox. 1986. Why Asians are going to the head of the class. *New York Times*. Special issue on education life. Section 12. August 3, pp. 18–23.
Clark, Timothy B. 1981. Affirmative action may fall victim to Reagan's regulatory reform drive. *National Journal* 13(28):1248–1252.
Code of Federal Regulations. 1986. Vol. 41. Section 60. July 1. Washington, DC: U.S. Government Printing Office.
Cost of Government Regulations Study for Business Roundtable. 1979. Chicago: Arthur Andersen.
Davis, George, and Glegg Watson. 1982. *Black life in corporate America*. New York: Anchor Press.
Dickens, Floyd, Jr., and Jacqueline B. Dickens. 1982. *The black manager: Making it in the corporate world*. New York: AMACOM.
Fernandez, John P. 1975. *Black managers in white corporations*. New York: Wiley.
Fernandez, John P. 1981. *Racism and sexism in corporate life: Changing values in American business*. Lexington, MA: D. C. Heath.
Fisher, A. B. 1985. Businessmen like to hire by the numbers. *Fortune*, September 16, pp. 26–29.
Hirschman, C., and M. G. Wong. 1984. Socioeconomic gains of Asian-Americans, blacks, and Hispanics: 1960–1976. *American Journal of Sociology* 90(3):584–607.
Jencks, Christopher. 1985. Affirmative action for blacks: past, present, and future. *American Behavioral Scientist* 28:731–760.
Jones, W. L., and S. H. Shoen. 1977. The new minority managers: how far, how fast. *MBA: Master in Business Administration* 11(1):47–50.
Kluegel, James R. 1985. If there isn't a problem, you don't need a solution. *American Behavioral Scientist* 28:761–784.
National Center for Education Statistics. 1983–1984. *Digest of education statistics*. Washington, DC: U.S. Government Printing Office.
Ramirez, Anthony. 1986. America's super minority. *Fortune*, November 24, pp. 148–164.
Smith, James P., and Finis R. Welch. 1986. *Closing the gap: Forty years of economic progress for blacks*. Santa Monica, CA: RAND Corporation Report.
Thompson, J. A., H. Steinberg, and J. Sharkey. 1976. The vanguard generation moves up. *MBA: Master in Business Administration* 10(1):21–42.
Wall Street Journal. 1986. Report on Higher Education. September 23, p. 33.

II

Just How Far Have We Come?

So much has been written about disadvantage, discrimination, and minority–majority relations that one often feels there is nothing more to say. Indeed, the first response when the topic is broached is that it has all been heard or said or tried before. Although much less has been written about minorities in corporate careers than about minorities in other contexts, this topic, too frequently, generates the same reactions. For this reason, we wanted to discuss the advancement of minority managers in the corporate world in both a positive and facilitative manner, rather than simply reiterating that there is a problem. We therefore chose to use a problem-solving framework for this book. The first step in the problem-solving process is to gather the facts of the situation. Part II of the volume includes a set of research-based papers that provide important background to understanding the current situation for minorities in corporate management. In subsequent parts, we complete the problem-solving process: Part III reviews the perspectives of key players in order to properly identify the problems; Part IV outlines potential solutions for managers and corporations; and Part V recommends action.

The article by Spilerman examines the sources of minority underrepresentation in management jobs by tracing the pattern of school completion, field of specialization, and occupational representation for whites compared to blacks, Hispanics, and Asians. By examining college completion rates by age cohort and what Spilerman calls survivorship rates (i.e., the percentage at each educational level who go on to complete the next level), Spilerman is able to identify both the trends over time in school completion and the decision points where educational achievement diverges by group. He finds that the dropout rate for Hispanics increases substantially at the end of primary school but after that point is similar to the rate for blacks. In contrast, the point at which blacks drop out in large numbers is their high-school sophomore year. Although these are the key points of major divergence, both blacks and Hispanics consistently fall below the percentages for whites or Asians in their school completion rates. The consequence is that the candidate pool of college graduates for blacks and Hispanics is proportionally far below that for either whites or Asians. Asians are similar in their survivorship to whites through high school but exceed whites from that point on. Although

21

there has been an increase in the educational attainment of both blacks and Hispanics in recent years, the same has been true for whites and Asians. Thus the racial distribution of the applicant pool for managerial jobs has not changed in 20 years, according to Spilerman. Perhaps even more important is that of those who complete college, a smaller percentage of blacks and Hispanics major in business-relevant fields, whereas Asians, again, exceed whites in this regard.

Smith and Tienda analyze the demographic characteristics of black, Hispanic, and Asian women compared to white, non-Hispanic women, in terms of labor force characteristics, occupational segregation, and earnings. They also compare the changes over a 10-year period. The labor force characteristics of black and Hispanic women place them at a disadvantage in the labor market compared to non-Hispanic, white women, whereas Asian women exceed white women in many labor force characteristics. Smith and Tienda show, however, that there are differences between black and Hispanic women and among different groups of Hispanic women. Black women are more likely to have child care responsibilities and more likely to have marital disruption. Hispanic women are more likely to have lower educational attainment. Both sets of circumstances make it difficult for these minority women to fare well in the labor force. In addition, Smith and Tienda show that, on top of the substantial gender-based job segregation for all women, minority women—especially blacks and Hispanics—are even more concentrated into a few job categories. Those women who are in higher status jobs are more likely to be in professional than in managerial jobs, and this too is even more likely for black and Hispanic women.

The picture of earnings, however, is more complex. Non-Hispanic white women in higher status jobs earn about the same as Cubans, more than Mexicans, but less than other minority women. This seeming anomaly, however, is due to specifics of their labor force participation. It appears that more non-Hispanic white women are working part time than previously, whereas black and Asian women are more likely to work full time. Even so, the earnings of minority women in higher status jobs has improved in the last decade. Smith and Tienda further detail the sources of earnings differences across groups. They confirm the importance of human capital investment for determining income but also find effects of occupational segregation by gender and race and ethnicity. The Spilerman and the Smith and Tienda chapters provide important context to the subject of minority success in management careers.

The Ford chapter summarizes the results of three studies on minority managers. In the first study, he more specifically compares the progress of minority and nonminority MBAs in terms of job progress and salary growth after several years on the job. He finds that minority MBAs are less likely to have been promoted and their salary progression is likely to have been slower than for a comparable set of white MBAs. The second study compares the physiological and psychological symptoms of stress for black and white women in management. Ford finds that black women managers are more likely to say they experience various forms of psychological stress. Based on answers to related questions, he interprets this as due to these black women managers having a lack of control over their work. In the third study, Ford looks at the effects of mentoring on the careers of black public officials. He finds that those administrators with mentors were less likely to experience negative work outcomes (like stress) but only somewhat more likely to experience positive work outcomes. Mentoring had no effect on such factors as pay and promotion.

Fernandez challenges what he takes to be common wisdom about the aftereffects of the civil rights movement and programs of affirmative action, namely that there is no longer a problem for minorities and women in corporate life. His title refers to efforts made by the Reagan administration in the mid-1980s to eliminate goals and timetables from affirmative action programs (see discussion in Chapter 1), ostensibly to ensure that all employment decisions are color- and gender-blind. In other words, the administration has sought to eliminate what it feels is "reverse discrimination" against whites. Using data from his two previous works as well as a new study of 9,000 employees in 13 companies, Fernandez tries to show both the pervasiveness and perniciousness of continuing racism and sexism on the job. Even more, he argues that the situation, far from getting better, has been getting worse over the last several years of the Reagan administration. For example, Fernandez finds that, although the proportion of employees in his samples who accept racist stereotypes declined between 1971 and 1977, it increased in 1984–1985. Fernandez finds the same trends in the acceptance of sexist stereotypes, but the data are mixed. He also presents data that suggest that discriminatory behavior has followed the same path as discriminatory attitudes, for both racism and sexism.

Fernandez supplements survey data with open-ended comments from the survey participants on a number of topics. The comments clearly show that there is a consciousness of race and sex in the work world, and it underlines the often made claim that each group charges that others receive favored treatment compared to their own. Fernandez ends his paper with a set of recommendations for corporations that he argues, will reduce the opportunities for racism and sexism and provide positive incentives for truly color- and gender-blind employment decisions.

The final chapter in this section of the book, by Davis, outlines the changes over the last several decades in the position of black managers in corporate careers. Davis and his colleague, Glegg Watson, interviewed both black and white, male and female managers in major corporations to get an understanding of the "human side" of the issue. Davis, a journalist, provides a qualitative summary of how black managers, as he says, operate in "foreign social space." Davis argues that there are three periods that define the place of black managers in major corporations: tokenism, racial turbulence, and backlash. He argues that all three of these periods continue simultaneously, depending on which company one considers, but that a fourth—and as yet undefined—stage is in the process of developing.

"Tokenism" defines a time when blacks were few in management jobs. As such, they were often showcased whenever a black face was needed, but they were rarely given significant job assignments that could warrant promotion up the corporate ladder. A second period that Davis calls "racial turbulence" describes the height of the civil rights movement, when, according to Davis, blacks in corporate life underwent a psychological revolution by mentally overthrowing the rule of white men. It was during this time, according to David, that "black blacks" entered corporate positions. Having a greater positive racial consciousness, these blacks were more ambivalent about assimilation to the white world. "Backlash" is Davis's term for the third period. According to Davis, the key question for black managers during this period is survival in corporate careers, as more whites claim reverse discrimination. The future suggests both positive and negative signs, according to Davis. Young MBA students feel they will do fine if given a chance, but at the same time, they still are not sure how to interact in a white corporate world.

Because the advancement of minority managers in corporate careers, like many issues of inequality, is an emotionally charged issue, it is important that we begin this book with what we know, rather than with what we think. These papers are intended to lay a foundation of facts for much of what follows in Part III, which includes facts of a different sort, namely what people firmly believe to be true because it makes sense in their experience. As for all controversial issues, facts seldom settle things, but they sometimes help sharpen the points of disagreement. Once we review how key actors define the problems of minority advancement in corporate careers, we will then turn in Parts IV and V to proposed solutions and recommendations for future action.

2

Sources of Minority Underrepresentation in Corporate Employment

Seymour Spilerman

The purpose of this chapter is to provide a context for understanding the attainments of minorities and, in particular, the career prospects of minority individuals in large corporations. The account I will provide emphasizes the limitations on what corporations can do to increase minority employment in high occupational positions but also suggests strategies that business organizations should follow to promote equity. Further, I note what minority individuals must themselves do in order to be situated favorably with respect to corporate careers.

In past decades, the objective of incorporating minorities into the mainstream of American economic life has been pursued through a policy of seeking to eliminate discriminatory barriers to entrance and promotion in large corporations. Although concerns about these matters still remain, in recent years there has been a shift to a more active role by business organizations, with the intent of locating and recruiting capable minority individuals and sponsoring their careers within the corporation.

What I wish to discuss are some basic demographic facts that make clear the need for a continued active role by business organizations, if they are to achieve a minority presence that approaches the representation rates of the various groups in the larger society. At the same time, the demographic statistics are sobering with respect to the extent that corporate America can be expected to influence its own prospects of becoming racially representative.

I develop these themes using a formulation in which entrance into a

Seymour Spilerman • Department of Sociology, Columbia University, New York, New York 10027.

career in a large company can be viewed as the terminus of a sequence of decisions by individuals regarding their occupational preferences, together with a parallel set of experiences by youth in prior institutional settings. Some of the experiences may foster opportunity and encourage an achievement orientation, whereas others may be discriminatory and might discourage competitiveness and striving. A sequence of experiences of the latter kind can progressively close options for young individuals; we expect that this sort of process is particularly severe for black and Hispanic youth.

I. EDUCATIONAL ATTAINMENT

In most corporations, entrance into management and professional ranks is now principally by educational qualifications. With increasing levels of educational attainment in the national population, it has become difficult for an able blue-collar or clerical worker, without a college degree, to move into management, especially into the middle-management ranks.

Yet, if we examine college completion rates—an initial measure of the pool from which management and professional personnel are recruited—it is evident that this pool is much smaller for blacks and Hispanics than for whites and some other minorities, such as Asians. Summary data on this point are reported in Table 1.

In 1980, in the 25 to 29 age cohort, 23.9% of whites completed college, as did 38% of Asian-Americans but only 11.4% of blacks and 9.0% of Hispanics. Further, by examining college completion rates across the age cohorts, it is clear that although there has been an increase in the *absolute* rate for each group over time,[1] there has been little change in the *relative* completion rates of the groups. For example, the ratio of the black/white rates is 49% in the 45–49 age cohort and 48% in the 25–29 age cohort. Comparable values for the Hispanic/white ratio in the two cohorts are 42% and 38%, whereas the Asian/white ratios are 177% and 159%. Thus, judging by college completion rates in the different age cohorts, the racial shares of the college graduate pool have not changed significantly in the past 20 years.

The importance of this datum arises from the fact that the most prevalent avenue of recruitment by corporations into entry-level management and professional positions is from the college graduate pool. The fact that black and Hispanic completion rates continue to hover below 50% of the white rate portends poorly for the prospects of increasing minority representation in industrial organizations to approximate the makeup of the larger society. This comment is emphatically not true, incidentally, for Asian-Americans, who have a college graduation rate that exceeds that of the white population.

---

[1] It should be noted that changes in college completion rates by different age cohorts will reflect, to some extent, changes in within-group heterogeneity. In particular, the increase over time by Asians may result from a decline in immigration to the United States of mature individuals (who lack a college degree) as much as from a trend to more education among U.S.-born Asians.

Table 1. College Completion Rates, by Race and Age, 1980

Age group	Percentage of age group that has completed college			
	White	Black	Hispanic	Asian
25–29[a]	23.9	11.4	9.0	38.0
30–34	26.4	12.0	9.7	44.2
35–39	22.4	10.3	8.6	45.6
40–44	18.6	8.7	7.9	39.8
45–49	17.0	8.3	7.2	30.1
54–59	14.8	6.9	6.4	21.3

[a]The somewhat lower completion rates for this age group, relative to the 30–34 cohort, may reflect a tendency by a small proportion of eventual college completers to graduate after age 30.
Source: U.S. Bureau of the Census (1980, Table 262), total population aged 15 or older.

A. Survivorship Rates

To gain some insight into the sources of minority differences in college completion, we examined survivorship rates for the different groups over the course of the educational career. These values measure the percentage of an age cohort that has completed the noted educational level. In particular, consider the cohort aged 30 to 34 in 1980—the last that can be viewed as having, by and large, completed its formal educational training. Table 2 reports the survivorship rates for this cohort separately by racial group; the same material is presented in graphical form in Figure 1.

By the time of completion of primary education, a clear pattern of racial differentiation begins to emerge in the form of a substantially lower survivorship rate for Hispanics. Twenty-two percent of the age cohort of this group has failed to complete primary schooling.[2] At this early point in the educational career, no other sharp differences stand out among the racial categories.

This pattern of lower completion rates by Hispanics is accentuated during the high-school years; only 55% of the age group has completed secondary school, in comparison with 86% for whites and Asians. A second racial pattern appears by the second year of high school—an increasingly lower rate of survivorship in the educational system by black youth. By high-school graduation, only 73% of blacks remain in the school system.

The trends in completion rates established in the high-school years continue during college and are even accentuated. Forty-nine percent of the white cohort completes 1 year of college, whereas the rates for blacks and Hispanics are much lower. Fully one-quarter of the white cohort has com-

[2]We emphasize that many in this group did not drop out of a U.S. educational program but emigrated to the United States after finishing their education. Thus our interpretation of the completion rates as a survivorship process in the school system is a simplification of the responsible factors.

Table 2.   Survivorship Rates Over the Educational Career, by Race,
for the Age Group 30–34 in 1980

School year	Percentage of age group that has completed college			
(k)	White	Black	Hispanic	Asian
Primary school				
1–4	99	99	98	99
5,6	99	99	92	97
7	98	97	81	95
8	97	95	78	94
High school				
1	95	92	72	93
2	93	87	66	91
3	89	80	61	88
4	86	73	55	86
College and postgraduate				
1	49	34	26	65
2	40	25	20	60
3	31	16	13	50
4	26	12	10	44
5 and more	13	6	5	24

Source: U.S. Bureau of the Census (1980). Computed from Table 262.

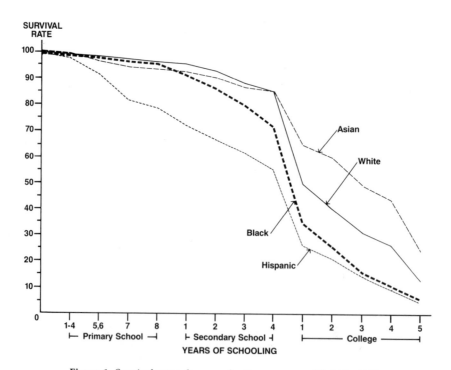

Figure 1. Survival rates, by race, for the age group 30–34 in 1980.

pleted college; the figure for blacks (12%) is less than half the white value, and the rate for Hispanics is even lower.

I have said little about the survivorship pattern of Asian-Americans because it is so anomalous. Over the primary and high-school grades, the completion rates parallel those of whites; indeed, in both groups, 86% of the age cohort survives in the educational system through high school. From this point, however, a striking divergence begins. Sixty-five percent of Asians complete 1 year of college (versus 49% of whites); almost one-quarter complete a year of postgraduate education (versus 13% for whites). Asians are four times as likely as blacks to finish a year of postgraduate education, and five times as likely as Hispanics to reach this educational level.

B. Continuation Ratios

A somewhat different perspective on the same material can be obtained by examining continuation ratios in regard to the educational career. Survival rates, presented previously, are indexed on the total cohort for a racial group. Thus, the figure 86%, for whites completing 4 years of high school means that 86% of the age group has completed this amount of schooling. Continuation ratios look at completion rates indexed on the size of the input into the particular school year. They are relevant to the issue of discovering where in the educational process the disadvantage occurs for a racial group. Continuation ratios for the four groups are presented in Figure 2.

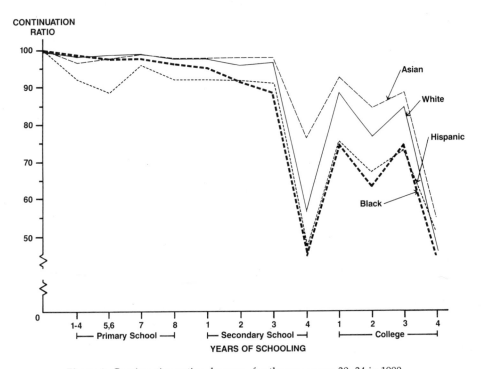

Figure 2. Continuation ratios, by race, for the age group 30–34 in 1980.

To understand this material, note that for Hispanics with 5 to 6 years of schooling, the ratio is .88. This value reveals that 88% of students completing 5 to 6 years also finish the seventh grade. The figure .88 is computed from the ratio 81/92, which compares the survivorship rate for Hispanics with 5 to 6 years of schooling and the rate for 7 years of schooling (Table 2).

Note that the graphs for blacks and Hispanics are very similar after 2 years of high school; indeed, from this point, Hispanics appear to have slightly higher continuation ratios than blacks. This result indicates that the higher survivorship rates of blacks in high school and in college, relative to Hispanics (Table 2), result *entirely* from the dropout of Hispanic youth during grade school and at the beginning of high school. In brief, the higher completion rates of blacks at the upper levels of schooling reflect their greater numbers in the middle years of high school, and not a tendency to lower attrition during the college years.

The continuation ratios also reveal the points of advantage for Asians. After 1 year of high school, the continuation ratio for Asians always exceeds that of whites. This means there is an increasing cumulative advantage to Asians in their survival rate over the grade levels in the education system. In addition, Figure 2 shows that there are two transition points at which Asians do exceptionally well, relative to the other racial groups: at continuation from high school to college, and at continuation from 2 to 3 years of college. Cumulatively, these advantages lead to the considerably higher college completion rates by Asians, noted in Table 2.

It is not my purpose here to try to explain the substantial differences in educational attainment among the racial groups, important and fascinating as the subject may be. This issue has been addressed by many authors (e.g., Clark, 1965; Jencks, 1972; Moynihan, 1966; Sowell, 1975), who have emphasized the effects of poverty, family structure, role models, and job opportunities on educational aspirations and educational attainment. It *is* my purpose to point out the consequences of the very disparate educational completion rates for subsequent achievement in the corporate world. To this effect, it is evident that one might reasonably expect blacks and Hispanics to be underrepresented in management and professional ranks, as a consequence of their lesser educational attainments.

C. Field of Specialization

In recruiting for management and professional positions and in promotion decisions to middle-level management, many firms seek not simply individuals with college credentials but candidates with particular majors. Mathematics, engineering, computer sciences, economics, and business school backgrounds are generally the most valued, not only for positions that require the formal skills associated with these majors but more widely because they signify a familiarity with analyzing complex information. In contrast, majors in education, humanities, and the social sciences are usually less attractive to industrial and financial organizations.

This argument suggests that our initial specification of the pool of potential recruits for management and professional jobs in large corporations should be modified by taking into account field of concentration by college graduates from the four race and ethnic categories. Because in some fields (e.g., business and management specialties), the degree of accreditation is at the master's level, we discuss area of specialization as reflected in the distribution of master's degrees.

From Table 3 we observe that blacks and Hispanics are heavily concentrated in the fields of education, social sciences (which include social work), and in the humanities; whites and especially Asians specialize, in comparison, in the physical sciences, engineering, and in business and management. In particular, 13.5% of master's degrees awarded to blacks and 16.6% of the degrees awarded to Hispanics have gone to majors in the quantitative fields, versus 24.3% for whites and 45.6% for Asians.

Thus not only is the pool of potential black and Hispanic recruits small relative to whites and Asians because of lower college completion rates, but their fields of concentration put them at a disadvantage in light of the presumed hiring preferences of large corporations. Relevant to this point, a past report by the National Advisory Committee on Black Higher Education (1980, p. 26) concludes that:

> Education and social sciences remain the principal fields of concentration for the majority of black students in higher education. Since both areas will offer severely reduced academic and non-academic occupational opportunities in the 1980s and 90s, this lack of educational diversification seems to doom black graduates to an ever decreasing portion of the job market. . . . Furthermore, 63.7 percent of all black doctorates stated that they expected to use their degrees to secure employment in educational institutions as opposed to only 4.9 percent who planned to seek industry or business employment.

Table 3. Percentage Distribution of Master's Degrees, by General Field of Study, 1978–1979[a]

Field of study	White	Black	Hispanic	Asian
Physical sciences[b]	3.6	1.1	1.9	7.5
Engineering	4.0	1.3	3.6	15.5
Life sciences	9.0	5.6	5.2	12.4
Business and management	16.7	11.1	11.1	22.6
Social sciences[c]	13.5	16.9	17.6	11.4
Humanities	7.2	3.3	9.0	6.1
Education	37.7	55.7	46.0	17.2
Other	8.3	5.1	5.7	7.4
All fields	100.0	100.1	100.1	100.1

[a]Calculations exclude nonresident aliens.
[b]Includes mathematics and computer sciences.
[c]Includes social work.
Source: Computed from Table 3 of Brown (1982).

II. OCCUPATIONAL PATTERNS

The disparities in occupational representation among the groups are fairly consistent with the distribution of educational outcomes. Data on occupational affiliation, from the 1980 Census of Population, are in Table 4.

The entries in the top row indicate that the representation of blacks and Hispanics in executive, administrative, and managerial positions (EAM) is approximately one-half the rate of whites. Analogous figures for professional occupations (PO)—sixth row—reveal virtually the same sort of concentration pattern for these three groups. Asians, in contrast, appear similar to the white population in their presence in EAM (overrepresented in reference to the other minorities) but are 1.8 times more likely than whites to be employed in a PO specialty (19.6% versus 11.0%).

These figures parallel the college completion rates of the different groups; further, the very high concentration of Asians in professional occupations is hardly surprising in light of their educational choices: mathematics, the physical sciences, and engineering. Somewhat more informative about the career consequences of college majors are the representation rates of the various groups in *detailed* occupations. Several lines of work, associated with each of the two major occupational categories, are presented in the body of Table 4.

Table 4. Some Patterns of Racial Concentration in Administrative and Professional Occupations, 1980

Occupation	White	Black	Hispanic	Asian
Executive, administrative, and managerial occupations (EAM), as a percentage of group's labor force	13.0	5.3	6.3	12.9
Public administrators, as a percentage of EAM	3.1	6.0	3.6	2.5
Education administrators, as a percentage of EAM	3.2	7.1	2.7	1.5
Financial managers, as a percentage of EAM	4.0	2.4	3.3	4.4
Manufacturing managers, as a percentage of EAM	13.1	6.0	9.7	8.9
Professional Occupations (PO), as a percentage of the group's labor force	11.0	5.6	5.1	19.6
Engineering occupations, as a percentage of PO	23.7	11.9	19.1	35.1
Physical scientists, as a percentage of PO	8.0	6.1	5.6	10.0
Primary and secondary school teachers, as a percentage of PO	17.3	26.3	17.5	6.4
Social, recreation, religious workers, writers, artists, entertainers, as a percentage of PO	19.9	29.4	27.9	11.4

Source: U.S. Bureau of the Census (1980). Computed from Table 277.

The employment figures for these detailed kinds of endeavors are conditional on membership in the respective major category and therefore do not reflect group differences in the propensity to be in one or another broad occupational class, that is, the rates in Rows 1 and 6.

From these data it is evident that the occupational outcomes are closely related to choice of educational specialty. In particular, within the EAM category, blacks (who tend, disproportionately, to major in education) are more than twice as likely as any other group to be education administrators. Asians (who have the lowest tendency to major in education) are the least likely to be employed in this EAM category. It is also more common for whites and Asians to be financial managers, and this outcome may reflect their greater tendency to specialize in technical fields in their education.

Probably the pattern of representation among detailed professional occupations is the most revealing datum with regard to the import of college majors on career direction. Among individuals in the PO category, it is far more common for whites and Asians, than the other groups, to be engaged in an engineering or physical science line of work. Blacks and Hispanics, in comparison, tend to be overrepresented in public school teaching and in social and humanistic occupations.

From a different source, we obtain figures that are consistent with the patterns of race and ethnic distribution in the national economy. IBM (1982, p. 3) has reported a breakdown of its work force, by major occupational category and race and ethnicity, for 1981. Calculations from these data indicate that, whereas 50% of white employees are classified as managers or professionals and 66% of Asians have these occupational designations, only 32% of blacks and 27% of Hispanics are in the categories. Even more striking, but consistent with the national data, are the representation rates of the four groups in professional employment alone: 36% of the white work force, 58% of Asians but only 23% of blacks and 20% of Hispanics.

The magnitude of these differences in achievement and occupational specialty is very large. The differences indicate that much more effort must be devoted to incorporating blacks and Hispanics into better jobs in the economy to achieve a representation that reflects their numbers in society. However, the findings also reveal that American society is sufficiently open and class boundaries permeable to permit high attainment by racial and ethnic minorities. Our analysis confirms what has been often said—that the most direct pathway to high occupational achievement is through the educational system. Indeed, it is likely that the principal source of the occupational disadvantage experienced by blacks and Hispanics, at the present time, with respect to corporate careers arises from their low college completion rates and from choice of major.

Should one fault minority individuals for majoring in education and social work rather than in mathematics or engineering? Clearly, there is a considerable need for capable individuals in the former fields, and a strong argument can be made to the effect that we should encourage and reward these sorts of career choices. However, if one inquires more narrowly about the sorts of skills in demand by large corporations or about the backgrounds that are likely to lead to high occupational attainment in business organizations—assuredly the concerns addressed in this volume—then, I contend, poor educational choices are being made by black and Hispanic youth.

III. ENHANCING MINORITY OPPORTUNITY FOR CORPORATE CAREERS

The analysis in this chapter makes clear that, in the long run, we must increase survivorship rates in the school system by minority youth and formulate strategies to raise their rates of college completion. I suspect that relatively little can be done by employers about the former matter because the dropout rate is already severe in high school and in the early college years, long before an opportunity for a corporate career becomes a serious inducement. Preventing this early dropout rate will probably remain the responsibility of family, educational institutions, and the larger society, as it is not evident how corporate actors can influence the early stages in the development of the pool of eventual college graduates.

Corporations can influence the choice of a college major by minority youth, through a process of emphasizing the linkage between specialization and career prospects. Although presentations on college campuses have value, large organizations should also consider a strategy of early recruitment: Hiring minority youth in, perhaps, their sophomore year, contingent upon successful completion of college with a particular specialization. Even if such a program carried only minimal payments while in college, the promise of an attractive entry-level position would be an inducement to complete college and to major in a field that is in demand by business organizations.

As a short-run strategy, accepting current completion rates and choices of college major as a given, corporations should actively recruit minority dropouts from college and graduates with majors in undesired fields. A variety of educational options would be made available to these recruits by employers, including specialized in-house training and tuition credits for coursework at neighboring universities. Most important, there should be clearly stated career rewards for completing college part-time or for retraining in a desired specialty.

Although these proposals are modest, they are based on an analysis of the sources of disadvantage experienced by black and Hispanic youth with regard to entry into a corporate career as well as an assessment of the developmental stages in the education process at which business organizations can intervene with some prospect of a potent impact. I have not addressed in this discussion the complementary but very important issue of the career course of minority individuals *within* a corporation, except to note that choice of college major has a residual effect and leaves many minority individuals poorly situated. Topics such as the importance of sponsorship, the contribution of role models, and the details of minority careers within corporations, more generally, are addressed in several other chapters in this volume.

ACKNOWLEDGMENT. This research was supported by NSF Grant SES-82-18534, by NIA Grant 1-RO1-AG04367-01A1, and by a grant from the Center for Research in Career Development, Graduate School of Business, Columbia University. The author is solely responsible for the conclusions.

IV. REFERENCES

Brown, George. 1982. *Earned degrees, by racial/ethnic status: 1978/79*. National Center for Education Statistics. U.S. Department of Education. Unpublished report.

Clark, Kenneth B. 1965. *Dark ghetto: Dilemmas of social power*. New York: Harper & Row.

International Business Machines. 1982. *Equal opportunity programs*. Document number SV04-0127-04 (January). Unpublished memo.

Jencks, Christopher. 1972. *Inequality: A reassessment of the effect of family and schooling in America*. New York: Basic.

Moynihan, Patrick. 1966. Employment, income, and the ordeal of the Negro family. In Talcott Parsons and Kenneth B. Clark (Eds.), *The Negro American* (pp. 134–159). Boston: Beacon.

National Advisory Committee on Black Higher Education and Black Colleges and Universities. 1980. *Target date, 2000 A.D.: Goals for achieving higher education equity for black Americans*. Washington, DC: U.S. Government Printing Office.

Sowell, Thomas. 1975. *Race and economics*. New York: McKay.

U.S. Bureau of the Census. 1980. *Census of population: Detailed population characteristics. U.S. summary*. Washington, DC: Government Printing Office.

3

Employment Prospects for Minority Women

Shelley A. Smith and Marta Tienda

One of the most controversial issues facing all levels of government today concerns current policies that provide equal employment opportunities for women and minorities in the United States labor force. The legality of previously enacted affirmative action legislation has recently been questioned on constitutional grounds, whereas research continues to confirm that women and members of minority populations are underrepresented in higher paying jobs and overrepresented in jobs that offer low economic rewards and few opportunities for advancement. This situation is particularly crucial for female minority group members, who carry the double burden of gender and color into an already segregated labor market.

In this chapter, we document some of the circumstances that account for persisting disadvantages experienced by minority women in the U.S. labor force. We accomplish this by evaluating the contemporary labor market position of minority women through an analysis of labor force characteristics, occupational segregation, and earnings differentials. Our primary interest is in black, Hispanic, and Asian women, whom we compare with non-Hispanic white women to show how the labor market standing of the former groups differs from that of the majority white female population. Central to our evaluation are premarket circumstances that critically shape women's labor market opportunities. In the previous chapter, Spilerman documented the crucial role of education in expanding employment opportunities prior to labor market entry. For women, and particularly women of color, additional factors—child care responsibilities, marital status, and being a single head of

Shelley A. Smith • Department of Sociology, University of South Carolina, Columbia, South Carolina 29208.   **Marta Tienda** • Department of Sociology, University of Chicago, Chicago, Illinois 60637.

household—not only affect labor market opportunities for higher paying jobs (Jacobsen, 1985) but also influence women's access to premarket education and training.

This chapter is organized into three sections. We begin with a sociodemographic overview of the female labor force in 1980 by race and national origin in which we selectively emphasize those characteristics associated with women's labor market activity. In Section 2 we consider the nature of work performed by employed women. This section compares the occupational configuration among women of different racial and ethnic groups. Additionally, we evaluate the extent of occupational segregation in the female labor force by sex and race in 1980. Section 3 documents earnings disparities among women of color and evaluates the importance of individual, household, and job characteristics that differentially influence earnings among minority women. We conclude by considering the future prospects for minority women in the U.S. labor market and comment on the barriers they face in the upcoming decade.

I. THE FEMALE LABOR FORCE: DEMOGRAPHIC CHARACTERISTICS

Our purpose in this section is to document socioeconomic differences among economically active minority women because of what they portend for the type of occupations they are likely to hold and their earnings levels. For women especially, the importance of evaluating social and demographic characteristics derives from the considerable impact of marriage and childbearing on their patterns of human capital investment and the role schooling plays in differentiating earnings among women of varying racial and ethnic origins.

The average age of the female labor force in the United States has risen steadily since the turn of the century, with rapid increases occurring since 1940 (Oppenheimer, 1970). In the recent past, greater numbers of women with children have reentered the labor force after bearing children (Sweet, 1975). Presently, a rising proportion of the female labor force continues to work throughout early childbearing years and spends more years in paid employment than has been true in the past. As a result of these trends, the average age of the female labor force has increased. In 1980, the mean age of the female labor force ranged between 32 and 40 years, and the modal age of employed women was between 25 and 44 years, irrespective of minority group membership (see Table 1). As a group, Cuban women are generally older than other minority women and non-Hispanic white women; this reflects the largely adult character of the Cuban refugee movement to the United States following the revolution of 1959. Not only were these refugees older, but the early cohorts (1960–1964) on average were more highly educated than other immigrant groups who have entered the U.S.

With the exception of black women, over half of all economically active women were married in 1980. Uniformly high rates of marital disruption characterize black and Puerto Rican working women who in 1980 had the

Table 1.   Selected Social and Demographic Characteristics of the
Female Labor Force, 1980 (in Percentages)

	White	Mexican	Puerto Rican	Cuban	Black	Asian
Percentage of the female labor force	81.4	2.7	0.5	0.4	11.1	1.9
Age						
Mean	36.7	32.7	34.1	39.7	36.7	36.0
16–24 years	24.4	30.9	25.6	19.3	19.5	17.5
25–44 years	45.4	51.0	53.7	40.6	53.2	58.4
45 + years	30.2	18.2	20.8	40.0	27.4	24.1
Marital status						
Married	57.0	55.2	53.0	59.7	43.6	63.9
Widowed	5.1	3.2	2.4	4.1	6.7	3.7
Divorced	10.8	9.2	11.6	11.3	12.4	5.7
Separated	2.2	4.2	7.0	2.6	9.6	1.9
Never married	25.0	28.3	26.1	22.3	27.6	24.9
Headship						
Household head	22.7	17.9	25.6	17.9	35.6	15.9
Education						
Mean	12.9	10.6	11.4	12.0	12.3	13.3
Percentage high-school graduates	64.6	48.8	52.3	51.9	58.7	49.3
Percentage college graduates	16.9	5.4	8.4	16.4	12.0	31.2
Employment status						
Percentage full-time/yr-round	48.8	44.1	48.4	52.2	50.9	50.4
Mean annual earnings	$8,227	$6,784	$7,754	$7,748	$8,287	$9,614

Source: 1980 Census, 1% Public Use Microdata Sample.

highest rates of marital disruption. Over 12% of employed black women and 11.6% of Puerto Rican women were divorced, and roughly 10% and 7%, respectively, were separated. This compares with less than 8% of Asian women who were divorced or separated in the same year.

The growing incidence of families headed by minority and nonminority women alike has propelled many women into the labor market out of economic necessity (Tienda & Glass, 1985). Over one-third of employed black women headed their own households in 1980, compared to one in four employed Puerto Rican women and 22% of non-Hispanic white women. Although the child care responsibilities demanded of single mothers often constrain their level of commitment to the labor market, economic pressures, nevertheless, compel many single heads of households into some form of paid employment. Particularly crucial for single mothers whose financial responsibilities propel them into the paid work force are foregone educational opportunities. Of all the prelabor market factors that contribute to labor market outcomes, perhaps none is as pivotal in predicting access to employment opportunities as education. This is true both in the short and long term.

Non-Hispanic white women have gradually closed the education gap between themselves and their male counterparts, but marked differences in educational attainment persist among minority working women that mirror differences in their occupational and earnings profiles. In 1980, Asian women had the highest average level of education, 13.3 years, followed by non-Hispanic white women at roughly 13 years, whereas Mexican and Puerto Rican women averaged less than a high-school degree. Although close to half or more of women in all groups were high-school graduates in 1980, a remarkable one-third of all Asian women were college graduates, nearly twice as many as Cuban or non-Hispanic white women, and sixfold the share of college-educated Mexican-origin working women.

In 1980, the percentage of women employed on a full-time, year-round basis hovered at 50% for all groups, with the exception of Mexican women, of whom 44% were so employed. The influence of minority group status on average annual earnings is made clear in the last row of Table 1. Not unexpectedly, we find that, in 1980, women of Asian origin received the highest annual earnings, which is consistent with the large proportion holding college degrees in this group. The earnings gap between non-Hispanic white and black women had nearly closed by 1980. However, because the data presented in Table 1 are based on all employed women *irrespective of full- or part-time employment status,* the earnings of black women show a slight edge over those of white women. Longer, uninterrupted work histories of black relative to white women and the greater seniority attained by black women (Wallace, 1980) largely explain the narrowed average earnings gap between white and black working women. Mexican women had the lowest annual earnings in 1980, receiving only 70% of their Asian counterparts and slightly more than 80% of the earnings of non-Hispanic white women.

In summary, Table 1 shows that female minority group members in the labor force are quite differentiated with respect to their contemporary sociodemographic characteristics. Asian women were at a comparative advantage to the other groups, including non-Hispanic white women, because of their low rates of marital disruption and female headship as well as higher educational credentials and average annual earnings. Women of Hispanic origin and black women exhibit characteristics that can pose difficult, often insurmountable barriers to access to labor market opportunities. Black women had very high rates of marital disruption and female headship in 1980. Mexican and Puerto Rican women were the most severely disadvantaged due to lesser human capital investments in higher education; only 5% and 8%, respectively, had acquired college degrees in 1980.

The disadvantages experienced by minority women in the labor market are partially illustrated in the comparisons of individual and household characteristics presented in Table 1. A clearer picture of how group sociodemographic differences shape the labor market experiences of minority women emerges from their allocation to different types of jobs. We review this question in the next section, in which we examine the kinds of work performed by female minority group members and the level of occupational segregation based on sex and race.

II. OCCUPATIONAL DISTRIBUTION AND COMPOSITION OF THE FEMALE LABOR FORCE IN 1980

A comparison of the 1980 occupational distributions of female minority group members reveals how race and ethnicity interact with gender to shape the labor market profile of employed women. That between 60% and 75% of all working women in 1980 were employed in just three occupations—clerical, service, and operative jobs—attests to the restricted access women have to the array of job opportunities in the U.S. labor market. Clerical jobs were the modal occupational category for all employed women in 1980, irrespective of their color, with the share of clerical workers ranging from 30% for Asian women to 37% for both Puerto Rican and non-Hispanic white women.

Although women of all origins in 1980 were concentrated in the three occupational categories mentioned before, the levels of schooling reported in Table 1 suggest that Asian and non-Hispanic white women, the two educationally advantaged groups, would have more access to professional occupations than other nonwhite women. The data reported in Table 2, which shows the allocation of women by race and ethnicity across 11 broad occupational categories in 1970 and 1980, supports this expectation. Asian women were most prominently represented in professional and technical occupations, followed by non-Hispanic white women. As early as 1970 almost 18% of Asian women held professional jobs, and only non-Hispanic white women attained a comparable level of professional employment by 1980. However, by that time, over one in five Asian women held professional jobs, thus maintaining their occupational advantage even over non-Hispanic white women.

Although all women increased their representation in higher status white-collar occupations between 1970 and 1980, proportionately fewer black and Hispanic women were employed in those occupations in both years compared to Asian and non-Hispanic white women. The presence of Puerto Rican, Cuban, and black women in managerial jobs roughly tripled, and the proportion of Mexican women approximately doubled between 1970 and 1980. Yet less than one-third of the women in any racial or ethnic group worked in upper-white-collar occupations in 1980, indicating the barriers faced by all women in securing higher paying occupations in both private and public sector industries. The relative success of Asian and non-Hispanic white women in securing higher paying occupations appears to be less a result of differential recruitment strategies by prospective employers than the product of higher education and lower levels of marital disruption compared to other women, a conclusion we verify further in a following section.

At the opposite end of the occupational spectrum, Hispanic-origin women continued to be heavily concentrated in skilled and unskilled blue-collar

Shelley A. Smith and Marta Tienda

Table 2. Occupational Distribution of Women in the Labor Force, 1970–1980.

Occupation	White		Mexican		Puerto Rican		Cuban		Black		Asian	
	1970	1980	1970	1980	1970	1980	1970	1980	1970	1980	1970	1980
Upper white collar												
Professional	15.1	17.6	5.5	8.8	6.0	12.2	7.7	10.3	10.2	15.0	17.6	21.6
Semi-professional	1.7	3.0	0.7	1.9	1.5	2.5	1.7	2.7	1.2	3.0	4.8	4.5
Manager	3.6	7.1	1.9	3.6	1.1	3.6	1.2	6.4	1.3	3.8	2.5	4.9
Lower white collar												
Clerical	38.4	37.1	26.9	31.4	27.3	36.9	25.2	35.0	20.9	29.4	31.7	29.8
Sales	7.8	6.9	6.4	4.3	5.0	3.2	6.1	5.9	2.5	2.8	5.4	4.4
Upper blue collar												
Crafts	1.9	2.0	2.1	2.7	2.4	2.7	2.3	2.0	1.5	1.8	1.5	1.5
Operative	13.9	9.9	23.8	21.8	43.2	23.7	40.7	25.4	16.4	14.8	14.7	15.2
Lower blue collar												
Service	16.6	14.9	25.7	20.9	12.4	12.9	13.0	10.9	43.7	27.3	19.9	16.6
Laborer	0.9	1.2	1.5	2.0	0.8	1.8	1.4	1.3	1.5	1.8	1.0	0.9
Farmer/farm manager	0.1	0.1	0.1	0.0	0.0	0.0	0.0	0.0	0.1	0.0	0.3	0.1
Farm laborer	0.2	0.3	5.4	2.8	0.3	0.6	0.6	0.3	0.8	0.4	0.8	0.6

Source: 1970 and 1980 census, 1% Public Use Microdata Samples.

occupations in 1980. Between 20% and 25% of employed Hispanic-origin women worked in blue-collar operative occupations in 1980, in sharp contrast to black, Asian, and non-Hispanic white women. Factory work has in the past provided employment for many Hispanic-origin workers, particularly those who have migrated to the midwestern and northeastern states where manufacturing in textile, food, and other light manufacturing industries thrived for many years. This situation seems to have changed in the Northeast in recent years, as many textile and garment firms have migrated south and overseas in search of lower priced labor.

Despite the secular decrease in the availability of laborer jobs as the structure of production in the United States shifted from goods to services between 1970 and 1980 (Singelmann and Tienda, 1985), all but Cuban and Asian women *increased* their representation in laborer occupations during this period. Only Puerto Rican and non-Hispanic white women, however, increased their representation among farm laborer positions, although they still represent far less in proportion than do Mexican women in farm laborer jobs. Just under 3% of Mexican-origin women held farm laborer jobs in 1980, down from over 5% in 1970. The higher representation of Mexican women compared to other women in agricultural occupations reflects their historical roles in the development of U.S. agriculture (Tienda, 1981) and especially their widespread participation in the migratory farm worker streams until the early 1970s.

A comparison of the 1970 and 1980 occupational distributions of the female work force shows some upgrading in occupational attainment over the decade, largely because women made gains in the traditionally male-dominated professional, technical, and managerial occupations, whereas the share of women employed in the low-paying service jobs declined or remained steady. The decline in service employment during the 1970s, which largely resulted from the declining demand for domestic service workers, was most pronounced for black and Mexican-origin women. Cuban and Puerto Rican women experienced greatest declines in operative employment over the decade; this ceased to be their modal employment category, owing partly to the substantial expansion of clerical employment for them and most other minority women.

The significance of the occupational profiles presented in Table 2 resides not only in the social standing and earnings these jobs portend for their incumbents but also in the level of gender-based occupational segregation. This is starkly shown by the disproportionate concentration of women in a small number of occupational categories. Research that examines the relationship between gender segregation of jobs and earnings has established the importance of distinguishing between earning differences arising from the uneven allocation of women and men in the occupational structure, versus those arising from paying men and women differently for similar work (England and McLaughlin, 1979; Tienda and Ortiz, 1987). Moreover, although much of the earnings disparity between men and women arises from the concentration of women in lower paying "feminized" jobs, some researchers suggest that certain jobs pay less precisely because they are dominated by women (England & McLaughlin, 1979; Shack-Marquez, 1984).

Although in Table 2 we observed that women were overwhelmingly concentrated in just three occupations, we also saw that certain minority groups were disproportionately concentrated in lower paying occupations compared to non-Hispanic white women. The extent to which certain occupations are open or closed to women of color is, along with gender segregation, an indication of the progress made by employed non-white women in access to well-paying jobs. Table 3 provides further information for evaluating how occupations were structured by gender and race in 1980.

Column 1 of Table 3 shows that, in 1980, clerical and service occupations were the most highly feminized; in these occupations, respectively, 80% and 67% of the workers were women. On a pessimistic note, these data indicate little retrenchment in the concentration of women in lower-white-collar and "pink-collar ghettos"; on a more optimistic note, roughly 60% of professional and semiprofessional workers, and one-third of all managers, were women in 1980. That the percentage of women engaged in managerial occupations was roughly one-half that of the other two upper-white-collar occupations testifies to the difficulty women face entering this traditionally male field. The rapid expansion of public sector jobs between 1960 and 1975 provided many opportunities for women to enter professional fields (as teachers, social workers, etc.) particularly in government and education (Tienda and Ortiz, 1987; Tienda and Smith, 1986). Nevertheless, women's access to managerial positions was primarily confined to social service industries in the public sector, whereas management positions in transformative, distributive, and producer ser-

Table 3. Gender and Ethnic Composition of Major Occupation Groups, 1980

Occupation	Percentage female	Percentage Hispanic	Percentage black
Upper white collar			
Professional	59.2	2.1	9.6
Semiprofessional	61.8	2.4	11.1
Manager	33.6	2.2	6.4
Lower white collar			
Clerical	80.0	3.5	9.0
Sales	51.0	2.6	4.7
Upper blue collar			
Craft	13.1	4.9	10.1
Operative	45.3	7.3	14.7
Lower blue collar			
Service	67.4	4.2	18.3
Laborer	19.1	5.6	15.1
Farmer/farm manager	9.8	0.0	5.0
Farm laborer	23.7	20.6	10.8

Source: 1980 Census, 1% Public Use Microdata Sample.

vices industries, which are predominantly private sector industries, continue to be largely closed to them.

Limited access to well-paying jobs in the occupational structure is even more pronounced among women of color, particularly blacks and women of Hispanic origin. Female minority group members comprised roughly 20% of the female labor force in 1980. Over half of these were black women (11%), 3.6% were women of Hispanic origin, about 2% Asian, and approximately 3% who do not fit any of the categories used here but are not non-Hispanic white women (see Row 1, Table 1). Hispanic origin women were uniformly underrepresented in professional, semiprofessional and managerial occupations in 1980 and overrepresented in lower paying blue-collar craft, operative, service, and laborer occupations. Only about 2% of all women engaged in the three upper-white-collar occupations in 1980 were Hispanics, compared to between 5% and 7% in craft and operative occupations. Essentially these comparisons show that relative to their 4% share of the total female labor force, Hispanics were underrepresented in upper status jobs and overrepresented in lower status jobs.

Black women, who comprised 11% of the female labor force in 1980, were more highly represented than Hispanic women in semiprofessional occupations. Yet like all employed women, blacks remained slightly underrepresented in professional, and especially managerial, jobs. In 1980, roughly 6% of all women employed in managerial occupations were black. The declining pace of expansion in service industries during the latter half of the 1970s (Singelmann and Tienda, 1985) coupled with the increasing competition for service jobs from men and the declining demand for domestic service workers (Tienda and Smith, 1986) has reduced the percentage of female service workers who were black over the past decade. Although the percentage of black women employed in service occupations decreased 50% between 1970 and 1980, nearly one in five female service employees was black in 1980.

In summary, the descriptive data on the occupational placement of women suggests that all women, but particularly minority women, had restricted access to the array of occupations available in 1980. Before discussing women's earnings in 1980, we wish to emphasize the importance of linking gender and race or ethnicity with both individual and institutional determinants of labor market activity. The occupational distribution of women in the labor force mirrors, but does not identically reproduce, the differential distribution of educational qualifications. Similarly, different levels of economic need and household composition—marital status, single headship, and the presence of young children—delineate not only access to premarket training among women and hence labor market placement but also determine levels of labor market commitment among women. Institutionally, occupational segregation based on gender and race further defines labor market opportunities by reserving a disproportionate share of low-paying jobs for women and minorities. To the extent that these allocative criteria are additive, then minority women are doubly disadvantaged—once because they are women and once more because they are nonwhite.

Despite recent and dramatic increases in the supply of women entering and remaining in the labor market, downward pressure on the earnings of women and minorities can be exacerbated if the increased rate of female labor force participation reinforces existing patterns of gender- and color-based occupational segregation. Therefore, in our analyses of women's earnings, we investigate whether such structural measures as gender and racial composition of women's occupations influenced the economic rewards received by female workers above and beyond their individual productivity characteristics. Evidence that the racial and gender composition of jobs determined the rewards associated with them will lend support to prevailing arguments about the importance of institutionalized discrimination in differentiating earnings between men and women, and among various minority groups.

III. WOMEN'S EARNINGS IN 1980

We begin our analysis of the determinants of women's earnings by first evaluating variation in annual earnings by race and ethnicity across four broad occupational categories. Table 4 displays annual earnings for women of color in 1969 and 1979 adjusted for full-time, year-round employment status. Our adjustment procedure differentially weights the average annual earnings in an occupational category by the relative numbers of women in full versus part-time employment.

The comparison of women's annual earnings in 1969 and 1979 accentuates the complexity of the combined effects of gender and race on labor market outcomes. Not unexpectedly, women in upper-white-collar occupations, traditionally higher paying and dominated by men, received the highest earnings in both years. In 1979, a fairly linear pattern emerged between annual earnings and the ranked occupational groups. To wit, women in

Table 4. Occupational Distribution of 1969 and 1979 Annual Earnings, Women[a]

Occupation	White	Mexican	Puerto Rican	Cuban	Black	Asian
			1979			
Upper white collar	$10,981	$9,253	$11,044	$10,581	$11,633	$13,874
Lower white collar	7,545	6,941	7,340	7,655	8,253	8,392
Upper blue collar	7,573	6,702	6,625	6,466	7,841	7,219
Lower blue collar	5,883	5,277	6,844	6,494	6,110	6,871
			1969			
Upper white collar	$12,493	$3,779	$4,076	$4,293	$9,258	$12,995
Lower white collar	6,709	2,296	2,750	2,665	5,070	6,780
Upper blue collar	6,052	2,099	2,291	2,755	4,274	10,650
Lower blue collar	10,168	1,232	1,898	1,948	4,506	9,215

[a]Adjusted for full-time year-round employment status.
Source: 1980 and 1970 Census, 1% Public Use Microdata Samples.

lower-blue-collar jobs had the lowest earnings, and for all but non-Hispanic white women, upper-blue-collar and lower-white-collar occupations paid incrementally higher annual earnings.

Substantial earnings differences exist among and between white and nonwhite women holding higher paying occupations. Among Hispanic-origin women engaged in upper-white-collar occupations, the annual earnings of Mexican origin women were approximately 85%, and those of Cuban women, roughly 95% as high as the earnings of Puerto Rican women, who received the highest average earnings among professional Hispanic-origin women. Black and Asian women holding professional, semiprofessional, and managerial jobs in 1979 received the highest annual earnings among all minority women. Their average earnings, and those of white-collar Puerto Rican women, exceeded those of non-Hispanic white women holding comparable positions. Payoffs to higher levels of human capital investment among Asian women and longer uninterrupted years of work experience among black women are two factors largely responsible for these earning differentials among the four occupational categories.

Comparisons of the earnings of women employed in upper-white-collar occupations in 1969 and 1979 illustrate the extent to which the demographic characteristics of the female labor force continue to change. With the exception of Asian and non-Hispanic white women, annual earnings for women employed in upper-white-collar occupations rose substantially over the decade. Non-Hispanic white women had *lower* average earnings in 1979 than 1969, which is an artifact of their patterns of labor-force participation.[1] The majority of non-Hispanic white women holding higher paying occupations in 1969 most probably worked on a full-time, year-round basis; in 1979, a higher proportion probably worked part-time, hence giving more weight to the lower earnings of part-time workers in these occupations.

The differential earnings levels accruing to women of varying racial and ethnic origins in 1979 suggest that even when women attain higher paying jobs, their earnings are not always commensurate with the prestige or status commonly associated with a particular occupational position. We address the question of unequal treatment based on race and ethnicity by estimating women's earnings functions for each group separately in 1979. For this analysis, we include all women aged 16 or over who were in the labor force for whom nonmissing industry and occupation data were available. We con-

---

[1]This result was initially puzzling to us. Although the annual earnings of nonwhite women realized increases over the decade, this was not the case for non-Hispanic white women when we controlled for employment status. We believe that gains in labor-force participation rates for non-Hispanic white women, particularly among those who are married or have children, have been largely in part-time employment relative to their participation in 1970. For example, the percentage of non-Hispanic white women employed in low-paying clerical and service occupations on a part-time basis increased between 1970 and 1980, whereas the percentage of black women so employed decreased. This results in weighting *down* women's 1979 earnings with the lower earnings of those occupations.

trolled for full-time versus part-time employment status in order to adjust for the effects of labor supply differences on earnings.

In order to portray the effects of occupational segregation by gender and race, we computed three structural measures from a matrix of occupation by industry cells for the 1980 female labor force, which depicted the relative percentage of female, black, and Hispanic incumbents in each occupation by industry cell. We subsequently assigned these aggregate measures to each individual based on their job incumbency in 1980 (as defined by broad occupation and detailed industry codes).

The results of the regression analysis predicting women's 1979 earnings are reported in Table 5. On balance, productivity characteristics were related to women's earnings in the way human capital theory predicts, but there are several notable differences between women of differing racial and ethnic origins. Marital status was significantly and positively related to earnings for all groups; without exception, married women in 1979 earned between 15% and 26% more on an average annual basis than their never-married counterparts. Similarly, with the exception of Puerto Rican and Asian women, divorced women also earned significantly more than their race counterparts who were never married, indicating the economic pressures of family responsibilities often associated with disrupted unions.

Economic returns to education reveal the most striking differences among women of color. All women benefited in the form of higher earnings from having completed college, but the penalty for college noncompletion was most severe for black and non-Hispanic white women. Black women with no college degree earned nearly 80% less than their otherwise comparable sisters holding college degrees. Cuban, Puerto Rican, and Asian women were penalized least by college noncompletion: Cuban women with no college degree earned 53% less than their college-educated counterparts, whereas comparable differentials for Asian and Puerto Rican women were 57% lower. In the case of Puerto Rican women, the smaller differential between college completion and noncompletion results from the relative scarcity of women with college degrees (see Tienda and Guhleman, 1985; also Nelson, 1984). This scarcity drives up the wage rate for college-educated Puerto Rican women, thus partly explaining the unusually high earnings of upper-white-collar Puerto Rican women.

At the opposite end of the educational spectrum, the economic disadvantage associated with high-school noncompletion is clearly evident. Black women lacking a high-school degree were the most disadvantaged, earning 34% less than their counterparts who had completed high school. The figure for non-Hispanic white women is 31%. Among Puerto Rican and Asian women, the earnings differentials associated with no high school degree versus high-school completion were only between 21% and 22%. The narrower earnings differential among Asian women arises from the relative scarcity of Asian women with less than a high-school education in 1980 (see Table 1).

As demonstrated in earlier research (Chiswick, 1978, 1979; Reimers, 1985), immigrants often earn less than otherwise similar native-born workers,

Table 5. Effects of Individual, Household, and Work Characteristics on Women's 1979 Log Earnings (Beta Coefficients in Parentheses)[a]

Independent variables	White	Mexican	Puerto Rican	Cuban	Black	Asian
Individual characteristics						
Age[b]						
16 to 25 years	−.371**	−.348**	−.404**	−.319**	−.506**	−.501**
	(−.160)	(−.163)	(−.189)	(−.138)	(−.195)	(−.193)
25 to 44 years	−.094**	−.038	−.112*	.004	−.035*	−.053*
	(−.047)	(−.019)	(−.060)	(.002)	(−.017)	(−.027)
Marital status[c]						
Married	.181**	.156**	.261**	.247**	.249**	.200**
	(.090)	(.079)	(.140)	(.133)	(.120)	(.097)
Widowed	−.101**	−.100+	.090	.137	−.064*	−.077
	(−.022)	(−.018)	(.015)	(.030)	(−.016)	(−.015)
Divorced	.040*	.072*	.088	.200*	.097**	.071
	(.021)	(.021)	(.030)	(.069)	(.031)	(.017)
Separated	−.054+	.009	.018	.073	.045*	−.028
	(−.008)	(.002)	(.005)	(.018)	(.013)	(−.004)
Education						
High-school degree	.313**	.299**	.211**	.283**	.340**	.223**
	(.150)	(.151)	(.113)	(.155)	(.163)	(.113)
College degree	.733**	.671**	.573**	.531**	.786**	.565**
	(.275)	(.154)	(.170)	(.216)	(.249)	(.266)
Immigrant status						
Foreign born	.053*	.035+	−.013	.059	.107**	−.039+
	(.010)	(.016)	(−.003)	(.020)	(.020)	(−.019)
Household characteristics						
Single head of	.304**	.203**	.252**	.143+	.246**	.267**
household	(.128)	(.079)	(.118)	(.060)	(.115)	(.099)
Presence of children	−.047*	.003	.047	.112	.008	.012
under 6	(−.012)	(.001)	(.015)	(.031)	(.002)	(.004)
Job characteristics						
Percentage female	−.002**	−.003**	−.002*	−.003*	−.004**	−.002**
	(−.054)	(−.066)	(−.054)	(−.066)	(−.082)	(−.036)
Percentage black	−.005**	−.010**	−.004	−.0003	−.010**	−.005*
	(−.032)	(−.076)	(−.029)	(−.002)	(−.090)	(−.031)
Percentage Hispanic	−.011**	−.007*	−.029**	−.017+	−.023**	−.033**
	(−.022)	(−.025)	(−.077)	(−.045)	(−.051)	(−.081)
Constant	8.086	8.254	8.351	8.082	8.383	8.403
R^2	.371	.289	.328	.294	.324	.347
[N]	[38,965]	[10,372]	[2,008]	[1,639]	[42,369]	[7,160]

[a] Adjusted for full-time, year-round employment status.
[b] Reference category: 45+ years
[c] Reference category: Never married
Source: 1980 Census, 1% Public Use Microdata Sample. **$p < .001$ *$p < .05$ +$p < .10$.

particularly immediately following their arrival in the United States. However, such earnings discrepancies narrow with increasing time spent in the U.S. labor market (Chiswick, 1979; Massey, 1984). In part, this results because of increasing proficiency with English and in part because, with the passing of time, immigrants encounter more opportunities to match their array of skills with specific jobs and to acquire job-specific training.

Our results show that foreign birth significantly influenced the earnings for all but Puerto Rican and Cuban women. Asian women born in the United States received earnings that averaged 4% above those received by their counterparts born abroad. That a statistically significant earnings advantage emerged for native-born Asian women is less surprising than the positive effect for Mexican-origin women. Although many Hispanic-origin women are immigrants, this apparently did not depress their wages with respect to non-immigrants in 1980. Some Hispanic women were able to find employment in their ethnic communities where language proficiency is less important than in the general labor market. For example, Cubans have formed an ethnic enclave in Miami that employs and caters to the Cuban population. Many Puerto Rican women are likely to have developed English skills because many have lived on the mainland for prolonged periods in their lives. Whether and how much poor English proficiency is a barrier to labor market success depends on the types of jobs sought by women of color. Mexican women who are migrant farm workers in the Southwest are less likely to be handicapped by poor English language skills than women employed in an occupation that requires extensive communication skills.

The negative effect of native birth associated with the earnings of black women indicates that black immigrant women fare comparatively better in the labor market than their U.S.-born sisters. Although this result may seem counterintuitive, it is consistent with other research (Bach and Tienda, 1984) that demonstrates the selectivity of black migration to the United States. Compared to Asian and Hispanic women, there are relatively fewer foreign-born among the black and non-Hispanic white populations. For both of these groups, the foreign-born fare better than their native-born counterparts. Immigrant women from Europe, who are usually white, are likely to come from professional and technical occupational backgrounds (Tienda, 1983). This affords them a distinct advantage over those born in the United States, particularly if they come from English-speaking countries.

The same holds for black foreign-born women, many of whom immigrate from the West Indies and the African continent. In the United States, there is a well-established community of West Indians that has had certain advantages, especially in education, over native-born blacks (Marshall, 1983). Similarly, African immigrants are most heavily concentrated in professional and technical occupations (Kelley and Elwell, 1981), partly because they are recruited to fill occupations where the supply of domestic labor is inadequate to satisfy demand. These factors gave black immigrant women an earning advantage of nearly 11% over U.S.-born black women in 1980 and non-Hispanic white immigrants a 5% advantage over their native-born counterparts.

Family and household characteristics impact women's labor-market outcomes above and beyond their influence on the labor force participation decision. Female headship was associated with a uniformly positive earnings effect for all groups considered, with spouse-absent household heads earning 15% to 30% more than single women or women in intact unions of like race or ethnicity. For these women, assuming the role of sole family provider was a dominant factor governing the economic value of their time. Recall that this earnings analysis is based on the subset of women in the labor force rather than the entire adult female population; hence, for our sample of employed women, the decision to enter the labor market means that the opportunity costs for not working exceeded those associated with entering the market.

With the sole exception of non-Hispanic white women, the presence of young children exerted no significant effect on women's earnings. The depressing effect of young children on the earnings of non-Hispanic white women resulted from the mediating influences of low levels of labor market commitment relative to women of color (Smith and Tienda, 1988) and spouses' earnings. The small number of non-Hispanic white women who remain in the labor force in early childbearing years are likely to have employed spouses; their presence would decrease their aggregate level of economic need relative to women of other racial and ethnic origins.

The effects of gender- and race-based occupational segregation on annual earnings is explored in the final set of characteristics included in our regression analysis. Our three measures of occupational segregation—gender composition, percentage black and percentage Hispanic—reveal clear indications of the existence of institutional segregation in the occupational structure.

The argument that gender segregation in the labor force depresses women's earnings finds support in our results. All women were uniformly penalized for incumbency in female-typed jobs, but this penalty was most severe for black women. That the completion of either high-school or college degrees was sufficient to offset the negative effects of gender composition on annual earnings (this can be seen by comparing beta coefficients) testifies to the importance of human capital investment as a strategy to improve women's earnings, even if this does not automatically ensure decreased levels of gender segregation among jobs.

The uneven impact of the racial and ethnic composition of jobs on women's earnings is troublesome because, like the influence of gender composition, it reflects a tendency toward depressed earnings for incumbents of occupations in which minority workers are concentrated. The finding that not all women are equally penalized also is disturbing. The racial and ethnic composition terms exerted significantly negative effects on the 1979 earnings of most women.

By examining the beta coefficients associated with the percentage black measure, we observe that Mexican and black women were the most penalized from incumbency in jobs employing a high percentage of black women in 1980. Similarly, Hispanic composition exerted uniformly negative effects on women's 1979 earnings; with the exception of Mexicans, we find that non-

Hispanic white women were penalized less than women of color. That women of Asian origin suffered more from incumbency in jobs dominated by Hispanic workers than from those dominated by black workers indicates not only the extent to which these jobs are underpaid but also the extent to which uneducated Asian women compete with Hispanics in securing employment. Their overlapping residential configurations make such competition plausible. However, the differing educational characteristics of these two groups probably serves to reduce labor market competition along racial and ethnic lines, despite the disproportionate representation of Asians and Hispanics in the western United States.

In summary, we find that racial and ethnic differences among women, coupled with occupational segregation, significantly differentiated women's 1979 earnings. Although educational credentials clearly contributed to higher earnings for all women, the effects of higher educational thresholds differed among groups, indicating the existence of discrimination in the evaluation of schooling for women, depending on their race or ethnicity. Our findings that gender, racial, and ethnic composition of jobs significantly lowered the economic rewards women received, above and beyond their productivity characteristics, are more problematic from a policy standpoint. Evidence of racial and ethnic stratification *within* jobs concurs with other work showing the importance of gender composition in stratifying jobs on the basis of sex (Tienda, Smith, and Ortiz, 1987). The general indication that both gender and racial/ethnic composition of jobs effectively holds down women's earnings requires further verification using alternative data sets to ascertain whether we are justified in concluding that institutionalized discrimination persists as a significant determinant of women's earnings.

IV. CONCLUSION

Our story provides grounds for optimism and pessimism about the prospects for women of color in the U.S. labor force. On the positive side, we observed occupational upgrading for all women between 1970 and 1980, and an increased share of women in all groups engaged in professional, semiprofessional, and managerial occupations. Further, we observed positive earnings effects of educational thresholds on women's average annual earnings. However, because not all women benefited equally from higher educational credentials, the completion of additional schooling is necessary but not sufficient for narrowing the earnings gap among women of color. One key to understanding why higher education does not reduce the earnings disparities among women stems from the constraints they face as sole family providers. The distribution of sociodemographic characteristics among women translates into substantial differences in opportunity costs. Among these, the decision to continue investing in education versus entering the labor market is perhaps the most critical.

Educational differences notwithstanding, our results strongly indicate the existence of occupational segregation based on gender and color, both of which clearly depress women's earnings. Further, the unequal earnings penalties among women, in which non-Hispanic white women were penalized less than many women of color as incumbents in jobs dominated by black or Hispanic women, suggests that stratification based on color as well as gender contributes to lower earnings.

Although our results afford insights into the economic position of minority and nonminority women in the labor force, they are more suggestive than conclusive about the mechanisms that differentially allocate women into occupations and determine their economic rewards. They do invite consideration of innovative ways to lessen the impact of childbearing, marital status, and single headship on women's labor market outcomes. As recent trends away from social spending progressively eliminate many services that employed women depend on, the role of employers in facilitating their labor market entry becomes increasingly critical. Internships, training, and other educational opportunities provided by employers could result in considerable economic payoffs offered at no opportunity cost to women who assume financial responsibilities as single heads and sole breadwinners. Further, the provision of child care could significantly raise women's labor market commitment, and hence their earnings.

Our results also raise theoretical questions that deserve careful consideration. For example, why does the influence of gender and racial or ethnic occupational composition render different levels of economic rewards to women of differing racial and ethnic origins? What are the mechanisms that perpetuate societal-level gender and racial stratification within occupational niches? These questions are crucial to understanding the unequal treatment of women and minorities in the labor market and should be considered by both employers and policymakers alike.

The current discussion about the impact of comparable worth policy strategies for narrowing male–female earnings differentials should also be discussed in the context of race- and ethnicity-based earnings differentials. A discouraging possibility is that the *sources* of earnings discrimination that stratify the earnings of women and minorities could be left essentially untouched by comparable worth policies. With current trends toward the increased use of technology and the coming obsolescence of once dominant industries, it is likely that the occupational structure will continue to experience major changes through the end of the century. Although changes in the economic structure appear to have provided some benefits to the occupational position of women thus far, the issues raised in this chapter must be more thoroughly explored if eliminating the earnings gap among women and between women and men is to move beyond academic domains and hypotheticals.

ACKNOWLEDGMENTS. This research was supported by the College of Agriculture and Life Sciences, University of Wisconsin—Madison, Hatch Project No. 2886. Computational support is from a grant to the Center for Demography and Ecology from the Center for Population of NICHD (HD-05876). We gratefully acknowledge technical assistance from Yu Xie and Ronald Miller.

V. REFERENCES

Bach, Robert L., and Marta Tienda. 1984. Contemporary immigration and refugee movements and employment adjustment policies. In Vernon M. Briggs, Jr. and Marta Tienda (Eds.), *Immigration: Issues and policy* (pp. 37–82). Salt Lake City, UT: Olympia.

Chiswick, Barry R. 1978. The effect of Americanization on the earnings of foreign-born men. *Journal of Political Economy* 86(5):897–921.

Chiswick, Barry R. 1979. The economic progress of immigrants: Some apparently universal patterns. In W. Fellner (Ed.), *Contemporary economic problems* (pp. 357–399). Washington, DC: American Enterprise Institute.

England, Paula, and Steven D. McLaughlin. 1979. Sex segregation of jobs and male-female income differentials. In Rodolfo Alvarez et al. (Eds.), *Discrimination in organizations* (pp. 189–213). San Francisco: Jossey-Bass.

Jacobsen, Linda A. 1985. *Women's education, occupational training, and work experience: Patterns, determinants and returns.* Unpublished doctoral dissertation, University of Wisconsin—Madison.

Kelly, Charles B., and Patricia J. Elwell. 1981. International migration: Canada and the United States. In M. Kritz, Charles B. Kelly, and Sylvano M. Tomasi (Eds.), *Global trends in migration: Theory and research on international population movements* (pp. 181–207). New York: The Center for Migration Studies of New York, Inc.

Marshall, Dawn I. 1983. Toward an understanding of Caribbean migration. In M. Kritz (Ed.), *U.S. immigration and refugee policy* (pp. 113–131). Lexington, MA: Lexington.

Massey, Douglas S. 1984. The settlement process among Mexican migrants to the United States: New methods and findings. Appendix III in *Immigration statistics, A story of neglect.* Final Report of the Panel on Immigration Statistics, Research Committee on National Statistics of the National Research Council. Washington, DC: National Academy of Sciences.

Nelson, Candace. 1984. Hispanic educational attainment: An ethnic issue? Unpublished master's thesis. University of Wisconsin—Madison.

Oppenheimer, Valerie Kincade. 1970. *The female labor force in the United States.* Berkeley: University of California Press.

Reimers, Cordelia W. 1985. A comparative analysis of the wages of Hispanics, blacks and non-Hispanic whites. In George Borjas and Marta Tienda (Eds.), *Hispanics in the U.S. Economy* (pp. 27–75). New York: Academic.

Shack-Marquez, Janice. 1984. Earnings differences between men and women: An introductory note. *Monthly Labor Review* 107(June):15–16.

Singelmann, Joachim, and Marta Tienda. 1985. The process of occupational change in a service society: The case of the United States, 1960–1980. In Bryan Roberts, Ruth Finnegan, and Duncan Gallie (Eds.), *New approaches to economic life: Economic restructuring, unemployment and social division of labor* (pp. 48–67). Manchester, England: University of Manchester Press.

Smith, Shelley A., and Marta Tienda. 1988. The doubly disadvantaged: Women of color in the U.S. labor force. In Ann Stromberg and Shirley Harkness (Eds.), *Working Women* (2nd ed., pp. 61–80). Palo Alto: Mayfield.

Sweet, James A. 1975. Recent trends in the employment of American women. Working Paper 75-14, Center for Demography and Ecology, University of Wisconsin—Madison.

Tienda, Marta. 1981. The Mexican-American population. In Amos Hawley and Sara Mills Maize (Eds.), *Nonmetropolitan American in transition* (pp. 502–548). Chapel Hill: The University of North Carolina Press.

Tienda, Marta. 1983. Socioeconomic and labor force characteristics of U.S. immigrants: Issues and approaches. In Mary M. Kritz (Ed.), *U.S. immigration and refugee policy: Global and domestic issues* (pp. 211–231). Lexington, MA: D. C. Heath.

Tienda, Marta, and Jennifer Glass. 1985. "Extended household composition and female labor force participation." *Demography* 22(3):381–394.

Tienda, Marta, and Patricia Guhleman. 1985. The occupational position of employed Hispanic women. In George Borjas and Marta Tienda (Eds.), *Hispanics in the U.S. economy* (pp. 243–274). New York: Academic.

Tienda, Marta, and Shelley A. Smith. 1986. *The structural transformation of employment in Wisconsin: 1960–1980.* Research Bulletin. College of Agriculture and Life Sciences, University of Wisconsin—Madison.

Tienda, Marta, and Vilma Ortiz. 1987. Intra-industry occupational recomposition and gender inequality in earnings. In Christine Bose and Glenna Spitze (Eds.), *Ingredients for women's employment policy* (pp. 23–51). New York: SUNY Press.

Tienda, Marta, Shelley A. Smith, and Vilma Ortiz. 1987. Industrial restructuring, gender segregation, and sex differences in earnings. *American Sociological Review* 52(April):195–210.

Wallace, Phyllis. 1980. *Black women in the labor force.* Cambridge: M.I.T. Press.

4

Minority and Nonminority MBA
Progress in Business

David L. Ford, Jr.

The minority MBA may be thought of as a relative "newcomer" on the corporate business scene. In fact, until recently, minority representation was so sparse in the managerial ranks of corporate business that it would almost be termed "nonexistent" without greatly exaggerating the situation. However, the civil rights activities of the 1960s along with the affirmative action decisions of the 1970s have helped overcome the previously "lilly-white" management structures of many organizations that now include black and other minority members. In limited numbers and often in special roles, blacks have entered the management ranks of predominately white organizations. Furthermore, Alderfer, Tucker, Morgan, and Drasgow (1983) have observed that such changes in the composition of the managerial work force have brought the tensions associated with contemporary race relations to an arena that previously had been without racial problems largely because it had been without racial differences.

The realization in recent years that blacks who are qualified for managerial positions were very scarce in number led to the decision to increase the number of black MBAs as the quickest way of increasing the supply of potential black managerial talent. As a result, the Consortium Program for Graduate Study in Management and similar educational programs that fund graduate business study for minorities came into being. One report on the responses of 21 consortium program graduates concerning their reasons for seeking the MBA degree and the value of their education revealed that the respondents perceived the MBA degree as a vehicle for (a) strengthening their promotional

David L. Ford, Jr. • School of Management, The University of Texas at Dallas, Richardson, Texas 75080.

opportunities, (b) receiving more job responsibility, and (c) obtaining an improved salary (Hemphill & Reddick, 1974).

With the findings from this study on the reasons for blacks to seek an MBA degree as background, I undertook an extensive study, in collaboration with another colleague, to determine the extent to which these expected payoffs actually accrued to minority MBAs. At the time this study was completed, very little data existed about the job progress of minority MBA graduates. Some of the results of this study, identified here as Study I, are provided later.

Study I was the start of a series of investigations into the nature and outcomes from the work experiences of minority professionals in predominately white organizations. Surprisingly, over the years a consistent pattern or trend in the results has emerged that points toward less positive work experiences and outcomes for minority professionals compared to their white counterparts. These trends have been corroborated in the work of Fernandez (1981), Davis and Watson (1982), and Almquist (1979), to name a few. The results of several of the subsequent investigations by me are also briefly discussed here as Studies II and III. Study II compares minority and non-minority female managers regarding their experiences of stress in the workplace. Study III examines the impact of the mentoring processes on the work outcomes of minority management professionals in public sector jobs. Because only brief descriptions of these studies are provided here, the interested reader is referred to Brown and Ford (1977), Ford (1984), and Ford and Wells (1985) for more detailed descriptions of these findings.

I. RESULTS

A. Study I

This study incorporated several objectives related to the career goals and perceptions of the future of minority MBAs as professionals, their employment experiences before and after the master's degree, and their graduate educational experiences. More specifically, the research sought to determine:

1. Whether the job progression experienced by respondents was different from that of whites with similar training and experience.
2. The extent to which the graduate degree made a difference in the types of positions held before and after graduation.
3. The degree to which the respondents' satisfaction with their graduate program was consistent with their current career attitudes.

The subjects included 161 minority (95% black) MBA graduates of the Consortium Program for Graduate Study in Management and 20 black MBA graduates of two predominately black institutions. All had received their graduate degrees between 1969 and 1974. The subjects were contacted by mail and were asked to complete a research questionnaire. The 181 (161 from the consortium and 20 others) respondents represented a response rate of 63.4%. Although no data were collected directly from white MBA graduates, the findings from the respondents were compared to those reported in a study of 680 white MBAs (Gutteridge, 1974).

Job progression of the respondents was based on both subjective and objective data. The respondents' perceptions of their own job progression was assessed by having them respond to a question indicating whether or not they had received any promotions with their employer and, if so, to indicate whether the promotion came slower, faster, or in step with promotions of their white colleagues with comparable training and experience. More objective indicators of job progression were reflected in (a) the level of the positions respondents held in their organizations relative to whites with comparable training and experience and (b) the salaries received by respondents relative to whites.

Table 1 presents the subjective data regarding respondents' job progression. Column 2 indicates that one-third of the respondents felt their promotions had been in line with normal or average job progression, and 14% felt their progression had been faster than that of their white peers. When corrected for nonresponses and nonpromotions, the results are dramatic. Column 3 of Table 1 indicates that 27% felt their progress to be faster than that of their white peers. Only 5% perceived their progress to be slower than that for white colleagues with comparable training and experience. However, when juxtaposed against the objective data concerning job progress, dramatic differences between perceptions and reality are apparent.

Table 2 indicates the organization level of the respondents' positions with

Table 1. Respondents' Perceptions of Job Progression with Present Employer

Progression index	N	(N/161)	Percentage corrected for nonresponses and nonpromotions (N/81)
In step with normal or average progression for those in the same field	55	34	68
Slower for respondent than for white colleagues with comparable training, ability, and experience	4	2	5
Faster for respondent than for white colleagues with comparable training, ability, and experience	22	14	27
Can't say—promotion involved transfer into unit	1	1	—
Had not received promotions with present employer	76	47	—
No response	4	2	—
Total	162	100	100

Table 2. Organizational Level of Present Position of Respondents by Years since Graduation

Years since graduation	Total		Management trainee		First-level supervisor		First-step middle management		Middle management		Upper management		No response	
	N	%[a]	N	%	N	%	N	%	N	%	N	%	N	%
0–1	60	33	10	5	36	20	—	—	10	6	3	1	1	1
2–3	95	52	7	4	57	32	2	1	24	14	2	1	3	1
4–5	16	15	2	1	16	8	—	—	6	3	1	1	1	1
Total	171	100	19	10	109	60	2	1	40	23	6	3	5	3
Comparable data from Gutteridge (1974)	680	100	21	3.0	166	24.4	133	19.6	231	34.0	129	19		

[a] Percentage of row total.

their employers. The percentages of respondents at each level were compared with the percentages reported by Gutteridge (1974). As seen from Table 2, the most discouraging result concerning job progression of minority MBAs compared to their white counterparts is that a total of 70% of the minority respondents were in trainee or first-level supervisory positions, whereas only 27.4% of white MBAs were in these entry-level positions. This difference in proportions is statistically significant beyond the .01 level.

When the mean current salary of the minority MBAs was compared to that reported by Gutteridge for white MBAs, it was found that the salary progression of minorities was slower than that for whites. Table 3 presents these results. Several things stand out in Table 3: (a) the mean salary increase for minority MBAs compared to whites was $1,508 versus $2,100; (b) there is approximately a $2,500 differential between mean current salaries of graduates from the consortium program and white MBAs and over a $5,000 differential between mean current salaries of graduates from black universities and white MBAs; and (c) although minority MBAs from the consortium received similar higher starting salaries as their white counterparts, on the average, they quickly lost ground to them in subsequent years.

To examine the extent to which the graduate degree made a difference in the types of positions minority MBAs held after receiving the MBA as opposed to before graduate school, the percentage of graduates in each of several functional areas (e.g., accounting, finance, personnel, production, engineering, sales, etc.) were rank ordered for both the respondent's first job after the bachelor's degree and the first job after the master's degree. Only consortium graduates with undergraduate majors in business and economics were considered in this analysis. The Spearman rank order correlation coefficient between the two jobs, corrected for ties, was $r = .433$, which is not significant at the .05 level. Therefore, at least with respect to the functional areas of the jobs held before and after the MBA degree, the graduate degree did make a difference. Many persons worked in different functional areas after the MBA than they did before getting the degree.

Table 3.   Mean Current Salary by Graduating Classes in Comparison to Gutteridge, 1974

Years since graduation	Consortium (N = 153)	Nonconsortium (N = 20)	The Gutteridge study
0–1	$15,543 (N = 46)	$14,550 (N = 10)	$16,287
2–3	17,829 (N = 82)	14,889 (N = 9)	19,515
4–5	20,269 (N = 25)	20,500 (N = 1)	21,107
Mean current salary	$17,539	$15,000	$20,259
Mean starting salary	$14,326	$11,800	$14,037

Finally, the extent to which the respondents' satisfaction with their graduate program was consistent with their current attitudes was assessed. Job satisfaction was measured using a 10-point Likert scale ranging from very dissatisfied (0) to very satisfied (9). In addition, the respondents were asked to rate the extent to which their present work situation was consistent with their work expectations and the extent to which their present job was consistent with their career goals, again using a 10-point Likert scale ranging from very inconsistent (0) to very consistent (9). The respondents' job satisfaction scores correlated significantly with their expectations ($r = .63$, $p < .01$). Additionally, the respondents' job satisfaction scores correlated significantly with the ratings of the extent to which their present job was consistent with their career goals ($r = .525$, $p < .01$).

Therefore, in general, it appeared that the work experiences of the minority MBAs were consistent with their career goals and expectations. Yet, their perceptions of their own progress vis-à-vis that of their white counterparts appeared to be out of touch with reality. Implications of these findings are discussed later.

B. Study II

This study was undertaken to examine the stress experiences resulting from work for a group of black women managers and to compare these results with the experiences of a group of white managerial women reported recently in the literature (cf. Cooper and Davidson, 1982). Another purpose was to suggest directions for future research on issues of importance to minority women in the world of work. The study sample included 74 black supervisory, managerial, and professional women employed in geographically dispersed organizational subunits of a large manufacturing and sales organization headquartered in the Southwest. They had worked for their employers an average of 4.7 years and had been in their present careers an average of 6.5 years. The average age of the women was 34 years.

Participants in the study, all of whom volunteered, responded to a self-report research questionnaire that assessed the participants' perceptions of various aspects of the work environment in terms of job-related stressors, job satisfaction, and reports of experienced phsyiological or health conditions (e.g., backache, ulcers, high blood pressure) and psychological strains (e.g., feeling depressed, feeling tired, having trouble sleeping).

Table 4 presents the proportion of the study participants who reported experiencing various physiological and psychological symptoms and conditions associated with stress. The comparable proportions of white women managers experiencing similar conditions as reported by Cooper and Davidson (1982) are also shown in Table 4. One might question the validity of comparing a black U.S. sample of women to an essentially white British sample. Although there are certainly some demographic and cultural differences, I believe that the work experiences and roles played by women in both samples are similar enough to warrant the comparisons.

The results in Table 4 indicate that the physical ailment most experienced by all respondents was muscle tension. Less than 10% of the participants reported experiencing any of the other physical ailments, with the exception of 27% of the white women, experiencing migraine headaches. Black women were more likely to suffer from muscle tension and heart disease, whereas white women were more likely to experience migraine headaches and arthritis. However, compared with physical ailments in general, a much greater percentage of the black study participants reported having experienced psychological maladies, with tiredness, anxiety, frustration, irritation, and depression being experienced by at least 80% of the black respondents. Compared to the sample of white women reported by Cooper and Davidson (1982) a significantly greater percentage of black as opposed to white women professionals reported experiencing these psychological ailments ($p < .01$ to .001).

Other physiological symptoms reported by a large percentage of the black women professionals in the present study but not shown on the tables because comparable data are not available for whites included backache (41.7%), common cold (50.0%), allergy (25.1%), and diarrhea or constipation (48.6%). Other psychological symptoms reported by a large percentage of the black respondents included difficulty in concentrating (73.3%), becoming less communicative with others (71.6%), forgetfulness (54.1%), and interpersonal problems with spouse or loved ones (75%).

These findings on the physiological and psychological symptoms for black women managers illustrate the high cost of stress on black women

Table 4. Physiological and Psychological Symptoms of Black Women Professionals in Comparison to White Women Professionals

Symptom/condition	Proportion reporting condition		
	Black women (N = 74)	White women (N = 135)[a]	z[b]
Physiological condition			
Migraine headache	8.3%	27.4%	−3.82***
Muscle tension	59.5	42.2	2.51
High blood pressure	9.7	9.6	NS
Heart disease	2.8	0.0	2.0*
Arthritis	0.0	8.1	−2.25*
Ulcers	2.8	4.4	NS
Psychological condition			
Tiredness	90.5	69.6	4.18***
Irritation	82.5	60.0	3.17**
Anxiety	89.3	54.4	4.98***
Frustration	85.1	34.8	7.18***
Sleeplessness	61.3	34.1	3.88***
Depression	80.0	23.7	8.04***

[a]Reported in Cooper and Davidson (1982).
[b]NS = nonsignificant results.
Note: *$p < .05$ (two-tailed); **$p < .01$ (two tailed); ***$p < .001$ (two tailed).

managers in terms of maintaining social relationships and maintaining acceptable levels of performance. Forgetfulness and difficulty in concentrating certainly must affect job performance to some extent. Cooper and Davidson (1982) reported that for the white women managers, in their sample, the reason many seem to suffer stress-related manifestations at work related to their lack of control of the work environment. The black women participants in the present study may be victims of similar work circumstances.

These results are found in Table 5, which shows the five work conditions with the highest percentage of respondents reporting them as stressful to very stressful (scores of 5, 6, or 7). Of these five, at least three suggest a lack of control over the work environment: decisions that are made without the participants' input, fighting fires, and interruptions of work for new priorities. Perhaps such lack of control is a reflection of the lower level of job complexity and job scope associated with the work the black women managers are doing. More than half of these women felt they were overqualified for the work they were performing. However, only 2.4% of the respondents reported that they felt they were underqualified for their work. Thus, it is no wonder that the stress experiences of these women are manifested in the conditions discussed previously. Implications of these findings are discussed in the conclusion of this paper.

C. Study III

Recent work by several noted researchers have documented the benefits that blacks have received as proteges of mentors or sponsors in organizations (e.g., challenging work, promotions, etc.; cf. Campbell, 1982; Davis and Watson, 1982; Dickens and Dickens, 1982). However, these accounts are not of a nature that would allow for the systematic and empirical examination of several factors of importance in the mentoring processes in organizations,

Table 5. Work Conditions Reported by Black Women Professionals as Most Stressful

Work condition	Percentage reporting condition as stressful	Subjective ranking[a]
Decisions or changes that affect me are made "above" without my involvement	55.6%	3
Management (my boss and above) expects me to interrupt my work for new "priorities."	51.8%	4
I feel overqualified for the work I actually do.	50.6%	1
I spend my time fighting fires rather than working from a plan	50.6%	2
I am cautious about what I say in meetings.	45.0%	5

[a]The subjective ranking is based on the proportion of respondents who reported the condition as "most stressful."

such as an examination of race and sex effects. Additionally, much of the available research on mentoring processes has focused on the work experiences of persons employed in the private sector. Therefore, Study III was undertaken to examine several factors related to the job progress of black administrators in the public sector. Indeed, Graves (1982) stressed the value and importance of a mentor in guiding the professional development of black urban administrators. The impact of having a mentor versus not having a mentor on a number of positive and negative work outcomes was examined in this study.

The sample included 134 black executive/managerial and professional personnel employed in various positions in municipal, county, state, and federal government agencies across the country. Several in the sample were elected officials. The sample consisted of 78 men and 56 women whose ages ranged from 21 to 62 years (average age = 37 years). The average length of time each participant had worked in his or her respective job was 41 months. Twenty-two percent of the participants held bachelor's degrees, 54% held master's degrees, 18% held doctorate degrees, and 6% had no degree.

Participants in the study responded to a research questionnaire that measured perceptions of various aspects of the work environment, race, and sex identification of the respondent and his or her supervisor and mentor, if the person had one, and the nature of the mentor–protege relationship. All participants volunteered for participation in the study and the participation rate was approximately 60% of those eligible to respond. Included in the research questionnaire were measures of positive work outcomes, such as amount of pay, number of promotions, job satisfaction, and social support. Measures of negative work outcomes included variables such as job-related stress, health symptoms, frustration, and emotional exhaustion.

To examine the impact of having a mentor versus not having one, two research hypotheses were tested:

1. Measurement of positive work outcomes will be significantly higher for public administrators who have mentors than for those who do not.
2. Measurements of negative work outcomes will be significantly lower for public administrators who have mentors than for those who do not.

The preceding two hypotheses were tested using a series of t-tests that compared the work outcomes of those participants who both indicated they had a mentor in their organization and who saw a direct association between the efforts of their mentor and their subsequent career success vis-à-vis those participants who indicated they did not have a mentor at the present time. Sixty-nine (51%) of the 134 respondents in the study indicated they had a mentor, and 60 (87% of these) indicated that having a mentor had had a bearing on their subsequent career success. Those with mentors included the following: 52 managers and executives had mentors (34 males and 18 females), whereas 17 professional personnel had mentors (7 males and 10 females).

Thus, for management personnel, a greater percentage of males as opposed to females had mentors (65% vs. 35%), whereas, for professional personnel, a greater percentage of females as opposed to males had mentors (50% vs. 41%). Sixty percent of the respondents reported having acted in the role of a sponsor or mentor themselves. Of their proteges, the overwhelming majority of mentors were black (92%), with an almost even split among male (47%) and female (53%) proteges.

Table 6 presents the results of the t-tests associated with the two research hypotheses in the study. Hypothesis 1 predicted that the positive work outcomes would be significantly higher for mentored versus nonmentored administrators. The results in Table 6 indicate that this was true for four out of seven positive work outcomes. Administrators with mentors reported significantly higher levels of extrinsic job satisfaction and significantly higher levels of all three facets of social support than did administrators who did not have mentors. Surprising was the fact that amount of pay, number of promotions, and intrinsic satisfaction were not significantly impacted by having a mentor. One would expect that these latter areas would be the ones that definitely would be affected by mentorship. Mentors of these administrators may engage more in the career functions of coaching, protecting, and providing exposure, as well as in the psychosocial function of providing friendship, counseling, and role modeling. Upward mobility for this sample does not

Table 6. *T*-Test Results for Differences in Mean Work Outcome Values between Mentored and Nonmentored Administrators

Variable	Administrators with mentors (N = 69)	Administrators without mentors (N = 36)	T-value
Positive work outcomes			
Pay	$34,069.66	$33,905.61	0.07
Number of promotions	2.08	2.16	−0.17
Intrinsic satisfaction	50.21	48.56	1.32
Extrinsic satisfaction	21.23	17.79	3.36***
Structural support	32.67	27.64	3.11**
Informational support	31.20	26.69	3.28***
Emotional support	34.69	29.13	3.73***
Negative work outcomes			
Chronic job stress	67.45	84.70	4.85***
Relations with management	26.16	32.91	3.68***
Autonomy and support	13.45	17.74	4.06***
Utilization of skills	7.08	9.66	3.63***
Departmental interdependence	12.82	14.86	2.22*
Peer clarity regarding work	6.78	7.83	1.74
Health symptoms	1.94	2.55	2.05*
Frustration	8.42	9.58	2.07*
Emotional exhaustion	20.02	27.67	2.08**

Note: *$p < .05$ (two-tailed); **$p < .01$ (two-tailed); ***$p < .001$ (two-tailed).

appear to be significantly affected by having a mentor. Overall, Hypothesis 1 was only partially supported.

The importance of mentor psychosocial functions, however, is more readily apparent when one examines the negative work outcomes in Table 6. The results indicate that administrators without mentors reported significantly higher levels of overall chronic job stress as well as higher levels on four of five facets of chronic job stress than did administrators with mentors. Additionally, significantly higher levels of emotional exhaustion. frustration, and health symptoms were also reported by administrators without mentors. These results suggest that perhaps more important than influencing upward mobility and pay for their proteges, mentors provide informational support, emotional support, and structural support of a nature that helps to remove roadblocks associated with work, and thus mentors impact significantly the stress and frustration experienced in the work lives of their proteges. Overall, Hypothesis 2 was strongly supported. The implications of these results and those of the other two studies are discussed later.

II. CONCLUSION

One strategy that has been proposed to help minorities and others overcome the roadblocks to upward organizational mobility is to secure a mentor or sponsor (Ford, 1983; Kanter, 1977). Indeed, mentorship has been shown to be an important training and development tool for upward professional progression in organizations (Jennings, 1971; Kram, 1983; Missirian, 1980; Shapiro, Haseltine, and Rowe, 1978). However, the evidence from Study III was not as strong in supporting the generally accepted and hypothesized notion that mentors have an important influence on promotion decisions and upward mobility of proteges, particularly black proteges, at least in the public sector. Administrators who had mentors did not report having received significantly more promotions or receiving significantly more pay, on the average, than administrators who did not have a mentor. Rather, the primary benefits of mentorship for these black professionals appear to be in the provision of informational and emotional support along with some coaching and counseling that helped to "buffer" the administrators from the negative consequences associated with work stress.

Studies I and II, which included samples from the private sector, suggest that few, if any, of the managers and professionals in these samples receive the benefits of mentorship of any type. This is seen in the lack of upward mobility, slower rates of promotion, and lower pay for black MBAs relative to their white counterparts, and the very high levels of psychological distress suffered by black female managers due to a lack of control over their environments. If minority managers and professionals are to be able to grow and advance in organizations, then clearly the benefits that accrue to them from mentorship and other processes must be of a structural nature that attacks the organizational norms and practices that contribute to discriminatory treatment.

It is not possible to say definitively, but I can speculate as to why MBAs from predominately black institutions are shortchanged several thousand dollars in terms of starting salaries. Factors such as lower competition for MBAs from black schools, the fact that many had general management degrees rather than specializations, or stigmatization of black schools by companies could have contributed to this state of affairs. I can also speculate as to the reasons for the lack of upward mobility for minority managers in general, compared to whites. This situation may be attributed to several factors: (a) personal choice in not accepting promotions in locations with small minority communities; (b) lack of social mobility in the "right" corporate circles; (c) discriminatory practices of management; and (d) problems of corporate "fit" that impede minority progress in management.

The presence of discrimination in organizations as experienced by minority managers suggests the need for continued efforts in making employment opportunities truly equal. Organizational development efforts directed at changing organizational norms and culture and multicultural training programs aimed at aiding organizations and individuals to manage the interface between different groups of people might well be put to good use in overcoming these barriers to progress for minority managers.

Several implications of the research results reported herein seem apparent. First, there is a need for organizations to review their salary administration and career planning systems to ensure that minority managers are being given a "fair deal" by these systems. Also, supervisors of minority managers need to be held accountable for the development and growth of minority subordinates, as well as white subordinates. Second, an implication of Study II is that work assignments and tasks of minority female managers, especially, need to be scrutinized for potential underutilization of their skills and abilities. Consistent with this, organizations will also need to devote more attention to the roles they can play in fostering meaningful and significant mentor–protege relationships for minority managers to help provide them with exposure and visibility to upper management and challenging job assignments in "bottom-line" related functions.

When senior management becomes concerned and committed to ensuring minority management success in business, articulates this commitment to all levels of the organization, and holds decision makers accountable for implementation of this commitment, then many of the problems identified in the research reported herein will begin to be addressed head-on and hopefully minimized if not eliminated altogether.

III. REFERENCES

Alderfer, C. P., R. C. Tucker, D. R. Morgan. and F. Drasgow. 1983. Black and white cognitions of changing race relations in management. *Journal of Occupational Behavior* 4:105–136.
Almquist, E. M. 1979. *Minorities, gender, and work.* Lexington, MA: Lexington.

Brown, H. A., and D. L. Ford. 1977. An exploratory analysis of discrimination in the employment of black MBA graduates. *Journal of Applied Psychology* 62:50–56.

Campbell, B. M. 1982. Black executive and corporate stress. *New York Times Magazine*, December 12, p. 36.

Cooper, C. L., and M. J. Davidson. 1982. The high cost of stress on women managers. *Organizational Dynamics* 10:44–53.

Davis, G., and G. Watson. 1982. *Black life in corporate America*. New York: Doubleday.

Dickens, F., and J. B. Dickens. 1982. *The black manager*. New York: Amacom.

Fernandez, J. L. 1981. *Racism and sexism in corporate life: Changing values in American business*. Lexington, MA: Lexington.

Ford, D. L. 1983. Black professionals and organizational stress. In A. Sargent and R. Ritvo (Eds.), *NTL Managers Handbook* (pp. 130–136). Arlington, VA: NTL Institute for Applied Behavioral Science.

Ford, D. L. 1984. The high cost of stress on black women Professionals: A comparative analysis. *Journal of Social and Behavioral Sciences* 30:15–22.

Ford, D. L., and L. Wells. 1985. Upward mobility factors among black public administrators: The role of mentors. *Centerboard-Journal of the SW for Human Relations Studies* 3:38–48.

Graves, C. W. 1982. The future for black urban administrators. *Public Management*, June, pp. 15–16.

Gutteridge, T. D. 1974. The composite MBA: A new computer anlysis. *MBA Magazine*, April, pp. 23–30.

Hemphill, J. M., and N. E. Reddick. 1974. A minority MBA program: Views of its graduates. *Collegiate News and Views*, Fall, pp. 5–6.

Jennings, E. E. 1971. *Route to the executive suite*. New York: McGraw-Hill.

Kanter, R. M. 1977. *Men and women of the corporation*. New York: Basic.

Kram, K. E. 1983. Phases of the mentor relationship. *Academy of Management Journal* 26:608–625.

Missirian, B. 1982. *The corporate connection: Why executive women need mentors to reach the top*. Englewood Cliffs, NJ: Prentice-Hall.

Shapiro, E., F. Haseltine, and M. Rowe. 1978. Moving up: role models, mentors, and the patron system. *Sloan Management Review* 19:51–58.

5

Racism and Sexism in Corporate America
Still Not Color- or Gender-Blind in the 1980s

John P. Fernandez

The following comments drawn from the responses of 9,000 employees in 13 companies to surveys conducted in 1984 and 1985 stand in stark contrast to President Reagan's avowal that America in the 1980's, is color- and gender-blind.

- Unfortunately, the fraternal "good buddy" syndrome still exists in our society. To a large degree, WASP males are still reluctant to utilize talented minorities and women in making advancement decisions. Unless we become seriously committed to looking at our work force of minorities and women, we will continue to lose them to companies that don't have the hangups (black, woman, middle-level manager).
- As a female, I would have to say that being "measured up" by males is one of the sexist things that is hardest to overcome. Not only are your credentials and background scrutinized, but your physical characteristics are always taken into account as if—to males—your lack of knowledge can be accepted if you are attractive or stimulating enough to compensate for this lack of knowledge. The older I become, the more I see this. Also, the more serious I become about my career, the more men seem to find this to be funny (Hispanic, woman, lower level manager).
- In this company, racism and sexism have gradually turned, in the last 5 years, to the point of reversal. For management advancement, the

John P. Fernandez • Division Manager, Human Resource Forecasting and Planning, AT&T, Basking Ridge, New Jersey 07920.

white male is the one who is now discriminated against (white, male, lower level manager).

- I feel that if they [blacks] are qualified for the job, color should have nothing to do with it. I've known of at least two or three black people who were qualified, but they had to fight to get the positions they wanted, whereas if they had been white, they would not have had to (American Indian, female, craftsperson).
- Please return to the practice of publishing the numbers of white, blacks, male and female, etc. in all positions. The white male believes he is being discriminated against, and I believe the figures will disprove their charges (white, female, middle-level manager).
- It has been my experience that people support affirmative action when it benefits them personally or enhances their careers. For example, I support pluralism up to and including my own level; however, I resent it any time anyone is promoted above me. Pluralism gives an edge to females and minorities that I can't have. I wonder how much support our offices would have provided if a female or minority had been competing with them for their jobs. Another fact: When a woman strives to be the equal to a man, she turns out to be less than a man—but also less than a woman (white, male, middle-level manager).
- Throughout the country, the pendulum has swung from discriminating against minorities to discrimination against whites. All companies are suffering the same problem (white, male, craftsperson).
- The company is not truly interested in ridding itself of racism. It promotes women only to get the heat off (white, female, upper-level manager).
- It is interesting and important, in my opinion, to perpetuate ethnic values, for example, Irish, Italian, "black," "brown," "yellow." The female issue is presently the most discriminatory *obsession* that is depressing and deflating the white male manager. He is now the victim of sex and race discrimination (white, male, middle-level manager).
- Despite some initial reluctance, I realize that in the 11 years since the consent decree was signed, I have been privileged to work with many women and minorities. I have been enriched and enlightened by their presence in the work force, and my earlier stereotypical views of their capabilities have been shattered forever. Unfortunately, middle- and upper-level management still seem to be the near-exclusive realm of white maledom. That it remains so is their loss as individuals and our loss as a company (white, male, lower level manager).
- At this point in time, women appear to "have it made" in this company regardless of their competency. I have met very few really smart women in responsible positions in this company. For every intelligent woman I've met in management, I've met about 16 dumb ones. Unfortunately, the company does *not* realize this yet. This worries me about our future. Now I've hired on with a woman whose scenario is very similar to mine. I feel that I'm more qualified, more intelligent, and get

along *much* better with people, and yet I feel that she is getting special treatment up the ass (she's also Hispanic). She is not respected at all by many of her peers including myself; yet she'll probably be able to write her own ticket. Scenes like those are going to kill employee morale (Hispanic, male, lower level manager).

- Women must do 52% to get credit for 20% of the work with a male partner (white, female, craftsperson).
- Our company hires many minorities; however, they are put in tedious and less challenging jobs in the company. They also have less opportunities for advancement (Asian, male, craftsperson).
- I believe society has an important role in racism. I don't believe that there is freedom and justice for all. I feel it's money and race that determine justice and success and freedom for all. I believe that being a woman and a mother and black has held my success down in a growing company like this (black, female, lower level manager).
- It's obvious racism and sexism exist in this company. How many Hispanics are promoted to management positions? How many Indians? Aside from the blacks, all minorities take a further backseat. Granted, in general, Hispanics do not have college educations, but how many promoted whites and blacks do? How many female executives are there in comparison to male executives? (Hispanic, female, lower level manager).
- Recent promotions to director have involved females where the qualifications and even the need could be questioned. It is obvious that we must have a black VP and a female VP, corporate level ASAP in order to solve a perception problem. This is illustrated by our high interest in bringing a black director from another company ASAP and the fact that a female who was surplus at middle level suddenly being promoted to director level. This is reverse discrimination (white, male, middle manager).

After more than 20 years of affirmative action, what is the true situation in corporate America? Is it, as the Reagan administration and most white males claim, a situation of reverse discrimination against white males? Or does there remain significant discrimination against minorities and women with white males still the most privileged group in society? What progress has been made in ridding corporations of race and gender discrimination? In short, to what extent is corporate America truly "color- and gender-blind" as the Reagan administration claims? This chapter addresses those questions and answers them with some hard facts. Before doing so, however, it is important to define our terms.

I. RACISM AND SEXISM DEFINED

In this chapter, *racism* and *sexism* are defined as basic cultural ideologies that state that whites and men are inherently superior to minorities and women solely on the basis of race and gender and that whites and men, especially white men, have the power over societal institutions to develop, evolve, nurture, spread, impose, and enforce the very myths and stereotypes that are basic foundations of racism and sexism not only in the minds of white males but also in the minds of some women and minorities. These myths and stereotypes are used to maintain and justify the whites' and men's, especially the white men's, dominant social, economic, and political position.

Underlying racism and sexism are power struggles between the dominant white men who want to maintain their privileged positions in society and the minorities and women who are determined to change the status quo. Even although they maintain total control over all of society's institutions, white men are subject to great fear, engendered by power struggles—a fear of losing their privileged positions that drive white men to develop myths and stereotypes in order to preserve these positions (Fernandez, 1981:304).

The past 100 years have seen new political and social values gradually taking hold in the United States, and steady progression of laws has challenged white men's preferred positions and monopoly on power. Although these laws contain mechanisms for putting some of the new values into practice, they cannot eradicate the pervasive, unconscious ideologies that have a tremendously negative effect on all people, both morally and psychologically. In addition, the recent attacks by the Reagan administration on civil rights, especially affirmative action, have created a generally hostile nationwide attitude against affirmative action that has weakened the effectiveness of these laws.

Thus racism and sexism are still two of the most powerful and complex social forces affecting every institution in American society and most aspects of Americans' lives. The form of these forces, however, has changed drastically, especially since 1964. Our present laws are trying to correct the obvious forms of discrimination that are called *overt* racism and sexism, but little impact has been made on the more subtle forms of discrimination that influence policies, practices, and patterns of decision making—*institutional* racism and sexism—or on the still subtler, covert neoracism and neosexism. Comments of some of our participants demonstrate that the less blatant sexism of the 1980s is much more difficult to see:

- Whites are very slow to accept people of color as equal. They outwardly appear to be playing fair, but "some" are "very" prejudiced and do only what is necessary to keep from being caught at discrimination. But most of them practice it (black, female, lower level manager).
- True racism and sexism are not as blatant in our society or company, yet they exist and they will continue to exist. Why? Because they both exist on a very insidious, down-played level. We, the employees and citizens, cannot fight intangibles that exist as a "gentleman's agreement." [Note the word *choice:* we say "gentle*man*," not "woman," nor "person."] Even our language is structured to reflect and reinforce that

vague kind of prejudice inherent in our society. (white, female, upper level manager).

- If you view any type of group activity that combines men and women, you'll notice just by body language alone that the men don't listen and respond to what the women say. I'va been in a situation where I did a job jointly with a man, but everyone, including my female boss, deferred to him. Yet I'm sure this was something my male co-worker didn't even notice (white, female, lower level manager).
- Racism is practiced undercover. By that I mean, no one is going to tell you he/she is a racist; however, actions and talk show it. Sexism is practiced more openly. I think the biggest problem here is that everyone was raised with the idea this is a job for men and this is a job for women. Women are homemakers; men are the breadwinners (black, female, craftsperson).
- In times of social or economic stress, racism seems more rampant as if it were an exercise. At work during stressful times, the comments seem more frequent and more derogatory. Sexism is often present in an office where the women are being called "girls" (Hispanic, female, lower level manager).
- Racism and sexism in the company are less overt than they once were; however, I believe that, for the most part, the attitudes are as strongly racist and sexist as ever (American Indian, male, middle-level manager).
- Racism and sexism are very much part of the work life. Cases are not always reported or directed towards specific people; the attack is mostly indirect and secret (Hispanic, male, craftsperson).

The reader should remember that despite the difficulties in seeing racism and sexism, these evil forces are no less destructive to the profitability of corporations because vast numbers of employees are not fully utilized and developed because of their race and/or gender.

II. THE DEVELOPMENT OF RACIST AND SEXIST ATTITUDES AND BEHAVIORS

Racism and sexism are developed and nurtured by all societal institutions controlled by the dominant white male group. Children learn racist and sexist attitudes and behaviors at a very early age. Families, schools, churches, other social groups, government, and the media socialize the population by communicating what is "good" behavior and what is "bad" behavior. They teach us what to expect of ourselves, our friends, and our families. They teach us how to relate to society. Governments resolve conflicts within the society in accordance with prevailing values.

As a result of their socialization, children learn how to be minorities or whites, men or women. They acquire a sense of the worth of their social group and of self from their earliest contacts with other members of their family and with peers and teachers, from what they see in the movies, on television, and in advertisements, from what they read, from conversations they overhear, and from their daily observations.

Some social scientists argue that children acquire racist and sexist attitudes indirectly, mostly through parental instructions or admonitions and through conversations designed to transmit prejudicial attitudes. (Goodman, 1964:36–46; Singh and Yancey, 1974; Willie, Kramer, and Brown, 1973).

Innumerable studies have explored the development of racist attitudes in white children at very early ages. One study found that very young children strongly prefer the color *white* over *black* and that their regard for the color *black* is transferred to their perception of black people. (Singh and Yancey, 1974). Another study found very young black children already entrenched in negative concepts about their blackness (Willie *et al.*, 1973).

These studies were done after the "black is beautiful" movement reached its peak. A prior study came up with similar findings—specifically, that white 4-year-olds had already internalized feelings of superiority to blacks (Goodman, 1964:36–46). This research clearly shows that the control of society's institutions by whites dominates children's perceptions. No matter how strongly the black community says "black is beautiful," the Hispanic community says "brown is beautiful," or the Native-American community says "red is beautiful," few of society's members will believe it unless most of society's institutions support these propositions.

With regard to sexual socialization, little boys are aware of their sex role as early as the age of 2, according to Helen Lewis. She observed that they seem compelled to show that they are different from their mothers and to renounce all characteristics that may be considered unmanly. She wrote:

> No wonder they have more trouble with the gender identity than little girls. And no wonder men are more prone than women to obsessional neurosis and schizophrenia (Lewis, 1976:85)

Experimenting with the role of the opposite gender is much more acceptable for little girls than for little boys. Girls learn at a young age that the male role is to be envied and imitated. Girls are free to dress in boys' clothes, but the reverse is certainly not the case. Parents who are amused to see their daughter become a "tomboy" are genuinely distressed if they have a son who is a "sissy" (Nilsen, Bosmajaan, Gershuny, and Stanley, 1977:30–31).

The result of these role-modeling techniques is that the woman's need to achieve is, ever so gently, sublimated into the need to nurture and serve:

> She is discouraged and protected from taking risks by her parents. At the same time she is subjected to peer pressure to fit the mold. "If you take chemistry, you won't have time to date"; "If you really swim, your hair will look a fright and your muscles will bulge"; "If you get good grades you're a drag"; "If you always win at tennis, no one will want to play with you." (Nilsen *et al.*, 1977)

The result of all this is that she follows tradition:

> She doesn't plan for the long range and doesn't recognize choice points but begins
> to back into or avoid decisionmaking. She becomes more dependent on others
> because it is easy and comfortable. She ceases her formal education, takes a job,
> finds a man, and becomes the role model. (Nilsen *et al.*, 1977)

As young children, we have little, if any, control over how we are so-cialized; thus racist and sexist attitudes and behaviors might seem normal. As we become teenagers and adults, the socialization process continues; howev-er, we become better able to determine what our own value systems and beliefs should be. Nevertheless, as a white male craftsperson currently notes, much of the information we are given as teenagers and adults is also very racist and sexist. He says that "sexism and racism are everywhere. We are bombarded daily with peoples' attitudes, prejudice, advertising, TV, movies, talk of liberation and integration: It goes on being used and abused. Positive understanding and redirection of priorities set by good example in manage-ment would be a good start."

Given this climate and the influences that pervade our lives from the day of birth, it is not surprising that only about 13% of the approximately 9,000 study participants do not agree with any racist stereotype, and about the same percentage do not agree with any sexist stereotypes.

It also is not surprising that more than 90% of the study participants believe that racism and sexism exist at least to some extent today in this country. Less than 5% believe there is no racism and/or sexism—a clear indication that few corporate employees believe that we live in a color- and gender-blind society.

What may be surprising to some, however, is the evidence, gathered in three different surveys conducted over a 15-year period, that both the preva-lence of racial and sexual stereotypes and the perception of the extent of racism and sexism have increased markedly during the Reagan years despite the president's insistence that America has no race problem.

III. RACIST STEREOTYPES ABOUT MINORITY EMPLOYEES

Common to the history of every minority group is the power struggle with the dominant white population. Many whites view minority groups as a threat to the status quo, and to their power, control, and social position.

Although whites have developed negative stereotypes to justify the ex-ploitation of and discrimination against all minorities, the most common and persistent negative stereotypes are about blacks and blackness. Public at-titudes toward other minorities have varied over the years, negatively and positively, but positive concepts of blacks have not prevailed in any period of white history.

How much have stereotypes about minorities (and about blacks, in par-ticular) in corporations changed? In 1972, I found in research for my book, *Black Managers in White Corporations*, that 83% of the white managers believed at least one stereotype about blacks, for example, they use race as an alibi, they have different life-styles, or they lack the intelligence to be effective managers (Fernandez, 1975:102–105).

In 1977, I found in the study done for my book, *Racism and Sexism in Corporate Life,* a significant drop in the percentages (60% of the white males and 46% of the white women) who believed at least one of the following stereotypes about minorities: They come from different cultural backgrounds that are not conducive to business; they use race as an alibi for job difficulties; or most are not as qualified as most white managers (Fernandez, 1981:44–47).

Even so, a comparison of the 1977 data with 1984–1985 data reveals a general increase in stereotypes about minorities. For example, in 1977, 13% of 4,200 managers believed minorities use race as an alibi. In 1984–1985 the percentage believing this was 38%, a significant increase. Predictably, minorities are much less likely to believe in stereotypes than whites: However, more than 20% of minorities held these views. Thus, despite an increase in the number of minorities employed by corporate America, the new conservatism of the 1980s seems to have been translated to increasing stereotypes, even among minorities themselves.

Let us now look at a more detailed analysis of stereotypes about minorities in the 1984–1985 time frame. In the studies I conducted in this period, I found that about two out of three white employees, more than two out of five Hispanic, American Indian, and Asian, and only about one out of five blacks believed, in general, that minority managers are no longer viewed in stereotypical ways by white employees.

To test this concept we asked the participants to agree or disagree with the following stereotypical assumptions about minority managers:

- The affirmative action program is forcing us to lower our hiring and promotion standards.
- Many minorities who are managers are as dependable as most white managers.
- Many minorities who are managers are as qualified as many white managers.
- Many minorities who are managers use race as an alibi for many difficulties they have on the job.
- Many minorities of color who are managers come from different cultural backgrounds that are not conducive to their success in this company.
- Many minorities of color need special training to be successful in management.
- A minority could not be demoted, even if inadequate in his or her new role, without undeserved charges of discrimination being made.
- Many minorities do not have the intelligence to be effective as managers in our company.

Only approximately 1 out of 8 employees hold no racist stereotypes about minorities. Overall, there are no significant differences between men and women in the same race group. As one might expect, more than 1 out of 4 blacks, 1 out of 5 of other minorities, and less than 1 out of 10 whites do not agree with any of the previously listed racist stereotypes. These responses belie the claims of many whites that minorities are no longer viewed in a stereotypical fashion. In addition, all the data presented thus far show that not only are whites socialized into racist stereotypical attitudes but that some minorities have also developed these negative, self-destructive perceptions.

Table 1 shows the responses of the employees by race, gender, and occupation to these questions when the questions are formed into an index. Those who did not agree with any stereotypes are obviously recorded as none, those who agreed with one to three are considered to have limited stereotypes, four to five a moderate degree, and six to eight a great deal of stereotypes. Table 1 illustrates that white males and white craftsmen hold the most racist stereotypes. Black craftspeople are least likely to have racist stereotypes.

It should be pointed out that the extent to which employees interact frequently with minorities at work does not have a significant impact on the employees' responses to racist statements. However, those who have more external social contact with minorities have fewer racist preconceptions. What these findings suggest is that many people who have racist stereotypes about minorities in corporations have developed them without experience in dealing with minorities in corporations.

Despite these findings, there is some hope. For example:

- White women and men at the higher levels of management are more likely than those at lower levels to agree to *no* racist statements. For example, 22% of the women and 23% of the men at director level and above, compared to 9% of the women and 6% of the men at lower levels, do not agree with any racist statements.
- Among whites (but not among minorities), the younger, more educated workers are less likely to hold racist stereotypes than older, less educated ones.

In order to give an added dimension to the statistics, let us look at some of the employees' comments that are stereotypical or indicate awareness of stereotypes in their companies:

- Blacks are always using their race. Why don't they work like others? (white, male, lower level manager)
- I have nothing against minorities. I just think God made us different and we shouldn't mix (white, male, middle-level manager).
- We have fallen behind because of no movement and unqualified women/minorities (white, male, middle-level manager).
- Currently, minorities are suspected of bad work ethics and create uncomfortableness among the work force. Special training for all managers might eliminate this (black, male, craftsperson).
- Being Indian, I get very upset when co-workers classify us as "drunken

Table 1. Racist Stereotypes by Race/Gender and Occupation (Numbers in Each Cell Are Percentages Summed across Rows, within Occupation)

Women

	None (0)		Limited (1–3)		Moderate (4–5)		A great deal (6–8)	
	Craft	Management	Craft	Management	Craft	Management	Craft	Management
Blacks	27	24	58	68	13	8	2	0
Whites	7	12	50	57	36	25	9	7
Others[a]	18	18	65	69	16	13	1	0

Men

	None (0)		Limited (1–3)		Moderate (4–5)		A great deal (6–8)	
	Craft	Management	Craft	Management	Craft	Management	Craft	Management
Blacks	30	20	50	67	15	13	5	0
Whites	6	10	41	46	38	35	15	9
Others[a]	18	23	64	53	19	20	2	2

[a]Others means Hispanic, American Indian, or Asian.

Indians" or "squaws." I feel they should have the sense to be quiet (Native American, female, lower level manager).

- Mexican minorities encourage stereotypes by speaking Spanish as often as they can in the office. It is not only rude but emphasizes their inability to express themselves in English. Management encourages this by responding in Spanish. I resent organizations such as SOMOS [Success Oriented Managers Offering Support] that cater exclusively to Mexicans to the exclusion of all other minorities (white, female, craftsperson).
- Minorities fall in two groups. They are either good employees or feel the company and everyone owes them (white, male, craftsperson).
- Minorities are lazy and not together (white, female, middle-level manager).

Employees who have such stereotypes about minorities cannot effectively work with them. This costs the corporation much money in lost efficiency and thus lost profits. Racial stereotyping is, obviously, still very much a part of corporate life. So, as we will see in the next section, is sexist stereotyping.

IV. SEXIST STEREOTYPES

Overall, in a 1977 study, about three out of five of the men and one out of five of the women agree with at least one of the following sexist stereotypes (Fernandez, 1981:79–82):

- Most women are not as qualified as most male managers.
- Women use their gender as an alibi for difficulties on the job.
- Women are too emotional to be competent managers.
- Women are not serious about professional careers.

The increasing trend toward racist stereotyping that we saw in the previous section between 1977 and 1984–1985 is also evident for sexist stereotyping. For example, when we compare the responses to the question about women's seriousness about their careers, we find that in 1977, 16% of the men and 7% of the women agreed that women are not serious about their professional careers. In 1984–1985, 22% of the women and 31% of the men agreed. This pronounced increase in such a negative stereotype flies in the face both of the increasing numbers of women in the permanent, full-time, work force and the findings by one high-tech company study that 82% of the men and 85% of the women categorize their careers as either extremely or very important. In addition, in this same study, 68% of the women compared to 53% of the men said career development was their top priority in life.[1]

In order to get a look at the strength of sexist stereotypes in 1984–1985, let

[1]Unpublished report used with permission, with the understanding that the name of the company would not be used.

us look at the responses as we did in the previous section to a series of questions formed into an index.

The questions that make up the sexist stereotype index are as follows:

- Chester I. Barnard, a former Bell System president, wrote in his book, *The Function of the Executive* (1940), that a culturally homogeneous (all the same) group of managers was necessary for the smooth, efficient functioning of a corporation. To what extent do you agree or disagree with his statement?
- Many women managers are as qualified as most men managers.
- Many women need special training to be successful in management.
- Many women use their gender as an alibi for many difficulties they have on the job.
- Many women managers are not really serious about professional careers.
- The affirmative action program is forcing us to lower our hiring and promotion standards.
- How would you feel about having a woman as an immediate boss?
- If you had a choice, would you prefer to work in a group that is pre- dominantly men or women?

It is important to note that more than one out of three women and about two out of three men believe women employees are no longer looked at in a stereotypical way by men employees.

Considering the preceding reviews, it is surprising and contradictory that so few women and men have no stereotyped views about women. When we gave the employees a chance to respond to 11 sexist stereotypes and the questions were formed into an index, we found that 18% of the women versus 8% of the men *do not* agree to any sexist attitudes. A higher percentage of blacks than other races are likely *not to agree* to sexist attitudes (24%). They were followed by other people of color (16%) and whites (12%). These overall results suggest that there is denial on the part of some women and many men about women no longer being viewed in a stereotypical fashion. Table 2 shows the responses by race, gender, and occupation. Note black managers, male and female, are least likely to express sexist stereotypes. White men, followed by other people of color, are most likely to express sexist stereo- types.

There is no relationship between the level of management held by white men and their expression of sexist stereotypes: 7% at the lower level, 13% at the middle level, and 12% at the upper level express *no* sexist stereotypes. For white women, however, the higher the management level, the fewer with stereotypical views: 16% at lower level, 25% at middle, and 35% at upper level express *no* sexist stereotypes. Among minorities, the pattern is similar; the higher the level of the person of color, the less likely he or she is to express sexist stereotypes.

As was the case with racist stereotypes, younger, more highly educated

Table 2. Sexist Stereotypes by Race/Gender and Occupation (Numbers in Each Cell Are Percentages Summed across Rows, within Occupation).

Women

	None (0)		A few (1–4)		Some (5–7)		A great deal (9–11)	
	Craft	Management	Craft	Management	Craft	Management	Craft	Management
Blacks	16	28	82	64	2	9	0	0
Whites	12	18	71	68	15	13	2	1
Others[a]	13	9	76	68	10	23	2	0

Men

	None (0)		A few (1–4)		Some (5–7)		A great deal (9–11)	
	Craft	Management	Craft	Management	Craft	Management	Craft	Management
Blacks	9	26	75	66	16	6	0	3
Whites	2	7	50	62	33	26	15	5
Others[a]	14	14	55	45	21	36	10	5

[a] Others means Hispanic, American Indian, or Asian.

employees are less likely than older, less educated employees to believe sexist stereotypes. This is a hopeful sign for the future.

The following employees' comments provide additional insight into statistical data:

- I believe women should be at home and men should be the bread-winners (Hispanic, male, lower level manager).
- Women want to work 9:00–3:00. Men, in most cases, work 11 hours a day (white, male, lower level manager).
- Is a pregnant manager an effective manager? (white, male, crafts-person)
- If my company would use *men* for work instead of all *married* women who do not need to work, there would be better work relationships and more output. Bitchy women just create problems throughout the company. Look around you for yourself (American Indian, male, crafts-person).
- Affirmative action is a good thing if used properly—especially with women. But if things keep going as they are, the company is going to lose a lot of good male and female employees who are frustrated by all the incompetence in female managers. It is now a state of *female overkill* to raise them into low and high management ranks even if they're not qualified (Hispanic, male, lower level manager).
- Although women can be as capable as men, they do not take the right courses in school or think seriously about a career. I see this slowly changing (white, female, lower level manager).
- Women managers can't handle it when the going gets tough. Women are too emotional (American Indian, male, lower level manager).
- The majority of women managers I've worked under do one hell of a good job. Some of them are too emotional and scare easily (Hispanic, female, craftsperson).
- Women managers tend to take things to heart, react on a personal level. If something goes wrong, they take it as a personal attack against them. They also let personality conflicts become involved with the judgments they make (Hispanic, female, middle-level manager).
- Affirmative action places emphasis on women, and some of these recent female promotions are not qualified or deserving. I agree we need a mix, but the more qualified women are not being selected; it's the pushy ones and sycophants. It is evident to many that they are more impressed with their new position than with doing a good job (white, male, middle-level manager).
- Many lack job experience in what they are managing. I personally haven't had women supervisors but would desire a young, good-looking one with a nice body or one that could do the job (white, male, lower level manager).

Two comments that criticize stereotypes also suggest that it is the insecure, not the top performing males, who are most likely to have stereotypes—

positions with which I strongly agree:

- Most men are so insecure with their own manhood and position on their jobs that a woman is a complete threat if she shows any signs of wanting to get ahead (black, male, middle-level manager).
- I have been a "nontraditional" employee my entire career. The men and women who think that women are, by virtue of their sex, inferior, are in the majority. The people who don't think that way are often our high performers. They are wonderful. Their results are highly competitive. You show me poor results in a mixed work force, and I'll show you sexism and racism at work. How long can we afford to "humor" these attitudes? (white, male, middle-level manager)

Gershuny makes some cogent observations on the negative effects of gender stereotypes. Her remarks serve as a fitting summary for this section:

> The trouble with stereotypes is that they restrict behavior and understanding by constructing a static image of both sexes. Furthermore, assigning verbal qualities to each sex creates an illusion of biologically determined traits instead of suggesting their socio-cultural origins or even an interplay of biology and environment. It is as though emotionality and passivity, usually assigned to the female stereotype, are qualities inherently absent in men. The passive man and the assertive woman are "unnatural" anomalies and are urged into psychotherapy to remedy behavior unbecoming the stereotype. (in Nilsen *et al.*, 1977:143)

Earlier in this chapter, I noted that many employees will argue that their racist and sexist attitudes do not affect how they deal with people at work. The following sections will clearly demonstrate the problems that racist and sexist stereotypes have created for the effective functioning and full utilization of minorities and women in corporations. Because minorities and women represent 50% or more of the work force in many companies, the cost to corporate productivity is extremely high.

V. RACE DISCRIMINATION IN CORPORATE AMERICA: A HISTORICAL VIEW

The racist stereotypes to which all Americans are socialized from their earliest years manifest themselves in discriminatory behavior toward minority employees. Recognizing the initial decrease in stereotypes in the 1970s and the subsequent increase in the 1980s, we would expect to see a decrease in discrimination in the 1970s and an increase in racial discrimination in the 1980s. An historical perspective bears this point out.

In 1964, Garda W. Bowman found in her study of 2,000 corporate employees, most of whom were white, that 77% believed that being black, 71% believed that being Chicano, and 68% believed that being Asian was harmful for advancement in business. In 1972, I found substantially decreased responses to similar questions. For example, 68% of the blacks compared to 58%

of the whites believed that being black was harmful to advancement in business (Fernandez, 1975:133).

In research conducted for my book, *Racism and Sexism in Corporate Life* (1977 data), the question was revised to ask whether employees believed their race would be harmful, irrelevant, or helpful to *their* career advancement rather than in a general sense as was the case in the 1964 and 1972 studies. Black males (46%) and white males (45%) were most likely to believe their race would be harmful, whereas only 6% to 16% of the other race/gender groups felt this way.

In 1984–1985, there was a dramatic decrease in the number of white males who believed their race to be a handicap. By contrast, 65% of black males and 27% of other minorities saw race as a problem. These figures correspond with the increase in racist views by whites and the sense that, under the Reagan administration, things are going backwards in terms of equality for minorities.

In comparing data on a number of identical questions asked in 1972, 1977, and 1984–1985 (i.e., minorities have a more difficult time finding a mentor, minorities are excluded from informal work groups, and minorities must be better performers than whites), it is clear that most employees, regardless of race, believed racial discrimination had decreased between 1972 and 1977 and that it increased between 1977 and 1984–1985. For example, on the question of whether blacks had to be better performers, 88% of the black managers and 33% of the white managers believed in 1971–1972 that the statement was true. The figures dropped in 1977 to 82% of the black managers and 17% of the white managers. By 1985, however, the figures had swung higher: 94% of the blacks and 32% of the whites believe this to be the case. In addition, in 1977 about 40% of the other minorities concurred, but in 1984–1985 the figure jumped to 66%.

VI. RACE DISCRIMINATION IN PRESENT-DAY CORPORATE AMERICA, 1984–1985

In the 1984–1985 surveys, more than 50% of the employees believed that racism exists, at least to some extent, in their companies. As one might expect, a much higher percentage of blacks (82%) than other minorities (69%) and whites (51%) agree. The following comments are revealing:

- I honestly believe I have been discriminated against by my second-level manager. However, the only reason I do not file a discrimination suit is because of my family. He already has destroyed me financially (Hispanic, male, lower level manager).
- There is no question in my mind that black men have a very tough problem of discrimination within the company that must be resolved. In general, I believe some black men represent a physical threat to white men (white, male, middle-level manager).

- Do black men exist? In 13 years with the company, why have I only met four black male employees? (white, male, lower level manager)
- I feel women have progressed faster than people of color because of subconscious racism. Women are a majority and *white* (black, male, middle-level manager).

In order to get a more accurate measure of the extent of employee perceptions of racism in corporate America, the participants in the 1984–1985 survey were asked a series of questions that were formed into an index. The questions were:

- Today, to what extent do you believe racism exists in your company?
- Other employees accept the authority of a minority who is a manager as much as they accept a white person's in a similar situation?
- Many minorities who are managers have a harder time finding a sponsor or mentor than white managers.
- Minorities who are managers have to be better performers than white managers to get ahead.
- White managers are generally unable to work comfortably with minorities who are managers; they bypass them and go to their superiors.

Table 3 shows the employees' responses by race, gender, and occupation. Overall, 25% of the employees believe there is *no* racism in their company, whereas 12% believe there is a *great deal* of racism. More specifically, a much greater percentage of blacks than other minorities of color or whites feel that there is a *great deal* of racism at their company. Fifty percent of the black women and 64% of the black men believe this. Only 15% of the other minority women, 23% of the other men of color, 13% of the white women, and 7% of the white men feel there is a great deal of racism in their company.

White men at the various managerial levels responded in a mixed fashion to the concept of racism: 5% at the lower level, 10% at the middle level, and 8% at the upper level believe that a great deal of racism exists. The reverse is true for white women. Higher level female managers are more likely to see more racism than those at lower levels: 17% at the lower level, 20% at the middle level and 64% at the upper level and above concur that a great deal of racism exists in their company. There are few differences among levels for all people of color.

Contact *on the job* with people of color does not have a significant impact on employees' perceptions of racism in their company just as it had little effect on their proclivity to stereotype. For example, 23% of the managers who have very frequent contact say there is *no* racism, and 28% who never have contact concur. However, there are significant differences with regard to social contact. Managers and craftspeople who have frequent contact outside of work with people of color are much more likely than those who do not to believe there is a great deal of racism. For example, 41% of those managers who have very frequent contact compared to 12% who never have any contact believe there is a great deal of racism. What these findings demonstrate is that

Table 3. Beliefs about Racism in the Company by Race/Gender and Occupation (Numbers in Each Cell Are Percentages Summed across Rows, within Occupation)

	None (0)		A little (1–2)		Moderate (3–5)		A great deal (6–7)	
Women	Craft	Management	Craft	Management	Craft	Management	Craft	Management
Blacks	0	0	11	2	47	31	42	67
Whites	28	12	44	34	22	33	6	21
Others[a]	14	10	34	24	40	43	12	24

	None (0)		A little (1–2)		Moderate (3–5)		A great deal (6–7)	
Men	Craft	Management	Craft	Management	Craft	Management	Craft	Management
Blacks	5	0	13	0	42	13	39	87
Whites	29	33	42	38	20	22	9	6
Others[a]	17	27	31	23	29	27	24	23

[a]Others means Hispanic, American Indian, or Asian.

perceptions of racial discrimination on the job against minorities, in many cases, has nothing to do with actual experience in working with minorities on the job but on personal feelings.

The following comments flesh out the statistics:

- Being a black and a woman makes it double hard to find a mentor (black, female, lower level manager).
- In this company, I feel that you still have to do better than average to get ahead if you are black. I see so many whites with inferior talents get ahead every day because of a mentor. It is hard for a person of color to get a mentor or sponsor (black, male, lower level manager).
- I feel that politics on the job has a lot to do with how one gets paid, rewards, promotions, etc. It seems that if you don't play the game by the rules set, you lose out. Quite a lot of discrimination is going on. You need a mentor (Hispanic, male, lower level manager).
- Some minorities get handed jobs they are not qualified for because of a quota. Some minorities want to get a position because they deserve it, not to be handed it (white, male, craftsperson).
- I believe whites, especially males, exclude minorities because they feel uncomfortable with them (white, male, craftsperson).
- Minorities continue to have problems in advancing up the company ladder because they are excluded from the informal work network. This is where the sponsors, mentors, and patrons can be found, but due to exclusion, these relations rarely develop (black, female, lower level manager).

The issue of minorities having to be better performers than whites has created the greatest differences in views between whites and blacks in all the surveys I have conducted in the past 16 years. The following comments address this subject:

- It is common knowledge among "people of color" that we have to be twice as good at our jobs to even be noticed, let alone promoted. Therefore, I feel that those managers of color are *very* capable of being managers. Sometimes they may even be a threat to their white co-workers (black, male, craftsperson).
- I feel that a person of color is expected to do more and keep things in a more orderly fashion than other managers. They are expected to actually know their jobs well, where other managers are permitted to do little for long periods of time (black, female, lower level manager).
- All I can say is that the record speaks for itself: There are no minorities above third level. Come on—you want me to believe there are none qualified? (black, male, lower level manager)
- Regardless of qualifications, I have not seen very many minorities in the upper management ranks, only at the first level (Hispanic, male, lower-level manager).

- Minorities are always expected to work twice as hard to achieve any higher positions in the company! Will this ever change? (black, female, lower level manager)

These data clearly show that there still is much racism in corporate America and that the Reagan administration's belief that this is a color-blind society is believed by few employees regardless of race and gender. Now let us look at gender discrimination.

VII. GENDER DISCRIMINATION: A HISTORICAL PERSPECTIVE

Following the same historical analysis format we used in the section on race discrimination, we find similar trends with regard to gender discrimination. Between 1964 and 1972, there was a significant decrease in the percentage of employees who believed that being a woman would be harmful to advancement in their company. For example, Bowman found that 77% of the employees in 1964 believed being a woman was harmful in business (1964:16–22). In 1972, 68% of the white managers believed this to be the case (Fernandez, 1975:133).

In the 1977 and 1984–1985 surveys, I changed the question to relate specifically to the respondent's own career. In the earlier study, overall, 19% of the women and 21% of the men believed their gender was harmful to their career advancement. However, 47% of the white men believed this (Fernandez, 1981:116). Eight years later, the percentage of minority women, (33%) and of white women (30%) who believed their gender would be harmful had increased, but the percentage of white men who believed this decreased to 29%. The responses of minority men were consistent over the time period, 15% in 1977 and 14% in 1984–1985 perceived gender to be harmful to their careers. These findings also suggest that affirmative action efforts have slipped under the Reagan administration.

When comparing questions in the two surveys such as those related to the exclusion of women from informal work groups and the necessity for women to be better performers than men, we find a general trend toward increased discrimination against women, at least in the minds of women. Male responses remained fairly constant. In 1977, about 63% of the women and 57% of the men agreed with the fact that women were excluded from informal work groups, whereas in 1984–1985, 85% of the women compared to 57% of the men agreed with the fact that women are excluded from informal work groups. About 7 out of 10 women surveyed in 1977 believed that women must outperform men. By 1984–1985, this percentage had increased to almost 9 out of 10. In 1977, about 1 in 4 men concurred; in 1984–1985, the figure was about the same.

In several cases, men also see things getting worse for women. For example, only 20% of the men in 1977 compared to 43% in 1984–1985 believed many men are unable to work comfortably with women, that they bypass them and go to their superiors.

These data clearly demonstrate the fact that there is a perception among many corporate women employees that women are having a more difficult time at present advancing because of their gender. The data also show that men do not believe there has been any decrease in gender discrimination in the past 8 years. Once again, this is a strong sign that the Reagan administration's attack on affirmative action has had a negative impact on women's careers.

VIII. GENDER DISCRIMINATION IN 1984–1985

When asked the specific question about the extent to which gender discrimination exists in 1984–1985 in their companies, 60% of the employees believe there is gender discrimination at least to some extent. The following comments are illuminating:

- Efforts to place women and minorities for director or officer positions have been only nominal. We have a few women and minority upper-middle levels and no efforts to develop middle levels to assume these positions in the future. We have good pools at lower levels to move into middle-level positions—but there is little support to move women/minorities into the "old boy power network" (white, female, middle-level manager).
- Take a look at the "numbers" in the officer and upper-level ranks of our company (white, male, middle-level manager).
- Even though our company claims to be sexually unbiased, very few inroads have been made by women into jobs that have traditionally been considered male-oriented. Also, the higher up the ladder in management you go, the fewer women you find occupying these jobs (white, female, lower level manager).

Using the same technique discussed in the previous sections, we posed a series of questions measuring gender discrimination to the participants and formed their responses into an index. The questions were:

- Today, to what extent do you believe sexism exists in your company?
- Other employees accept a woman manager's authority as much as they accept a man's in a similar situation.
- Many men in work groups listen less to work-related opinions of women managers than they do to those of other men managers.
- Many women are often excluded from informal work networks by men.
- Many women managers have a difficult time initiating informal work-related activities such as lunch and socializing after work, because men misinterpret their behavior as a "come-on."

- Women have a much easier time finding a sponsor or mentor than men do.
- Women managers have to be better performers than men to get ahead.
- Many women managers have the same power as men in similar positions.
- Many men are unable to work comfortably with women; they bypass them and go to their superiors.
- Many women are faced with some type of sexual harassment on the job.

Table 4 shows the responses by race, gender, and occupation. Responses revealed that only 2% of the employees do not believe there is any sexism in the company. By contrast, 25% believe there is *a great deal* of sexism in the company.

Women and minorities were most likely to say that sexism exists in their company. More than half (53%) of the black women, 35% of the black men, 33% of the other women of color, and 20% of the other men of color agree that *a great deal* of sexism exists in their company. The most significant difference is apparent between white women and men; 40% of the white women, compared to only 10% of the white men, agree that there is a great deal of sexism in their company.

These data also show the tremendous differences in opinion among blacks and whites and other people of color, between the genders, and between craft and management employees. For example, 56% of the black management men versus 10% of the white management men and 53% of the white women managers versus 26% of the white craftswomen say there is a great deal of sexism. It is interesting to note as well that, on this index, black management men respond very similarly to white women and other women of color who are managers.

The level of management has an impact on white men's responses. For example, 8% of the lower levels say there is a great deal of sexism, compared to 31% of the middle levels, 17% of the upper-middle levels, and 29% of the upper levels. A higher percentage of white women at the upper levels believe there is a great deal of sexism than those at the lower levels: 50% of the white women at the lower level, 63% at the middle level, and 68% at the upper level believe this to be the case. Even though the numbers are small, there is a definite trend for other people of color at higher levels to see more sexism than those at lower levels. For blacks, the responses are high regardless of level.

The following statements by study participants will give the reader a better picture about employees' concepts of gender discrimination including sexual harassment and related power issues, having to work harder than men, and mentorship:

- Sexual harassment is alive and well. It is covert. In our organization, the director's feeling about women in management is widely well known, and nothing he has done proves differently. Even the men feel

Table 4. Beliefs about Sexism by Race/Gender and Occupation (Numbers in Each Cell Are Percentages Summed across Rows, within Occupation

Women

	None (0)		A little (1–3)		Moderate (4–7)		A great deal (8–10)	
	Craft	Management	Craft	Management	Craft	Management	Craft	Management
Blacks	0	0	11	0	56	12	33	88
Whites	0	0	18	9	56	38	26	53
Others[a]	0	0	23	10	48	35	28	55

Men

	None (0)		A little (1–2)		Moderate (3–5)		A great deal (6–7)	
	Craft	Management	Craft	Management	Craft	Management	Craft	Management
Blacks	0	0	17	6	69	39	14	56
Whites	2	6	32	44	56	40	10	10
Others[a]	0	0	35	22	47	57	19	22

[a]Others means Hispanic, American Indian, or Asian.

it and are appalled. The company is not as progressive towards upgrading women as it was in previous years (white, female, lower level manager).

- Harassment is alive and well. A new management hire showed me a "diary" (documentation) of the times, dates, and places a district-level manager asked her to lunch, what she was doing over the weekend . . . and so on (white, female, middle-level manager).
- I think many women managers are faced with a "blind spot" effect when attending meetings predominantly occupied by male managers. The women are invisible (I use that rather than ignored, only to give men the benefit of the doubt that they wouldn't intentionally be that rude.) The men in the conference, meeting, or presentation simply do not see them (white, female, middle-level manager).
- I feel men are now at the point where they *will* ask for a woman's opinion, but they do it strictly out of courtesy or something they're obliged to do. In a recent incident, for example, my boss (a man) asked me (a woman) and another man for advice. He listened to both of us and then said, "Thanks, Fred. That's what I'll do." I felt invisible (white, female, middle-level manager).
- Men do not accept women as their equal. They give me the impression that women are here, and men are expected to deal with them but not as equals. They (men) define a position for you and you stay there. They think women are dumb and scatterbrained. Most of them don't even understand their own wives: How can you expect them to understand women in the workplace? (black, female, middle-level manager)
- The old saying, "a woman has to work twice as hard as a man to get the same pay and recognition," is true today (white, female, craftsperson).
- I have noticed that a woman has to prove herself whereas a man can just sit around and not worry about it (American Indian, female, lower level manager).
- Women today know they have to work hard if they are going to accomplish their goals. In this company, I believe that women are now starting to move quickly up the ladder. This is good (black, male, middle-level manager).
- Traditional male employees are still resistant to women in our work force (at their level of pay). Advancement to upper management at upper middle level and up still is difficult for women to achieve. They have no help (white, female, craftsperson).
- Men in this company have the potential to be groomed for success. Women are often left on their own to be frustrated by a male-dominated system. Prejudice against women in the company, based on my own experience, ranges from the blatant and destructive to subtle and often unconscious manifestations. If women move into an area previously dominated by men, men invariably devalue that area. The company needs to prove its commitment to women by grooming them for

more hardcore technical jobs, not just for the so-called administrative jobs that are often clerical in nature (Hispanic, female, lower level manager).

- Even though our company has made improvements in first-level and second-level positions, the company is still paying only lip service to equality in middle- and upper-level positions. The records speak for themselves. In our five-state area, only small sections of the total company work force are women in middle-level and above positions. Is it possible that there are no women capable of being district managers and above? (white, male, lower level manager)

IX. CONCLUSION

The previous sections clearly answer the questions as to whether this is or is not a color-blind and gender-blind society and the extent to which racism and sexism are still present in corporate America. In both cases, the answer is that we have a long way to go before racism and sexism are eliminated in this society and women and minorities have equal opportunities in corporate America. In fact, historical data show that many employees, regardless of race and/or gender, believed that equal opportunities for women and minorities were increasing from the mid-1960s through the late 1970s. But, the 1980s brought a marked increase in racist and sexist stereotypes, and consequently, in race and gender discrimination despite a pervasive tendency to deny the very great impacts of race and gender on corporate life and the careers of women and minority managers. America, in general, and white men, in particular, do not like to think of themselves as unfair.

Deep cultural and psychological conflicts occur among Americans because they hold ideals of equality, freedom, and individual dignity on the one hand, and on the other, they engage in practices of discrimination, humiliation, insult, and denial of opportunities to minorities and women. Many women and minorities are paranoid because of their treatment by the dominant society. Some minorities often retreat into a self-imposed ghetto as the only psychological defense against the unbearable pain perpetrated upon them by a racist society.

Although some black psychiatrists have found healthy aspects in this paranoia, they note how difficult it is to keep the paranoia positive and not self-destructive: "To maintain a high degree of suspicion toward the motives of every white man, and at the same time never allow their suspicion to impair the grasp of reality, is walking a very thin tightrope" (Grier and Cobbs, 1968:161).

Women respond to the constant message that they are the weaker, inferior sex to be controlled, harassed, and exploited by developing defense mechanisms that allow them to retain a sense of their dignity, respect, humanness, and importance. That some women question the motives of men and develop a sense of paranoia is a sign not of unhealthiness in most cases but of recognizing and trying to deal effectively in a sexist society. As was the case with minorities, trying to maintain a balance between a healthy and a self-destructive paranoia is a very difficult and delicate act for women. Certainly, occasions do occur in which women and minorities, because of their socialization and experiences, interpret specific acts as sexist and/or racist when they really are not. The new forms of racism and sexism, however, are difficult to detect and to document, and too often complaints are dismissed as unfounded, but to conclude that women and minorities are simply paranoid and unnecessarily critical would be shortsighted.

The support that women and minorities receive from men and whites clearly suggests that there is much validity in the charges that racism and sexism are still alive and well in American society and corporate America. Remember that 90% of the participants believe racism and sexism exist at least to some extent in American society, and more than 50% believe these two evils exist at least to some extent in their company. The vast majority of the employees in our survey hold some degree of sexist stereotypes, and a significant majority, especially of whites, hold racist stereotypes about minorities.

These racist and sexist stereotypes are translated into discrimination against women and minorities. Less than 5% of the employees believe there is no gender discrimination in their company, and less than 25% believe there is no race discrimination. It is a fact that in many companies women and minorities make up more than 50% of the work force. In fact, in a number of large companies, about 70% of the work forces are made up of minorities and women. No corporation can compete effectively and efficiently if more than half of their work force is stereotyped, excluded from informal work groups, held to unreasonable performance standards, and denied the power and authority to effectively do their jobs.

To ensure the full utilization of this heterogeneous work force so that the companies can be optimally competitive and profitable, several strategies are in order. The following recommendations focus on an overall strategy to try to deal with the employees' racist and sexist stereotypes and behaviors. No one method will solve these problems because, in large part, they are so inbred and reinforced from so many different sources that an all-out, multifaceted approach needs to be implemented. Such an approach should encompass (a) comprehensive training for employees at all levels, including top management and (b) integration of affirmative action/equal opportunity awareness and activities throughout the company's existing functions in all departments and at all levels.

A. Training

An overall training program focused on evaluation and staff development should be developed to give supervisors effective and bias-free tools to better evaluate their subordinates' performance and potential and to prepare managers to deal with their subordinates' career development and planning needs. Parallel sessions for subordinates should aim to enhance their understanding of the programs and to stress their individual responsibilities in these processes. A crucial element of these programs is training for the supervisors in the skills of clear, honest, supportive, and knowledgeable communication.

Many excellent training programs and policies are never or seldom properly used because there are no incentives, beyond individual interest and initiative, for the employees to use them. An effective reward system recognizes, with bonuses, special assignments, and promotions those managers who have a good track record of developing and utilizing all of their work force and those employees who take the initiative to improve their skills and marketability.

B. Equal Opportunity Emphasis

With specific regard to the issues of equal employment opportunity a company can:

- Establish goals and timetables for all departments and levels of the corporation, with respect to hiring and promotion of minorities and women.
- Conduct multicultural events and strongly encourage employees to attend.
- Take concrete, well-publicized action, such as on-the-spot awards for individuals who have contributed in a significant manner to the company's efforts, to demonstrate the company's commitment to equal employment opportunities.
- Develop and implement race and gender awareness workshops as an ongoing part of the company's training and development programs and expand and/or revise these programs as the company continues its efforts to eliminate racism and sexism. Make participation in such workshops mandatory and use trained volunteer facilitators drawn from high-potential district managers and above.
- Require employees to attend workshops that deal with *both* racism and sexism because they are interrelated. Previous studies have shown that attending workshops on both issues has a greater positive impact on the employees than attending sessions that deal with only one or the other.
- Make certain that all training programs and systems related to managerial/supervisory skills development have modules that deal with some aspect of racism, sexism, and pluralism.
- Require higher level managers to become mentors/sponsors to high-potential women and minorities. Measure and reward their success in this task.
- Develop concrete performance measurement criteria to evaluate all managers' efforts in the equal opportunity (EO) area. Establish rewards

for those who demonstrate a positive record in these areas and penalties for those who do not.

- Demonstrate the company's commitment to EO by promoting individuals who directly or indirectly work in these areas and who do an outstanding job.
- Make EO-related jobs necessary work assignments for high-potential people and for any person being considered for promotion to third-level and above. These tours should be for at least a year.
- Provide those in EO-related jobs extra pay incentives above and beyond normal incentives, when they do an outstanding job.
- Require all high-potential managers and those being considered for promotion to third-level and above to belong to and be active participants in community organizations that are concerned with the elimination of racism and sexism and support their involvement by channeling corporate community service contributions, both financial and in-kind to the organizations' activities and programs.
- Make certain that issues concerning EO and pluralism have time slots on all middle- and upper-management meetings.

Implementation of these recommendations will make EO an integral part of corporate culture and create an atmosphere in which all employees are fully utilized and developed. The end result will be a more efficient and productive corporation that will be able to compete effectively in the new competitive environment.

Companies, on the other hand, that deny—as the federal government is doing—the continued presence of racist and sexist attitudes in their work force and fail to take appropriate measures to diffuse them, will, in the long run, short-circuit their own productivity and competitiveness. Whatever the cost of the preventive measures described here, it is far less than the cost of ignoring the issues, as Kathleen Welds so graphically demonstrates:

> Many unanticipated conflicts may occur overtly, but there are also more subtle, self-destructive displacements when conflict is ignored altogether. Besides decreasing an organization's potential for an open, creative, and friendly atmosphere, hidden conflict can also be reflected in tardiness and absenteeism; high turnover and production errors; increased accidents, grievance, and transfer requests; plus decreased productivity. In addition, there are stress-related physical symptoms: insomnia; headache; hypertension; asthma and cardiac irregularities, weight changes; ulcers and colitis; uncontrolled use of drugs, cigarettes, or food; anxiety; and depression. These all suggest unresolved conflict in the workplace and lead to occupational burnout (1979:380–383).

X. REFERENCES

Fernandez, J. P. 1975. *Black managers in white corporations.* New York: Wiley.
Fernandez, J. P. 1981. *Racism and sexism in corporate life: Changing values in American business.* Lexington, MA: Lexington.
Goodman, M. E. 1964. *Race awareness in young children.* New York: Collier.

Grier, W. H., and P. M. Cobbs. 1968. *Black rage.* New York: Basic.

Lewis, H. B. 1976. *Psychic war in men and women.* New York: New York University Press.

Nilsen, Alleen Pace, Haig Bosmajaan, H. Lee Gershuny, and Julia P. Stanley. 1977. *Sexism and language.* Urbana, IL: National Council of Teachers of English.

Singh, J., and A. Yancey. 1974. Racial attitudes in white first grade children. *Journal of Educational Research* 67:370–372.

Welds, K. 1979. It's a question of stereotype vs. reality limits vs. potential. *Personnel Journal* (June):380–383.

Willie, Charles V., B. Kramer, and B. Brown (Eds.). 1973. *Racism and mental health.* Pittsburgh: University of Pittsburgh Press.

6

The Changing Agenda
New Era, New Perspectives

George Davis

Black Life in Corporate America, which I published with a colleague in 1982, attempted to look at aspects of the mostly hidden effects on the personal lives of these men and women who, in ever-increasing numbers, are trying to "make it" in the mainstream. It is also an attempt to give a view of the mainstream itself from the point of view of black managers as they attempt to swim ahead or simply to survive in these multibillion-dollar organizations— these uniquely modern ways of organizing a good percentage of the world's trained personnel into entities called Exxons and AT&Ts, IBMs, Sears, Fords, and U.S. Steels. *Black Life in Corporate America* (1982) is a vision of the human side of the story of men and women operating in foreign social space with unfamiliar protocol, with habits, manners, values, and styles of thinking that until recently were very new to them.

Our work is deliberately nonstatistical. Although statistics may provide some insight to the success of minorities in business, there are many things that statistics cannot tell us. Statistics cannot answer for us such vexing questions as "What is it like to be black in a place like this?" "How have you been received?" "What was the hardest thing for you to get used to?" "How do you feel about your chances of making it to the top?" "Do you still feel like a token?" "Of all your options, why did you choose the life of a corporate manager?" "Is life harder here for a black man or black woman?" "Have you ever felt you wanted to quit?" "Do you really feel you're in the mainstream or off in some special tributary set up by the company just to comply with EEO [equal employment opportunity] directives?" "In what ways do you feel the white woman qualifies as a minority, and in what ways does she not?"

George Davis • Department of English, Rutgers, The State University of New Jersey, Newark, New Jersey 07102.

These are questions that must be answered before we can go about the job of assuring minority success in business. In a sense, they must be answered before we can ensure the continued success of American business, because in the future, minorities and nonminority women (who face many of the same problems) will become an ever more powerful presence in the work force of our nation. According to U.S. Department of Labor statistics, by 1995, three of every five new entrants into the labor force will be either minority members or women. Companies that learn to make the best use of this pool of trained and talented players will have a decided advantage in putting together the best teams to tackle the difficult tasks facing American industry in the twenty-first century.

The challenge is not simply to hire more minorities and women, which is what affirmative action policies have attempted to achieve over the past two decades. Nor is the primary challenge simply to assure equal pay and equal opportunities, as difficult as that may be to accomplish. The real challenge is much more subtle. The intrinsic problem is much more difficult to address directly—which is not to say that it can, with any reasonable justification, be ignored. It involves changing the culture of corporate America or changing the environment of a particular company so that minorities and women will be able to make the full contributions they are qualified to make and that companies sorely need them to make. At present, corporate culture allows— even encourages—the underutilization of minorities and women, who all too often are not expected, or permitted, to take on levels of responsibility commensurate with their talents, training, and aspirations.

While doing research for *Black Life in Corporate America* (1982), we interviewed a black male manager at a Fortune 500 company. He said the major leagues of American industry are still:

> . . . like baseball before Jackie Robinson: There are a lot of could be stars and superstars who cannot make it to the majors because they happen to be black or female. Aspects of their style and their appearance are different, and so they are just not trusted as much, or in the same way.

Senior white male executives we talked to for our research on this subject agreed there was much truth to this assertion, but they were not inclined to tackle the difficulties involved with bringing minorities and women into the levels they themselves occupy. An instinct for short-term self-preservation would seem to be involved in their attitudes. They do not want to disrupt the old-boy network or the boy-wonder system that feeds into it.

To break up this long-standing continuity would amount to breaking up what Rosabeth Moss Kanter calls a system of homosocial reproduction (1977), which is the natural impulse of senior management to (a) perceive as most competent, (b) feel more comfortable with and affinity for, and (c) have a greater willingness to promote aspiring managers who look and act most like themselves. Homosocial reproduction is often justified with such statements as "They [blacks and women] are just not as good in business situations as white males are." These justifications are similar to arguments advanced during the 1920s and 1930s that "they [in this case, blacks] are just not fitted by nature for organized major-league sports."

As laughable as those arguments now seem, they were part of our national culture in the same way that the "not-as-well-fitted-for-business" arguments are a part of corporate culture today. We can sigh with relief when we think of those brave white males who saw the potential in developing athletes who might have looked a little different, who surely spoke differently, and who perhaps threw the ball or patrolled centerfield with different style and determination. In the competitive search for corporate excellence, business leaders who put together the winning teams will be those brave enough to be among the first to learn how to use fully the diverse talents of our racially and sexually diverse population.

The point that I have been making is: Ensuring minority success in business is more intimately connected with ensuring the success of business and ensuring the success of this republic and the world than we might at first think.

It is good, then, to consider where we are. Where are we? We are in a time warp. It is as if characteristics of three distinct periods of racial integration are existing simultaneously with the emergence of a fourth phase. It all depends on which company we are looking at. The three periods can be called: tokenism, racial turbulence, and backlash. The emerging period has not yet named itself, but before we can understand it, we must review the three prior periods and examine the extent to which characteristics of each still exist today.

I. TOKENISM

"It was very different when I came in," said a man whom we identified in our book as the grand old black man of the corporate mainstream. We interviewed him in 1980. "Back then [1947] you could go for days in one of these places without seeing anyone black, except the messengers and the janitors. The elevator starters were black, and they would grin and say, 'Yes, sir, good morning, sir' when you came in. I couldn't exactly say I was a manager because I didn't manage anything or anybody. You have no idea how different it was back then," he said. "You yourself representing the company on so many occasions that were outside your area of expertise—I'm an accountant by training. Whenever they needed a black face for a particular gathering, they would come in and get me. I'm sure this made it impossible for my supervisor to take me seriously as a member of his department," he said and laughed. "But being a token can work to your advantage, too. If they need a black face at a certain level in the company, they'd put you on a fast track and promote you to that level. The disadvantage was they would never promote you above that level, or out of that particular area, never pull you back here." He held his clenched fist close to his chest, as a cog in the machine. "But this promotion still caused resentment among the white guys in the department because I was being moved to a higher salary level faster than they. Some of this so-called backlash comes from this source. The guys in today's middle and top management remember how tokens were treated when they were working their way up. They are the guys who are yelling about reverse discrimination. You see the double bind you're in? There's no such thing as reverse discrimination if you're talking about a fast track to the executive suite in a significant job in the company. But I've been the affirmative action manager, the equal opportunity director, and the vice-president of special markets—not the comptroller."

What is still true in corporate America today is that in some companies you can still go for days without seeing a black manager with a substantial job. The janitors are often still black, but one indication of progress is that they are often the employees of a black-owned cleaning service that has a substantial contract with the Fortune 500 firm. There are few elevator starters, but often the mailroom staff and low-level clerical personnel are visible black faces. There are still far too many black managers who do not manage anything or anybody, and there are a great number who are in window-dressing jobs that are not really taken seriously by the company.

Blacks report that they still have to work harder than whites to make far fewer gains in the environment. Blacks are still placed in situations that are not going to lead to important positions in their companies, which is why there is still such a cluster of them in personnel departments and public affairs departments.

This is not to say that these jobs are not important, but they are certainly not the kinds of jobs that are going to lead to the power positions. What Steven M. Gelber said in *Black Men and Businessmen* back in 1974 is still true in 1984:

> Employers sought and frequently found overqualified black applicants for managerial positions. . . . Hired for decorative rather than functional purposes, the token black manager could serve their purposes just as well in powerless junior positions as in senior positions where they might have some real power in the company.

What was a rather standard practice is now only a tendency in major companies, but as a tendency it traps many minorities and women in situations of underutilization. Many race and gender pioneers bear these burdens of tokenism, however, because they sense that they are doing something to advance their sex or race. They are understandably more impatient and more frustrated to have to endure the same kind of environmental restrictions on their progress as blacks and women bore 20 years ago—the same kind of racist and sexist jokes, the same kind of doubts of their proven abilities, the same restrictions with regard to important assignments, and thus the same handicaps with regard to upward mobility.

II. RACIAL TURBULENCE

Corporate America has never been a very racially turbulent environment, but during the 1960s and early 1970s American society was so racially turbulent that corporate life was affected as well. It is instructive to look at the affect that the 1960s had on the minds of black people and therefore on the minds of black managers. In the 1960s, there was a revolution. The revolution can be called successful even though no one overthrew the dominion of white males over America and the world. We blacks, however, overthrew the rule of white men in our minds. We underwent a psychological revolution.

Before the 1960s, only a few among us actively questioned the rightness of whiteness. The march of civilization was toward the white way of being. The ideas behind the long battle to integrate public schools was to give black children an opportunity to mix with children of the ruling caste, and thereby join the march.

It seems that no one intended to alter all this, and certainly few people outside of psychological circles knew that such a revolution was needed. There was no psychological intent to the 1955 Montgomery bus boycott. Rosa Parks was simply too tired to get up and give a white man her seat on an Alabama bus. At first, Martin Luther King. Jr. intended nothing more psychologically profound than racial integration. The nine kids who were stoned and spat upon at Little Rock Central High School in 1957 could hardly have known the full psychological impact of their defiance of social custom.

The sit-ins began as simple efforts to win blacks the right to sit and drink coffee at the lunch counter of a dinky Woolworth's in Greensboro, North Carolina. Blacks and whites confronted each other in Birmingham, Alabama, where whites used police dogs, cattle prods, and fire hoses. Four young girls were killed in an Alabama church bombing. The bombers went free. Civil rights workers were mutilated and killed in several southern states. The nation watched on TV. Guilt swelled like a knot in white throats. Gunnar Myrdal had said in *The American Dilemma* (1962) that racism kept a moral uneasiness simmering just below the surface of American life. TV brought it to the surface as never before since the Civil War.

In 1965, President Lyndon Johnson signed into law massive amounts of civil rights legislation. "It is the glorious opportunity of this generation to end the one huge wrong of the American nation," Johnson said to a black audience at Howard University in June of 1965:

> The barriers [to freedom] are tumbling down. Freedom is the right to share, share fully and equally, in American society—to vote, to hold a job, to enter a public place, to go to school. It is the right to be treated in every part of our national life as a person equal in dignity and promise to all others.

The promise came too late for the bad dudes of the northern streets: They began burning things down. At first the incidents were small. In the summer of 1964, the first of a series of urban uprisings flared in Rochester, New York.

It lasted 2 days and the National Guard was called in to put it down. In 1965, the bigger uprising in Los Angeles shocked the nation. Thirty-four people were killed. Thousands more were injured, and more than $35 million in property was burned, wrecked, looted, or defiled.

The following year Newark burned. LBJ's promise came too late for that city's 20 thousand pupils who were on double sessions, for thousands of dropouts who comprised about 33% of the city's high-school-aged youth. (Of 13,600 blacks in Newark, between 16 and 19, more than 6,000 were not in school at that time.) In 1960, over half of the adult population of Newark had less than an eighth grade education. "The typical ghetto cycle of high unemployment, family breakup, and crime was present in all its elements. An estimated 40 percent of Negro children lived in broken homes," said the Kerner Commission Report (U.S. President's National Advisory Committee on Civil Disorders, 1968).

Newark was not different; it was only worse than other big cities plagued by violent urban unrest. The growing power of the Equal Employment Opportunity Commission (EEOC) was one of the responses to this unrest. The EEOC gained enough power to bring suit against corporations who did not open opportunities to minorities and women. AT&T had to pay $38 million to people it had discriminated against. Sears, General Motors, and General Electric also lost money and face.

Doors were forced opened, and what we might call "black" blacks rushed in—ones who had not accepted the automatic rightness of whiteness. These black managers had a not-too-unexpected ambivalence toward what they perceived as a need to clone their white male corporate superiors in order to get ahead. Their ambivalence was quite natural. During this time, blacks outside the corporation were trying to separate themselves entirely from American life, which they felt to be spiritually sterile, overly mechanistic, and "packaged."

"They want you to be like them," said one scientist–manager:

> They want you to suppress certain aspects of your racial identity—your life-style, sense of humor, way of dressing, existential things that are part of your racial heritage. I can do it. I can "behave." Behave means act the way they want you to. "Behaving" is a problem for me because I'm from an entirely different background.
>
> I have doubts about my ability—no, I doubt my desire to behave much longer. Soon I might do something "real." Like wear the wrong clothes to work—a pair of patent leather shoes with three inch heels just to mess with their minds. Something ridiculous like that.

Another scientist, with a master's degree in engineering and a PhD in chemistry, was very happy with his new job. He was part of management, but he did not manage anyone but himself and three junior scientists who aided him on a special project. He loved the money he made—about $20,000 a year (in 1977)—but he was ambivalent about the subtle corporate demands on his taste and life-style:

> For example, most people in the scientific community drive Volkswagens or Volvos to work. They question my scientific dedication when they see my Cadillac in the

staff parking lot. They want me to accept their values. They probably feel that all a black wants is a Cadillac. They want me to give up my values and accept theirs before they can feel completely safe about me. They want me to wear Robert Hall suits and Hush Puppies before they can accept the fact that I'm a good physicist, an excellent one.

It was certainly the black revolution of the 1960s that created such disinclination to assimilate. It was the force of the Civil Rights Act of 1964 that brought so many "black" blacks into the mainstream. These were not members of the established black middle class, as most of the tokens were. This new black man or black woman might have come from a stable family background but could just as easily have come from one of those broken homes that crowd the statistics on black life. He or she was likely to be from a churchgoing family, but the church could easily have been one of the temple-of-fire gospel churches that taught that God's relationship to life on earth was immediate, judgmental, rewarding, or punitive, as the situation demanded.

As likely as not, this new black manager came from a turbulent childhood full of extremes of agony and ecstasy, defeat and victory. Hunger and obsession may have affected him or her, but usually not in the extremes that would prevent the young man or woman from getting through Howard, Morgan State, Harvard, or Michigan and into corporate management. The memories of childhood hungers and obsessions were usually strong enough to fill the manager with the fear of ever having to return to that life or of ever having to raise children in a similar climate.

To some degree, many of these black men and women had experienced the system as victims. Some were ambivalent about any implication that by joining the system they had become victimizers. Some did everything they could to avoid identifying with the black masses from which they sprang, whereas others wanted to cling tenaciously to an identification with the past and culture, sometimes in rebelliously immature ways. Many encountered a great deal of racist resistance, but sometimes what they interpreted as racism was not racism at all. Some of their problems stemmed from their own unfamiliarity with the way big impersonal organizations operate. For example, some blacks complained that it is dishonest to pretend to like someone you do not really like, as corporate life demands that you do. Wilbert Moore, in *The Conduct of the Corporation* (1975), points out that this kind of "emotional dishonesty" is necessary. The single greatest advantage of the corporation "over other forms of human interaction is the capacity for inducing strangers and even potential enemies to cooperate in accomplishing the collective mission."

This aspect of corporate life was harder for blacks to adjust to because they had more potential enemies who were more unreasonably hostile than they perceived whites to have. Many young blacks felt that there was something wrong with grinning in the face of someone you did not like and who did not like you. Their parents had had to do too much of that. Blacks had gotten used to "telling it like it is," "being for real," and "letting it all hang out."

Conformity was difficult, and even dress codes became a source of contention. All jobs in corporations do not necessarily preclude spontaneity, honesty of feeling, and integrity, but many of them do. "But if you want to play the game you've got to pay for a ticket," one black manager said. "Getting used to this atmosphere is the price of the ticket."

Most black managers, even during the hot 1960s and early 1970s, tried very hard to conform, and usually, with greater effort than their white counterparts, they were able to do so. Most admitted they were glad to be in corporate life, and they acknowledged that they were there because civil rights groups and the federal government pressured their companies into giving blacks a chance, but all felt fully qualified, often overqualified.

The patterns of their adjustment were similar in many ways to those of countless generations of European immigrants adjusting to America. But the visible racial difference and hundreds of years of systematic attempts to dehumanize black people made adjustment more difficult for them in many ways. And many of them seemed to be saying that there was some persistent blackness of their spirits that kept them from wanting to assimilate.

Among many blacks there was much anomie, a condition resulting from the breakdown of traditional values and norms of an individual who cannot or does not want to assimilate the values of a new, more complex, and often inhospitable environment. Anomie, according to Don A. Martindale in *The Nature and Types of Sociological Theory* (1960), often results in feelings of isolation and the loss of the intimacy found in traditional cultures.

Several interviewees admitted that they may have had a touch of something like that. Some of the black managers we met in corporate America in 1984 still suffered from such identity problems, but much less so. Nonetheless, many blacks still find that the path to success lies in cloning white male behavior. Some do it cheerfully. "If you want to be someone in life, imitate people who've already attained what you hope to attain," said one black manager. Another black manager rode around Connecticut all winter with skies on the back of his Mercedes even though he couldn't ski, simply trying to convince whites that he was more like them than they themselves were.

The pressures to overconform are not as great as they once were. Whites and blacks have been together in the environment long enough for whites to accept some of those subtle differences between members of different races as inconsequential as far as effectiveness is concerned. Yet the pressure is still there, prompting one University of Tennessee student to ask: "Can I go into corporate America without giving up my blackness?" Giving up his blackness was his way of asking if he must give up many of those existential parts of the self that makes each of us a unique individual.

The answer, of course, is yes—to some extent you do have to give up part of your identity. Everyone, white or black, male or female, must give up some portions of what they might consider their individual identities in order to become what the company wants them to be. Blacks simply have to give up more.

III. BACKLASH

During tough times, questions of identity are not nearly so important as questions of survival. Survival became the important question during the last few years of the 1970s and the already completed years of this decade. This can be called the period of backlash. *Backlash* is the word that came into vogue in the early 1970s to describe the actions of the privileged to preserve their positions from the inroads of the underprivileged.

There is no doubt that much backlash was based on open racism and sexism, but there is also no doubt that some of it comes from sources more complex.

One manager we interviewed described the period of backlash very well:

> I think there are some of us with good jobs in the mainstream who will hold on to those jobs. There will be some rollback, and some attrition due to the fact that when some blacks get fed up and drop out, their places will be taken by nonblacks; but on the other hand I think that corporations will continue to hire young, well-trained blacks for entry-level positions, and some of these will work their way up in the system. Yes, definitely, the door won't be open as wide, but it will remain open in many instances.

He closed his office door behind him and told a red-haired secretary that he was going out to lunch and that he would be back in about an hour. "I do think there are going to be a lot of careers put on hold. White people really believe in this reverse discrimination thing," he said. White males began to accuse companies of reverse discrimination when a minority candidate or woman got a job that a white male "should have gotten." He also said:

> Some people believe in this reverse discrimination thing and it just depends on whether the ones who know that it's bullshit will stand up to the ones who want to use it as an excuse. I don't think there's going to be a complete turn around but I think that it's going to be rough for a while . . . it's going to be tough with Ronald Reagan's people in there.

Certainly Ronald Reagan was not elected president in 1980 in order to put an end to affirmative action programs. He was elected because he proposed a new approach to the nation's problems—an approach that was different from that of previous administrations, even from the administration of Richard Nixon, who was of the same political party.

Reagan's style was different. He was friendly, cool, and businesslike. He seemed almost corporate. He convinced many people that big government was responsible for many of the nation's troubles. Charmingly, he promised to "take the government off the backs of the American people." Plainly, to the enemies of affirmative action, this meant that he wanted to get the government out of the business of forcing companies to end racial and sexual discrimination. In fact, he said that he was philosophically opposed to affirmative action.

And so during the first year of his administration, the government began quietly putting this philosophy into practice: The administration told corporations with a combined total of more than 7.5 million workers that they no longer had to draw up detailed plans for hiring and promoting women and minorities. It changed the rules under which female and minority workers could sue to collect back pay for jobs or promotions they did not get. It forbade any employer with a government contract from hiring women and minorities over equally qualified white males even to atone for the effects of past discrimination.

These measures, the September 7, 1981, edition of *Time* argued, were trial balloons to see how politically wise it might be to take further anti-affirmative action steps. Being philosophically opposed to affirmative action, the administration was testing to see how wise it would be to be operationally opposed as well.

Of course there were other reasons for the ridiculous charge by white males that minorities and women were being favored over them. The economic infrastructure of the country was still overwhelmingly based on the white male wage earner. When inflation went into double digits and unemployment, in some sectors of the economy, surpassed the rate of inflation, a tightness of spirit set in, and meanness came out. Competition grew more fierce, and charity began to dissolve. This played right into the hands of those who had been angry since the early 1970s when the federal government first stepped up the drive to end employment discrimination.

In November of 1984, Ronald Reagan was again elected president—by an unprecedented majority. Ninety percent of all black voters voted against him. Almost 80% of all white voters voted for him. This certainly should not lead one to claim that 80% of all white voters are racially conservative, but it is safe to assume that a majority of the white voters in the country are in a conservative mood.

IV. THE OPEN FUTURE

This is the social situation in which corporations now exist. These corporations are beset by all of the problems that I have so far mentioned, and on the brighter side, many companies are still nominally proaffirmative action. But a greater burden has been placed on upwardly mobile blacks to find their own means of gaining equal treatment inside their respective companies.

Many blacks now find themselves in jobs that they would not have dreamed of 20 years ago. Looking at the forest that is corporate America, we see fewer black trees, but those we find are sturdier, and they find themselves in many vital and diversified parts of their companies. For those blacks who are very qualified, substantial positions can be achieved, said more than one member of the National Black MBA Association at the association's fifth Annual Conference in Atlanta. "American industry is at a crossroad," said Ray Carter (a pseudonym) whom I interviewed on the first day of the conference.

Carter was an intense individual with an MBA in finance. At 47, he was older than most of the attendees at the conference. He had been in corporate life for 22 years. He could speak from experience. He acknowledged that there were many visible indications that might lead one to believe things had gotten better. However, he was still not persuaded even when we pointed out that more than half the front-desk staff of the fashionable hotel where the conference was being held were black; that Atlanta's past and present mayors are black; that the busy midtown area in Atlanta was full of well-dressed black men and women going about the affairs of one of America's most important cities.

Was not that proof of how far Atlanta, the State of Georgia, and the nation had come since the 1960s? Were not the 550 bright, mostly young MBAs—themselves representing hundreds of the nation's blue-chip organizations—proof of the progress American industry has made in the past 20 years? "But American industry is at a crossroad," Carter argued. "It has been forced to take these people in. It now has to decide, deep in the bowels of each organization. what it wants to do with them. That's the period we're in now. And it's tough, day to day, in each company, division, department, team."

I surveyed more than 180 of these MBAs by written questionnaire and follow-up sessions. Here is what I found: Only 25 of them cited backlash and the "racially repressive political climate" of the 1980s as their major problem. Only 37 cited specific instances of overtly discriminatory practices. However, to the question, "What do you feel is the greatest problem faced by black managers in corporate America," 102 mentioned or alluded to, exclusion from the informal structure of the company:

> I think the problem stems from the fact that, as a black, you are still perceived as an outsider, an unknown quantity [said an MBA who works as a strategic planner for a West Coast electronics firm.] Because of social, cultural and physical differences, you don't become part of the real information flow and the real decision-making processes of the company.

Another manager said:

> The cultural and social differences between black managers and white managers create a level of social discomfort that results in noncommunication. Your [white] manager doesn't talk with you frankly and informally, and so you don't really know him and he doesn't know you. You don't then pick up the nuances of his expectations, and he doesn't really sense your strengths and weaknesses. So, quite naturally, you are not given the high-risk, or plum, assignments. The tendency is to put you in assignments where you cannot possibly: (1) build your own skills or (2) increase your confidence in yourself, or, more importantly, increase senior management's confidence in you.

A third manager added:

> The real business of a company is carried on by people sitting down over coffee, or face-to-face over drinks, or laughing together in each other's homes, or walking together down the fairway of a golf course, or at 32,000 feet in the corporate jet. This is how it is done. What takes place in offices is often no more than pro forma, and

even when decisions are not made in informal settings, the stage is set for them, the rapport is developed. People come to understand each other's real feelings on matters. This is the only way it can happen—jawboning, horse trading, back slapping, arguing; and to the extent that some blacks and women don't fit in comfortably, they work under a handicap.

These managers are not alluding to a "black" problem so much as a structural one for which the black problem is only the latest hyperbole for the environment that other minority entrants have come up against. They are concerned about problems that make the cultures of their companies segmented, rather than unified, that make them individual contributors performing in fish bowls, rather than team players. For them, the likelihood of quitting seems more real than the likelihood of getting fired.

"I left my old job to start my own business because I knew I had topped out," said one black executive. "The company was not going to allow a black to get any higher. And you talk about frustration—to be dead-ended at 31. Try that!"

This individual realized that even many white males face the same problem but not in the same percentage or to the same final degree. His fate forced him to contemplate how many other talented people that same company had lost because of the vast differences between the way things were and the way things were supposed to be.

"For example, they are not sure about having you manage white employees," he said. "And in many cases, white employees perceive, quite correctly, that you are relatively powerless, or that you are on perpetual probation with senior management. Often your employees—especially if they are white males—are better wired than you are. They are inside the information flow."

We have interviewed black managers who have gone to ridiculous extremes to get whites to be comfortable with them. We know of one smart, young black manager, who was graduated from Harvard University. Surely, he thought, this would make him "acceptable." However, his manager kept trying to make his badge of acceptability a counterfeit. This young man was 6'5", so his manager maintained that he must have gotten into Harvard on a basketball scholarship—certainly not by being bright.

The company wanted energetic salespeople, but he was very tall and dark-skinned. He knew, on the one hand, that he could easily be perceived as hostile, yet he knew on the other hand that, if he was not forceful, he would not be considered aggressive enough. He developed the habit of always sitting when he talked to his manager so he would not appear to tower over him. He never mentioned basketball, although he loved the game and he knew his manager loved it, too. Finally, he raised his voice an octave. So, here was this big black guy from Harvard running around corporate America saying "super," "fantastic," and "sure" in soprano.

He was fired. He moved to another company where management encouraged and trained its managers in good cross-cultural communications. He became a district manager in 2 years.

A black female manager told us, "I have been with my company for 10 years, and I still don't know how to 'be' in order to gain the trust of the inner circle." If black males have a problem being accepted as "one of the guys," we can imagine how much greater the problem is for black females; how much more difficult the informal exchanges that get so much of the company's "real" business done.

An entire book could be written about the chemistry of the interaction between black and white men and women in the informal structure of American life. It would not ignore the historical parallels with the entry of the offspring of this country's immigrant cultures into the business world. The conclusion would have to be that the failure of real communication, based on mutual respect, is probably the greatest productivity problem we have.

Surveys, like the one conducted by Rosabeth Kanter for her book, *The Change Masters* (1983), show that companies with the most enlightened policies toward minorities and women are generally better at solving the many human problems that have a more profound effect on the bottom line than corporate theorists had once supposed. Kanter's work suggests that the complaints that the 180 black managers we interviewed made about exclusion from the informal structure were nothing more or less than the most obvious statement of what can happen to many others in organizational life.

No theorists of organizational life would argue that there are not positive, indeed necessary, contributions made via informal relationships and alliances within organizations. But because blacks are not usually part of the most important of these relationships, they are often the victims of them. They are victims in all the ways that people in the system can become victims. It happens when informal relationships and alliances short-circuit the structure, preventing a lot of talented people, black and white, male and female, from having the information and support they need to get the job done.

V. REFERENCES

Davis, George, and Glegg Watson. 1982. *Black life in corporate America*. New York: Doubleday.
Gelber, Steven M. 1974. *Black men and businessmen*. Port Washington, NY: Kennikat.
Kanter, Rosabeth Moss. 1977. *Men and women of the corporation*. New York: Basic.
Kanter, Rosabeth Moss. 1983. *The change masters*. New York: Simon and Schuster.
Martindale, Don M. 1960. *The nature and types of sociological theory*. Boston: Houghton Mifflin.
Moore, Wilbert. 1975. *The conduct of the corporation*. Westport, CT: Greenwood.
Myrdal, Gunnar *et al*. 1962. *An American dilemma*. New York: Harper & Row.
U.S. President's National Advisory Commission on Civil Disorders. 1968. *Report of the National Advisory Commission on Civil Disorders*. New York: Bantam.

III

Defining the Critical Issues
Problems and Concerns

The second step in the problem-solving process is to identify the positions of each important actor. Part III of this book includes several key actors: corporations, current students and recent MBA graduates, and more advanced minority managers and academics. This part, more than any other in the book, underlines the depth of the barriers to minority advancement. It is not just a matter of this or that particular problem or issue. More important is that the key actors do not agree in fundamental ways. Of course, disagreement can mean that each is looking at different parts of the same problem or choosing to emphasize different things, but that is not the case here. Instead, some of the key actors aggressively deny that the views of the others have merit. And, some deny that there is a problem at all. These are the sorts of gaps that must be confronted and bridged for a more positive approach to problem solving. Only part of the material in this section of the book is based on generalizable research, but all of it reflects firmly held beliefs about this important human resource issue. Even those parts of the section that summarize small group discussions with experienced managers or interviews with recent graduates provide important insight about the thinking which goes on in management circles about the advancement of minority managers. Although not based on random or large samples, this material, nevertheless, uncovers opinions which are widely held, even if publicly suppressed or minimized. The following provides an overview of the differing perspectives.

    The first paper in this section, by DiTomaso, Thompson, and Blake, reports corporate perspectives on minority advancement based on the results of a survey of 218 top corporations. Three problem areas were identified for the corporate respondents: organizational policies and procedures; relations between minority managers and others; and the preparation of minority managers for their careers. The organizational factors considered most problematic for the corporate respondents are the lack of promotion opportunities and lack of company planning for minority career development. The relationship factors considered of most concern are the lack of other minority managers to provide support as well as the lack of role models and mentors.

And, far and away the most frequently mentioned factor in terms of the preparation of minority managers is the insufficient number of qualified minority candidates. It may be equally revealing to note what was not mentioned as problematic for these corporate respondents: Pay was not considered a problem; there was not much concern about the reactions of others to working with a minority; and there was very little concern about issues such as motivation and ambition.

From the point of view of corporations, the problems in the advancement of minority managers into top-level positions are primarily a matter of time. That is, in their view, once a sufficient number of minority managers get the requisite training and skills, there appears to be confidence they will be promoted. As they are, the concern with networks, role models, and mentors will be arrested. A possible obstacle, however, will be corporate structure itself. The current trends toward mergers, acquisitions, and downsizing suggests that there will be even fewer opportunities for advancement in the future than there have been in the recent past. Minority managers may be ready for promotions just as the openings disappear, and this concerns our corporate respondents. This view of the situation, however, is somewhat at odds with the views given by experienced managers and academics.

Chapter 8 summarizes discussions of 10 small groups from a conference on minority advancement in management. Each group included experienced managers (both minority and nonminority) and academics who have done research on minorities in the work force. The groups were structured to allow free and open discussion, but it is quite clear that, in the context of the conference and given the strong minority presence in each of the groups, the white participants might present different views than they would on an anonymous and written survey. Discussions were lively, but there were not, on the bottom line, strongly divergent views expressed within each group. At the same time, the 10 groups did not talk about the same things.

Three issues emerged from the discussion groups as being most important (although only half of the groups discussed any one of these issues). On one, there is agreement with the corporate respondents discussed in Chapter 7, namely the need for mentors, sponsors, coaches, and role models for minority managers. Of the other two issues considered most important by these experienced managers and academics, one, the need for strong company commitment, was also considered a problem by the corporate respondents in Chapter 7, but it was not at the top of their list. The third issue, the need for accountability or rewards in meeting affirmative action goals and developing minority managers, was not asked directly of the corporate respondents. It could have been mentioned by them, however, in a series of open-ended questions on the survey, but only 12% of the 117 respondents who answered the relevant question mentioned accountability (see discussion in Chapter 12 of this part of the survey).

On the whole, it appears that the participants in these small-group discussions see minority advancement primarily as a matter of policy and practice, rather than a matter of time. In fact, there was a clear sense in their discussions that minority advancement could not be left to develop without clear commitment and monitoring by top management. Whereas the corporate respondents discussed in Chapter 7 may feel that minorities who want to enter management careers need to do more to prepare themselves, the experienced managers and academics whose views are discussed in Chapter 8 feel that minorities have already done their part and that now the responsibility lies with the corporation. At the same time, they indicated some pessimism about the prospects for any increased corporate commitment, given recent problems of competition and the general nature of changes going on in the corporate world. They were especially concerned about the role of middle management in making the crucial difference in the advancement of minority managers and yet noted the limited accountability that is present on affirmative action and equal opportunity goals in most corporations.

The perspectives of current and recent MBA graduates who are just beginning their careers in management are discussed in Chapter 9. In contrast to the guarded pessimism of the experienced managers and academics in Chapter 8, the younger minority managers discussed in Chapter 9 report optimism about their future in the corporate world. These new MBAs want their minority status downplayed and expect that to be possible in their future careers. In contrast, the more advanced minority managers feel that there needs to be continuing strong support from top management to ensure minority success in most corporations. Although the younger managers-to-be want their minority status to be invisible and irrelevant to their career progress, the older managers want accountability for what happens to minority managers, and as such, they want to stand out.

These new MBAs indicate strong family ties and usually some extra help in their educational preparation. Although many attended inner-city public schools and in later contexts found that their educations had been lacking, most of these found ways to augment their educational experiences. While attending college, most stayed close to home and few attended Ivy League schools. Most majored in business-relevant subjects, and most had some, but limited, work experience before getting their MBAs. The career aspirations of most of these new MBAs is rather moderate compared to the images often portrayed in the media about MBAs wanting to be president of the company overnight. In fact, only one or two saw themselves as reaching top management in a major corporation; many of the others planned to start their own businesses after a short time in the corporate world. All in all, the responses indicate very little concern about discrimination, and instead, a strong sense of determination and confidence that they will get ahead because of what they have to offer and because of how hard they will work. They want role models and mentors, not so much to actively help them, as to help them help themselves. And, although they recognize the need for networks, none of them has them at this point. The orientation to self-help that many of these respondents exhibited helps explain that few thought of themselves as minorities. They want their own experiences to be color-blind—and gender-blind—and they feel some sense of confidence that they will fare well in such an environment. In addition, there is some genuine ambivalence about the legacy of the civil rights movement, especially affirmative action or any programs that will make their minority status a prominent part of their corporate identities.

There are both differences and similarities in the perspectives of the various actors discussed here. The possibilities for reconciliation depend on a better understanding among the actors about how their views differ and on developing solutions that meet their respective interests. Part of developing feasible solutions is for each of the parties to agree that whatever is proposed is better for them and for others as well, but we will save this discussion for later parts of this volume. In Part IV we examine solutions by looking at the careers of successful minority managers who tell us how they did it and by reviewing successful programs at some of the corporations that are known for their success in the advancement of minority managers. That there are so few successful minority managers in terms of the goals outlined in this book, namely holding top, line management positions in major corporations, suggests that there is much more to be done. That so few corporations are well recognized for their success in promoting minority managers—and there is a decided lack of concensus about which companies should be included in the category—indicates that we do not already know how it should be done. The next part is intended to stimulate ideas and generate more discussion about these issues. Part V provides a summary and recommends specific actions.

7

Corporate Perspectives on the Advancement of Minority Managers

Nancy DiTomaso, Donna E. Thompson, and David H. Blake

An important determinant of minority management success in the corporate world is the interpretation that the top managements of corporations give to the problems and solutions of the current underrepresentation of minority managers in higher level management positions. For this reason, we felt it was necessary to include among the various perspectives on the problems and issues of minority managers in corporate careers, the perspective of corporations. Obviously, corporations do not themselves speak or think, but we surveyed the top managements of major corporations and asked them to speak for the corporation in their responses. A report of our findings is the purpose of this chapter.

The corporate perspective on minority advancement in corporate careers is a glaringly absent omission from the existing literature on this topic. And, yet it is important to understand both the similarities and differences between the corporate perspective and the minority perspective, if minority under-representation in top management positions is to be eliminated. As noted in the first chapter of this volume, there are two distinct stories about minority advancement, one from minority managers (represented by what has been written about black managers) and one from white managers in key positions in corporations. On the face of it, these stories are divergent in their premises and their conclusions.

The explanations given by minority managers (as noted, we are summarizing the published view of black managers) for their limited success in management careers are consistent across the existing literature. First and foremost, minority managers argue that they have been discriminated against

Nancy DiTomaso, Donna E. Thompson, and David H. Blake • Rutgers Graduate School of Management, Newark, New Jersey 07102.

and that this is the primary reason for their underrepresentation in top management positions. Discrimination is said to take several forms. Before government regulations forced open the doors, access was limited to even entry-level jobs. Access is now more readily available, according to minority managers, but they still face an "invisible ceiling" on their advancement, which ends somewhere in middle management—or before (Brown and Ford, 1977, 1977; Crotty and Timmons, 1974; Hicks, 1985; Hymowitz, 1984).

A second explanation given by minority managers for their lack of advancement is their exclusion from social and political networks that can provide them with the information and resources for getting their jobs done, knowing when opportunities are available, and providing support when choices are made about promotions. This issue is discussed in two forms, the lack of connections to mentors, coaches, and role models, and the inability to fit into white corporate culture, due both to discrimination and to genuine differences in interpersonal styles.

Minority managers, however, reject an explanation attributed to white corporate managers, namely that there are an insufficient number of qualified minority candidates. In the view of minority managers, such an explanation is a smokescreen, which hides discriminatory and biased evaluations of minority performance, while unnecessarily emphasizing degrees and credentials which may not be necessary for adequate performance on the job (Fernandez, 1975, 1981; Morgan and Van Dyke, 1970). Fernandez (1975) finds, for example, that in a comparison of a sample of black and white managers in 12 corporations that blacks were, on the average, more highly educated and equally as likely as whites in the same companies to have degrees in business and technical fields.

This chapter provides some elaboration of the corporate view beyond what was discussed in Chapter 1. The focus here is on the corporate view of problems and issues; corporate practices and policies are examined in Chapter 12. The results reported here are taken from a mail survey to the 808 firms on the *Forbes* combined 500s lists of the top, publicly owned U.S. companies in sales, profits, assets, and market value for 1983. A total of 218 questionnaires were returned for a response rate of 27%, which we consider adequate for the purposes of this analysis. Responses were well distributed across industry type, with the primary concentration in durable and nondurable goods manufacturing; transportation, communications, and other public utilities; and finance, insurance, and real estate. Also included in the sample are companies from retail trade; mining; business and repair services; personal service (excluding private household); professional and related services; agriculture, forestry, and fisheries; wholesale trade; and construction; as well as 16 firms that identified themselves as conglomerates. See Table 1 for a distribution of our sample compared with the *Forbes* list.

Although respondents were asked to speak for the corporation and not for themselves, it is obvious that one's own views on this topic may shade what one thinks to be the corporate view. Indeed, the very existence of two stories as we describe them in Chapter 1 indicates that perspectives differ by

Table 1. Distribution of Respondents and of Sampling Frame[a]

Industry	Respondents		Sampling frame	
	Number	Percentage	Number	Percentage
Finance, insurance, and real estate	57	26.1	219	27.1
Transportation, communication, and public utilities	43	19.7	162	20.0
Nondurable goods manufacturing	25	11.5	114	14.1
Durable goods manufacturing	23	10.6	115	14.2
Conglomerate	16	7.3	30	3.7
Retail trade	8	3.7	46	5.7
Mining (including oil)	7	3.2	54	6.7
Business and repair services	3	1.4	11	1.4
Personal service, exluding private household	2	.9	5	.6
Professional and related services	2	.9	—	—
Agriculture, forestry, and fisheries	2	.9	—	—
Wholesale trade	1	.5	41	5.1
Construction	1	.5	5	.6
No response	28	12.8	—	—
Total	218	100.0	808	99.2[b]

[a]Discrepancies are due to the differences in the type of information available for coding, as well as to any sampling biases. Respondents were asked to provide industry information in an open-ended question. Their responses were then coded into census categories. The industry information for the sampling frame is taken from the *Forbes* list of companies that was used as a sampling frame.
The *Forbes* list does not use the same census categories, and therefore it is possible that some minor differences in coding occurred. For example, one of our respondents might have indicated being in the "lumber" business and thus was coded as "agriculture, forestry, and fisheries." Companies on the *Forbes* list that we know are in the lumber business are listed by *Forbes* as "building materials," which suggests that it should be coded as "wholesale trade" (and we did code it as such) rather than as "agriculture, forestry, and fisheries." It was particularly difficult to distinguish given the information provided by either source, manufacturing from wholesale trade, as it is not always clear from industry categories alone whether a company makes a product or only sells it to other companies. Also, our sample has a larger percentage of "conglomerates" than does the *Forbes* list. This may have occurred because *Forbes* may consider a particular company to be *primarily* in a given type of industry, whereas the respondent for that same company, if it is included in our sample, may have indicated on the questionnaire that it was a "multiproduct company." If so, we had no choice but to code the firm as a "conglomerate."
All responses to our questionnaire were anonymous, and some respondents may have felt that if they identified the type of industry, along with other requested information, such as number of employees and size of assets, that it would be possible to identify the firm. Given the imprecision of the information available for coding, there is, nevertheless, a remarkably similar distribution between our respondents and the sampling frame.
[b]Less than 100 due to rounding error.

race. This is true for sex as well. In separate analyses, we found that white and male respondents were more optimistic than were blacks or females. Whites and males were more likely to view their companies as being successful in supporting the advancement of minority managers and less likely to see continuing problems in their firms compared to black and female respondents in our sample. Hispanic and other respondents were sometimes consistent with whites—Anglos—and sometimes consistent with blacks. Respondent characteristics for our sample are summarized in Table 2.

We do not want to overemphasize these differences in our sample. They

Table 2. Respondent Characteristics

	Number	Percentage
Sex		
Male	148	67.9
Female	63	28.9
No response	7	3.3
Total number of respondents	218	100.1
Race/ethnicity		
White/Anglo	162	74.3
Black	39	17.9
Hispanic	7	3.2
Other	1	.05
No response	9	4.1
Total number of respondents	218	99.6

exist but are not marked. Their existence confirms our claim that there are two stories, but given that the majority of our respondents are white and that we asked all respondents to speak for their corporations, we feel that we can treat these data, by and large, as a representation of the circumstances in corporate America.

As discussed in Chapter 1, we see the problems and issues associated with minority advancement in management careers in terms of three categories: problems having to do with the policies and practices of organizations; problems having to do with the relationship between minority managers and other people; and problems having to do with the preparation of minority managers for corporate careers. Following this assumption, our questionnaire identified problems within these three issue areas and asked respondents to indicate the extent to which the item was a problem in their company as a factor hindering minority success. For each item, there was a 7-point scale, ranging from "no problem at all" to "a very serious problem." A list of the questions is given in Table 3 and differences by race and sex in Table 4. As can be seen, the black respondents were more likely to think that organizational and relational items were problems and less likely to see individual items as problems than were white respondents. Other respondents were mixed in their responses. Female respondents tended to respond like black respondents, but the differences are not marked.

For many of the items, considerable judgment had to be made by the respondent to answer for the corporation. We, somewhat arbitrarily, divided the responses into "high," "medium," and "low." High was defined as a mean response on the item above 3.0 (on a scale of 1 to 7); medium as between 2.5 and 3.0; and low as below 2.5. Given a restricted range on most of the items and the general tendency of the respondents to present their companies in a favorable light, we felt this division was reasonable. More

Table 3. Questionnaire Items for Three Problem Areas:
Organizational, Relational, and Individual

Each question (scaled 1, no problem at all, to 7, a very serious problem) asked the following: For each of the following items, please indicate how much of a problem, if any, you think each has been as a factor which hinders the success of minorities in management positions. We are asking you to generalize about these issues, even though we know there is wide variation in your company's experience. There are no right or wrong answers, so please be frank.

Organizational issue

1. The recent economic conditions of the company
2. The lack of strong company commitment regarding minorities
3. Lack of planning for minority career development
4. Lack of sufficiently rapid promotion opportunities for everyone
5. Minority managers too often get assigned to jobs which deal mostly with minorities or minority issues
6. Minority managers too often get assigned to staff, rather than line positions
7. The ability of the company to provide necessary support to get the job done
8. The supervision received by minority managers
9. The training provided for minority managers
0. The pay for minority managers compared to what they expect
11. The quality of the work assignments available for new minority managers compared to what they expect

Issues having to do with relations with other people

12. Minority mangers' lack of social/business connections which help in business success
13. Minority mangers' lack of familiarity with company politics
14. The ability to "fit in" (i.e., whether others feel comfortable with minority managers)
15. The responses of peers
16. The responses of subordinates
17. The responses of managers to minority subordinates
18. The responses of customers or clients
19. The lack of appropriate role models for minority managers
20. The lack of appropriate mentors for minority managers
21. An insufficient number of other minority managers to provide support

Issues regarding the preparation of minority managers themselves

22. The educational preparation they have
23. Their technical competence
24. Their interpersonal skills
25. Their writing skills
26. Their oral communication skills
27. Their level of ambition to make it to the top
28. Their level of motivation to get the job done
29. Their concern about details
30. Their ability to plan
31. Their ability to follow through
32. Their ability to learn new assignments quickly
33. Their loyalty to the company
34. Their lack of self-confidence
35. Being too self-confident
36. Lack of clearly defined career goals
37. Insufficient number of qualified minority candidates in the fields in which your company most needs to hire

Table 4. Mean Responses of Questionnaire Items by Race/Ethnicity and Sex

Item	Total	Black	White	Other	Male	Female
	Item mean					

Item	Total	Black	White	Other	Male	Female
Organizational items						
Economic conditions	3.216	3.436	3.230	3.500	3.401	2.952
Lack of company commitment	2.963	3.846	2.863	1.875	2.946	3.222
Lack of company career planning	3.862	4.821	3.786	3.374	3.878	4.197
Lack of promotion opportunities	4.115	4.026	4.173	3.750	4.196	3.968
Assignment to jobs with minorities	2.206	3.184	1.975	3.125	2.211	2.387
Assignment to staff jobs	3.014	4.243	2.800	3.857	3.110	3.148
Ability for company to provide support	2.775	3.769	2.559	2.750	2.701	3.016
Supervision received	3.009	3.949	2.857	2.625	3.041	3.129
Training provided	2.734	3.590	2.586	2.500	2.797	2.730
Pay received	2.266	2.923	2.155	2.750	2.286	2.413
Work assignment	2.899	3.564	2.764	3.000	2.939	2.952
Relational issues						
Lack of connections	3.321	4.282	3.124	3.250	3.299	3.524
Not knowing politics	3.110	4.359	2.876	3.500	3.075	3.476
Ability to fit in	3.307	4.385	3.136	2.500	3.270	3.571
Response of peers	2.835	3.789	2.761	2.375	2.979	2.855
Response of subordinates	2.697	3.333	2.615	2.625	2.803	2.651
Response of managers	2.927	3.769	2.789	3.000	2.986	3.016
Response of clients	2.633	2.769	2.694	2.375	2.733	2.619
Lack of role models	4.225	4.718	4.179	4.125	4.264	4.349
Lack of mentors	3.927	4.897	3.923	3.250	3.979	4.387
Lack of other minorities to provide support	4.266	4.974	4.237	3.875	4.361	4.403
Individual items						
Educational preparation	3.463	3.189	3.711	2.625	3.722	3.194
Technical competence	3.261	3.027	3.541	2.500	3.483	3.213
Interpersonal skills	2.798	2.972	2.994	2.500	3.042	2.803
Writing skills	3.523	3.378	3.732	3.625	3.748	3.492
Oral communication skills	3.243	3.351	3.433	3.125	3.503	3.197
Ambition	2.312	2.378	2.458	2.500	2.475	2.393
Motivation	2.417	2.270	2.639	2.500	2.613	2.483
Concern with details	2.376	2.568	2.573	2.500	2.590	2.517
Ability to plan	2.367	2.622	2.570	2.500	2.590	2.526
Ability to follow through	2.326	2.514	2.541	2.625	2.504	2.621
Ability to learn new assignments	2.206	2.243	2.395	2.125	2.343	2.407
Loyalty	2.202	2.054	2.419	2.125	2.423	2.150
Lack of self-confidence	2.679	2.676	2.928	2.750	3.021	2.569
Too self-confident	2.183	2.378	2.349	2.500	2.291	2.483
Lack of career goals	2.982	3.541	3.045	3.750	3.171	3.148
Insufficient qualified candidates	5.050	4.444	5.538	4.500	5.385	5.082

important than the precise cutoff points for the items, however, is the ordering of the responses. We show the results in two ways: first, within each of the three issue areas and second, combining all of the items together.

I. RESULTS: THE CORPORATE PERSPECTIVE ON PROBLEMS HINDERING MINORITY SUCCESS

A. Organizational Policies and Practices

The first issue area, organizational factors, was included in the questionnaire both to balance the personal and interpersonal orientation that often predominates when the topic of minority success is discussed and to account for dramatic changes that are taking place in many companies across the country. Especially since the economic downturn of 1982, many large companies have been the target of mergers, acquisitions, or reorganizations. A primary effect of these changes has been to reduce the number of positions available in middle, if not upper, management in many companies. The results for organizational factors are given in Table 5.

As expected, high on the list of factors is the "lack of promotion opportunities" available in the company. This factor is considered even more important than "recent economic conditions," which we interpret to mean that even companies that are doing well may be reducing or leveling off the number of management positions. If this is so, then minority managers may be facing both increased competition and scarcer resources just as more of them are reaching the threshold of upper management. Also among the more important problems is the "lack of planning for minority career development," which may reflect two things. First, there is concern often expressed

Table 5. Corporate Perspectives on Organizational Factors That Hinder Minority Success

High	
4.115	Lack of promotion opportunities
3.862	Lack of planning for minority career development
3.216	Recent economic conditions
3.014	Minority managers assigned to staff jobs
3.009	Supervision received
Medium	
2.963	Lack of strong company commitment
2.899	Quality of the work assignments
2.775	Abiity of company to provide support
2.734	Training provided
Low	
2.266	Pay received
2.206	Assignment to jobs which deal with minorities

that minority advancement will not occur inadvertently, because reaching upper management has as much to do with connections and political skill as it does with job competence. For this reason, many have argued, as will be seen elsewhere in this volume, minority advancement must be incorporated into the business plans of companies so that upper level managers are accountable for seeing that barriers are removed within their own jurisdictions. Second, there is general agreement that many companies do not do a very good job with any of their employees in planning career development. If this is so, then minority managers may find it even more difficult to determine the best strategies for career success and may be even more likely to get lost in the shuffle.

Also high on the list of organizational factors (although not clearly differentiated from our "medium"-level items) is the tendency for minority managers to be "assigned to staff jobs" and the "supervision received" by minority managers. Staff assignments are widely recognized as less powerful positions in many companies in the sense that they have fewer ties to the top jobs (Kanter, 1977), in part because they are likely to involve the supervision or management of fewer people and lesser resources. If getting ahead means learning to manage well, then minority managers may be denied the opportunity to learn to manage people and resources by being concentrated into staff jobs. In addition to not learning necessary skills, people in staff jobs may also not have as much contact with powerful people, who can then help them or even mentor them in their career development. Although the fast-trackers in any corporation may spend some time in staff jobs (e.g., as assistants to powerful people), they more typically spend only part of their careers in staff jobs but circulate as well through key line positions. In contrast, many minority managers complain that they get pigeonholed and stuck in staff positions.

A related issue is the supervision that minority managers themselves receive. If minority managers are denied both the constructive criticism and the insider advice that comes with a good relationship with one's boss, they will be further hampered in their rise to the top. They may act under a mistaken impression that everything is fine because no one ever told them otherwise, whereas those around them wonder why they do not "straighten up." Or, minority managers who do not receive good feedback from their supervisors may expend more effort than is needed on things that do not matter in their companies, while neglecting the more important things. Finally, getting good supervision is an important means of learning how to do the job. Unlike production jobs where there may be a defined set of skills that one can learn and easily quantifiable output measures, management jobs tend to be more ambiguous in their content and less easy to evaluate in terms of output. Thus, it would be easy for someone who has been denied good feedback to do the job less well or with far more effort than would otherwise be needed.

Almost as important within the category of organizational factors are lack of strong company commitment, quality of the work assignment, ability of the company to provide support, and the training provided. Factors that are not considered problematic, however, are both pay and assignments to jobs that deal with minorities. Evidently, there is not much consciousness of overt discrimination of minority managers. Omission appears to be more important than commission within this category.

B. Relationships of Minority Managers with Others

The second issue area about which we asked respondents is the relationships of minority managers with other people. The results for relationship factors are given in Table 6. In the pre-civil rights era, one would expect that the primary problems facing minority managers would have been the overt discrimination of those around them. As noted before, there is an assumption currently that overt discrimination is no longer a problem, and this is evident in the findings on the relationship of minority managers with others. The responses of managers, peers, subordinates, and clients or customers fall at the bottom of the list; although based on our arbitrary division, they constitute "medium"-level problems.

Considered far more problematic for minority managers according to our corporate respondents is the "lack of other minority managers to provide support," the "lack of role models," and the "lack of mentors." That these items show up at the top of the list within this issue area undoubtedly reflects the commonly accepted wisdom these days that networks, role models, and mentors are necessary for success. But, whether it is common wisdom or not, an important assumption underlies the fact that these items appear at the top of the list. That is that minority managers will succeed if they are clued into the rules of the game. In other words, success for minority managers is seen as a function of specific knowledge of the business world that comes through

Table 6.   Corporate Perspectives on Factors Regarding the
Relationships with Other People That May Hinder the
Success of Minority Managers

High	
4.266	Lack of other minority managers to provide support
4.225	Lack of role models
3.927	Lack of mentors
3.321	Lack of social/business connections
3.307	Ability to "fit in"
3.110	Familiarity with company politics
Medium	
2.927	Responses of the managers of minorities
2.835	Responses of peers
2.697	Responses of subordinates
2.633	Responses of clients or customers
Low	
[None]	

contacts and experience. Given that the same aids are assumed to be necessary for any manager to make it in the corporate world, this appears to be a positive view of the capabilities and promise of minority managers in the pipeline.

However, other items ranked high on the list of relationship factors must temper the optimisim evident in the top items. Minority managers are also said to be hindered by "lack of social or business connections," the "ability to fit in," and "familiarity with company politics" (or lack thereof). These items are of a different nature than networks, role models, and mentors. They have less to do with understanding the business world and more to do with having contact and experience outside of it. Social connections are clearly related to family and friends, and business connections may be. Similarly, the ability to fit in presumably has to do with life-style and culture more than with training and qualifications. In both senses, minority managers may be placed at a disadvantage, which would be true even if they came from well-to-do but nonbusiness backgrounds. Thus, if connections rather than skill are the bases of rewards and upward mobility in corporations, then anyone without the requisite background will be hampered in making it in the corporate world.

Networks with other minority managers, role models, and mentors can help mitigate the lack of familiarity with the norms of the corporate world and can perhaps help provide the necessary social and business connections. But, apparently, the former is insufficient without the latter. It is not enough to learn normative behavior if one is not put in the right places, around the right people, and at the right times so the relevant similarities are evident and fruitful. If, as has been suggested (e.g., Kanter, 1977; Pfeffer and Salancik, 1977), trust that grows out of familiarity is increasingly important as one moves up the corporate ladder, then special attention must be given to the ways minority managers are incorporated into the group, which would be true for anyone marked for upward mobility.

C. Preparation of Minority Managers

The third issue area about which respondents were asked has to do with the preparation of minority managers themselves. Recognizing the controversial nature of such questions, we, nevertheless, have included these items because they come up in conversation, if not in published work on the topic of minority upward mobility. In addition, it is important to note that these questions are not about the inherent abilities or potential of minority managers, but about their current level of preparation in different areas assumed to be associated with getting ahead, which may reflect the quality of education and training available as much as anything else. Given that the quality of schools, along with job opportunities, has been of major concern to the minority community for years, it seems somewhat inconsistent to us to then argue that there are no possible differences in the educational preparation of some minority persons. It seems apparent, therefore, that there are other unspoken issues of concern about this topic, and it would be well to address them before we discuss the results of this part of our survey.

The instructions given to our respondents in the questionnaire noted that there may be wide variation among minority persons but that we were asking the respondents to generalize. We do not, therefore, assume that the responses are about all minority managers but about minority managers, on the average. If some, and presumably a substantial number, of minorities now in management careers attended schools that were largely segregated, in inner city or rural areas, and/or in poorer neighborhoods, then the chances are that they did not receive the same quality of education in the same proportion as white students now in management careers. Furthermore, as has been noted previously (e.g., Spilerman, Chapter 2), minority managers are likely to have majored disproportionately in nonbusiness and nontechnical areas. Both blacks and Hispanics are substantially underepresented in engineering, science, and business fields, whereas Asians are overrepresented in both engineering and science and holding their own in business (see also, Sowell, 1984; Williams, 1986). Both the quality of schools and the chosen field of study may contribute to less adequate preparation for minority managers.

Although hard work and extra effort may compensate for less adequate formal preparation, there still may be differences evident in day-to-day interaction. This is an issue on which there is some controversy, because, it has been argued by some (see, e.g., Davis and Watson, 1982, and Fernandez, 1975 and 1981) that (a) what is learned in school may not be relevant to job performance, especially at the upper management level and (b) that many whites are equally unprepared for the promotions they obtain. Let us look at each issue in turn.

Although it is commonly accepted that what one learns on the job may have only remote relation with what one learns in school, technical skills and general educational preparation are not superfluous to getting ahead in any career. Formal education clearly varies in content, but there are many jobs in management, especially at entry levels, which require specific technical skills that are learned in school. Doing well at this level is likely to be a prerequisite for moving up the corporate ladder. In addition, what formal education is supposed to do is to prepare one to recognize when certain skills or abilities are needed and when they are applicable, and one who does not possess a specific skill may not know that it was applicable to a given situation or circumstance. The same is true for general education, including the use of correct grammar, mathematical skills, general social knowledge, and so on. Although there may not be a direct relation between school knowledge and job knowledge, the former clearly contributes to learning and applying the latter.

That many whites are promoted who are unqualified for the jobs they receive may indeed be true, but it is not necessarily relevant to the situation for minority managers. As we have already discussed, politics and connections may have much to do with getting a job, especially as one moves up the corporate ladder. In addition, good timing and good luck often have as much to do with obtaining a job as do skills and qualifications. But, if minority managers are less attuned to politics and have fewer social and business connections, then they must "compensate" by presenting exceptional credentials. Even if we grant, as some have argued, that at the upper levels of management, everyone is qualified because of screening at lower levels, this does not negate the fact that choices are made among candidates and that judgments about who is "most" qualified are going to be made at all promotion levels. The quality and type of education is therefore relevant to upper-level positions, especially for minority managers, and any presumed deficiencies in preparation are going to be even more problematic when such decisions are made.

Another unspoken issue that may, in part, underlie the concern with raising questions about the preparation of minority managers is the implication for minority managers who are already on the job and finished with their formal training. If there is an assumption that minority managers are somehow less qualified, even "on the average," than their nonminority counterparts, then one might assume that the future career prospects for current minority managers will be restricted. This need not be true, even if it were true that minority managers had less adequate or less appropriate preparation for jobs in upper management, because education and training are lifelong processes and both self-improvement and additional formal education and training are available in most corporations. Whether it means taking classes, getting another degree, or participating in workshops or self-study, the option is always open to improve one's preparation. The difficulty may be not knowing what the problem areas are and how best to use limited time and resources efficiently.

Finally, there is clearly a concern that even discussing issues like preparation, whether in education, training, experience, or attitude, may lead to "statistical discrimination." That is, any open discussion of the preparation of minority managers, "on the average," will create difficulties for those minority managers who do have adequate or superior qualifications and relevant business background and experience because it will be assumed that because they are minorities, they too fit the "average." This may be, but we feel that it is more likely to exist if the issues are not addressed openly and the misconceptions, as well as perceptions, laid to rest. The same can be said about the claim that discrimination is operative against minority managers in the process of performance evaluations, where individual judgments may be affected by conscious or unconscious biases. Although this clearly is a problem in some companies and for some managers, it seems likely that it is even more likely to take place if the issue is never discussed and the facts separated from the fancy.

With this long preamble, we want to discuss the results from our survey regarding the preparation of minority managers. Table 7 shows the distribution of responses. Far and away the item considered most important from the view of corporate representatives is the "insufficient number of qualified candidates." We assume that this reflects all of the issues that we have already discussed: underpresentation of minorities in business, science, and engineering education, especially at the graduate level; the quality of education available for many minority students that undoubtedly has affected some

Table 7. Corporate Perspectives on Preparation of
Minorities Themselves That Hinder Their Success in
Business

High
5.050	Insufficient number of qualified candidates
3.523	Writing skills
3.463	Educational preparation
3.261	Technical competence
3.243	Oral communication skills

Medium
2.982	Lack of clearly defined career goals
2.798	Interpersonal skills
2.679	Lack of self-confidence

Low
2.417	Level of motivation
2.376	Concern with details
2.367	Ability to plan
2.326	Ability to follow through
2.312	Level of ambition
2.206	Ability to learn new assignments quickly
2.202	Loyalty to the company
2.183	Being too self-confident

now in management careers; and judgments that may or may not be accurate on the part of those making hiring decisions for corporations.

Also high on the list, although at a lower level of importance than the number of qualified candidates available, are "writing skills," "educational preparation," "technical competence," and "oral communication skills." We already discussed education and technical training, but we have not explicitly discussed the areas of written and oral communication.

Although communication skills are frequently associated with general educational preparation, they are of particular concern to minority groups, albeit for different reasons. Among Asians and Hispanics, the large number of immigrants within these subpopulations means that a substantial number of managers from these backgrounds either themselves speak English as a second language or their parents did in their homes when they were growing up. They may, therefore, speak with foreign accents, unknowingly use incorrect idiomatic English, and perhaps sprinkle their speech with phrases and words translated loosely from their first (or parents' first) language.

Blacks born in the United States are sensitive about the issue of communication skills because they associate it with assumptions about their inherent abilities. The issue gets raised, in part, because of the existence of what is called "black English" (see Stevens, 1985) or variations in dialect specific to some segments of the black community. Although many blacks speak what is called standard English, many others, as we discussed for Asians and Hispanics, learned speech patterns from home or family that is divergent in some respects from standard English. These blacks claim that black English is a legitimate dialect that should be accepted by white culture as readily as regional white dialects are and that black English is not incorrect English, just different. Whatever one thinks about this claim, a recent study suggests that due to the level of segregation in the United States, black English is becoming increasingly distinct from standard English, as is true for certain white dialects (Stevens, 1985). The characteristics of black English vernacular in some respects violate the rules of standard English, for example, dropping the "s" on singular verbs in sentences with singular subjects. Even those blacks who learned standard English in their own homes and in their education may inadvertently use some elements of black English in their speech and be unaware of the distinctions and the assumptions associated with them.

That written communication skills are higher on the list than oral communication skills may reflect the fact that errors in grammar or idiomatic variations from standard English may be less evident in spoken than in written speech. The generally poor preparation in the writing skills of many managers, including whites, may contribute to a presumption about minorities that is true instead for a whole generation.

Also considered of importance but falling into our "medium" category are the "lack of clearly defined career goals," "interpersonal skills," and "lack of self-confidence." Career goals are undoubtedly related to exposure to those who have achieved what one may want to emulate. It is difficult to aspire to something one does not know about or has only casual knowledge of. If minority managers are less likely than whites to have parents who pursued corporate careers—and we know this to be true or there would not be underrepresentation of minorities in upper management—then they may have less clear ideas about what options may be open to them. For the same reasons, they may have less clear knowledge about careers, in the sense of what jobs provide necessary training and experience for future jobs. And they may not have conceived of themselves as reaching top levels of management because they have not seen other minority persons doing so. Career goal planning is problematic in most corporations for most managers, and this is likely to be even more so for minority managers. This issue is discussed in more detail in Chapter 12.

Interpersonal skills may be related to communication skills, as well as to networks, role models, and mentors. There are at least two things usually associated with interpersonal skills that may be relevant to the advancement opportunities of minority managers. First is the similarity in culture and experience that translate into appropriate "cocktail" behavior. That is, the ability to make small talk, to respond appropriately in all those "formal informal" occasions around which business takes place, whether lunches, receptions, recreation, or around the water cooler. Because of widespread segregation in the country, a pattern of segregation often continues in the corporation, maybe especially at the level of management because of the fewer number of minorities in such positions. Both because of the need to network and to learn informal rules of behavior as well as because of overt exclusion from other groups, minority managers may be more prone to associate with other minorities and be less comfortable—or perceived to be—among whites in interpersonal interaction.

In addition to cultural differences, there may also be class differences in the background of many minority managers compared to the average nonminority manager. Many minority managers have been upwardly mobile in two senses, both in terms of intragenerational and intergenerational mobility. They have improved their occupational attainment over their own lifetimes, and they have attained a higher level of position than their parents had done. In either case, but especially in the latter, they may not have learned the cultural norms that go with upper-level positions. Although it may seem trivial, learning how to eat, to dress, what to read, and how to entertain oneself goes with having more status and higher salaries. Much of the corporate chitchat that surrounds decision making includes discussion of music, theater, art, travel, food, and so on, which may or may not be part of the experience and background of minority managers from middle-, working-, or lower-class backgrounds.

A second aspect of interpersonal skill may have to do with other kinds of assumptions made about interpersonal behavior. Cultures and subcultures differ in terms of things like how close one stands, how loud one speaks, whether eye contact is made or not, how direct one is, and so on. What nonminorities may interpret as lack of interpersonal skills may reflect differences in culture or subculture as much as true differences in skills. Black males, for example, are often interpreted by whites as being too aggressive, Hispanics as too familiar, and Asians as too mysterious. Although many stereotypes are founded more on perception than reality, often there are real behaviors that simply have different meanings for different groups. For example, within some segments of the Hispanic culture there are strong norms about the obligations to family and friends that may translate on the job to crossing an arbitrary line that whites feel is too familiar. Whites, in turn, may be perceived by Hispanics as being too cold and distant. The point is that such differences in culture and subculture, when they exist, are often unconsciously evaluated in terms of one's own culture and then translated into an evaluation of the other person's interpersonal skills.

Another area of concern is the "lack of self-confidence" of minority managers. Confidence may have to do with a sense of security about one's abilities, which may or may not be a problem for minority managers. But, lack of confidence is also sometimes a temporary response to an unfamiliar situation. To the extent that many minority managers are new to the business environment and may not know the rules of the game and the limits of internal politics, they are likely to be cautious in their interaction with others, and this may be interpreted as lack of confidence in themselves. At any rate, confidence in oneself is easily gained by success and therefore is not likely to be a major barrier to job performance for minority managers in most cases. Where the job requires risk taking, however, lack of confidence may be a serious liability that will need work if the minority manager is to succeed.

Finally, there are a number of items regarding the preparation of minority managers that were not considered major problem areas for minority managers. These include "lack of motivation," "concern with details," "ability to plan," "ability to follow through," "level of ambition," "ability to learn new assignments quickly," "loyalty to the company," and "being too self-confident." These items have to do with doing the job and wanting to do it, and evidently neither is considered a major problem for minority managers from the corporate perspective.

Table 8 shows the combined ranking of the items from each of the three problem areas in terms of those considered high, medium, and low as we have defined them. The purpose of combining the lists is to provide a sense of the relative importance of the items. An insufficient number of qualified candidates is considered the major problem across all three issue areas, and concern for this item stands apart from all the others in magnitude. Also at the top of the list are networks (other minority managers to provide support), role models, and mentors and the need for companies to plan minority career development and to provide greater promotion opportunities.

II. CONCLUSION

If we assume that the identification of problems reflects the need for solutions, then a number of things may be suggested at this stage. It follows that if there are not enough qualified candidates, then there are also likely to be an insufficient number of role models, mentors, and people to provide support in networks. It would, therefore, be even more important than otherwise for organizations to foster the minority candidates that they have through better career planning and development support. Doing so, however, may be increasingly difficult if organizations are themselves trimming staff and reorganizing through mergers and acquisitions, as has been occurring in the last several years.

Given the situation, it appears that an added responsibility is placed on both the minority managers who want to get ahead and on the organizational hierarchies that would like to see them do so. Minority managers need, now more than ever, to take responsibility for their own career development, which means both to set specific goals and find out what they need to do to achieve them. And they need to be more directive in their relations with their employers about the experience they want to gain and for what purposes. Where there are roadblocks, they need to hurdle them if they expect to attain their goals. For organizations, they need to be more attuned to the wise use of human resources, which includes providing opportunity for development and assistance for goal setting. What employers are doing is explored further in Chapters 11 and 12, and what minority managers themselves have done to enhance their chances for success is discussed in Chapter 10. Suffice it to say that solutions do not always match the definitions of the problems and must be examined in the broader context of human resource management.

The purpose of this chapter has been to provide information on the

Table 8. Corporate Perspectives on All Factors That May
Hinder the Success of Minorities

High
5.050	Insufficient number of qualified candidates
4.266	Lack of other minority managers to provide support
4.225	Lack of role models
4.115	Lack of promotion opportunities
3.927	Lack of mentors
3.862	Lack of planning for minority career development
3.523	Writing skills
3.463	Educational preparation
3.321	Lack of social/business connections
3.307	Ability to "fit in"
3.261	Technical competence
3.243	Oral communication skills
3.216	Recent economic conditions
3.110	Familiarity with company politics
3.014	Minority managers assigned to staff jobs
3.009	Supervision received

Medium
2.982	Lack of clearly defined career goals
2.963	Lack of strong company commitment
2.927	Responses of the managers of minorities
2.899	Quality of the work assignments
2.835	Responses of peers
2.798	Interpersonal skills
2.775	Ability of the company to provide support
2.734	Training provided
2.697	Responses of subordinates
2.679	Lack of self-confidence
2.633	Responses of clients or customers

Low
2.417	Level of motivation
2.376	Concern with details
2.367	Ability to plan
2.326	Ability to follow through
2.312	Level of ambition
2.266	Pay received
2.206	Ability to learn new assignments quickly
2.206	Assignment to jobs which deal with minorities
2.202	Loyalty to the company
2.183	Being too self-confident

corporate perspective of minority advancement in management careers. Although a single survey is necessarily limited, we feel that two general conclusions can be drawn. First, to the extent that the corporate perspective as discussed here represents the white or Anglo view of the problems facing minority managers, there is clearly divergence between the view of minority managers and their employers on issues regarding qualifications, educational and technical preparation, communication skills, and the circumstances of "fitting in." But, second, it appears that the perspective of minority managers and their employers may not be so divergent on other issues. There are many items about which minority managers and their employers agree are critical to the success of minorities in management careers: networks, role models, mentors, increased promotion opportunities, career planning, connections, culture, and politics. Whether one sees these findings as encouraging or discouraging depends on whether it is possible to reconcile the differences of perspective in specific solutions that are both feasible and operative.

III. REFERENCES

Brown, H. A., and David L. Ford, Jr. 1977. An exploratory analysis of discrimination in the employment of black MBA graduates. *Journal of Applied Psychology* 62(1):50–56.

Crotty, P. T., and J. A. Timmons. 1974. "Older minorities—'roadblocked' in the organization." *Business Horizons* 17(June):27–34.

Davis, George, and Glegg Watson. 1982. *Black life in corporate America: Swimming in the mainstream.* New York: Doubleday.

Fernandez, John P. 1975. *Black managers in white corporations.* New York: Wiley.

Fernandez, John P. 1981. *Racism and sexism in corporate life: Changing values in American business.* Lexington, MA: Lexington.

Hicks, J. P. 1985. Black professionals refashion their careers. *New York Times,* November 29, pp. A1, D2.

Hymowitz, C. 1984. Many blacks jump off the corporate ladder to be entrepreneurs. *Wall Street Journal,* August 2, pp. 1, 16.

Kanter, Rosabeth Moss. 1977. *Men and women of the corporation.* New York: Basic.

Morgan, J. S., and R. L. Van Dyke. 1970. *White-collar blacks: A breakthrough?* New York: American Management Association, Inc.

Pfeffer, Jeffrey, and Gerald Salancik. 1977. Toward an examination of stratification in organizations. *Administrative Science Quarterly* 22:553–567.

Sowell, Thomas. 1984. Math dropouts aren't going to integrate science. *Wall Street Journal,* February 8, p. 32.

Stevens, William K. 1985. Study finds blacks' English increasingly different. *New York Times,* March 15, p. A14.

Williams, Lena. 1986. Trend studied as fewer blacks choose science. *New York Times,* September 23, p. C10.

8

A Summary of Small-Group Discussions on the Advancement of Minority Managers
Perspectives of Academics and Experienced Managers

Nancy DiTomaso and Donna E. Thompson

As part of the conference sponsored by Rutgers Graduate School of Management on Ensuring Minority Success in Business, held September 24–25, 1984, 10 small discussion groups met to assimilate the presentations and provide a forum for defining critical issues regarding minority advancement in management careers (See preface for further description of the conference). The composition of each group included representation of academics and experienced managers, both minority and nonminority and male and female. Most of the minority participants in both the conference and the small-group discussions were black, with only limited participation by Hispanics and Asians. The representation partly reflects the specific networks that developed as the conference was being planned and partly the current distribution of minority managers, especially in the affirmative action and equal employment opportunity positions from which many of the conference participants were drawn. There was an attempt to balance the discussion groups in terms of type of industry represented. Each group had two cofacilitators, one a manager and one an academic.

Each group met twice during the conference, and accordingly, the charge to each discussion group was twofold. On the first meeting, following initial conference presentations on the current state of affairs for minority managers,

Nancy DiTomaso and Donna E. Thompson • Rutgers Graduate School of Management, Newark, New Jersey 07102.

each discussion group was asked to generate a list of critical issues that affect the advancement of minority managers in large corporations through a process of brainstorming and then from that list select three as the most important issues. To further facilitate thinking about the issues in the first meeting, each group was asked to consider the expectations for minority managers, concerns about ensuring the success of minority managers, and resources needed and available in their organizations. The presentations that preceded the first small-group discussions included the chapters in this book by Spilerman (Chapter 2), Ford (Chapter 4), Davis (Chapter 6), and DiTomaso, Thompson, and Blake (Chapter 7). Otherwise, the participants were not prompted with a prepared list of issues.

The second meeting followed presentations on specific programs and policies at major corporations. The groups were then asked to take the issues that they had identified earlier and to turn them into goal statements and discuss the factors that are likely to help the attainment of the goals as well as the factors that are likely to hinder their attainment. This chapter reports the results of the first meeting that defined issues and problems and the subsequent discussion regarding factors that help or hinder. The suggested action is discussed in Chapter 15, which also follows discussion in this book of specific policies and practices by major corporations (Chapter 12).

I. PROBLEMS AND ISSUES AS DEFINED BY SMALL GROUPS

The 10 discussion groups came up with a diverse list of potential problems or issues affecting the advancement of minorities in management careers. Table 1 provides a list of the issues, both in terms of being "most important" and in terms of how many groups discussed them in the process of identifying the three most important.

We had expected that there would be a fairly clear concensus across groups on what the most important issues were, but only three issues identified as most important were selected by three or more groups: top management commitment (noted by five groups), need for accountability or rewards to those meeting affirmative action goals and developing minority subordinates (noted by six groups), and the important role of mentors, sponsors, coaches, and role models for minority managers (noted by three groups). All three issues were also discussed by half or more of all the groups, even if not selected as most important. These three issues can be thought of as a prescription for how to ensure minority success in management careers, given the diverse backgrounds and experiences of the conference participants who collectively identified these as most important. The three are also seen as interrelated.

Accountability is not possible without top management commitment to the goal of increasing the number of minority managers in upper-level positions. And, commitment is not sufficient if it is only spoken but not acted upon. The discussion groups concentrated on the relationship between top

Table 1. Problems and Issues Identified in 10 Small-Group Discussions

Issue	Number of groups ranking issue as most important	Number of groups discussing issue
Top management commitment	5	7
Accountability/rewards for meeting affirmative action goals and developing subordinates	6	6
Job assignment in first jobs/assignment to staff jobs	1	6
Mentors, coaches, role models, sponsors	3	5
Career planning (by individuals and corporations)	2	5
Political, social, and economic conditions (including law enforcement)	1	5
Criteria used for success/evaluation (including existence of double standard)	2	5
Discrimination/stereotypes	2	4
Corporate/university exchanges (especially whether schools teach what it takes to get ahead in corporations)	2	4
Political, social skill development (including corporate culture)	1	4
Middle management resistance (including decentralized structure of corporations that leaves decision-making in hands of middle management)	2	4
Technical/educational skill development	2	3
Reverse discrimination/backlash as problem	1	3
Networks/help from peers	0	3
Lack of candidates (as excuse or fiction)	2	2
Visibility (lack of and need for)	0	2
Need to identify high potential candidates	0	2
Need for human resource training for everyone	1	1
Need to treat minority managers as individuals	0	1
Verbal fatigue about issue in organizations	0	1
Isolation of minorities in a majority world	0	1

managers and their middle management subordinates and agreed that middle managers, who are the ones making most of the decisions about promotion, job assignments, and atmosphere on the job in most corporations, will attend themselves to the things that bring themselves the most rewards. If they are rewarded only for the numbers on the bottom line in the short term, they will act in such a way to maximize those numbers. But, if people skills and the development of their subordinates partly determine their reward package, they will be more cognizant of their people skills and find creative ways to make sure that their subordinates get the training and development necessary to succeed. Accountability for affirmative action goals will create strong incentives for middle managers to attend to the career progress and training needs of their minority subordinates.

Furthermore, the general agreement that there is a need for more mentoring, coaching, and sponsorship for minority managers recognizes the widely held assumption that as one moves up the corporate ladder, who you know and who knows you are as important as what you know. This, too, is linked to the desire to have affirmative action goals a top priority for upper-level management and part of the reward structure. People help others in corporations, not primarily because of altruism, but because they see the other people as like themselves and identify with them or because they see them as helping them get their own jobs done. If minority managers are identified as different in style or culture from the white male managers in top positions in most corporations, then, in order for minority managers to gain the assistance and support of top managers, it is necessary for them to see minority managers as an asset to their own career success. Being rewarded for meeting affirmative action goals will, at minimum, call the attention of other managers to their minority subordinates and provide incentives to provide coaching and mentoring. One of the primary effects of top management commitment, making managers accountable for affirmative action goals and providing incentives for coaching and mentoring of minority managers, is that there will be more minority managers, undoubtedly, who make it to the top and, in their own success, become role models for other minority managers.

Beyond these three issues, there was a wide disparity in the issues identified as most important by the discussion groups, although many of the groups talked about the same issues. Four issues were discussed by at least half of the groups but were not selected as most important by more than one or two. These include the nature of job assignments given to minority managers; the need for both individual and corporate career planning; the current state of political, economic, and social conditions surrounding corporations, including a perceived lack of enforcement of affirmative action laws; and issues regarding the criteria for success, including the need for a clearer understanding by minority managers of what it takes to get ahead and a claim that there is a double standard by which minority and nonminority managers are evaluated in their performance, with the assumption that minority managers are evaluated unfairly.

Only one group identified job assignments as one of the most important problems, although six groups discussed it. Two kinds of issues were of concern: the career paths to which minority managers are directed because of their first or early job assignments and the prevalence for isolating minority managers in staff jobs that are unlikely to lead to top management positions. The discussion groups acknowledged that part of the problem in the the early job experience of minority managers is their own lack of knowledge of what kinds of training they need to make it to the top and their reluctance to take certain kinds of assignments. But most of the small-group participants assumed that nonminority managers in corporations are primarily responsible for the job assignments given to minority managers. The participants felt strongly that nonminority managers held stereotypes about what minority managers should be doing and even felt that nonminority managers seem to think that minority managers should be grateful for the chance to enter corporate careers and thus be content with "their place." Although these may be unconscious motivations of nonminority managers who make decisions about placement, in one sense it is a problem easily dealt with as more minority managers seek out line positions and the stereotypes are overcome by education and experience.

More difficult to address is another reason for the isolation of minority managers in less powerful and less visible job assignments, and that is the unwillingness of nonminority managers to take a chance with minority managers. The conference participants felt that minority managers are not allowed to fail, and thus not allowed to learn, in the same way as is true for nonminority managers. Two reasons may be likely. On the one hand, nonminority managers may think that they are doing a favor for minority managers who are given assignments in which they can clearly perform well. But at the same time, the assignments are such that they are unable to show what they can do. They are unable to shine, as it were, and also unable to learn the full range of skills and abilities that would help them go further in the corporation. Such "assistance" from nonminority managers may be motivated by good intentions, but it masks underlying stereotypes and therefore discrimination against minority manageers. On the other hand, nonminority managers may be unwilling to place minority manager subordinates in "risky" assignments because the nonminority supervisor sees his or her own job as being affected. That is, presumably all managers in corporations want to do their jobs well and be recognized for their successful performance. To get many jobs done depends on the ability to motivate and manage subordinates to do their part, to not drop the ball, and not to embarass or allow one's supervisor to be caught off guard. Some nonminority managers may feel, unconsciously or otherwise, that they cannot trust minority managers in risky assignments to follow through successfully. Whether due to unconscious prejudice or even to an understanding of the extra pressures placed on minority managers, the effects for the career development of minority managers are adverse.

Given the problems that minority managers have in getting good assignments that will serve them well for advancing to higher positions in corporations, the conference participants also saw career planning as a special need for minority managers. Minority managers themselves must take responsibility for their own career development and not be passive about the kind of assignments or the training that they receive. Otherwise, they are likely to end up in less desirable positions from which they cannot easily move. To do so requires good information about what it takes to get ahead in a chosen field or specific corporation, and that is likely to be obtained only through networks and social contacts, if not mentors or coaches. Many, if not most, corporations do not have clearly defined job ladders for managerial positions, and so knowledge of likely promotion steps must come from informal grapevines.

For the same reasons that minority managers must be cognizant of how their own careers are developing, the conference participants also felt that corporations should identify and monitor the careers of high-potential minority managers in their hire. This was seen as a primary means to protect minority managers from the biases of middle management decisions, whether intended for good or ill, as well as a means to make minority managers less dependent on informal networks to which they may not be privy.

Half of the 10 discussion groups also noted the importance of the current political, social, and economic environments that are shaping the career prospects for all managers. Of particular concern to the conference participants have been the actions of the Reagan administration to change the direction of affirmative action guidelines, and even more so, the perceived lack of enforcement of existing affirmative action regulations. Many thought that their own, as well as other corporations, would not continue being concerned about the advancement of minority managers without such external pressure, and they felt concerned that discrimination would again become more accepted in informal decision making, if not in formal policies. Aside from the legal environment in which corporations operate, there was also recognition that the social environment may have shifted toward a more conservative direction, with a consequent impatience regarding issues of equal opportunity and affirmative action (see, for example, Fernandez, Chapter 5).

In addition to changes in the political and social environments, the conference participants also recognized that changing economic conditions have changed the rules of the game in many corporations. The size of middle management has been reduced in many companies, both as a result of and a response to the increased numbers of mergers and acquisitions across the country. In addition, many companies have been facing competition from Japan and elsewhere that has forced them into cost cutting and understaffing. All managers are facing an increased risk of displacement and perhaps unemployment, minority managers included. As one person commented, minority managers may be "getting to the station just as the gravy train is pulling out."

Concern about the criteria used for success is related to two other issues that were discussed by 4 of the 10 groups and identified as most important by 2 of them: the continued existence of discrimination and stereotypes and the need for more corporate and university interchanges. Because there was some feeling among participants that it is not clear what it takes to get ahead in different occupations and industries, some argued that corporations should make performance criteria more explicit. It was felt that discrimination would be less possible if performance criteria were, as much as possible, based on objective behaviors rather than subjective evaluations—a lament frequently heard by organizational specialists about problems in performance appraisal. Universities, it was said, could help by better research on career paths in different industries and on the criteria actually used in evaluating candidates for promotion in different kinds of jobs.

Of particular concern in this regard is that there is a double standard operating for minority and nonminority managers, which, whether conscious or unconscious, is nevertheless a critical factor hindering minority advancement. Such a double standard works in two ways. First, the same behavior is evaluated positively when exhibited by a nonminority manager and negatively when exhibited by a minority manager. For example, self-directed behavior may be interpreted as high motivation and ambition in a nonminority manager but as unacceptable aggression in a minority manager. Second, participants felt that minority managers are often evaluated as less competent regardless of their performance due to prejudice about minorities in general. In both cases, it was felt by participants that the fate of minority managers could not simply be left to the chance workings of organizations without special attention from outside enforcement of the law and top management. Continued awareness training, backed up by bottomline accountability, was seen as needed to overcome these largely unconscious or unadmitted prejudices.

Four groups also discussed the need for more understanding by minority managers of the politics and corporate culture in their organizations and the need for more attention to the actions of middle managers in perpetuating the status quo in corporations. The conference participants felt that management schools should take more responsibility to teach their graduates about the "soft" side of the corporation. At the same time, on the assumption that politics and social skills are not easily taught out of context, the need to learn about the underbelly of corporate life, where careers may be made or unmade, was seen as another reason that mentors, sponsors, coaches, and networks are so important for minority managers, as for all managers.

That middle managers play a key role in what happens in corporations was acknowledged. Even if top management is committed to increasing the numbers of minority managers in top positions, they may not be aware of potentially qualified candidates if they are not given the opportunity to be seen and to show what they can do. As important, high potential may never become known if minority managers are not provided with the kinds of training and experience that would teach them the necessary skills to move ahead. If crossing the line from middle management to top management requires broader knowledge about the corporation and refined social skills, as many have claimed, then the kinds of assignments, exposure, and support given to minority managers, as is true for all managers on their way up, are critical. The conference participants saw nonminority, middle managers as important gatekeepers of these processes that required more attention and monitoring from the top. The general assumption of conference participants was that there was still much resistance, if not outright discrimination, to minority managers from many nonminority managers in the middle, many of whom are presumably competing for the same top spots and who see minority managers as being both unqualified and yet favored over them.

There were other issues, as noted on Table 1, which were discussed by only a few of the small groups but were then judged by them to be among the most important. For example, the technical and educational qualifications of minority managers on the average were said to need improving, concern was expressed that nonminority managers used the lack of qualified candidates as an excuse or a ruse, and the problems posed by a backlash regarding reverse discrimination were mentioned. In addition, at least one group felt that all managers need better people skills and that providing them would in itself enhance the career prospects for minority managers by improving communication and understanding of diversity among people.

Interestingly, one of the issues not often discussed in these groups, despite the prior presentations by both Ford and Davis (see Chapters 4 and 6 in this volume), are the psychological costs felt to be incurred by minority managers because of the experience of discrimination and being a minority in a majority world. As these issues are discussed elsewhere in this volume, they will not be further raised here.

On the whole, it is clear that the participants in this conference felt that much of the responsibility for minority success in management careers rests with corporations and their top managements, on the assumption that minority managers had themselves already done what they could to prepare themselves and perform on the job. As might be expected in this context, aside from the issues of the quality of education available to minority people in the country, none of the participants claimed that minority managers have been given their due. Unlike the corporate respondents in the survey discussed in Chapter 7, many of whom argued in open-ended questions that minority advancement is a matter of time, the conference participants whose perspectives are discussed in this chapter saw improvements in the career prospects for minority managers as matters of policy changes and commitment.

II. FACTORS THAT HINDER THE SUCCESS OF MINORITY MANAGERS

As noted, in the second meeting of the small groups, the participants were asked to turn the problems that they had identified as most important into goal statements and then to discuss what factors in their organizations were most likely to help or hinder the accomplishment of these goals. The intention of this assignment was to force participants to think about why the programs and policies that they saw as solutions were perhaps slow in the making in many corporations and schools of management. A further purpose was so that the groups would focus on the real levers of change, rather than simply to develop wish lists. As in the earlier discussion, there was a broad range of factors that the groups identified, but they can be summarized in terms of several general sets of issues.

The group assignment was to consider both corporations and schools of management and to identify factors specific to one or the other. Most of the factors discussed for corporations can be related to either the need for commitment to affirmative action goals or for tying managerial rewards to them. The participants identified reasons why commitment may be lacking and why it may be difficult to generate, as well as why accountability is so problematic.

Many participants felt that both the time and money required to be more thorough in affirmative action added an administrative burden that many corporations are not willing to bear, especially in the midst of increased foreign competition and retrenchment. Along these lines, participants felt that companies were more fearful of their competition and thus were cutting back on all costs. Affirmative action and equal opportunity programs, according to some participants, are not seen as critical to the business and thus not likely to be expanded. Furthermore, many felt that affirmative action and EEO had negative images in many corporations, both because people do not really understand what the purposes are and because there is continued discrimination and prejudice. Some even expressed a sense of hopelessness because they felt that without active external pressure, their organizations were not likely to maintain their commitments to affirmative action and EEO.

For all these reasons, participants were uncertain about the chances for greater top management commitment to the goal of minority success in management. But they also recognized that even if top management were committed, there are still obstacles to success for minority managers. Top management is often isolated from what takes place throughout their corporations, especially at the level of middle management. Due to the decentralization of many companies and to the complexity of organizational structure, it is not possible for top management to closely monitor what goes on in all parts of the organization without much difficulty. This is a general problem, no matter what the outcome goals, but for affirmative action, it may be even more difficult. Because many managers throughout corporations do not understand what affirmative action is all about, are frequently intolerant of its purpose, and otherwise have underdeveloped people skills, they may work at odds with formal company policies. And, even if one could assume that middle managers were committed to affirmative action goals—which is highly unlikely in many corporations—the widespread lack of leadership skills necessary to be coaches or mentors creates another obstacle to successful corporate policy.

Organizational complexity adds another dimension to developing a successful corporate policy for insuring minority manager success. For many jobs at many levels in corporations, responsibility for performance is not truly individual but dependent on the contributions of a team of interdependent managers. This is true of people goals, as well as production goals. Furthermore, it may be more difficult for some areas of the corporation to improve their contribution to affirmative action and equal opportunity than for others, depending on the pool of candidates from which they have to draw and the difficulties of the training that they need to provide to make successful managers.

Again, even if we assumed good will, there are obstacles to ensuring equal opportunity. Performance appraisal systems that are objective and eliminate biases are notoriously difficult to develop. In addition, there are, according to some participants, unwritten rules in most corporations about time in grade, which make it difficult to be flexible about how much training may be necessary before a promotion is warranted. Minority managers, for very good reasons, may need either more or less time and not be given the benefit of the doubt. Thus, even if corporations have systems to identify "high-potential" minority candidates, they may face obstacles in moving them successfully through the range of jobs needed to prepare them for top management. And, this assumes that one knows what such a range of jobs would or should be, but as we have already noted, there is very imperfect knowledge about the nature of career paths and the most likely links to the top.

Because there are no foolproof evaluation systems, most corporations still maintain pockets of favoritism, and some more than others. Political and social skills, as we noted, may be just as important in one's evaluation as technical skills, and there are no easy ways to guard against this. In some cases, one may not even want to do so. Some small-group participants talked about how difficult it is to learn corporate culture if one begins as an outsider. There are unspoken, taken-for-granted values that may have to do with family background or school affiliation, and top managers may feel more comfortable with people they think of as like themselves. Favoritism and politics are the other side of discrimination, which can manifest itself in many subtle ways in decisions made about peformance and promotion.

The obstacles in schools of management are related to some of the same issues. Most schools do not provide enough assistance to any of their students, including minority students, on job-hunting skills, career planning, and life management. In addition, the curricula of many schools favor the "hard" skills but not the "soft" side of the corporation that many participants felt make the critical difference in getting ahead. That is, schools do not teach students about the politics and culture of corporate life and are weak in their training of people skills in general, including coaching, leadership, and how to influence peers, subordinates, and superiors. Yet, according to some participants, many business students do seem to learn along with their hard skills an inflated view of the contributions they are likely to make in the corporate world, and accordingly, they develop inflated expectations about how far they can go how quickly. Schools could do much better, according to the participants, in teaching students realistic expectations about their likely career paths and could make their paths smoother by also teaching the students about how to receive criticism.

In addition to teaching what we already know but underemphasize, the participants also felt that schools of management had a large role to play in furthering research on selection, performance appraisal, careers, and cross-cultural and multicultural management. As new knowledge is generated, the participants also felt that schools should make an active effort to disseminate it by sponsoring conferences and workshops (such as the one discussed here) and otherwise providing managers and prospective managers with the benefits of their learning.

Finally, some participants felt that schools of management were too far removed from the everyday activities of corporate life and that they consequently did not teach their students what it really takes to get ahead. They recommended more hands-on experience in management training, including internships for both students and faculty. Closer contact of this sort, according to the participants, would help keep students and faculty honest in their expectations by maintaining a greater sense of realism about corporate life. It would also make students more aware of what are the most relevant skills they can acquire on their way to corporate success.

The participants in the small groups were hopeful that increased success for minority managers was possible and likely, given sufficient attention and commitment on the part of corporations and schools of management, but they were also sober about the hurdles. In this chapter, we have primarily discussed the problems that they identified, Other parts of the book focus on solutions.

9

Perspectives of Current and Recent Minority MBA Students on Advancement in Management Careers

Nancy DiTomaso and Donna E. Thompson

The record clearly shows that prior to the civil rights movement, there were few minorities in top management positions in major corporations (see, for example, Davis's article in this volume for documentation of this claim). And, even today, as discussed in Chapters 1 and 2, minorities are overrepresented in humanities and social science fields and in the public sector, whereas they are underrepresented in business, science, and engineering. Given the history of minority concentration in nonbusiness fields, it is also clear that those minorities who entered management jobs during and just after the civil rights movement often came from nonbusiness backgrounds. Many, therefore, entered jobs within corporations, namely personnel, public relations, and other related staff jobs, which were closest to the fields of training that they had outside corporations. Thus, some have argued that the ceiling on minority advancement is partly a reflection of the composition of the group of minority managers who entered corporate careers long enough ago to now be in middle management and therefore part of the pool of potential candidates for top management positions. This group, by and large, does not have the training or experience to make them likely choices for further advancement. (Of course, this is not the whole story, as there are minorities who have pursued

Nancy DiTomaso and Donna E. Thompson • Rutgers Graduate School of Management, Newark, New Jersey 07102.

business and technical education who have also found it difficult to get beyond middle management, but that issue is dealt with in other parts of this book.)

A critical part of defining the issues on minority advancement in management careers, then, are the perspectives of current MBA students and recent minority MBA graduates, who clearly do not fit the old models of being trained in the "wrong" disciplines or having started careers in the "wrong" sorts of jobs. This chapter provides some insight into the current pool of talent for future minority advancement in management. Thirteen minority MBA students or recent graduates of Rutgers Graduate School of Management were interviewed about their backgrounds, their career aspirations, and their expectations for the future. As for the successful minority managers discussed in Chapter 10, these current minority students were asked what they think might help them the most in attaining their career goals, what they think may hinder them the most, and what they would most like to have available to assist them in their career development, if it were possible. In addition, they were asked about their sense of their minority status and their view of the civil rights movement. Some of their answers may surprise readers.

The 13 MBA students and recent graduates were diverse in their background and ethnicity. Included are 7 blacks (4 female and 3 male), 4 Hispanics (3 female and 1 male), and 2 Asians (both female). As is evident from this list, it was easier to find female rather than male students, which parallels the impressions of experienced managers that there are fewer problems finding qualified minority women than minority men. Although we were primarily interested in U.S.-born minorities and Puerto Ricans (who are U.S. citizens whether born on the island or in the States), our list includes 4 non-Puerto Rican immigrants (1 black, 1 Hispanic, and both Asians). We did not, however, include any recent immigrants, and all of our interviewees are planning to make their careers in the United States. The Hispanic participants included in the list are either Mexican-American, Puerto Rican, or Central American. None is Cuban in ethnicity, although one lived in a predominantly Cuban neighborhood.

The interviews were unstructured, although each participant was asked a set of general questions as noted before. Although no claim is made that this group is representative of the current entering cohort of minority managers, we did make an effort to include a diversity of types of minority students. Their responses do provide insight into the definition of the problems and issues as seen by new minority job entrants. Because we did not interview a comparable group of white students to contrast to these minority students, we must be tentative in some of our conclusions. We purposely chose open-ended interviews for this part of the book because such data are most conducive to understanding problems that are not already well defined. Also, other parts of this manuscript provide hard numbers about the current status and future prospects for minority managers.

I. FAMILY BACKGROUND

Family relationships take on even more importance for upwardly mobile minority persons than for nonminority persons who might find extrafamilial support groups more readily available. In addition, poor neighborhoods often are characterized by the kind of added pressure that truly makes family a haven in a heartless world for those lucky enough to have good family relations. The closeness these minority managers have to their families is marked and most likely a major factor for most of them in their ability to achieve.

Some of these new and prospective minority managers faced a great deal of hardship growing up and had to overcome the odds to make it to their current levels of achievement. But, only a few come from the most disadvantaged backgrounds, and even these are more accurately characterized as the working poor. At the same time, most do not come from advantaged backgrounds either. Of the 13, only 4 or 5 have parents (i.e., either a father or a mother) who are professionals, and *none have parents who are themselves managers*. Complete information is not available in all cases, but only 4 had fathers and 5 had mothers with more than a high-school education (not all of these are college graduates). Only 3 or 4 had parents with less than a high-school education (most of these are Hispanic). Two of the respondents were orphans (one lived with relatives and the other with foster and then adoptive parents). Only 3 of the respondents were from broken homes (1 black and 2 Hispanic), and of these, 2 were at various times, while growing up, on public assistance. In each of these cases, the mothers with whom the respondents lived undertook to finish their educations or strongly encouraged the respondents to do so. Also, in most of the families, both parents worked outside the home; only 2 or 3 had mothers who were housewives. On the other side of the scale, the professional occupations of either the fathers or mothers were in most cases in social service, education, and in one case, nursing. Only 1 respondent (an Asian) had parents in the better paid professions, and in this case both parents fell into this category (one a medical doctor and the other a dentist).

One would most likely conclude, therefore, that these new minority managers are from the middle strata of minority families. This is even more evident if we consider their siblings. In most cases, these respondents come from small families. Ten of the 13 had 2 or fewer siblings, 2 had 3 siblings, and only 1 had more than 3. And, 12 of the 13 (information was missing in the case of 1 of the orphans) had at least one sibling who graduated from college (or was about to), and most of these were in professional occupations. So, in addition to their parents, who often provided the strongest influence for their own educational attainment and occupational aspirations, these respondents in many cases also had brothers and sisters who had done reasonably well.

For most of these prospective minority managers, there was family encouragement, even if not much financial support, for educational attainment. In only one or two cases was this not mentioned, and in one of these, there was apparently active resistance to the career goals of the respondent. But even with a close family life, the picture is not all rosy for these respondents. Many lived in poor neighborhoods and most lived in segregated neighborhoods. In a few cases, where the respondent's family moved, for example, from predominantly black to predominantly white neighborhoods, the new neighborhoods changed within only a few years back to the black majority. Most of these respondents lived in inner-city neighborhoods, where as one said, "the incentives were there to be a bum." But, most also thought of themselves as different and capable of achieving more than their circumstances might warrant.

For most of these prospective managers, there is a very strong sense of obligation to do well for the family. This is especially evident for the Hispanic and Asian respondents but also true for some of the black respondents. In all but one case, the respondents from the poorest backgrounds mentioned the strong influence that their mothers had on their own aspirations, sense of worth, and desire to pursue their education. One respondent told of how her mother, who although on public assistance after a divorce, nevertheless, always worked and herself pursued a college degree while trying to support her family. She not only obtained the degree but graduated with honors. The respondent said of her mother, "She has a lot of class, is nice and sophisticated." The respondent also indicated how grateful she was that her mother purposely limited her own social life so as not to create a confusing or unhealthy environment for her children. Another respondent who saw his mother as the strongest influence on his achievement also mentioned the positive influence of his father. He said that he can only remember his father staying home from work 1 day in his life, not because he was never sick, but because he had such a strong sense of duty. From him, he said he learned a sense of responsibility. A sense of moral or ethical behavior was also indicated by several of the respondents.

II. EDUCATION

Education is the primary pathway to success for those who do not have family connections to get them there. At the same time, research has shown that education often does not "pay off" for minorities in the same way that it does for nonminority persons. Some assume this is because the quality of education is not as good, a charge with which minority persons are continually faced. Others assume it is because of discrimination. It is, therefore, important to have a sense of the educational histories of these minority managers before we discuss their career aspirations and prospects.

A. Primary and Secondary School

For most of these prospective minority managers, there was something special about their educational experiences in primary and secondary schools. Three of the recent immigrants did not provide any information on their precollege educations, except to indicate that they had always done well in school. Another immigrant attended a company-sponsored school in the foreign country where her parents worked. Of the other 9, only 1 mentioned going to an inner-city public school without also mentioning some special attention or assistance received.

This leaves 8 of the 13 with experiences that set them apart from many minorities who attend inner-city public schools. Four of the 8 attended private schools, 2 prep schools and 2 private, religious schools, although 1 later transferred to a public school. When transferring, the respondent was so far ahead of the other students in the school that the principal of the school made special arrangements for her to transfer to another public school with higher academic standards, even though it meant living temporarily with her divorced father. The 2 who attended prep schools (both males) mentioned the importance of the prep school environment for shaping their aspirations. In both cases, they indicated that they learned what was available to them in the world by being around students from wealthy backgrounds. In both cases, the experiences were positive. Both attended on scholarships.

Of the 4 others who attended public schools, 1 started in inner-city public schools for the first several years, but following the urban riots, her parents moved to the suburbs to avoid the problems of the city and to find better education for their children. She says that she does not think her parents were aware of how bad the inner-city schools were in comparison to those in the suburbs until they moved. She was able to transfer to the same grade, but her brother was held back a year for being so far behind. The 3 other respondents all attended inner-city public schools, and each in their own way found later that their educations had been lacking. But they were able to get the best out of what the public schools had to offer. One talked admiringly of the role models and mentors she had had (a teacher and a coach). The other 2 were clearly student leaders and were active in many clubs and sports. But, even for them, when they attended predominantly white colleges, they found themselves having to work extra hard to keep up, and 1 of these flunked out before getting himself together and becoming an "A" student elsewhere.

B. College

Although primary and secondary education provides the foundation for future learning on and off the job, a college education is an important transition to the workplace. A good college education provides not only training but also socialization. It contributes to the presentation of self to those who would enter the corporate world. It also provides information about available career options and potential networks to use in the climb to success. One's choice of a college, academic record, and savvy for translating the college experience into the adult work world are all important contributors to later success in one's career.

While attending college, most of the students stayed close to home, both for financial and for social reasons. Only 5 of the 13 graduated from schools far away from their homes, and even among these, 3 went to schools near relatives or friends. Five of the 13 attended large state schools (2 blacks, 2 Hispanics, and 1 Asian). Three others (all black) started out in large schools (one in a military academy, the others in state schools) but transferred in midstream to small, liberal arts institutions (2 of them, predominantly black schools). Two of these had flunked out and so had to transfer; the third could not afford the out-of-state tuition after giving up a sports scholarship that took too much time away from studying. Three other respondents went to small, private liberal arts schools (1 black, 2 Hispanics), 1 of these only after having to transfer from school to school over a 10-year period for financial reasons. Thus, only 2 of the 13 graduated from Ivy League schools (1 black and 1 Asian), and 1 of these after transferring from a local community college and only by attending on a scholarship.

All of these prospective managers said they knew that they would attend college, even those who came from very poor backgrounds. The sense of determination and of accomplishment is evident as they talk about their college experiences. One got into a very good school after having been rejected by writing a forceful letter saying they should take him. Many others had to overcome "culture shock," moving from their segregated neighborhoods to the more cosmopolitan environments of the colleges they attended. It is for this reason that 2 transferred from large public schools to all black schools and most of the others attended other small, private schools. Of the 5 who did attend large state schools, all did so close to home.

Almost all of these minority managers majored in business, science, or other technical fields: 3 in accounting or business (all black), 2 in computer science (1 black, 1 Asian), 2 in chemistry (1 black, 1 Asian), and 2 in economics (both Hispanic). The 3 who majored in the social sciences (excluding economics) or the humanities all were oriented toward general liberal arts educations and not to social work, education, or other traditional fields for minority graduates. In some cases, the career direction chosen by these prospective managers occurred almost by chance: the comments of a teacher or college adviser, and in one case, a lucky conversation with someone in the library.

Most of these prospective managers described themselves in positive terms. They indicated that they had done well, were involved, and had friends. For some of these students, this may be a false sense of accomplishment, as they described themselves as having done "well" when their grade point averages indicated less. But this was true of only a few. In most cases, they did do well, and there is a seriousness with which they took their educations. One described himself as "driven" and "hungry for an education," whereas another described dropping a whole semester's worth of courses rather than take C's when travel for work made it difficult for her to finish the term with the A's she was otherwise getting.

Although most of these prospective managers are relatively young, most had work experience before going on for the MBA. Only 1, an Asian without a green card permitting her to work, entered graduate school directly after completing a bachelor's. Only 2 of the 13 moved to New Jersey or the metropolitan area in order to attend Rutgers; the others are all nearby residents.

Only a few indicated that they had applied to or even considered one of the top 10 business schools. One tried one for a while, but left for personal reasons following a divorce. One received only a partial scholarship and so could not afford the more prestigious school. And another considered it but was too intimidated to apply. Four of the 13 chose Rutgers because it offered a part-time MBA, and they wanted to continue working. The others chose Rutgers because it was convenient to their homes, because they could more easily afford it than other area schools, or because they received financial aid.

III. WORK EXPERIENCE AND CAREER ASPIRATIONS

It is difficult to pinpoint exactly when a "career" begins because many people have early work experiences, especially while in school, that are discontinuous with their later career development. But, whether or not it is a step to future movement on a career ladder or one stage of a natural career progression, early work experience is important for several reasons. It helps one sort out what he or she wants to do in life, and it provides exposure to the differences between school and work. If one is fortunate, it also can provide contacts, experience, and access to more responsible positions in a given field.

A. Work Experience

As indicated, all but 1 of these 13 minority managers worked either full or part-time before or while attending school for their MBA degrees. In more than half the cases, they found their previous work experiences negative and are seeking the MBA to find better opportunities, most likely in different types of jobs. In the other cases, the MBA degree is seen as a means to advancement within the fields they have been working. Three are working in scientific or technical fields and want opportunities for advancement—and more money—"off the bench." Four had worked in various parts of the insurance industry (mostly doing underwriting or claims adjusting) and wanted out, usually to find a faster paced field. One working in government and another in accounting plan to continue in these areas. The rest have worked in a variety of retail or wholesale trade, usually in small businesses.

Three of the respondents described significant racist incidents which occurred while on the job. All of these respondents are black. One attended a "routine" lunch with a senior executive who proceeded to make explicitly racist comments to the respondent. One found a racist note attached to his car and generally found the environment of the organization inhospitable. The third was called incompetent to her face and in writing after an accident caused some damage to company equipment, and she interpreted the remarks and the subsequent actions as racially motivated.

One of the respondents who has already completed her degree received one of the best jobs in one of the most prestigious firms in her chosen field—after going through 28 interviews with various departments and levels of management. She was 1 of only 6 people hired at the firm in her area, out of 2,000 applicants, and she started far above the median MBA salary for that year. She is also 1 of the only ones in her firm, of which she is aware, with a degree from Rutgers, rather than one of the Ivy League or other top business schools.

B. Career Aspirations

One decides what one wants to be in life from many different sources of influence: family, peers, educational experience, early work experience, and luck. Although many children have a very restricted view of the world of work, with many wanting to be fire fighters, police officers, nurses, doctors, truck drivers, and astronauts, those aspirations change dramatically as one gets closer to graduation in both high school and college. Given that many students, it is said, are more oriented toward getting the educational training that will help them get good jobs, we would expect that there will be very self-conscious choices made to facilitate future career plans. Before we can talk about whether minorities are likely to reach top management positions, we have to consider what sorts of positions they are aiming for.

Given the family and educational profiles of these thirteen prospective minority managers, it is perhaps not surprising that their career goals reflect moderate aspirations for most of them. Only 3 of them (all black) saw themselves in positions that could in any way be construed as "top management." The highest aspiration mentioned was to be CEO of a major corporation but given the academic record of this respondent, most likely this is not a realistic expectation. Two others, both interested in banking and both male, expected to achieve responsible positions, but neither were orienting themselves toward the very top. One wanted to be a vice president of a commercial bank; the other expected to reach senior vice president of a division (or executive vice president, he said, of a "very enlightened firm"). Three or 4 (depending on how one interprets the comments) saw themselves as department managers (all of these are women). One explicitly stated that she did not want the responsibility of top management; another said she had never thought about the possibility of reaching top management.

Four others planned to work for a short time for someone else and then begin their own firms, 2 in financial consulting, 1 in retail, and the other probably in finance, but open to possibilities. They view the opportunity to be rewarded to the extent that their abilities will take them a positive incentive for being entrepreneurs, and they all want the control that owning one's own firm provides. A fifth saw herself as president of a small firm in her industry. She did not make it clear whether she expected to own the firm or not.

One of the respondents did not fit into any of these categories, and her response stands out. Although still young, she had more work experience than most of the other respondents, and she also had struggled more .to complete her education than any of the others. Coming from a very poor background and from parents who, she said, accepted their fate in life, she instead planned from very early on to make something of herself and to rise above the life circumstances she had been dealt. She said that at one time in her life she might have thought about wanting to be a president or a vice president but that she had since come to see positional titles as not very meaningful. Instead, she says, she thinks in terms of monetary goals, and with a strong sense of determination and self-confidence, she said she planned to be making a million dollars a year within 3 years. She was already working in an industry where that aspiration may have been possible to fulfill but she did not count on fate to get her there. She had a work plan for herself that broke down what she needed to do each month, each week, and each day to reach her goals. After feeling humiliated by some of the early experiences in her life, where others controlled what happened to her, she said she vowed then to never let herself again be in that circumstance. She said her response to poverty and misfortune were to have a healthy respect for herself, to *know* that she did not belong in that situation. Throughout her early work experiences, and even in her initial job search, she set out to do what others said she could not. It is easy to believe that she will reach her monetary goals as well.

On balance, then, and excepting the last case, these prospective minority managers are more or less oriented toward solid middle management positions or to owning their own, most likely, small firms. There was only an implied sense of fear of discrimination because of their race, ethnicity, or gender, although some comments were made to the effect of finding congenial environments, where they would be most likely to succeed. Also, there was strong concern about finding work situations where they would be evaluated on their performance alone—the proverbial bottom line—and not on, to them, irrelevant social characteristics. As one said, if your performance shows on the bottom line, you will gain respect, however grudgingly, "whether green, or brown, or black." If this group were representative of the cohort of minority managers and the pool of talent for major corporations interested in increasing the number of minorities in top management, it is clear that motivational issues would be as important a factor to consider as technical competence or social or political fit.

IV. WHAT WILL HELP MOST, WHAT WILL HINDER MOST, AND WHAT WOULD THEY WISH FOR IF THEY COULD?

When respondents are asked what is most likely to help them attain their career goals, one is struck that the primary, but unspoken, response is their belief in themselves. They express this, however, in predictable ways. Although most respondents mentioned several things that they thought would contribute to their success, the most frequently mentioned items are education, hard work (or energy), and contacts. In one sense, these are very realistic answers. Most minority people who get ahead do so through the educational system, but qualifications and competence are assumed for many of the jobs they will be competing for, so education and hard work may not differentiate them from their competition. (By the way, all 4 of those whose highest aspirations for themselves were to be department managers mentioned education as the most important factor in their success.) Knowing the right people or having the right contacts was equally considered a factor in success, but importantly, all but one of those who mentioned this did not already have such contacts. Instead, they recognized the importance of connections but found themselves in a situation of having to create or foster them. The other saw her extended family as providing essential assistance for making it.

In addition to these factors, a few mentioned their interpersonal skills, their positive attitudes, and their ethical commitments. As important was finding the right kind of supportive environment and also one where they would be judged on the bottom line. Only one mentioned the ability to bring in business, indicating perceptively, that "the MBA is only a ticket to the dance." In addition to hard work, education, and contacts, one mentioned the role of luck. Another focused primarily on the ability to escape family responsibilities until her career was established. Others mentioned this as well—both male and female—in response to other questions.

Summarizing these responses does not provide a full enough sense of what these prospective minority managers had in mind, especially of the expressed expectation that they would each somehow control their own careers. One mentioned not only interpersonal skills but also underlined that she would be aided by the fact that she would like her co-workers and be willing to spend time with them. Another had plans for building networks and letting her presence be known in her company, by applying for lots of jobs, so that her vita would get around. Another feared that she may not get the kind of assignments that would make it possible for her to learn the business as well as she felt she needed. And another wanted a supportive environment but was clear that he did not want to be put into a situation where he would have to, in his words, "sink or swim." Some talked about being organized and getting done whatever they set their minds to. Another talked about not only hard work and being willing to pay the price for success but also the need to choose goals that are worth it. Regarding having a good education, one of the Asians indicated that education itself was not the key but having a good U.S. education.

In response to being asked what things may hinder their success, there is almost no overlap in the answers, with two exceptions. Three mentioned that "maybe" being female may be a problem, but one said it would be the only thing to hinder her and she did not expect it to do so, and another said she had not ever thought about something hindering her success but perhaps being a female would. Two mentioned that being black may hinder them, but again in the context that it would be the only thing and that it was not expected to be an issue. Aside from these, the other responses are all unique and thoughtful.

A list of their responses follows:

- Being too passive and having meekness interpreted as weakness
- An internal battle she will have to fight over the need to spend time with her family and helping others, versus working on career goals

- Having a boss threatened by him
- Being an "advanced" MBA (in his mid-30s)
- Not finding the right people to help him start his own business, that is, people who will be driven by accomplishment and not just a "pot of gold"
- Being on the wrong side of key political issues in her environment
- A lack of confidence, fearing her own ideas (for someone with very high aspirations)
- Giving up or having a negative attitude
- Not postponing family plans
- Poor communication skills
- Having her technical background pigeonhole her

Thus the overwhelming concerns of these prospective minority managers are not fears of discrimination because of their race, ethnicity, or sex. Instead, they fear sabotaging themselves, by not having the right presentation of self or because of the possibility of poor interpersonal relations in a given social environment. In general, it seemed clear that most of these prospective managers had not considered the possibility of what might stand in their way. They were decidedly positive in their orientations. As one said, "I cannot focus on reasons for not getting ahead, only on why I will."

When asked for a "wish list," that is, what would they like to have available to enhance their chances of success if it were possible, most gave only short responses. In only a few cases did they refer to race or family background. One male said he wished for the absence of racism, but added that he did not really know what the state of race relations are within corporations. Another black male said that if he were a "different color" (presumably white), that he could "set the world on fire." One of these same two people also mentioned that coming from a more affluent background would have helped him, and another respondent indicated that having the kind of useful family connections that she saw available for the students around her would make her life easier. But, as in the previous questions, there is not an overwhelming sense of concern that discrimination will be a major factor in their careers. In fact, one of the respondents made it clear that although he did not want to face racism, he also did not want any "special consideration" for being a minority.

The most frequent response to the question about what the respondents would like to have available if possible is the wish for a mentor or role model to discuss things with along the way. To some extent, the respondents were not hoping for someone to help them get ahead by opening doors, as much as someone to talk to when things got confusing or tough, when decisions had to be made, and someone to explain what it was like to face some of the same circumstances and win. One respondent talked of this as having access to the best minds in history, of people with "commitment, vision, and patience." The examples included inventors and entrepreneurs. The wish for mentors is consistent with the fact that the second most frequently mentioned "wish" is finding support, whether of an organization or of co-workers. In addition to these wishes, one respondent said having an Ivy League degree would have helped. And, one of the Asians wanted the green card she did not have (by support from a large corporation), and the other hoped for a guaranteed, ideal job, upon completing the MBA.

V. THE VIEW OF ONESELF AS A MINORITY PERSON IN THE POST-CIVIL-RIGHTS ERA

Because of the wide variety within the minority population and the ambiguity—as we discussed in Chapter 1—about who should be included within the category of a "minority," we asked the respondents whether they thought of themselves as minorities. We had expected that maybe the Asians, and perhaps some of the Hispanics, would disavow the minority label for themselves. For the same reasons, we had asked this question of the successful minority managers discussed in Chapter 10. All of them strongly indicated their awareness of their minority status, often providing anecdotes and stories of discrimination to underline how their minority identities were brought home to them. To our surprise, the prospective minority managers interviewed for this chapter said otherwise.

Ten out of 13 said they did not think of themselves as minorities, and the other 3 each said in various ways that, although they recognized their minority status, it was not an issue for them. One of these (a black female) said that, although she had to be realistic and recognize that "socially" she is seen as a minority, "Lord willing, this will change." Another (a black male) said that he had to recognize that he is a racial minority but that he did not see it as a "hindrance or an obstacle" and indicated that his minority status was more important off the job than on. He had almost always lived in a multiracial environment, in contrast to some of the others, although he did go to a black college. The third (one of the immigrants and black) said she was aware of her minority status only since coming to the United States. Further, she said, that because she was not a minority in her homeland, she felt she had a more positive attitude about herself than U.S.-born minorities. She was one of those to describe an explicitly racist incident on the job. Her consciousness of herself as a minority, it seemed, was also shaped by that incident.

All the others said they did not think of themselves as minorities, and their responses are of interest. One (a black woman) said, "I am a citizen of the world, not the U.S., and in the world, there are more people of color than not." She went on to say that to her, a minority, is just a "technical term," and one "which is damaging if you think of yourself that way." Another (a black male) said that racially he did not think of himself as a minority, but said, "I am a minority in terms of being well-disciplined, responsible, a good thinker, and smart." One of the other immigrants (a Hispanic male) said that he is a minority in this country because he speaks a minority language, but as someone who has been "Americanized to the nth degree," he does not fit the image of the "typical minority." Another (a black male) said, "To think of oneself as a minority is self-defeating. It means you accept limits upon yourself." Thus, he said he only thinks of his minority status if someone else raises it, but that otherwise "I was raised to think of myself as just as good as anyone else."

Two minority females (one black and one Hispanic) both said they did not think of themselves as minorities, and both added their reasons why. One said, "I do not have to blame everything on my color." The other said, "I do not look for discrimination. If I have a problem, I do not think of it as discrimination, because it may put a chip on my shoulder before I even meet people." Another (a Hispanic female) said, although she had and continues in various contexts to experience discrimination, that she had put it behind her. She said, "At the age of 21 or 22, I looked at life and said that this was a terrible life, why me, but then I hit bottom and decided to get on with it." From then on, she said, she did not focus on being a minority. The other three, all immigrants (one Hispanic female and both Asian females), said they had never thought of themselves as minorities either because of their ethnicity or their sex. Both Asians added that they had never been treated as minorities or been discriminated against. One added that discrimination was only a problem for Asians who had language problems (which she did not).

One might think that these are woefully unrealistic views and that with more experience, each of these minority managers will "find out." No one, of course, at this juncture can say. It is quite possible that as they have pursued nontraditional roles for minorities and been encouraged to do so from their families, various scholarship programs, and a general public awareness stemming from the civil rights movement, that their lives have been different so far from those of the experienced minority managers described elsewhere in this volume. By seeing themselves in a world context or defining themselves in terms of their character rather than their ethnicity, it may be both a healthy and realistic view of themselves for the life experiences they will face.

Given that few viewed themselves as minority people, we were also curious about their view of the civil rights movement. The responses are generally mixed. Although most feel a debt to the civil rights movement for opening doors for them that were closed to their forebears, for the most part, they do not want to rely on it now. One respondent (a black female) said that we are "beyond the civil rights movement": "At this stage, Afro-Americans need to network with each other. There is no more affirmative action; you are on your own now." Another (a black male) said that he was guardedly optimistic, which is what he feels should be the outlook for all minorities. But, he added, "One should not go around with a sense that people are out to get you." Two (both Hispanic) spoke somewhat negatively of the consequences of the civil rights movement. One (a female) said, "It started out to do what was needed, but it has also given minorities an excuse to keep using discrimination as a factor for not being qualified or to have the right skills." The other (a male) said that, as an immigrant, the movement did not apply to him (despite many years of minority scholarships at various levels of education). He added that "too much emphasis has been placed on civil rights and affirmative action" and that "people do not need these things to get ahead." Speaking of groups other than his own, he said, "Some minorities think things are owed to them and this has stymied their progress. In this country, everything should be earned rather than given to you." Another Hispanic female (an immigrant) said that minorities "have to fight to get ahead" but added that "not enough minorities prepare themselves by getting the necessary education and training."

Some felt grateful for the legacy that the civil rights movement had given to them, although they downplayed it for their own careers. And, some mentioned that more needed to be done, but often they had others in mind when they said this. One (a black male) said there was still work to do and changes to be made, but he said, "not only for blacks but also for women and other minorities, Asians, Latins, Spanish, and for foreigners." Another (an Asian female) said that discrimination must exist because so few minorities were in top management, but she herself felt optimistic about the future. Another (a Hispanic female) said that she works with "99.9% WASPS, but I do not focus on this fact." She said the only time she thought of being a minority is when she fears for her daughter.

Others viewed the civil rights movement more personally. One (a black female) said that, because some people still doubt the ability of blacks, equal access is still needed. And another (a black male) said of the civil rights movement, "Thank God for these people, but, quoting Churchill, it is only the end of the beginning." A black female indicated her gratitude for both the civil rights movement and the feminist movement but said she "prayed for new ideas because some members of the black race are too relaxed about what they have, while there are still problems." An immigrant (a black female) said the civil rights movement and pressure for affirmative action was "definitely relevant" to her current situation but added that because she did not herself live through the movement, she has a more positive attitude about herself and toward others.

Overall, it seems that the black respondents were grateful for the civil rights movement and saw it as providing them with opportunities that they would not have had if they had been born decades earlier. Some of the black respondents also expressed some concern about the need for continued progress in civil rights protection but just as many wanted to see it as behind them. To some extent, they did not, apparently, want it to intrude upon their own careers. They want to be treated just like everyone else, not have their minority status made an issue. They want to be judged on their merits alone and feel generally confident that if this were so, they would do just fine. The Hispanic respondents were less likely to see the civil rights movement as for them. One said it had made it "easier" for her but also made it clear that she was making it on her merits, not on her minority status. The other three all raised issues about whether the civil rights movement had been used as a substitute for personal accomplishment by "some groups." And, for the most part, they attributed their own success to date on their performance, not on special treatment. Even those who had minority scholarships claimed that their academic records (combined with the economic status of their families) would have merited them scholarships in any case. The Asians, both immigrants, did not see the civil rights movement as about them at all, but they acknowledged that "some groups" were discriminated against and therefore probably needed it.

Thus, for this new generation of minority managers, there is not much activism for legislative or other governmental support. Although many want the current legal guarantees to stay in place and be enforced—although some seem ambivalent about even this—their primary orientation, if any, is toward setting an example for others, to be role models to others, to show others how to do it by doing it themselves. A few spoke of a mission to their own group to show them the way. One (a black female) said she was a "pathbreaker" for her relatives, by showing them that it was possible to develop careers outside of the traditional social service fields. Although she wanted to get what she could out of her career at this stage, she ultimately talked of teaching in a business school and had taken some steps to pursue her PhD. Another (a Hispanic female), although currently very much oriented toward making it in her career, nevertheless wanted at some point in her future to do "public speaking" so, "I can reach out to as many people as I can that this is America and you can do whatever you want." She said that her sense of responsibility to help others see how to get ahead was almost a "burden" for her. She said, "The lives of so many children will be wasted if I don't show them the way. Many people are paralyzed because they don't know how to take the steps, and yet, they are little bitty steps." She also wanted to make a lot of money and ultimately fund a university chair for someone to deal with minority issues. On the whole, though, most of these prospective minority managers thought that being the very best that they could be was their contribution to civil rights.

VI. OTHER ISSUES

We gave each of the respondents an opportunity to comment on anything of interest to them that had not been covered in the interviews. Some chose not to, but most did. Three issues emerged from these comments: family life, the need for more minorities in management career tracks, and continued discussion of the ambiguities of the civil rights movement. The first and most frequently raised issue is the importance and problems that family life poses for prospective minority managers who want to make it. One (a black female) said, "I don't want to be successful alone, but this is a problem for many successful corporate women." Three others (1 black and 2 Hispanics) raised the other side of the family issue. Each of them were adamant about putting off any family obligations until their careers were established. They added that this was a trap for too many minorities. One said, "In Hispanic culture, there is so much pressure to get married by age 20." Another said, "Too many minorities end their chances for success by developing family commitments too young."

Their concerns were underlined by three of the female respondents who have children. One said that her husband has not helped at all but that she has taken responsibility for the children. She said that this has put a tremendous drain on her time and ability to do the job the way she prefers. Another, whose husband apparently does help, said that she is "torn between helping people and the feeling that she has to succeed and get ahead." The third, who also relies on her husband for a substantial part of the responsibility of child care, nevertheless, told of having to leave the house before her daughter was up for school and then returning late. She made a point to prepare a special daily message for her daughter, which she left for her to enjoy with breakfast. But, she said her biggest concern was that her hopes for her child would not be fulfilled. She said she wanted for her "even more than I want for myself, but she will not have the experiences which created in me the determination to get ahead." Another of the respondents with a child, whose extended family apparently has taken on the responsibility of child care for her said that there was "no problem" balancing motherhood and career. But then, she decidedly did not want a top management position. As she said, "The responsibility is overwhelming, and I don't want it put on me."

The second issue mentioned by some of the respondents is the need for getting the word out to other minorities about the opportunities in management. One (a black woman) said, "Blacks need to know how to play the games and need mentors and people on the inside to help them." She added that this is equally important for undergraduates as well as for MBA students and working managers. Another (a Hispanic female) said that there needed to be more minority MBA students, but she said that they had to be reached before they were teenagers. As she said, "Minority students are not dumb, but they develop a pattern of learning which is hard to change by the age of 18. So, many just give up. But, they have street smarts which indicates that they have abilities if they would develop them."

Finally, the issue was raised again by some that the situation was different for different minority groups and that civil rights meant different things to different people. One (a black female) indicated that many U.S.-born blacks have a very negative and cynical attitude, which she feels is not to their advantage. Because she was born and has spent a lot of time outside of the United States, she feels that her own sense of self-respect and self-worth—that is, her positive attitude—give her an advantage over U.S.-born blacks. Another (a Hispanic female) commented on how Asian parents spend the time to teach their children, but she said that many Hispanic parents leave education up to the teachers because they are so worried themselves about "their next meal." Finally, another said that he feared future problems because "certain minority groups are going to be demanding their share, but it is their own lack of skills and lack of desire to work which is the problem." He added, "In this country, with the opportunities available, there is no reason why you shouldn't succeed, no excuses. There are so many government programs and so many community programs that can get you going. If one is in poor economic conditions in this country, the only reason is because you want to be there." This is from someone whose own family worked hard, at low-skilled jobs, to provide for a house and an education for the children. Presumably he did not mean that one should be blamed for being poor but only if one stays poor over generations. These comments, like the interviews in general, belie a strong sense of self-confidence and a feeling that hard work and determination is what makes the difference—for minorities or anyone who wants to get ahead.

VII. CONCLUSION

Although as indicated earlier, this group of prospective minority managers are not representative of minority managers as a whole, their comments and concerns do provide some clues to how the next generation of minority managers view their career prospects. Admittedly the group is unrepresentative in several senses. They are all from the same graduate school and, therefore, also to some extent, all from the same environment. Their aspirations and expectations for themselves may be decidedly different—as we hear is true for white students as well—if they were getting degrees from one of the more prestigious business schools that orient their training to top decision makers. At the same time, they are all from the East Coast, in the midst of a concentration of corporate headquarters, and are, therefore, probably somewhat more cosmopolitan in their outlooks than might be true for a sample from somewhere else in the country. And, there are more females than males in the sample. What effects these particular characteristics may have on the career outlook of the respondents is not clear.

Presumably, it means that they are more familiar with the range of options that may be available to them, given the general environment, but that there is nothing in their personal environments to suggest to them to strive for the very top. Their rather limited aspirations may suggest that they are not being socialized through their educational experiences to think of themselves as candidates for top management, and at the same time, they are not getting exposure to such aspirations from their home life. Most attended small, liberal arts undergraduate schools or the same large state university where they are getting their MBAs. It, therefore, seems important that they have early and frequent contact with minority managers who have made it, as well as the opportunity to meet and interact with successful nonminority managers with whom they can identify.

The absence of extensive support groups in school may account for the very strong bond that most of these prospective minority managers seem to maintain with their families. Although we did not interview a comparable group of white students, it seems apparent that the norms for white children are quite different, with many seeking separation from their parents as early as possible. In a sense, some of these minority managers appear to be striving to get ahead for their families, more so than for themselves, which is counter to the self-seeking behavior often attributed to the typical white MBA students. It also may be counter to the norms expected in corporate life, where one's dedication to the company and career are to take priority over family and personal life. Although it is clear that the close family ties that these prospective minority managers maintain must provide the missing social support that we know is an important factor in the ability to cope well with stress and to work under pressure, it also must present to these minority managers a continuous ambiguity about what it is they are doing and for what purpose. There must be for many of them internal conflict about the lives they lead at home and in their segregated neighborhoods, and the presentation of self they are expected to maintain in a white, corporate world. Thus, their close family ties can be thought of as anchors for them in two senses. It holds them in place, giving them emotional stability and a sense of self, but it also may hold them back.

Another image that comes through of these prospective minority managers is the somewhat idealistic notion that most of them have about what it takes to get ahead. They have a strong belief that their education, hard work, and sheer determination will be enough for them to make it. This sense of drive and determination, to some extent, they share with the successful minority managers who are described in Chapter 10. One does not get as much of a sense that they are prepared for a world where subjective criteria count as much as objective performance for determining who will make it. Being young, most have been in a school environment for most of their lives, and schools are probably more objective in their evaluations than are corporations, where evaluations tend to be more subjective. If one does well on an exam, it usually means you get a good grade, no matter how you interact interpersonally. And, for the most part, assignments in school are individual assignments, where how you do indeed depends on your own effort and performance. Corporations, however, are much more characterized by interdependence and teamwork. How well you perform may depend as much on your ability to work with others and on their contributions to the team effort as it does on your own efforts. Equally important is that their performance will be measured by your contribution as well as your performance being measured by theirs.

Although the self-confidence that these prospective minority managers exhibit is probably going to be an important factor in their success, it also could be devastating for them if they fail. Some of them suggest that they are not only striving for themselves but also for their families, and indeed, sometimes, for their whole race or ethnicity. Putting so much pressure on themselves may be an unnecessary burden that can also potentially hamper their performance. They may take fewer risks and be less willing to try those things that have less assurance of success. This also may account for why it seems that many of them, although they have thought about their futures and planned at least the early stages of their careers, are not "ready to seize opportunity." That is, they are not risk takers, nor are they adventurers. As noted, most have stayed close to home, in comfortable environments, and although many have already achieved far beyond their own parents, they do not yet seem ready or even interested in setting the world on fire. As one of the respondents who has several years of work experience said, "I turned down many good opportunities. Maybe I should have been a bit more restless." Indeed, most of the respondents exhibit a sense of trust and faith in other people to recognize their achievements, if they just continue to apply themselves and do what is asked of them. But, they do not have as much of a sense of making their own way in a corporate environment, where initiative may make the difference between those who make it and those who do not. This also may be why so many of them ultimately want to own their own businesses—as soon as they feel they have enough experience and capital to do so. They want control over their own fate, and they want hard work to be the only thing that counts.

There is not, though, a clear sense either of the informal aspects of corporate life or the importance given to how one presents himself or herself. As mentioned, although many see the need for contacts, they themselves do not have them, and only a few mentioned any plans for how to get them. They want support and mentors, but there is a sense that having them is by luck and happenstance. Some of the successful minority managers described in Chapter 10, in contrast, downplayed the role of mentors and instead talked of how to make friends, wherever and whenever they have the chance. As we describe in other parts of this book, getting ahead for minority managers is partly a matter of organizational structure, policy, and practice, but it is equally a matter of personal effort on the part of minorities themselves. Saying so, however, means that many who try may fail. It is just that if one does not make the extra effort, he or she undoubtedly will fail. We want this book to be about success, so we make these observations not to discourage any prospective minority manager. On the contrary, we want to encourage them and to give them the necessary information on what it takes to make it.

IV

Finding Solutions
Coming To Grips With The Issues

Once problems have been identified and the stakes that people feel they hold are understood, one can begin the heart of the problem-solving process, namely finding solutions. Part IV of this volume incorporates ideas about how success can be achieved for minorities in management careers, both from a selection of autobiographical statements from successful minority managers and from corporations that have taken steps to improve their success in the advancement of minority managers. We feel that efforts must be made in both directions: from managers outward and from corporations inward.

Although none of this material is based on generalizable research, by providing insight into career strategies and corporate policies as they have been experienced in practice, we feel we can provide an important introduction to the issues which can be interpreted in the context of the research chapters in this volume.

Chapter 10 contains a series of selections from successful minority managers and Chapter 11 from corporations with successful policies or procedures. The contributors were each invited to be part of the volume because of the diversity of their solutions. In both sets of papers, there are some that were presented at the conference and some that were subsequently invited specifically for this volume to help round out the picture. The successful managers are from different racial and ethnic groups and include both men and women. The successful corporations function in different industries and face different labor markets and job structures. Chapter 12 then presents an overview of corporate policies and practices by reviewing the results of our survey of 218 corporations regarding what they are doing to ensure minority success in management careers. It also discusses actions that corporations believe that schools of management should undertake.

Because Chapter 10 and 11 both contain introductions that detail the main points of the selections within each chapter, only a brief overview will be provided here. In Chapter 10, successful minority managers discuss how they made it to their current positions. In almost all of the cases, these minority managers focus on hard work, perseverance, and determination. They also stress, however, that it is important to learn when, where, and how your efforts should be used. That implies setting both short- and long-term goals. Many mention the importance of mentors in their own careers, but they also indicate that it is important to make friends and to develop your own networks whenever you have the chance. Mentors actively look out for your interests; you actively foster friendships because you never know when you may need their help.

The successful minority managers included here said it was important to know how to use power, but they did not focus much on politics. Instead, they said that performance was more important than politics, and that to perform well, you need to know what kind of training to get and then to get it. You need to know your own strengths and weaknesses and use the information to fix the weaknesses. But they stress that technical skills are not enough. One must balance the technical and the nontechnical to reach top levels of management in the corporate world. At the same time, even with the right kind of training, friends, and breadth, minority managers must also realize that they will have to work harder than nonminorities if they want to make it. And they must be sure they understand that results are all that count.

Writing a book is a lengthy task, especially when so many authors and organizations are involved as is true in this volume. At the same time, as has been mentioned elsewhere in this book, corporations have been changing dramatically, with mergers and acquisitions changing the landscape of many companies faster than one can print the stationery. Because many of the selections included in this part of the manuscript were written very early in the process, it is understandable that positions, titles, and even organizations have changed since the pieces were first written. It was impossible for us to keep up with all the job changes of the contributors, especially to Chapter 10, and therefore, after a point we did not try to do so. Their comments are just as valid if we end their stories with the jobs they held when they agreed to be a contributor to the volume as if we had continuously revised while the rest of the manuscript was being completed. Consequently, some of the contributors are no longer with the employers they had worked for when their contributions for the volume were written.

Chapter 11 contains a series of papers from corporations that describe a policy or practice implemented in their company and that they consider to have been successful in improving the upward mobility of minority managers. Because there are so few minority managers at the highest levels of management in any company, we and they recognize that these programs and policies are not final solutions. Of course, they could not be because as we know from other parts of the manuscript, the contributing factors to minority underrepresentation in management careers are not limited to what corporations are or are not doing. But they are an important part of the story, especially because most of the companies included here are recognized within the minority community and elsewhere in the corporate world as having done better than many others in their commitment to and success in advancing minority managers.

When we were putting together this manuscript, we had assumed that most companies that we approached would be happy to be included in the volume because it would provide an opportunity for them to highlight their efforts and be recognized as a leader in this area. To our surprise, many companies we approached were not at all willing to be contributors, primarily, it seems, because they feared potential legal ramifications and in some cases, perhaps, because they were embarrassed at the gap between what they would like others to believe and what actually occurs in their firms. We are, therefore, most grateful to the companies that were willing to put themselves on the line—in writing. Needless to say, many of these companies also recognize that more needs to be done. But they were willing to share some of their best ideas because they feel it may be of use to others who are trying to rethink their strategies for improving equal opportunity.

The development of these programs or policies in each company, we are sure, resulted from hard thinking and careful analysis of ideas within the companies, but as far as we know, these programs are not directly the result of generalizable research. Although many of these companies hired consultants who may have done research as a basis for designing the programs or policies, the companies have been concerned primarily with the policy implications, especially for their own industries, more so than with the generalizability of effects to other kinds of firms in other kinds of industries.

The programs described in Chapter 11 cover five types of interventions: the role of top management support, accountability, recruiting, training and development programs, and external relations. These are not exhaustive of all that is being done in each company, but they represent major areas of emphasis in corporations that have undertaken systematic programs for improving minority advancement in management careers. Admittedly, all of the companies included here are large, established, and as such, are more targeted than some others for compliance with federal regulations. But they also, despite, or perhaps because of, rapidly changing environments, have expressed a strong commitment to the role that their human resources play in the success of their companies. An illustration of their human resource philosophies can be seen in that most of the programs described here were developed in participation with employees and often use employees, rather than paid consultants, for implementation. Perhaps most significant in the programs described here and what sets these companies apart from many others is the strong endorsement of top management to the programs, and in many cases this endorsement is backed up with incentive systems tied to performance in meeting human resource, including affirmative action, goals.

Chapter 12 further describes results from the survey we did of top corporations. The first part of the survey results were discussed in Chapter 7, where the problems these firms said they faced in ensuring minority success in management careers are described. In Chapter 12 results are provided on the perspectives these corporations have about the success their companies have had in advancing minority managers, the availability of various programs or policies in their firms, and their opinions on a number of related issues.

Although on all measures of attainment, the companies report only moderate success, they report their greatest success in retaining minority managers and educating nonminority managers about the issue. They also report less success in hiring minority managers but somewhat more in developing and promoting them. Very few of the companies, however, report success in promotion to top-level positions. These findings suggest that companies feel they have the necessary programs for development in place but that they cannot develop and promote the minority managers currently in middle-level positions in their companies and that they are still very concerned about selection and recruitment. Their success may also depend, however, on what kinds of programs they actually use. Many of the corporations reporting in the survey said they used feedback, training, and goal setting for all of their employees, and the use of such programs apparently facilitates their success in the promotion of minority managers to middle-level positions. However, many fewer corporations said they used the programs that were important for success in promoting minority managers to upper level positions, namely assignment to a variety of jobs early in the career and the use of career path planning. Even so, many of the respondents said such programs would be of special importance for minority managers to succeed.

The respondents were also asked a series of open-ended questions. Not all chose to respond. Of those that did, the most frequently mentioned item for each of the categories asked are as follows: the commitment of top management was seen as the most important organizational policy; the increase of awareness was seen as the most important agenda for nonminority managers; for minority managers, most respondents simply said to do the job; for schools of management, it was said they needed to better teach interpersonal and other people skills; for minority women, most respondents thought there were no special issues, although many thought presentation of self was important; and finally, the most important resource constraint mentioned was future limitations on promotion opportunity, but the lack of sufficient qualified candidates was also mentioned by many.

The variety of solutions discussed in different ways in this part of the book will be pulled together for specific recommendations in Part V. The same themes emerge repeatedly. Minority managers are told to keep at it no matter what and, if necessary, to make setbacks stepping stones to the next level of progress. But finding oneself in the process and engaging the support of friends and others are important means for finding the personal resources to persevere. Corporations are also told to keep at it, but they must do so in the ways that count, namely making it clear that equal opportunity is a fundamental corporate value to which top management is strongly enough commited to make it part of the bottom line for everyone in the corporation. Schools of management also have a role. They must provide all students, including minorities, with the knowledge about the people skills they will need for managing both the technical and nontechnical aspects of their careers. Part V discusses each of these in more detail and raises some of the fundamental issues regarding successful implementation.

10

Making It in the Corporation
Retrospectives of Successful Minority Managers

To know how to get ahead is always easier in hindsight, but it still can provide both encouragement and insight for those in midstream who want to reflect on their own career progress or for those who are just beginning. The following contains a series of autobiographical statements from successful minority managers, including both male and female blacks, Hispanics, and Asian-Americans. Each of the people included in this chapter have attained a level of achievement that most of those around them—both minority and nonminority—would consider successful, and they discuss here what they think are the factors most important to their success and the success of future minority managers. Of the statements included here, those by Scott, Edwards, Stubblefield, Jackson, and Mariel were prepared for presentation at the conference. All contributors were asked to answer three questions: What helped them most in their career success, what hurt the most, and what would have helped had it been available? Each contributor chose to answer these questions more or less directly and in his or her own way. In this introduction, we provide an overview of the concerns and issues expressed in the autobiographical statements that follow.

Consistent with the often repeated assumption (in chapters in this volume as well as elsewhere), we find some support for the critical role that mentors and networks can play in the climb to the top. However, most of the successful managers included here focus instead on hard work, perseverance, determination, and knowing when, where, and how to apply them as well as to a positive attitude and sense of oneself. These managers do not deny that others helped them, but they see such help as a happy addition to their own efforts. That is, mentors are great if you can find them, but one should not rely on them to make your success happen. Of course, it is quite possible that these successful minority managers are not consciously aware of all the help they got from others. They are indeed self-efficacious.

The lessons for success recounted here can be divided into two levels, personal and professional. The personal level can also be divided into the attitudes or values that one should hold and the preparation that one should make. In the discussion of each, we are extrapolating from the collection of retrospective statements of the successful minority managers included here.

The reader must be cautious how he or she applies these recommendations. As the authors of the statements are black, Hispanic, and Asian-American and male and female, any one of them may be speaking to problems that are unique to their own ethnic group or sex. We obviously at this point do not have a large enough sample to generalize for others, but readers can use what feels right and makes sense to them. If we were to generalize, we would argue that the black managers included here emphasize the opportunity to take risks and to fail in order to learn without it counting against them; the Hispanic managers emphasize the process of learning Anglo culture and fitting in; and the Asian-American managers emphasize using positive stereotypes of Asians being hard working and clever while avoiding the negative stereotypes of Asians being weak on communication skills or timid. The important point is that for each to succeed, he or she found ways around whatever obstacles he or she faced and kept on going on.

I. PERSONAL ISSUES: ATTITUDES AND VALUES

The managers in this section stressed the need to accept yourself, to develop an equilibrium about who you are (concentrate on your strengths but recognize weaknesses), and to respect yourself. They talked of the need to know where you come from and what you owe to the past. Many talked about the important contributions of their parents, and a few mentioned their spouses. Interestingly, some also discussed the critical role religion has played in their careers.

To know what kind of contribution you want to make, you need to have a dream. Dreams, however, must be translated into both short- and long-range career goals. At the same time, these successful minority managers felt it necessary to learn realistic goals about how far one can move how fast in any given career path. To ensure success, you should know what you are worth and what rewards others in like circumstances are receiving. You can only demand your due if you know what is due you. Whatever the situation, as a minority manager, you need to learn to stand up for yourself without letting it interfere with your own effectiveness.

These managers also all felt that minority managers need to be aware of the obstacles they may face but that they can succeed by turning negatives into positives. The old adage about the glass being half-full or half-empty was used to explain the point. Minority managers need to learn to overcome adversity, to persevere, and not to take no for an answer. Once the hurdles have been overcome, it is important that minority managers let people know of their successes.

Minority managers who want to be successful must also learn to compete, to negotiate, and importantly, to want to win. Given that there are always costs along the way, it is also important at the outset to decide what you have to do and what you are willing to do to get ahead. Most likely, successful minority managers will use what is positive from their own minority culture in order to succeed. As one manager said, minority status can be an edge for you or against you.

Minority managers should not wait for mentors to come along, but they should make it easy for people to like them, which is related to maintaining a positive attitude. Even if people encountered along the way do not take the role of mentors, they may be willing to help in specific situations or on specific occasions if they like you.

II. PERSONAL ISSUES: PREPARATION FOR SUCCESS

That one must obtain the proper skills and training in order to be successful may seem self-evident, but often it is not, because of the assumption that politics and culture are what determine success. The managers included here, however, stressed that politics cannot substitute for performance. You must not only be well trained but also know what training and experience are needed for the position you want to obtain. Along with more narrowly defined technical training, you must also learn both oral and written communication skills. In addition, these managers recommended that you know your strengths and develop them and, likewise, know your weaknesses and do something about them.

Technical skills in and of themselves will probably not be sufficient for success in corporate management. To get to the top positions, you must have broad experience as well as well-developed skills in a particular area. It is important for minority managers to learn that just doing a good job is not enough for getting ahead. Doing a good job will only improve your position in that job but will not help you move beyond it.

These successful managers stressed that for proper preparation there must be a balance between technical and nontechnical training. If you are sincere about wanting to get to top management positions, then a good foundation in the humanities and in cultural and intellectual pursuits (art, music, food, how to behave, etc.) are also required. Although none of us think we have the time, success can be aided as well by involvement in civic, political, and social activities. Along the same lines, it is necessary that you know who your constituents are and what their interests and needs are. To do so may require being a quick study and to learn how to learn.

If necessary, minority managers must be willing to change themselves and to learn to fit in. If one does not already have networks, then it is necessary to create your own, in the minority community and outside of it. An important lesson for doing so is to create commonality wherever you are. But, it is not sufficient to be personable. To get to the top, you must learn how to sell yourself, while at the same time being a team player. And just as importantly, you need to learn how to acquire and use personal power.

III. PROFESSIONAL ISSUES

To succeed, minority managers will most likely have to work harder than nonminorities and be concerned with every detail. They will have to work weekends and evenings while others pursue personal pleasure, but according to managers here, it is a matter of priorities. Hard work in itself, however, is not sufficient if you do not know where you are heading. You need to do some research to know where you want to go and how to get there. Success may mean finding an environment where you will be judged on your performance objectively (as much as possible), and it may mean taking risks. To be successful clearly means to recognize opportunity when it comes along and to grasp it. At least one manager included here also recommends leveraging your background rather than taking steps back on the way to the top.

Opportunity may be difficult to recognize, and yet it is more important than money if you want to succeed. Short-term gains may be at the expense of long-term success. In this sense, it is more important to be on the right track than the fast track. Because opportunities involve risks as well as payoffs, coaches may be more important than mentors. That is, to succeed you will need someone who will help you understand and overcome your weaknesses and who will show you how to get ahead. This may mean also finding a situation where you can fail without it counting against your race, ethnicity, or sex. It also may mean getting to know people so that they are willing to take a risk with you. Coaches and mentors and even casual friends cannot contribute to your career, though, unless you learn to receive criticism, and equally important, learn how to give it.

One of the most important messages from these successful minority managers, however, is that the end result should be the focus. It is the outcome that counts and not your efforts toward it, because people will only see the results. They do not care what you had to do to achieve them. Thus minority managers need to remember that their goals should be getting the job done. Often that means to learn how to get things done through other people. Final results do not depend on prior experience. You can learn what you need to learn along the way if you believe in yourself and have learned how to learn. The important thing is to actively control your own environment and to find a way to do what you have to do successfully.

Although many of these recommendations may sound like "bootstrapping," the managers included in this section saw it more as determination. They said that it is important to learn how to survive and not to get stopped just because negative things happen along the way. To some extent, they seemed to subscribe to the notion, "Don't get mad, get even." The getting, however, was really for themselves and their families, not for others. They did not spend their efforts fruitlessly on worrying about the past, but instead, set their sights on the future and kept at it despite setbacks or disappointments.

It may appear from this summary that these successful minority managers had all of the answers and were completely self-confident in their abilities and their chances for success. This is not the case, however. Many were reluctant contributors to this volume because they had not fully thought through what they had had to do to make it in the corporate world. In many cases, the events and circumstances that led to their rise were painful to think about or seemed too precarious to them to put into writing. They all agreed to share their own experience with others, because they were convinced that some things about their own past may help encourage others. Because most were very conscious of their status as minorities, they wanted to contribute what they could to other minority managers who may feel discouraged or "beat." As they began to put their experiences into writing and to make them coherent, they often themselves felt encouraged and strengthened about what they had overcome. They also felt somewhat grateful, because many also recognized the important role of timing and luck, as well as hard work. Most saw the civil rights movement and the sacrifices made by others as important to their success, and they appreciated what doors others had opened for them.

The Fast Track or the Right Track?

James H. Scott

What cynics they are, those minorities who labor in profit-seeking organizations, who disbelieve the attainability of higher management jobs in their companies. My own experience tells me that they are far outnumbered by minority men and women of some position who think that they can continue to succeed, but who also think that the odds need improving. I would go further to say if the odds were modestly improved, a real breakthrough could be achieved in the near future.

My career has been characterized by a wide range of diverse experiences and a high level of involvement. In high school I was president of my class and student council. I earned three letters in varsity baseball and was on the public speaking team. I also worked at a supermarket during my high-school years. I graduated from Villanova University in 1965 with a major in electrical engineering. I later joined the Peace Corp that first sent me to Georgetown, Guyana, and later to Trinidad. After returning to the United States and attaining deferment, I earned my MBA in 1970 from Washington University, St. Louis. I then moved to New York where I joined Citibank and worked in the electronic and information systems department for 3 years. I then took a career jump to Gulf and Western where I worked for a year as the assistant to the vice president of finance. I then moved to Morgan Guaranty. I was appointed as a White House Fellow in 1978 and took a 1-year leave of absence from the bank. When I returned, Morgan Guaranty sent me overseas for 3½ years. After returning the United States, I remained with the bank until 1986 when I joined Amherst College.

My successful managerial career has been due, in part, I believe, to the kind of person that I am. I am basically a very happy person who enjoys doing exciting things. That is, I have always viewed life as a series of experiences and believe that you should want as much as you can get. I believe that

James H. Scott • Treasurer, Amherst College, Amherst, Massachusetts 01002.

it is important to remain flexible as well. One has to open one's eyes and take advantage of opportunities that avail themselves. So many people are afraid to take advantage of opportunities. You must push yourself and take chances.

My Christian faith and home life have also played a critical role in my success. My wife has been very important to my career. We have been married for 20 years. She has never worked outside the home, is very active in church activities, and does volunteer work at the local hospital. She has provided an important anchor for myself and our three children in the rather hectic life that we have had. My faith that things are going to work out and belief that there is a benevolent God have also sustained me in good times and bad. Together, strong faith and a good home life can provide an important balance in one's life.

These and other experiences have led me to believe that the challenge of business is to be fair and evenhanded in growing its managers, and vigorous and innovative in removing unnecessary hurdles that face their minority men and women. Three issues will be explored here: money, time frame, and risk taking. Each can have an important impact on the success of minorities in management. Breakthroughs by minorities will become more commonplace when business organizations address these fundamental issues innovatively.

I. MONEY

I have observed that minority managers focus on salary much more sharply than do nonminority managers, and the emphasis is much more exaggerated than it need be to ensure a healthy outlook on the job at hand. Intellectual and emotional energy that could be used on other things is thereby dissipated by an overconcern for money.

The preoccupation with money goes back to the first day on the first job that the manager got following school. Most likely, a new graduate will arrive with much less money in his or her pocket and in the bank than his or her peers had. Certainly, most minority managers had less than they needed to get started. Most likely they had less call on the family bankroll (if there was a bankroll, or family). They probably had more trouble finding an adequate apartment and raising enough money for a rent security deposit and furniture down payment. Their wardrobes were probably inappropriate or inadequate for business, compared to their peers, because of differing cultural norms. Thus, there is a reason for initial preoccupation with money on the part of minority managers.

A number of approaches might be used to overcome this initial problem with money and the repetition of this capital shortage later on in the career. Developing new approaches to compensation could ensure that more of the minority manager's energies could be used to develop job excellence, rather than be diverted to worrying about money. First, give the opportunity for more front ending of salary or subsequent raises. Start the young management trainee at, say, $25,000 per year plus $5,000 up front, instead of a

$30,000 salary; or $25,000 per year for 2 years, plus $10,000 up front, plus a 2-year contract calling for performance incentive raises in the second year. Likewise, for the $60,000 per year district manager, give the chance to receive his or her 11% raise up front. Use the management contract more frequently at the lower level and use it more creatively to address the reality of the minority manager's situation. Obviate or mitigate the need for borrowing, for example, for schooling. The children of white colleagues may look to the grandparents for tuition, whereas the children of a minority manager look to him or her.

Second, companies should work harder to shatter fantasies about achievable compensation levels. They should make it clearer to trainees and young managers what the upside earnings potential is for various achievable career tracks over a 5-year horizon. Monetary expectations can then be managed by the minority manager in his or her own evolving recognition of self-development and contribution. Borrowing from a football analogy, if you know your secondary is vulnerable to the pass, you had better expect a lot of passes. Similarly, minority managers will be sorely tested in this area by life circumstances, and they should be more adequately equipped to address the concern about money as they look forward.

Third, in companies there are sometimes truly advantageous salary earnings differentials in comparable jobs that are in different locations or divisions. Where this is so, minority managers should be given their fair share of temporary relocation opportunities to those specific jobs. The jobs should be offered, and the manager should be told directly that one of the reasons the job is being offered is the upside financial gain. The chance to "break out" financially will probably be gratefully received. All worthy organization growth is not just vertical movement, but those lateral moves can be professionally and, as importantly, financially rewarding.

As far as money is concerned, business can do more with what is available than it has done. These few suggestions are illustrative of some fiscally empowering aids for ensuring minority success.

II. TIME FRAME

How far up can one go and how fast can one get there? Corporations do very little generally to encourage realistic attitudes in this area. As a result, the upwardly mobile minority managers (and other managers as well) and the company suffer. The company suffers because managers imagine unfairness when it might not exist; the manager suffers inwardly because his or her every working day is an experience of being neglected or bypassed. The ultimate corporate insanity in this whole area is symbolized in executive vice presidents who are passed over for president. Have they failed or are they successes? Or the president when someone else is brought in to be a CEO. Companies should disclose more information about the statistical contours of the career path: the average experience years for a given level and the actual range of experience for those at that level; the average age of those at the next level up in the hierachy and their age range; the average years with the firm of senior management, as well as the range of those years. Many more statistics suggest themselves: the quality and depth of education; performance rating history; or critically, the number of managers at a given level who are practically eligible for the next level position! Disclosure of such information would force all managers to have more realistic, personal views of their progress.

There will always be room for superstars because superstars will see to it that management notices them. But the next performance level down is that which drives the organization. And it's that level that needs a healthier outlook on promotability, necessary in-service time, and discrimination versus sheer numbers. To ensure minority success, companies should recognize more practically the role that situation analysis plays in their young managers, the self-evaluation of success, and how much more vulnerable the minority manager is to a tempation of feeling overlooked or unfairly bypassed than white managers. Companies should stop titillating the tendency in all of us to aspire to the superstar fast track and encouraging people to think that that is where the action is. One either is a superstar or one is not. If yes, the company will notice, regardless of your race or sex. If no, which is the overwhelming probability for most managers, the company owes you the responsibility to help you evaluate where you are, where you are going, and what the odds are of your getting there.

III. RISK

There is something quite accurate in the observation that one cannot be a good banker unless one makes a bad loan. Opportunities or potential opportunities must be exploited, and too short a reach unnecessarily limits the organization's reward. Risks must be taken. And so it is with "surprise" promotions or demotions or firings.

I have come to believe that a (nearly) insurmountable internal hurdle for minority managers is the unwillingness of many corporations to risk failure of minorities. Whether driven by corporate defensiveness ("to make sure their peers don't get upset") or a fear of criticism if things don't work out, minorities who make breakthroughs in the corporate structure are often sure things. They will surely succeed at higher management levels. This is not necessarily bad, but the odds of finding minorities at the top will diminish to a level even lower than one might expect statistically, because real chances are just not being taken. But in whom should the chances be taken?

This problem will be difficult to solve because it is a product of the muscle-bound, administrative/procedural systems in our companies. Of course, high-potential candidates should be encouraged to take key slots when they are available. But the corporate system can never identify all candidates who belong at the top. There is always room for a wild card. I think we need more minority wild cards. Using another football analogy, the end around might be an effective approach. Senior management could go directly to its growing stable of minority managers, ask to be with them, and speak to them on a regular basis. They can look for that extra sparkle, the intangible signals that suggest that here perhaps is someone worth watching. Again, this is not the superstar, this is the young manager who is in the pack and doing a fine job, but one who needs a break. To the extent it is true that one doesn't take chances with people one doesn't know, this approach might produce results.

What is not suggested here is the proverbial cocktail party where the divisional staff, including the sparsely represented minority contingent, is present with senior management. These sessions should and must continue, of course, but the CEO's attention there will be drawn and monopolized by his divisional general managers, all invariably on the corporate make. No, I am calling for a segregated gathering, where the seniors can mix freely with their minority legions: where hard questions can be asked, where hierarchical barriers can be vaulted over, where the spark, if noticed, can help raise senior awareness of a presence, but if unnoticed, cannot hurt.

In summary, I feel that there are sufficient minorities in the corporate pipeline who have intelligence, ability, tenacity, discipline, interest, and motivation to ensure group minority success in business over time. That it may take longer than it need take troubles me. That corporations have failed to communicate what success in business, in general, means will make the timetable seem even more protracted than it should be. The process could be accelerated.

It can be accelerated if senior managers address more creatively the role of money in their minority managers' lives; if they learn to take more risks in their handling of their minority managers' careers; and if they work assiduously to supplant the superstar notion of progress with the reality of corporate life: the slow, arduous trek to the top.

Getting and Using Power

Horace B. Edwards

My own success as a top management executive has been due in part to a strong educational foundation as well as the additional knowledge and skills that I have acquired in the numerous positions that I have held throughout my career. I earned a BS degree in mechanical engineering and naval science at Marquette University and an MBA from Iona College. I also have a number of honorary degrees. A number of years in my career were spent working in systems engineering at Allis Chalmers, General Motors, Conrac Corp., and Northrop Corp. In 1967 I joined Atlantic Richfield Co., where I held a number of different management positions, including manager of special projects; assistant controller, marketing; controller, products division; assistant controller and manager of financial operations analysis; manager, planning and evaluation, transportation division; and vice president, planning and control, ARCO Transportation Co. In 1980 I became president of ARCO Pipe Line Co., a subsidiary of Atlantic Richfield, which is the number 1 pipeline operations in the United States, ranking between seventieth and eightieth on the *Fortune 500* list of corporations.

My success has also been due as well to the fact that I have always had high aspirations. I have always been very goal-oriented. Throughout my career, I think that the people who were in positions to make choices were aware of this. Consistent with this, I have also always been a very determined person with a strong sense of self. I am not easily dissuaded. I have always been prepared to deal with people who told me that I could not do something. For example, I became a commissioned officer in the Navy at a time when the likely expectation of such a promotion for a young black male was that you might as well quit. In essence, I have always believed that there are really no obstacles; that one must view life as a series of challenges and do your own thing if you are going to be successful.

Horace B. Edwards • Secretary of Transportation, State of Kansas, Topeka, Kansas 66614.

I grew up in Tuscaloosa, Alabama, where I graduated from high school at the age of 16. I was active in sports and student council. Both of my parents had high expectations for me and my two sisters. My father was a wise, ambitious man. My mother, equally wise, was a tremendous source of inspiration and "conned" us into believing that we were special folks. She also led us by example and was always very much in pursuit of education.

My experiences have led me to the conclusion that achieving success involves striking a balance between things that have economic and survival value, like technology and communication, and things that do not necessarily have economic values, like the humanities, the arts, science, and religion. An important link, I believe, also exists between fitness and optimum productivity. One of the first things I did when I became president of ARCO Pipe Line was to put in a fitness room. Fitness cuts down on health costs and absenteeism. Furthermore, I think that people must learn to cherish themselves as individuals if they are going to succeed. Great leaders come from those who want to be different.

A parallel can be drawn between the requirements business leaders face and the preparation and skills that should be developed by students, of whatever hue, to succeed in business. In essence, business and academic leaders and students need to balance the needs and interests of the various constituents that they serve. To illustrate this point, first consider the following requirements that leaders must attend to:

Constituents	Principal interests/needs
Owners/stockholders	Profits
	Cash flow
	Economic worth
	Growth
Employees	Fair compensation
	Opportunity to grow and succeed
	Sense of worth
Community	Service
	Financial support
	Enrichment of the quality of life
	Minimum disruption of other activities

Similarly, students and others who aspire to succeed in management or executive careers need assistance in dealing with competing requirements. Two factors that I feel help to advance upward mobility in American corporations the most are first, learning how to acquire and use power; and second, maintaining a sense of balance among all of the competing requirements one is forced to deal with on an ongoing basis. These two factors are critical in the development of any top executive.

In order to acquire and successfully use power, the individual must be competent, possess quality education and training, the discipline to work hard and persevere, good interpersonal skills, and a positive attitude. These characteristics contribute to the personal power of the individual. They should not be confused with conferred power that is derived from position, perks, and success within an organization.

The ability to balance competing requirements, in turn, depends on the ability to maintain some sense of balance between technological understanding and an appreciation of the humanities. Balancing cooperation and teamwork against individual responsibility, and independence of thought and action is essential as well. Lastly, one must be flexible, open to new ideas, and able to compromise. Although flexible, however, the individual must maintain a strong value system. Such a system does not permit situational ethics. Rather, it maintains appropriate nonnegotiables with regard to what may be right or wrong in *any* business situation.

Learning to Communicate

Lois M. Jackson

Let me help you better understand who I am by sharing with you in my remarks today some information about my background. I am a product of the Newark public school system. In high school, I was a college preparatory student, took advanced placement courses, and was regarded as bright, popular, and artistic. I was a cheerleader and active in other extracurricular activities as well. I graduated from Glassboro College in 1965 where I majored in history and English. There too, I was very active, involved in such activities as the newspaper and student government.

I have always been very goal-oriented. I have a lot of respect for authority as well. My parents were very hard working, blue-collar workers. My dad was a multidimensional person, "bigger than life" in many ways. He had a number of careers that included owning his own business, working in the coal mines, and working as a mechanic. My parents were also property owners. Above all, they were highly moral and ethical people. They taught me early on that there was a broader existence than the street corner and that I could be whatever I wanted to be in life.

Although neither of my parents had finished high school when I was growing up (my mom has since finished college), they placed a heavy emphasis on college. My goal was to become a doctor, and they encouraged me to pursue that goal throughout my teens. As an only child, I was sheltered and my parents kept me off the streets by sending me to summer school every summer.

I was somewhat aloof as a child. I received good grades and was not easily influenced by my peers. Fortunately, even as a child, I have been a person who is vicariously satisfied. I did not personally have to participate in drugs. It was enough to see others involved in such activities to know to stay

Lois M. Jackson • Manager, External Affairs, IBM World Trade Americas Group, International Business Machines Corporation, North Tarrytown, New York 10591.

away. I have also always been "negatively motivated." That is, if someone told me that I could not do something, my natural response would be, "I'll show you." I was also a kid who parents and teachers fought for. I went to schools outside of my district because my teachers felt I was a good student with considerable potential. The high school that I attended had a 97% Jewish population. This school provided me with the greatest intellectual challenge that I ever experienced. College just served to broaden the knowledge base that I acquired in high school. My experiences there also helped me learn a great deal about the political arena. I had a strong self-concept and was determined not to be defeated. I learned in high school that I could learn and achieve, that no one was better than I was, and not to be intimidated by others.

These lessons have stayed with me throughout my career. I have continued to cultivate my love of learning and have gone on to acquire three advanced degrees. I have maintained my openness to new experiences. I perceive myself as a highly ethical technocrat, an intuitively "right" person, and a perfectionist. In addition to my childhood experiences, I attribute my success in corporate America today to a number of factors. First, there are the skills that I have acquired through my educational and work experiences. Of utmost importance is that I have not ignored basic analytical skills. I think it is necessary to accept as a given right the need for basic skills before one even knocks on the door of corporate America. There have been a number of other skills that have been imperative to my success as well. They include but are not limited to the following:

- The ability to communicate effectively, both orally and in writing
- The ability to appear organized (the more organized an individual is the less pressure he/she imposes upon him-/herself)
- The ability to compete
- The ability to negotiate (always striving to ensure that each encounter is a "win–win" situation)
- The ability to manage and lead in a crisis
- Knowledge of people and organizations (e.g., simple recognition of the difference between an organization chart and a chart of the "power" centers within an organization)
- Being what I call a "quick study" (i.e., quick identification of a problem and who owns it in each encounter)

In addition to these skills, a second factor that has been instrumental to my success is that I have always maintained a willingness to question along with the security and creativity to break with the bonds of "conventional wisdom." I think that it is important to learn early on in one's career that your opinion is as valuable as anyone else's. A third factor invaluable to my success has been learning to receive and deliver criticism. Fourth, senior individuals (call them what you like—godfathers, godmothers, good coaches) have embraced me and taught me the system. Lastly, I have had lots of luck—timing is truly everything.

When I reflect on my career, a number of critical issues that I have had to deal with are very salient. I have had to convince a male-dominated society that I "understand their business" and that I was "tough enough." I also had to find enough time to be an executive, a mother, and a wife. At various points in my career, understanding and accepting my talent/ability and value to the organization has been a challenge. Moreover, the management of my own career has been critical. Though many corporations have executive resource programs, the responsibility does and should belong to the individual. You and your family must make the trade-offs required at each step.

I think that my trek up the management ladder would have been easier if I had had the opportunity to play a competitive sport in my youth. Learning early to be a team player and how to go for the "win" are invaluable skills in business. In addition, role models and networks often help eliminate the valuable time one spends teetering on the boundary of uncertainty. Few of either existed during my early years.

In conclusion and in looking toward the future, I think that there are things that both the academic and business communities can do to make it different for the generations behind us. The university must simulate the business environment and allow its students to practice critical skills. There is little margin for error when your competition is "biting at your heels." The university environment must be competitive and the rules explicit. Taking positions, making decisions, defending decisions and actions, both orally and in writing, should be stressed each classroom hour. This is particularly important for students whose fathers or mothers "didn't carry attache cases." The business community in turn needs to recognize the value of great teachers and coaches in assimilating the next generations into the corporate "family." The business community must also provide each of us with the opportunity to fail. Too often we are insulated from failure, for whatever reasons, and never allowed to grow.

The Value of the Right Coach

William Stubblefield

As managers our success is dependent on our ability to get things done through others. In fact our role as corporate managers is more like that of coaches than quarterbacks or team captains. The coach's ability to do the following are keys to success:

1. Accurately assess the strengths and weaknesses of the members of the team
2. Place individual participants where they can *immediately* capitalize on their strengths
3. Develop the member's skills

In this statement I want to share why I think I have been able to succeed in corporate America. To do so, I want to address two questions: (a) What helped most? and (b) what would have helped?

I opened my remarks by making a statement about managers being coaches. I did that because too many managers have not been trained to be good coaches. In fact, I believe the odds that a bad coach will be encountered are better than 50/50 early in one's career. Unfortunately, when this happens to minority entrants to the junior management pool, there is usually not an "informal" coaching group to offset the negative experiences.

What helped the most for me was that I had three good coaches in succession, coaches who pointed out behaviors of mine that created negative perceptions in others and how I could change to a style of management that was effective but still comfortable for me. Without the input of these coaches I probably would be struggling with my same weaknesses, making the same mistakes, and becoming very frustrated that others whom I perceived to have less talent than I being promoted faster than me. I would be one of the

William Stubblefield • Hilton Head Island, South Carolina 29338.

thousands of talented people in corporate America who are underutilized, confused about what it takes to succeed, and just waiting to escape.

Several other factors have contributed significantly to my successful career advancement. For example, the environments I have experienced, both academic and corporate, have played a critical role in my development. I attended private schools in grammar, high school, and college. As a result, I received a classical education in Latin, math, and English. This formal training in the classics was reinforced informally at home where I was surrounded by Aristotle and Socrates. My educational background was also characterized by a strong foundation in the natural sciences. I have a BS in biology and chemistry from Dubuque University in Iowa where I was a premed student. I can recall that in high school, I never even considered a business career. In continuing my education, I received an MBA from Northwestern University in Evanston, Illinois. My involvement in extracurricular activities was helpful as well. For example, in both high school and college, I was president of the student body and on the debating teams. I also ran track in high school.

My parents were both high-school graduates and put a strong emphasis on education. I was an only child. Both of my parents worked outside the home. My mother worked in the retail business, in sales and sales management. My father held numerous jobs that included working for the railroad, a race track, an insurance company as an agent, and as a waiter. He also had a cleaning business of his own. They raised me to believe that you can be whatever you want to be in life. Any limitations you have, you put on yourself. For example, I can recall one particular incident when after "clearing a hurdle," my father remarked that he was not surprised. He always told me that nothing would stop me but myself.

The corporate environments that I have experienced have played a critical role in my development as an executive. I have always had mentors who have helped me make my own personal style "mesh" or "fit" with the corporate culture with which I was working. Style is critical to successful advancement in most corporations. It refers to the way a person is presenting himself or herself. It includes such things as drive, results, performance, and impact. Mentors can be very useful in helping you learn how to best "package" yourself. Throughout my career, I have always had mentors who were "outside" of the corporation I was working in as well. These "outside" mentors were very useful in helping me wrestle with difficult career choices.

Consistent with this, I have found that networking has also been critical to my success. I have always had a set of supporters inside the corporation and a set outside of the corporation. My involvement in professional organizations has helped to build and foster these networks. These networks are important in building the perception that one can be trusted as a leader. Moreover, at the vice-president level or above in a corporation, one must understand how to get various teams of people to support you. For example, you must know how to get your competitors and people in staff functions who do not report to you in your own company to cooperate with you. Networks can greatly facilitate this process.

I also believe that it is important to ascertain what functional areas are important in your organization and maintain flexibility. My early career experiences were in the functional areas of business, with a strong bias in marketing. Initial assignments were natural building blocks to move up to the top. In order to facilitate this process, one needs only to look over the careers of their organization's CEOs and trace their background over a 15-year period.

On a more personal level, I have always been a very aggressive individual, who is very goal-oriented and has a strong self-concept. One of the obstacles I faced early on in my career was my height. I am only 5'6" tall. American leaders are tall. As I have aged, it has become more of an asset. Shorter people often look younger than they are and more virile. My experiences have also led me to believe that the home life of a senior executive can also have an impact on their promotability. At the higher levels of management, there are many social functions and how well your spouse can move in those circles can be critical to your success.

Now I would like to answer the second question, "What would have helped me in my climb to the top?" For me, what would have helped would have been a clear message from my former employer that my failure would be recognized as being just that, "my failure" as an individual, not the failure of a group. I did not want to fail as a black person, but I wanted to be able to take risks so that I could learn from my individual mistakes. In concluding, I would like to summarize what I see as important directions for corporations that want to enhance minority success in management:

1. Ensure that your managerial high potentials have supervisors who are good coaches.
2. Encourage an open discussion of the areas where improvement is needed for each manager.
3. Do not assume that the challenge to corporations is to identify and recruit exceptional talent; rather, it is to develop each manager.
4. Ensure that the accomplishments and failures of individuals are viewed as individual results.

If this advice were followed, I believe more minority managers would succeed in management positions.

Using Opportunities

Serafin U. Mariel

When I look back over my career, three things particularly stand out. First, I have always worked hard at what I have done. Second, I have always enjoyed the tasks that any job may have required. Third, I have always tried to take advantage of opportunities the various work environments that I have experienced have provided.

My career at Bankers Trust Company (BTCo.) is a good illustration of the latter point. In fact, I credit my progress at BTCo. from teller to vice president to the environment that existed at the company during my 17½ years of employment. Management established a decentralized decision-making process that allowed for the upstreaming of disputed decisions. It was my impression that although performance was recognized, failure was not punished.

Branch managers operated their branches as semifranchises; each lending officer had single-signature lending authority. Shortly after becoming a branch manager I was enrolled at the Stonier Graduate School of Banking. Based on the branch's profitability, I was allowed, with the aid of my staff, to completely redecorate our branch. Subsequently, I was given the opportunity to study the profitability of establishing a branch at the Meat Cooperative Market in the Hunts Point Peninsula. After successfully establishing that branch, I was given responsibility for both that branch and the branch I was already administering. Six months later I was promoted to cluster head with 11 branches reporting to me. Based on a study I initiated, I recommended that 5 of those branches be closed because it did not seem possible to operate them profitably. Four of the branches were closed, and we sold the fifth branch to Citibank.

At that point in my career, I was given the opportunity to transfer to the International Department. Upon my acceptance, I was given a 10-month sab-

Serafin U. Mariel • President, New York National Bank, Bronx, New York 10459.

batical during which I received training in areas that would equip me for a new job assignment. Initially I was managing the Venezuelan desk and subsequently was given responsibility for the North Andean group of countries (Venezuela, Colombia, Ecuador, and the Netherlands Antilles). During this period I was allowed to introduce our cash management products and account reconciliation to this section of the world.

It had been my personal goal that upon reaching the age of 35 I would look at three alternatives: (a) working at another bank; (b) working in the treasury of a large corporation; or (c) establishing my own business. If, after examining these alternatives I rejected them all, I planned to work at Bankers Trust Company for the rest of my career. An examination of these alternatives resulted in my deciding to establish a financial group to deal with the small business market. Our financial group includes a bank (New York National Bank), a venture capital company (TRIAD), and a financial consulting company (FISCO).

When I informed my superiors of my decision to establish this financial group, John Hannon, the then-president of Bankers Trust Company, suggested that I buy one of their branches, which we subsequently did. During my career at Bankers Trust, I had many opportunities to upstream disputed decisions with mixed results. Nevertheless, I got the feeling that my efforts were recognized and impacted upon the company for which I worked. Although I credit the business environment that existed at Bankers Trust Company as the main contributor to my successful career development, I would add that the educational opportunities given to me and the mentors (Michael Gill, William Knowles, and John Hannon) who showed an interest in my career gave me the opportunity to go from teller to vice president.

In reflecting on my career, a number of other factors are worth mentioning. My formal education included graduating from James Monroe High School and attending Hunter College where I was president of the freshman class. As indicated before, I later completed the program at Stonier Graduate School of Banking. Of all of the teachers and professors that I have had, one stands out as being particularly influential, Mrs. Bogner, my eighth-grade teacher. She really cared and involved herself in both the school life and personal life of myself and some of my peers.

With regard to my family background, my sister and I were raised by our grandparents. My grandmother was a very strong person and taught us responsibility from an early age. On Saturday mornings, for example, she gave us chores to do that we had to complete before we could go out with our friends or do the other things that we wanted to do. She would give us money every weekend to go to the movies. If we wanted to see more than one movie, however, we would have to wait until the next weekend or earn the money ourselves. So at a fairly early age, I learned what it means to work for those things that you want in life by taking on odd jobs to earn extra spending money. My grandmother was also a strict disciplinarian. She monitored closely what we were doing and often encouraged us to invite friends home. Most importantly, she continually stressed the importance of education, working hard, and getting ahead.

Buying New York National Bank brought me back to my roots, to the community I was brought up in. This has led, in turn, to my becoming actively involved in the economic development of the community. This involvement has been very motivating for me and has contributed greatly to my success. I have always been good at conceptualizing and financial structuring. My experiences in the local business communities have taught me that I am also very good at dealing with economic development-type issues.

Another factor that has contributed to my success is the fact that I am solution-oriented. That is, I focus on solutions, not problems. I also encourage my employees to be solution-oriented as well. When they are grappling with a problem, I tell them to walk into my office ready to discuss the alternative solutions they have generated to their problem. I am also somewhat pragmatic. In selecting decisions, I try to be realistic and focus on what we can actually accomplish. It may not be the "ideal" solution, but it is generally something that we *can* do.

Another critical factor in my success is the fact that I have always been relationship-oriented. People are important. There are several aspects to this orientation that I feel are worth mentioning. First of all, I believe in helping others. You never know who is going to help you: "Put your bread on water and eventually it may come back to you." I also sincerely rejoice in the success of others. My grandmother helped me learn very early in life how important it is to have humility. You do not need to take credit for everything. Unfortunately, people are generally not willing to be a part of something if they do not see something in it for themselves as individuals. That is, they are transaction-oriented and as a result, fail to build important networks. They do not invest in relationships but rather, focus on what they can get from another person at one point in time. They are not willing to share. To be a successful manager, you must promote leaders and be pleased with the progress that they make.

Second, I believe in looking at every person as a "whole." Everyone can make a contribution in some way. As a manager, one must learn how to capitalize on the unique talents that each individual brings to the work situation. You must learn to accept people for who and what they are and judge them for yourself. You should not rely on what others may have told you about an individual. For example, I see an activist as a gain to the community. Although he or she may have used tactics in the past that I would not feel comfortable with, the fact is that the person has made a substantial contribution in his or her own way to the community. You can't just "throw out" people who have made contributions.

That leads me to a third point. I believe that one can always find something in common with another person. That is, that one must be pragmatic, not emotional, when dealing with other people. This has been particularly true in the work that I have done with various community groups. Very often, I have found that members of these groups have not learned that you can disagree without being disagreeable. They highlight their differences and, by doing so, increase their distance from one another. Groups that appear to be in conflict with one another must focus on what they can do together. That is, we must learn to work together on agendas that we have in common if we are going to be successful. In the work that I have been doing with black and Hispanic business leaders, I have found that when we each put our own agendas on the table, we have found that we share common agendas. The same principles hold true within the context of any organization. We can be much more effective if we learn to work together given the time and resource constraints we must all deal with.

Spiritual and moral standards have also been important to my success. Happiness does not come from where you live and what you own. Such standards provide an anchor, some values to guide one's decision making. Having belief in a Creator is important. It provides some balance in one's life. This can be invaluable, particularly in light of the fact that most of us believe that we are not able to always accomplish as much as we would like.

I think that it is also important to note the importance of a good home life to career success as well. I always tell my employees that they do not work for me. They work for their families and that is why they should strive to do the best job that they possibly can. Home life has played a pivotal role in my own personal success. My wife is ambitious. She has always encouraged me to reach out, to strive for bigger and better things. She has really helped me advance. She has also been a strong source of support in the 25 years that we have been married. We function as a team. It is important to remember that close relationships need attention. Three c's have always been central to our family life: communication, cooperation, and consideration.

In sum, if I were giving advice to people just starting their careers, I would recommend first and foremost that they choose something they like to do, something that they will be happy doing. It is important for young people to take the time to determine what they would really like to do, and that means taking the time to make mistakes. They also need to have long-term objectives, such as the one I set for myself at age 35 when I reevaluated my career. I would also encourage them to go into business for themselves. That is what the capitalist system in this country is all about. However, I would also suggest that they go to work for a large corporation first where they can learn many of the technical and managerial skills they will need in running their own business. I would urge them to be relationship-oriented as well. They should strive to build a network of relationships through the people they meet. And, to always remember how important people can be in getting anything accomplished. Lastly, I think that it is important for them to maintain some spiritual and moral standards.

Learning to Fit In

Hector Juan Montes

To advance, minorities need to learn how to fit in, to assimilate into the power structure, while at the same time maintaining their own identities. Fitting in means to learn all of the external things that set the corporate culture apart from the experiences of many minorities: to learn how to communicate so that when you speak you are as eloquent as they are; to learn how to dress and groom yourself in the way it is expected in the corporate world; to learn how to behave in public, for example, how to order in restaurants and how to project yourself as a corporate leader. These may not be the most important social norms, but they are the things that get noticed first in the corporate world, and your qualifications and skills may not be properly evaluated, if you don't learn to fit in. It's their world, and you have to play by their rules.

Compared to many Hispanics, I had many advantages. Both my parents were educated; my mother attended college for 3 years at the University of Puerto Rico, and my father had earned his master's degree from Columbia University. They insisted on a good education and because I initially planned to become a priest I attended Cathedral Preparatory School in New York City. This provided me with an excellent educational foundation because the Catholic church educates its priests well. My father had an accounting background and managed several factories in Puerto Rico. This further helped make it possible for me to discuss my career plans with my parents. I feel all this guided me into making the correct decision to obtain a degree in economics. Despite all these advantages, I was still a product of the Hispanic community and had to learn about the corporate norms through observation and experience. If I had to do it all over again I would have attended an Ivy League college. Although I earned a degree in economics from Manhattan College and a master's degree from Fordham University, I never attempted to enroll in an Ivy League college and I could have. Had I tried, I would have obtained

Hector Juan Montes • Vice President, Matthews and Wright, Inc., New York, New York 10005.

the necessary contacts to have expanded my present network well beyond its present status.

Assimilation does not come naturally for many minorities. Whether Asian, black, or Hispanic, we often come from family and neighborhood backgrounds where the norms are different. Even those from relatively advantaged backgrounds in the minority community may have learned habits that will make them different in the corporate culture. Acceptable behavior can only be learned—and appreciated—by keen observation. Minorities who want to assimilate into the corporate culture should know that they need to step back, observe, and *learn*.

At the same time, it is very important for minorities in corporations to maintain their own identities as minority people. This means a number of things for minority managers, most important of which is to respect yourself and your heritage. Although it is likely that you will have to change external appearance and behaviors, you *must not* lose contact with your community, that is, the minority community from which you came, and you must not lose your sense of self. In my own career development, I learned two things about maintaining my identity that I feel have been extremely important to my success: (a) I learned to set boundaries from which I will not deviate as I traverse the corporate culture and (b) I learned that the minority community is a resource for my development as a business person. Let me explain both.

Although I feel that I have learned often through painful or frightening experience by not knowing just what to do, how to speak, dress, groom, or behave in public, nevertheless, I use whatever opportunities are available to reinforce my sense of self as a Hispanic. For example, whenever the occasion arises, I speak Spanish. It helps me remember my roots, and it provides a symbol to those around me that I have a heritage that may be distinct from theirs. Obviously, I am careful about the context and the timing of my expressions of self, but because I value my Hispanic heritage, I am not afraid to reinforce it—even in the corporate world and among non-Hispanic managers. Sometimes I also deviate from the norms, but within the limits of corporate propriety. For example, I sometimes wear cowboy boots, instead of wing-tipped shoes. In my career, that verges on the outrageous, but it is still within the bounds of appropriate behavior. It is fitting for me to wear cowboy boots because I travel a great deal to the Southwest. The lesson, for me, is that there are ways that I can reinforce my Hispanic culture through language and my identity by deviating from the norm and that there continues to be a significant contribution for me to make. Yet, at the same time, I have come to understand what the limits of acceptability are in the corporate culture. Actively, I do not try to thwart the corporate culture or to violate its norms, but I can be myself, as a Hispanic, within the corporate world.

The second lesson that I learned about maintaining my identity is that my community can be a business resource for me. Although I happen to be Puerto Rican, I think other minorities—whether black, Asian, Mexican-American, Puerto Rican, or whatever—are all considered the same within the business world. We are minorities in the corporate world and not differentiated by our distinct backgrounds within the minority community. That may be interpreted by some as a form of discrimination, but it also provides an opportunity. This is what minorities in management need to learn. They can help their communities, maintain their sense of self, and yet earn money, by cultivating their contacts.

My career began as a "street banker" at Chemical Bank with my territory being the South Bronx and Harlem. I used this as an opportunity to develop my skills as a banker, help the community, and develop contacts. Later, as assistant vice president and director of community affairs at the Seamen's Bank for Savings, then as director of Minority Financial Services for the State of New York's Department of Commerce, and recently as an investment banker in the Public Finance Department at Bear, Stearns & Co., I have been able to use these contacts to further my career, earn money for my company and myself, and to provide economic resources to my community. In my current position, I deal frequently with blacks and Hispanics in policymaking positions throughout the country, and these experiences have helped me to advance. I can use these experiences only because I have not lost my roots or my identity. And, I can do it without being isolated or classified in the corporate world, because it is directly related to my performance. These are important lessons for minorities who want to succeed in business.

This last point underscores two other things that I have learned in my own career, both of which I think are critically important for all minorities. It is absolutely essential that minorities in management have networks. Most minorities come into the business world without extensive networks and therefore must actively create their own. A network comes from your school friends, those you've trained with, and from those whom you meet on your way up. You must have these networks, use them, and you must develop them yourself. Networks are important not only because they provide "support" for minority managers to help them through difficulties, but in addition, networks are important because they provide contacts to solve those difficulties. They make it easier to get the information that may mean the difference in making critical decisions more quickly, which is a very important resource in business.

To get the most out of networks, you have to know where you want to go with your career. If you don't know what your ultimate career goals are, then you will not know what kinds of networks and contacts you need to develop. This is critically important, because it may be necessary for you to develop the networks you need by changing jobs. This was true in my case. After working at both Chemical Bank and Seaman's, I decided that if I were to make it in investment banking, especially in the kind of investment banking where I could use my contacts in the community, I needed to get public sector experience. I made the decision to leave the position I had at Seaman's to take a position with the State of New York's Department of Commerce for my career, because I knew I wanted to become more involved in public finance within an investment banking house, and I knew that I had to expand my contacts beyond those locally within New York City. The change in position allowed me to expand my networks, develop broader experience, and ultimately to target the position I have now.

As I reflect upon my experience, another important observation is how long it took me to get where I wanted to be at this time, and I assume this is true for other minority managers. This is a result of our inability to learn how to grasp opportunity. This grasping opportunity when it is presented involves two things: (a) knowing what you are worth and using that knowledge to negotiate rewards appropriate to your true worth and (b) recognizing opportunities when they are offered to you. Let me discuss two experiences from my background that illustrates these points.

It took me 7 years to learn the importance of taking risks and of how to recognize and develop opportunities. After a number of years of working at Chemical Bank, I learned of a position and was given the salary range by a friend. I applied for the job, and it was offered to me, but at a lower salary than what I expected. Although it was still more than what I was making, I explained what my understanding about the salary was, asked for that, and much to my surprise got it. For me, this was a real risk, because I wanted the position. But, it was also the means by which I learned that I had something to contribute to the corporate world and that I should demand that I get paid for my skills and experience.

Not only on this occasion but throughout my career, I learned how to recognize opportunities, often by developing my assignments into opportunities. For example, in my first position at Chemical Bank, some might think that being assigned to Harlem and the South Bronx was a limiting experience for me, but I turned it into an opportunity. This has been true of each of the position changes I have made. I never forget that my constituency is the minority community. Although I work and have done very well in the corporate world, I have done so by using my involvement in the minority community to help create business opportunities for myself. I have been able to create business opportunities, and that means making money. I have recognized and created opportunities out of situations that others might have found worthless.

Finally, let me discuss an issue that was important for me to understand as a minority manager. As a minority manager, I feel that first and foremost, I have to understand that there is racism in corporations. This is true because there is racism in society, and corporations are a microcosm of society. But—and this is important—I, too, am a racist, because I am also a product of society. This reciprocal racism could get in the way, and indeed, it often does for many minority and nonminority managers. But it need not, if you remember that your goal in the business world is to get the job done. If you feel secure about your own identity and maintain your roots, you can joke with nonminorities about your background and your differences with them, but when it is time for business, and for respect, then you perform. You can put your own racism aside and find ways to create commonality with others as you need to in order to accomplish the ultimate goal.

In my case, I remember a situation in which I was expected to attend daily lunches with other managers at my level, and I was the only minority. At first, I felt very uncomfortable and soon tried to avoid attending. But, I was told that it was expected of me, so I decided to make the most of it. Although I thought that I did not have much in common with the other managers, I tried to find something we did have in common—in this case, sports—and to use that as a bridge. It may be different in your case, but the important point is to create commonality wherever you can. To a large extent, it is your responsibility, because you are the one who will gain from it, and you may find that those to whom you extend yourself can become your friends and part of your network.

At this point in my career, I feel optimistic. Although I might have done things differently had I the opportunity to do it over, I feel that the lessons I have learned have helped me succeed, and I firmly believe that these are important fundamentals for all minorities in management.

Learning Corporate Culture

Antonio Acevedo

Making it in a corporate environment such as the one in which I work is due to hard work, perserverance, and luck, and it requires that one learn how to function in a corporate culture. To a large extent, I was a product of the inner city. However, I was fortunate to have a supportive family, to live in a mixed neighborhood, and to have become well acquainted with the non-Hispanic world by the time I was an adult. Although I obviously think of myself as culturally Hispanic, while growing up I was influenced in school, in my neighborhood and everyday life by non-Hispanics. If anything, I consider myself a typical New Yorker, with both the advantages and disadvantages that that implies. Contrary to common belief, corporate culture and Anglo culture (nonminority) are not synonymous inasmuch as the differences are socioeconomic, not racial. Thus, being an Anglo may allow one to assimilate more easily, but it does not necessarily facilitate functioning in a corporate environment.

I grew up in a predominantly black and Puerto Rican neighborhood fringed by Irish and Italian sections across an imaginary border. My father is Puerto Rican and my mother Cuban, and I had exposure to the extended family of my grandmother and aunt (on my mother's side). All of my family stressed the importance of education, and I feel that made a big difference in my life. Although my parents were not themselves well educated, they considered it essential for me and were very demanding about grades.

I attended Catholic schools, because my mother felt that the discipline under which they were run would compensate for my surroundings. Catholic schools brought two worlds together, the inner-city minority environment of the neighborhood and the nonminority environment portrayed by the priests and nuns, who were, for the most part, Anglo. Because the schools I attended were mixed with blacks, Puerto Ricans, Irish, and Italians, income level was

Antonio Acevedo • Vice President, Bankers Trust Company, New York, New York 10007.

the common denominator. I was exposed to many different types of backgrounds, but at the same time, there were always enough Hispanics so that maintaining my identity was not a problem.

The strong influence from my family and from the Catholic schools I attended helped me gain a sense of myself. In the inner city, there are strong values to avoid the peer pressure that causes many to become involved in drugs and gangs. They were not part of my background, and for that I consider myself lucky.

I attended Cardinal Hayes High School, also comprised of predominantly low- and middle-income students, but where it was possible to get a good education. For those who could take advantage of it, the school offered courses for which one could get college credit while in high school. On one hand, because of circumstances that existed, I am grateful for the opportunity to attend parochial schools, an affordable means to a sound education.

On the other hand, the tunnel vision of the staff at these schools did not permit me to become aware of the opportunities that existed. The counselor in the Catholic high school directed me only to local Catholic colleges, but then they did that for all the graduates. None of us considered applying to any schools outside of New York because we did not know that world was within our reach. In my own case, because neither of my parents, nor any of my family had attended, applying to college was foreign territory. Looking back, I think my academic record would have qualified me for other schools, but at the time, I did not even consider that an option. Had I been more actively involved in the Hispanic community at that time, I probably would have learned about special opportunities for minority scholarships.

For my undergraduate degree, I chose to go to St. John's, which is located in Queens and provides a very suburban environment where most of the students are Anglo and middle class. Because it was only an extension of my New York City background, I had no trouble fitting in. In fact, I ended up as president of my fraternity, was involved in intramural sports, and felt well integrated into the school. As a psychology major, my target was to eventually proceed into the social services.

By my senior year, I was becoming more involved with the Hispanic community. I worked in the Puerto Rican Community Development Program as a counselor in Bedford-Stuyvesant, a valuable experience in many respects. Through my involvement in the community, I learned about, applied for, and was awarded a scholarship to Columbia University Teachers College, for graduate study in psychology. Although fully intending to start the following September, the business world intrigued me, and I decided to accept a job in banking for 6 months. That temporary detour took place 14 years ago.

From the experiences of my initial job search, through my early years at the bank, and now in my current job, learning to deal with the corporate environment has been an ongoing education. It turned out to be a world apart from my experiences growing up, but it is something that can be learned without changing your basic personality. Those who have been exposed through their family background to the corporate world and to upper-class

Anglo culture obviously begin with an advantage. But those without initial exposure can also learn the behavior and comportment required by the corporate environment. To know that it is a matter of learning already puts you a step ahead. My learning required several years, during which time I made some mistakes. But I also learned my job and learned more about myself as a person.

If I were to identify one thing that would have simplified the learning process for myself and presumably for others, who like myself, did not know much about corporate culture, it would be having someone available to have given me advice. If I could have had someone explain to me along the way what was going on, how to respond, and what steps to have taken, I am sure that the road to my current position would have been smoother. Without such a person, I learned through the "empirical" method of trial and error, and this is not the most efficient way of doing so. But, then, that is the difference between learning about corporate culture around the dinner table at home versus learning it on the job. It can still be accomplished, only with more effort. Let me explain some of my experiences.

The most obvious things come to mind first, so let me just say a word about the proper appearance for the corporate world, that is, how to dress. Like most kids out of college, I had dressed casually for 4 years and had only one suit. When I began interviewing for jobs, I naturally wore that suit, only to be told by the placement officer with whom I was working that maybe I should wear "my other," more appropriate suit for the interview. I had to tell him that this was "my other" suit. I immediately bought another suit, and although it was sufficient for the purpose of interviewing and landing a job, I would probably spend an equivalent amount but not make the same choice today. This may seem like a small or insignificant issue, but talent and training can be overshadowed by appearance and mannerisms when trying to make a good first impression. Because of the emphasis on career training today, more and more students coming out of college know what the conventions of dress are in the corporate world, but they, like me, may still end up standing out, for the wrong reasons.

The second aspect of the corporate culture that comes to mind is social and professional behavior. Intellectual pursuits like the kind of art, music, theater, or food (what to eat and how), which are taken for granted by many corporate managers, all have to be learned. A good example of where this becomes relevant is the obligatory cocktail parties, of which there are many, even early in one's career. Cocktail parties are principally about people exchanging viewpoints on what they have in common. If you want to participate and succeed, you have to have things in common to talk about. My background had not exposed me to the wide range of topics that people in this environment would discuss. Again, it is not that I did not know how to behave. I had been actively involved in my fraternity in college and considered myself well skilled socially, but it is not sufficient just to be pleasant. You also have to share common interests and experiences, and that you can only learn through exposure to the corporate environment.

Another aspect of social and professional behavior that has to be learned is personal interaction, that is, corporate politics. We may all think that we are skilled in political behavior, especially those of us who grew up in a diverse environment like that of New York City, but corporate politics are different from street politics. In a corporation, you have to learn how to sell yourself, while at the same time remaining a team player. If you sell yourself too hard, you may be perceived as disloyal to the corporation or, importantly, the team with which you most immediately work, but if you do not sell yourself enough, you can get lost in the crowd. A sense of balance must be maintained, and understanding how to do that is something that must be learned as part of the corporate culture in which you find yourself.

Finally, as an example of some of the more obvious things one has to learn within a corporation is how to communicate. For me, speech itself was not a problem; after all, I had grown up in a cosmopolitan Anglo world. But the means of corporate communication were not easily familiar to me. In my early career, I was surely not direct enough, not precise enough, and not clear enough in my communication to suit the corporate environment. This was true in both my verbal and written communications. These, again, are things that one learns by observation if it is part of your family life. If that is not the case, then you resort to learning it by observation on the job and through trial and error.

In addition to these more general aspects of corporate culture, one must also learn how to respond to specific situations that arise, especially during the early part of your career. In my case, I feel that I made a major mistake, which may have cost me 2 or 3 years of time before I was able to get back on track toward my career goals. With more experience or a better understanding of corporate hierarchies, I probably would have handled the situation differently. This is what happened.

In an early job assignment, I was working for someone whom I felt was treating me unfairly. In spite of what I thought was above-average performance, I had received poor performance ratings, and I felt it was due to personality differences between myself and my supervisor. Rather than trying to clarify the situation and to come to some mutual understanding, I demanded a transfer, which I ultimately got. My outspokenness was a result of a lack of understanding of the system. My inability to handle the situation in a more professionally acceptable fashion was considered a weakness in my overall performance. Were the same thing to happen today, my feelings would be the same, but my reaction would be entirely different.

I began my career at Bankers Trust in the commercial banking side of the Metropolitan Department. (The bank has since sold the department.) It was a part of the bank into which those without business training could enter and be trained by the bank. Because of my degree in psychology, it was the natural place for me to begin a banking career. Because I was a New Yorker, with lots of city experience, it was a comfortable environment. My first assignment as an account officer was a very fortunate one. Although it was not one of the so-called glamour spots, the branch head took the development of his subordinates very seriously, and I benefited a great deal from his mentorship. He continually prodded us with questions that ensured our knowledge of the business by meeting his demands.

Being in this branch and under those circumstances helped me maintain my sense of self-respect during a time in which I otherwise might have been very insecure. It also provided me the opportunity to learn much more about banking than I might have otherwise learned over a period of years. Even so, I knew early on that I wanted to move into international banking, and that provided another challenge.

Although the Metropolitan Department provided an excellent learning environment, it was considered a less prestigious part of the bank compared to the international side. This was true in most money center banks, but it was especially true during the mid-1970s when revenues from international business soared with the interest rates. To move from the Metropolitan to the International Department was a difficult prospect, at best. However, a perfect fit of commercial experience and fluency in Spanish, during a time when these were being sought, and a better understanding of the system allowed me to accomplish the transition.

Transferring into the International Department was one of the greatest challenges offered me by Bankers Trust. The successful move to a foreign environment, both professionally and geographically, was greatly assisted by a better understanding of how the bank and my new customers functioned. Without my experience, I probably would not have fared as well, but it is unfortunate that it took me years to learn on the job what others learn growing up.

I feel fortunate to work at Bankers Trust in my present capacity. Although a major U.S. bank with all the bureaucracy that that implies, the internal environment promotes professional growth while not violating one's individuality. I have been able to maintain my sense of self, while learning positive things that were not part of my early upbringing. Having to deal with successful Latin American businessmen, I now know that corporate culture has less to do with ethnicity than it does with a professional behavioral norm to which we all try to subscribe. Although I had to learn what for others may be taken for granted, it was possible to do so because I had a supportive family and a sound education. Bankers Trust has challenged me throughout my career and recognized and rewarded my accomplishments. I have learned the importance of understanding the corporate culture. So much so, that I realize the need to continue my education.

Making a Way

Ernest D. Chu

To be successful as a minority person requires a positive attitude. Few minority people can get ahead with a chip on their shoulders. Although this may be true for all people, it is especially true for minorities. They must see the glass as half-full, rather than half-empty. Being positive helps in two specific ways: (a) Other people like you when you have a positive attitude because no one gets ahead without the help of others and (b) you are more likely to find a way to succeed because you will be unwilling to take no for an answer. Both of these outcomes of a positive attitude have been important in my own career.

People liked me because I made it easy for them to do so, and they in turn helped me at critical points. Meeting the right people may be a result of luck or the outcome of networking, but being ready to benefit from meeting them comes from the right attitude. In addition, there were a number of key situations in my life, including obtaining one of my first jobs, where the situation looked hopeless, but I persevered and found a way to turn *no* into *yes*. Call it determination or persistence, but it is an important aspect for getting ahead.

A positive attitude, alone, is not enough for success. You must also be willing to work hard. That means giving 110% all of the time, even to things you do not like, not because you are being paid for it, but because there is personal satisfaction and a commitment to give it your very best effort. Combine hard work with the luck and determination that often come from a positive attitude, and success is likely to follow. Because everybody only has 24 hours in the day, hard work often means sacrifices—if you would rather hang out with friends, watch sports on television, or go away on weekends, then you may not get much work done. Although everyone needs some balance in their lives, too often, work is rationalized away. I have worked many weekends, not because someone was going to see me doing it, but

Ernest D. Chu • Vice President and Chief Financial Officer, HABER, Inc., Towaco, New Jersey 10005.

because I had a personal commitment to getting results and being effective with what I was working on. The extra few hours gave me a chance to get more done during the week and increase my chances of being effective.

The United States is a very competitive place, and everyone who wants to get ahead looks for an edge over others. If you look different—as all minority individuals do—it can be an edge. But it is an edge that can work either for you or against you. Which way it works depends on whether your attitude is positive or negative. I know that I myself am also very competitive. I want to get ahead. I pursue the American dream of my generation. Therefore I work harder than I need to, and most likely harder than those around me. I also am continually looking for ways to get things done, no matter what the obstacles, and I look for ways to network with people who can help me. Success, in my judgment, is measured in absolute, not relative terms. It is not a matter of how good you are for your age, or given your background, or even given the obstacles you've faced; what matters is how good you are, period.

I would like to share with you some things in my growing up and my work experience that have helped to shape this philosophy. But perhaps I should preface this by saying that I've always been aware of being different— being a minority. How could I not be. I'm 5'6" tall in a culture where most men are taller and tallness is associated with authority. I also look and have always looked very young compared to those around me. Although I was born in New York, I used to be frequently asked during my formative years, what country I was from. Because Asians often look alike, I have variously been confused with a Korean musician, a Japanese engineering student, a Chinese maitre d' in a restaurant, being a chemist or technician rather than the senior vice president of finance—all this without opening my mouth.

Early in my business life, I've reached an equilibrium with myself about looking different. I think that most Chinese-American children go through two identity crises, especially in their teenage years. One is the usual one that all teenagers go through. The other is the crisis of realizing that you are different and wanting to look like everyone else—blond, blue-eyed, and six feet tall—rather than what you are. But you are what you are, and I feel every minority person who wants to get ahead has to come to terms with who he or she is. To me, the important part of coming to terms is not to use one's minority status as a crutch or to focus constantly on discrimination. Instead I feel it is important to concentrate on what is positive in your minority culture and to try to use these differences to your advantage, at the same time finding out what you need to do to get ahead despite potentially closed doors. When I walk into a room with a lot of people, I feel it is an advantage. People will remember me because there are generally few other Asians, and being remembered is an important first step in finding the doors to success.

I grew up in an affluent community in Chappaqua, New York, but my family was probably the least well off in the area. It certainly seemed that way to me. My father was an architect, and in the eyes of some, I am sure would be thought of as a success. He was more interested in designing beautiful buildings and did not care much about money. My mother, who held two master's degrees in psychology, did not work outside the house when I was growing up. She was a very frugal person. For example, the family drank powdered milk, rather than having it delivered. We never had a new car. We walked wherever we could, and we wore clothes that were purchased from clothing or church sales. Compared to my friends and classmates, I had to do without many things. The experiences of being a "poor" person in a rich environment gave me a lot of ambition. I knew I did not want to be poor, but I was not sure how I wanted to accomplish my goals.

Asian-Americans of my parents' generation (i.e., the 1940s) faced a lot of discrimination. That we were of Chinese-American ancestry, not Japanese, did not make much difference at that time. Most white, Anglo-Americans do not differentiate one Asian from another. The response to discrimination was a sense of uncertainty, so my parents, like other Asian-Americans, had a strong need for security. They expressed this need to their children by orienting them toward the professions, rather than toward business. They think of the professions, like medicine, law, or engineering, as holding more security than business careers. And they tend, in my judgment, to associate bigness with stability, so they also often directed their children to work for large corporations, as professionals.

I did not want to follow that mold. It helped that my mother supported me in my decision not to enter a professional field. She stressed in her children that they could do anything they wanted, and I am sure that I learned some of my sense of determination from her. By the way, she demonstrated this in her own life by beginning a career outside the home at the age of 52. She said at the time that she could do it, and she did.

Unlike many Chinese-Americans, I had a facility for language, unfortunately balanced off by the fact that I was not particularly good at mathematics or physics. While in college, I majored in English and history. Yet, I am now the chief financial officer in a publicly held company that is based around a major breakthrough in physics. A major part of my job is explaining to outsiders, potential investors and shareholders, and bankers, lawyers, and other corporations what the company is about. How I got from the humanities to business in my career development, I think, is instructive. I would like to think of myself as a good example of what a solid liberal arts background can do for you. Although I did not learn the substance of what I now need to know about business when I was in college, what I did learn was how to learn. I also learned to communicate well. Both have been very instrumental in helping me get to my current position.

I attended Amherst College, a very good, small liberal arts school in Massachusetts. Although my parents helped part way with college expenses, I basically earned a good bit of my way by teaching tennis and then investing some of the money I earned in the stock market. I began teaching tennis while in high school, continued in college, and have since found tennis to be very helpful for meeting people and getting to know them now that I am in business. Tennis provided more than money and exercise for me. It also helped me make friends and contacts that I would not otherwise have made. Early on, I realized that it afforded me the opportunity to meet the parents of my students. It was not that I set out to use it as a means of networking, but as I realized the potential, I used it.

In school, I was not a diligent student. It was not that I was a bad student either, but I could have done much better than I did. Instead, I looked on school as some kind of a game. I now regret I did not use my time more productively, for I now realize that there are many things I could have learned in a classroom, which I had to learn on the job the hard way. What I do not regret about my college experience is that I majored in liberal arts. The communication skills I learned have been invaluable in my career development. They are responsible for my being able to get my first job as a staff writer for the *Wall Street Journal*—in combination with luck and a positive attitude.

My lack of diligence helped me in a way. Through procrastination, I learned to write at the typewriter keyboard. By constantly doing my assignments at the last minute, I found it saved a great deal of time to write them directly on the typewriter (now a word processor). The ability to write off the top of my head, so to speak, not only helped with the *Wall Street Journal* job but has since been useful as well in my career. I find that I can get work done in a fraction of the time by typing it myself rather than going through secretaries. I also have found that the more I write, the better I write. Although I learned good writing and oral communication skills in college, I have also found that over the years as I worked on them, they have improved.

My writing rewarded me in an unexpected way. I had had no idea what I wanted to do with my life in the early years of college, and by my junior year, I was bored with school. But rather than dropping out or giving up, I looked around for an adventure in learning. My decision was to spend my junior year abroad, and I chose to go to India, rather than Europe or Mexico as many other students did. The University of Wisconsin had a program abroad in India, and I was fortunate enough to be selected to be part of it. What an adventure indeed it was: Besides attending Delhi University full-time, I traveled nearly 6,000 miles in India using nearly every conveyance conceivable. I saw poverty and misery as I have never seen before; until my junior year in India, I had never seen anyone die. In India I saw several people die. The adventure of India made me only long for more travel and to see the world in Southeast Asia and the Orient that were foreign to me but part of my heritage. Although my student stipend had ended, I did have a plane ticket. The next few weeks were spent variously living in a monastery in Thailand in exchange for food, sleeping in a mountain climbers' camp in Kathmandu, Nepal, hitchhiking in Cambodia, wandering the streets of Saigon during the war, talking myself into being allowed into the demilitarized zone in Korea, and seeing the Philippines, Japan, Hong Kong, and Taiwan.

My senior year was spent back at Amherst. The *Amherst Student*, a publication that is sent to all students, alumni, and other schools, got me to do a series of articles on my travels that included life in India and my travels in the demilitarized zone in Korea. During the year, one of my tennis partners was the high-school son of the president of the college. Probably because of that connection and the fact that my father was once involved in the design of the college library, I was invited to a dinner at the president's house for a few students and members of the board of trustees a couple of weeks before graduation. Fortuitously, I was seated next to Mrs. Helen Douglas, the wife of Louis Douglas, who was once the ambassador to the Court of St. James (Great Britain). She, by chance, had read my articles in the *Amherst Student* about India and had been fascinated by them. During the evening, she asked what I wanted to do when I finished college. When I told her I wanted to be a writer, she was impressed enough with my sincerity to offer to make some contacts for me. She certainly did: I was able to get interviews with *Look* magazine that contracted me immediately to do a free-lance piece, *Newsweek* magazine, and finally, the *Wall Street Journal* that hired me a couple of months later.

Although the particular events that led to this job were clearly due to luck, they were also due to my readiness to take advantage of the opportunities as they came to me. Although not the most diligent student in college, I, nevertheless, projected the image of someone who worked hard and I did. And as mentioned, I had a positive, sincere attitude that made it easy for people to befriend me and to help me. It is not that my family had connections, but like many Chinese-Americans, they know how to develop and use them. I sometimes think that the Chinese people have raised networking to an art, and in this way my mother helped a great deal. She made a point to introduce me to people from church and from the neighborhood and helped me to understand that although you should not use people, as you develop friendships, if people like you, they will help you. It was also through such connections that I got a summer job at IBM following graduation and before I started at the *Journal*.

I worked for the *Wall Street Journal* for under a year. Although I liked writing, I kept meeting people on Wall Street, who, in my opinion, barely knew the difference between a stock and a bond, and yet were able to make more money in a minute than I was making in a year. My childhood feelings of being poor, I am sure, contributed to my anxiety to get onto Wall Street rather than writing about it. The people I worked for at the *Journal* saw that I really liked the securities business and agreed to help me, but I set up most of the interviews myself. I called everyone I knew or had met through the *Journal* and asked them to whom I should talk at a given firm. I had thought it would be easy to get a job from the *Wall Street Journal,* but everyone I talked to viewed me as a corporate communications person. I wanted a job in marketing, because that was where the money was. Regardless of what was offered, they all wanted me to start in an entry-level position. I always believed that you should leverage your experience and never take a step backwards, so I felt I was ready for a real marketing position, even though I had been out of school only a year.

The firms that attracted me were not the ones where I had contacts. Also my youthful appearance kept getting in the way. One person I interviewed told me to join the Army and get married first, and then come back to look for a job. The firm in which I was most interested was Cogan Berlind and Weill, a small but dynamic firm. Just walking into the place gave me a sense of energy, and I knew that this was where I wanted to start my career. But they did not want me—they had never taken trainees, and I had no experience. My response when I received their rejection letter, though, was not dismay, but anger. So I wrote them a long letter that in effect said, "you are making a mistake in turning me down; here's what I can do for you." It had the effect I wanted. The vice president, who had interviewed me, was so taken aback and in a way impressed by the letter, he called me to come in for another interview, and they hired me.

I was correct about the firm as being a good place to start. It was a high-pressure, fast-moving environment and an excellent place to learn the skills I needed. Through acquisitions and mergers, the firm grew rapidly and is now the core of the second largest securities firm in this country (Shearson–American Express). Two of the original partners are still prominent in the financial community. Sanford Weill is formerly the CEO of Shearson–American Express and Arthur Levitt, Jr., is the chairman of the American Stock Exchange. In addition to learning how to sell while at this firm, I learned two other valuable lessons: (a) that anything is possible if you set your mind to it and (b) that for someone such as myself, a minority person without a business background, I needed an unstructured environment with lots of freedom and room to grow if I wanted to be successful.

I worked for that firm for about 2 years before changing jobs. In each new job, I looked for an environment where I had the opportunity to show what I could do and where I knew I would be judged on results. I realized very early that I would not get ahead in a large corporate Wall Street environment for quite a number of reasons, including my ethnicity. As it turned out, I worked mostly for Jewish firms. Like other groups, Jewish people tend to promote people they can relate to, with whom they are comfortable, and that usually means on Wall Street, other Jewish people. Rather than viewing this as another example of discrimination against me, I tried to turn it around. For example, I knew that many Jewish people are crazy about Chinese food, so I used this to my advantage by taking my colleagues to Chinese restaurants. I would be able to get the head of the firm or key people in the company on "my turf," so to speak, where they would be relaxed and where they might even see me in a different light. The lesson I learned from this experience is that not only must you know what kind of environment in which you can grow, but you must also learn that once you get to a certain level, you need to know that you can control the politics, rather than letting them control you.

But, let me underscore that none of my efforts would have been successful, if I had not learned to communicate well. In a way, I benefited doubly from having to write and speak with facility. There is a negative stereotype of Chinese people, particularly of those who speak with an accent and do not have facility with language. I not only did not fit that mold, but I was also able to use the positive stereotype about Asians being good in math and science to gain a foothold in a financial career, even though my past background had not indicated that this was where my strength was. Because I knew how to learn and to learn quickly and because I had a kind of determination born of hard work and a positive attitude, I was able to do what I needed to do.

I frequently took on projects for which I had limited qualifications, but felt I could do. I enjoyed the challenge of stretching my abilities, and I had an inner optimism that I could succeed. Most of the projects I was given to do were not straightforward—in fact, I was judged more on results than on the time actually spent on the project. The fact of life was that initially a great deal of front-end time and effort had to be spent to get results. But the difference between those who succeed and those who do not may be that those who do do not give up. Is someone uncooperative? Is information not available? Is the situation too hopelessly complex? Even when a project looked hopeless, I learned there was always an alternative—there is never just one way to do something. I put my mind to thinking of a way, and usually there was always another way.

Success, I think, is partly defined by the ability to overcome adversity. It is the unwillingness to fail. After all, people only see the results after you are successful; they do not know and often do not care what obstacles you had to overcome to make it happen. Such determination in my experience comes from a series of small victories. You need to really believe there is always a way to do something and not to take no for an answer. Ideally, an individual should look at this as a personal challenge that can bring out the best, and there is no better sense of satisfaction than the satisfaction of doing something that conventional wisdom says you can't do. Often the major difference between a big victory and a big defeat is getting just one person who wants to say *no* to say *yes.*

In my case, I did not have a career strategy, but I did have relatively short-term goals for myself, goals that I could reach in 3 to 4 years. Then, once I understood where I wanted to go, I would try to focus all my energy and intensity to get there. Along the way I had friends. They were not really *mentors* in the sense in which the term is used today, because it is not that they were particularly interested in helping my career. But as they became friends, they were willing to help me. Having a positive attitude and willingness to work hard reduced the risks that my friends would otherwise have had to take.

Let me summarize my experience in two incidents that I believe illustrate a lot of what I am trying to say. Both have to do with my understanding of my minority status. The first involves my application as a White House Fellow in 1975 under the Ford administration. It was the first time I realized the overt meaning of discrimination against me. I was one of 32 finalists out of several thousand applicants for the 15 or so positions as White House Fellow. The program is used to provide government experience through contact, education, and work to the brightest and most promising people who apply. The interview process alone is quite grueling; the honor is quite prestigous. As a finalist, I was invited along with the other finalists for a weekend of interviews. I gave it my best but was not selected. A subsequent action under the Freedom of Information Act brought by a number of women who were not selected apparently showed I was ranked ninth out of the 32 and should have, according to the program's own criteria, been selected. I later found out, as a result of a *Washington Star* investigation, that the selection committee apparently disregarded all the women and minorities among the finalists when they made their final choices.

My first reaction to this incident was that I should sue under Title VII, but I'm glad I did not. Suing would have turned this into a negative event; instead I chose to do what I think led to a very positive outcome. My decision was, in effect, to get new people to run the program by working for a change of administration, and in the process make people more aware of what happened. I began as a fund raiser for Jimmy Carter, working with the late Howard Samuels. I also worked with an Asian-American caucus group that was working for Carter. Subsequently, I met Dr. Peter Bourne, a special advisor to Governor Carter and the person who would later be responsible for the White House Fellows program. Along with others, I made Bourne aware of what had happened. Over the following 4 years, partly because of my efforts, partly because of the merits of the individuals involved, four Chinese-Americans were selected as White House Fellows, whereas prior to 1975, only one Asian—let alone a Chinese-American—had ever made it to even the regional interviews. Even though I told few people and claimed no credit, I felt a sense of immense satisfaction and vindication, more so than if I had sued.

A final incident helped me to understand something about what it means to look different. I was planning to take a business trip with a fellow with whom I had talked on the phone but had never met. We were to meet at a small waiting room of an airport terminal. I described myself as Chinese-American, 5'6", wearing a dark blue suit, gold-rimmed glasses and carrying a brown attache case. Assured that he would have no trouble recognizing me given the early hour and the deserted waiting room, I was chagrined to see a Japan Airlines Tour Bus pull up and 45 Japanese businessmen fill the terminal—all wearing dark blue suits, glasses, about 5'6", and carrying brown attache cases. To see the expression on my contact's face when he did arrive was something that brings a smile even today. Even though I include this incident among my repertoire of "ethnic" jokes about myself when I give speeches, I did realize that being different is a relative thing, and the term *minority* is what you make it to be.

Accentuating the Positive

Mutsuo Yasumura

All of us are a result of our past experiences, but we have different ways of understanding what that means for our futures. As I reflect on the development of my career, I see two things of special importance: (a) that I know where I am from and what that means and (b) that from my past I know how to turn the negatives into positives. Knowing where I have come from means several things to me. Most of all, it means that I have an obligation to improve upon my past. In the same way that my father's father passed onto my father opportunities that enabled him to go farther and do better than my father's father had done, I have an obligation to pass along to my children opportunities to go farther than I have been able to do. Turning negatives into positives, for a Japanese-American, means to accentuate the positive and to underplay the negative. Japanese people would rather die than show you their weaknesses. I have found that same to be true in my experience. When something goes wrong, I am silent. Often I disappear. But, when something goes right, I have learned that I must make it known to others. That does not mean that I respond only to what happens. Turning negatives into positives also means that I actively try to control my environment so that I have control over what happens to me. I do not merely accept things. I change them when I can so that there is both order and focus where only disorder may have been. Both of these lessons have been important for me to learn and to implement in the development of my career.

I and my 11 brothers and sisters were all born in the United States. When I was a child, the family lived on a farm in southern California. Numbers of Japanese people, including my father, had immigrated to the United States in the late 1800s and early 1900s. At that time Japan was having economic problems, forcing many into a jobless situation. Both North and South Amer-

Mutsuo Yasumura • Senior Vice President, Cato Yasumura Behaeghel, Inc. (a fully owned subsidiary of Young & Rubicam), New York, New York 10017.

ica were viewed by these many Japanese as lands with immense opportunity. My grandfather encouraged my father at the age of 17 to go to California to work for a cousin who owned a clock shop and to start a new life in a new world. My father's immigration to the United States was a fairly simple process, like that of many others who were encouraged by U.S. employers and the need for menial labor. It was not until later that quotas and restrictions began to be placed on their movement and activity in the United States. When jobs in the city became scarce, many Japanese bought farms, sometimes in the names of their U.S.-born children, until land ownership by Japanese people was also restricted. Such was only the beginning of my understanding of discrimination against people of Japanese descent in this country.

Like many other Japanese-Americans, I and my family were relocated when World War II broke out. *Relocation* is a euphemistic term for what really amounted to being sent to prison—or even more accurately, a concentration camp. During the time when Japanese-Americans were being assembled for the camps, we were put in the Santa Anita racetrack, where we lived in stables and slept on the hay. Then, as the war progressed, we were moved to the interior of the United States so that we would pose less of a threat in the eyes of Caucasians. We were sent to Jerome, Arkansas, and while there, lived in a real prison. The government cleared an area of about a mile square in the middle of the forest and built wooden barracks covered with black tar paper. We were then moved to Rohwer, Arkansas, where I and my family lived for the duration of the war. Incidentally, the Jerome Prison Camp then became the location where German prisoners of war were held until the end of the war. The Rohwer camp was organized into 36 blocks, each with a common laundry and bath. Each block had 12 to 14 barracks, and each barrack had about eight apartments. While the rest of the family lived in this prison, three of my older brothers were drafted—as was true of many draft-age Japanese-Americans at the time—and sent to Italy to fight for "our" country. Later I found it strange and ironic that they would come to visit in their American soldier uniforms. Although held behind barbed wire, search lights, machine guns, and U.S. armed sentries, after all, we were all Americans.

Living under such conditions, of course, is the most significant event of my life. It shaped me in many ways, and it is an experience that I cannot forget. I was only about 8 years old when the war began and about 12 or 13 when we were returned to California. During the time in the prison, I regret especially the effect on my education. Although there were schools provided for us in the camps, they were little more than social activities. No learning took place, as I recall. To pass the time, I began to draw and evidently developed my skills enough that drawing became a steppingstone to my career in advertising. Although a fortuitous outcome of a very negative part of my life, who knows what I might have accomplished in a more encouraging environment.

During the war, my family, like others, lost our land, and when we were returned to California, we were not even sent back to the area from which we had been displaced. We ended up in Long Beach, California, living in government-provided trailers because we had no home. Because my family was so large, we had to live in two trailers. Soon after, we were moved into low-income, public housing. By this time, I was in junior high school, but it was not an easy or pleasant experience for me. There was still a lot of discrimination against Japanese-Americans after the war, and almost every day Caucasian children called me and the others names. We were not willing to take such abuse willingly, so we got into many fights. In fact, in today's terms, I may have been considered a juvenile delinquent.

Even at this stage and with the adverse experience of the concentration camp, I was driven toward being a success. Being poor as we were, I wanted so many things, and I knew that my needs would continue to be unsatisfied unless I made money. This became an early and continual goal for me. While still in high school and just after, I worked at Douglas Aircraft Company. My hero during this time was James Dean. He drove a Porsche, and I wanted one too. I was fascinated by the design, as well as the image. Working at the airplane factory enabled me to buy a Porsche, which I purchased with a down payment and then sold a few years later for the same amount I had paid for it. But I learned from this experience that I did not want to work in a factory for the rest of my life and to have to punch a time clock just to prove that I was there. I knew that I had to find another way.

By 1950, my parents were able to move out of public housing into their own house. I was about 17 at the time and was looking forward to having my own front and back yards. Just as it appeared that I might have a normal life, I was drafted into the Army, and in effect, was sent back to camp. I was being sent to fight in Korea, but on the boat on the way over, the war ended. I was, then, stationed in Japan. This was the first time that I had seen so many Japanese people. It was like finding my identity. The circumstances made it a double-edged experience, though. On the one hand, I had a better sense of who I was, but on the other hand, I saw for the first time direct, physical abuse of Japanese people (especially of soldiers toward Japanese women) and the unsettling experience of seeing them begging for food (again, to soldiers on the troop trains moving them around the country).

During my time in Japan, I was able to reunite with my next older brother who had been sent to Japan before the war began to help my maiden aunt on her farm. He had only been about 10 years old when he left and so was not involved in the war. Although it had been over a decade since I had seen him, there was an immediate rapport. During the 20 months that I was in Japan, I was able to travel around and to get to know the country. Although I did not usually wear my uniform when away from the base, my relatives insisted that I wear it because they were proud of my being an American soldier. My unique status as a Japanese man in an American uniform also made me popular with the Japanese people. As might be imagined, the whole experience was significant in my life.

Two other things about my Army experience may be of interest. The first is that I was able to use my drawing skills to carve out a special role for myself in the Army. In a sense, I became an Army "artist," which gave me special privileges. Seeing my art as a means of making a living, I am sure, contributed to my decision to pursue a career where I could use these skills. The second incident, I think, shows my sense of determination to make a way. Army officers were looking for a translator, and although I actually spoke very little Japanese, I was able to speak enough to become an interpreter.

When I returned to the United States after my tour of duty, my primary concern was to find a way to get an education. I married and worked nights in the airplane factory, while attending Chouinard Art Institute in Los Angeles on the GI bill. My mother, especially, thought that I had made a mistake in my career choice. All of my brothers worked in factories, and that was her image of a safe and secure life-style. Not only was I in art school, but I also had grown a beard, something that Japanese men did not do. She was so concerned about being shamed before the neighbors, that I could only visit late at night, when no one was likely to see me.

I finished school by about 1960. One of my teachers encouraged me to go to New York, of which I knew nothing. But, I looked upon the journey as similar to my father moving from Japan to the United States, which for him was about as exotic as if he had been asked to go to the moon. I knew I had to be just as adventuresome, so I made the move. My first job was with Young & Rubicam, where I have stayed throughout my career. I was hired as an art director at a salary of $80 a week. Although against company policy, I also did free-lance work on the side to gain experience and to earn extra money. I was in a hurry to get the experience I needed and then to return to California, so I felt I could not afford to take my time to get experience in the usual way.

I chose advertising for a career because I knew I could make money at it, and making money was important because of the insecurity of my upbringing. Jobs were easy to come by at this time, and to a large extent, the timing was right for me. These were the years of Kennedy and King and the Beatles. The Beatles helped loosen up society. Kennedy focused attention on "the people." And King brought Kennedy's message to minorities. Suddenly, I was part of this thing called "people." Even the style of clothing had changed. Just prior to my joining Young & Rubicam, everyone in advertising wore dark business suits and white shirts, but soon after, a more artsy style was adopted, especially for people on the creative side.

Early in my career I learned that there were only two ways to get ahead: (a) one could socialize, drink, and politic and (b) one could win awards. I did not drink and did not feel comfortable socializing, so I decided that if I were to get ahead, I needed to win awards. I set out to do this in a very deliberate way, and I have been successful. Throughout my career, I have won over 100 awards. I feel that this has made a major difference in my career, as well as in my salary.

I approached winning awards as I have approached many things in my life. I decided that I needed to figure out what everyone else knew and then discover something in addition, something that would set my work apart from theirs. After analyzing the situation, I came up with a strategy. It was clear to me that the bigger the account one worked on that the more money one could make. But, there was also a downside to this fact, namely that there was also a great deal of competition for the largest accounts. I decided instead to go after the accounts that no one else seemed to want. These were smaller accounts, nonprofit or public sector accounts (like the Red Cross or the Peace Corps), and trade association accounts. Because there was less competition for accounts such as these, it meant that I had much more freedom to do with the accounts what I wanted. My work on these accounts led to awards. To my surprise, not only was I rewarded for winning awards, I was given large bonuses just for being in the shows.

As I gained experience and worked on the "less desirable" accounts, I also carved out for myself a somewhat unique role within advertising. I was both an art director and a designer. Most people in the field are either one or the other. This gave me both flexibility and broad experience and made me more valuable to the company. It was not enough, however, to be talented and to win awards. I also learned early on that Madison Avenue (i.e., the advertising business) is a big business. It is bigger than the movies, and as such, it is filled with a lot of politics. A second lesson that I learned and learned quickly was that to get ahead I was going to have to change myself. Again, my decision came about following a strategic analysis of the situation around me.

Advertising is populated by Caucasians, mostly Anglo-Saxons, some Jewish people, and some Italians. When I started, I think that I was one of the only minorities, and I do not remember seeing any blacks. Each of the different ethnic groups socialized among themselves and had their own way of doing things. As a minority, I realized that there was no way for me to fit in unless I changed myself, so I set out to make myself over. First, I made a point of trying to get to know the peculiarities of each group, although I spent most of my time with Jewish people, some time with Italians, and the least amount of time with Anglo-Saxons. With each, I tried to have lunch with them and to get to know them. As I got to know more about their different cultures, I noticed distinct differences. A good example is in the way they presented their work to others. Jewish people would show their work and say, "Isn't this terrific." Italian people would show their work and say, "What do you think?" But Anglo-Saxon people would tend not to show their work at all until it was finished because they did not seem to want any criticism. I made myself a conglomerate of what I thought was useful. When I show my work, I say, "Isn't this terrific. What do you think?"

In addition to learning how to interact, I also changed my style of dress so that I would look more like the Caucasians. I also learned how to socialize, even though it was difficult for me to do so. I would force myself to go into someone's office and talk with them. This was a big step for me, not only because of my natural shyness, but also, I suspect, because with my inadequate education, I was never sure that I knew how to talk with people. Over time I learned how to make it work and how to get rewarded in the process. I did not change companies in my career because I was always challenged with new opportunities in a company that was developing into the leader in the advertising industry. I was smart to stay where I knew and respected the corporate leaders. As I won more awards, I felt more respected and appreciated within the company. I am now a stockholder, a design director, a principal, and a senior vice president, and at a fortuitous time, I helped start a new wholly owned packaging and corporate identity design subsidiary of Young & Rubicam Inc. Originally called 285 Design Division, the name changed to Yasumura & Associates in 1975 and then to Cato Yasumura Behaeghel (CYB) Inc. in 1981 when it became a worldwide design company.

Despite my success, the road was not always smooth. There have been many incidents along the way where my minority status was quite evident to me and where my success was challenged because of it. One of the earliest and most poignant examples was after I won a gold medal for design, which in advertising is like winning an Academy Award. It is the highest award one can win in the field. A Caucasian fellow in the firm tried to take the award away from me by claiming that the idea was really his. Having learned from my childhood how to stand up for my rights, I did so in this case, and I won. I was able to establish that the idea was indeed mine, but it left an understandably bad impression on me. It showed me again that Caucasians seem to think that if you are a minority that you can be taken advantage of.

On another occasion I found out that someone within the corporation whom I had thought of as a good friend was trying to get me fired. My first reaction was to quit. I was so upset about the situation that I went to California for a week just to collect my thoughts and to rest. Instead of quitting, I decided to return and to challenge his motivations. By researching the situation, I discovered his vulnerabilities and found my own strengths. It was not too long after this confrontation that he was asked to leave the company.

A similar situation occurred several years later. Another art director/designer was to be hired at Young & Rubicam. Because this is a rare combination in advertising, the fellow represented a threat to my own status. Soon after he was hired, I caught him trying to steal one of my ideas. When I went to his office and confronted him, he simply apologized. This was another lesson to me. Here this fellow was doing the unthinkable, and yet he could get away with it just by apologizing. I did learn the lesson that apologies work, but this man was never again considered a friend, nor did his name ever leave my blacklist. He also was asked to leave the company several years later.

All of this may sound quite severe and cutthroat, but to me the advertising business is like that. There is a great deal of competition over ideas, titles, and power. Often people who would have been friends try to do each other in, and the only way to survive is to fight back. As a minority, I think that I have experienced this in a different way than if I had been a Caucasian. Perhaps people would not have been so blatant. They would have been more careful in their challenge to me and would have shown more respect. I believe that they were surprised that I was willing to challenge them, but they were also quite surprised that I was able, with time, to win.

The key to success, in my opinion, for a minority person is to be concerned with every little thing. Every job should be important, because minorities cannot afford to separate the big from the small jobs. I firmly believe that if you pay attention to each thing, then you will be way ahead of the others in the game. At the same time, balance is extremely important for a minority person, because minorities start the game off balance. You have to decide what is important to you and be willing to spend the time, the many hours at work, to accomplish what you want to do. A single person only has so much energy, so you have to make decisions at the outset. It is also the case that time is not really a factor when you are trying to establish your reputation. If you pay attention to the details, the accomplishments will follow. In other words, the behaviors that are necessary for getting the job done will come naturally to you. This does not mean that you should have only short-term goals. On the contrary, for proper balance you need to know where you are going, as well as from whence you came.

If I had to point to one factor that has contributed to my success, I would say that it is my focus on turning negatives into positives. At times, there seemed to be insurmountable barriers, but through determination, I found a way to overcome them. I have made a point to keep the advantages out front and to downplay the negatives. To do so, of course, I have to be very aware of what my positive qualities are. Also important is that I have done my homework. If others worked 8 hours, I would work 16. At least in the early days, I had to because I needed to experience as much in as short a time as possible. It is not just the number of hours, though, but rather what you produce for your time. I have tried assiduously to maximize my efforts. The only way to do that is to be able to see what others do not see, to figure out what others know, and then go beyond that. What perhaps has made the difference between myself and many other Asian-Americans is that I really wanted to get out of the ghetto. I had a dream. You have to.

Preparing for Responsibility

Ming Hsu

I was born in Peking, China, and during my early years lived through war between Japan and China and then World War II. Because of the wars, I moved a lot as a child and lived in many places in China and throughout Southeast Asia. At the time, I resented the constant moving and the hardships of the war years, but now I realize what a personal opportunity it was for me to learn and to experience new people, places, and events. I was educated in American, British, and Chinese schools in China, Singapore, and Hong Kong, as well as other places. My father was a high government official in the nationalist government of China, and as a consequence of his connections, I was able to meet foreign diplomats and correspondents at a very young age. Through these years, I was able to develop both my interests and my consciousness about foreign affairs.

Although it was not easy growing up under the circumstances of war and insecurity, it helped shape my character in an important way. Despite the hardships, as I look back, I can say that I was never really discouraged. On the contrary, I developed an optimism that has carried through in my life and in the development of my career. Doing something constructive with my life became the most important goal for me. As I realized from the hardships around me that there is so much to be done in this world, I decided that one must overcome difficulties if possible and use opportunities that are available to you. Through these experiences, I see myself as a survivor. That has made the difference in my life—to survive and to survive well.

Despite the disruptions of the war years, I managed to graduate from high school. At the age of 19, I left China via India to attend college in the United States. My parents had always planned for me to come to the United States to attend school. My father had been educated at Cambridge Univer-

Ming Hsu • Director, New Jersey State Division of International Trade, Newark, New Jersey 07102.

sity in England, and my mother attended Gunston Hall, an elite finishing school and junior college in Washington, DC. I began my college education at Barnard College in New York, but because of my interest in foreign affairs, I finished my undergraduate education at George Washington University's School of Government in Washington, DC, with a BA in foreign affairs. I was then awarded a Penfield Fellowship in International Affairs at New York University, where I finished all of the requirements for a PhD except the dissertation.

My career goals at the time were to attend law school and then to work in the public sector, but this route was barred to me. I was not only a minority, an immigrant, and a noncitizen, but under the immigration laws at the time, there was no way for me to become a citizen, and hence, no way for me to practice law. Even though the Exclusionary Act, which said that no person of the "yellow race" could be naturalized as a citizen, had been repealed, there were still very restrictive quotas for Chinese to gain permanent residence in the United States. To even apply for permanent residence, I would have had to leave the United States, make the application, and then wait, maybe 15 to 20 years, maybe even a lifetime, before I could be readmitted, given the limited quotas. In the meantime, I was in the United States on a student visa, which did not allow me to work, and I had to be reviewed every 6 months by the Immigration and Naturalization Service. In effect, I risked deportation every 6 months. At the same time, I could not return to the land where I had grown up, because the revolution in China in 1949 closed off that option to me as well. I, therefore, had no sense of permanence about my situation, and for years, faced a great deal of uncertainty. Despite my interest in public affairs, when I was finally granted permission to work in the United States, I had no choice but to go into the private sector. My first job was with NBC in the research and planning department, during which time I did some of the early sales promotion for innovative television programs. I had not given up my goal of working in foreign affairs. I tried at one point to get into NBC's news department. With my background and experience, I thought it was a natural alternative for me to consider journalism, but at the time, there were no women at all in NBC news. My chance to pursue my interests in international affairs came when I was asked to do a presentation to top management at NBC on the potential for developing international markets. Following a successful presentation, I made my real interests known. Because there was no prospect at the time for NBC to develop an international department, it was suggested that I try to transfer to the parent company, RCA.

After 5 years at NBC, I did move to RCA into the International Division. The transition was made through the organizational development departments in both NBC and RCA, which in itself was a milestone, because no other women had advanced in the company through organizational development at the time. Such career development programs were reserved for men. I worked as an analyst in the International Division of RCA for over a decade. This was an extremely frustrating time for me because of the limitations placed on my advancement, again because of my status as a minority, a woman, and a noncitizen. I firmly believe that RCA was no different than any other company would have been in this regard. The International Division was primarily a manufacturing, engineering-oriented operation. Most definitely, it was an inhospitable place for a woman.

During my years in the International Division, I would say that I experienced every kind of problem you can think of because I was not a white male. As I look around me now, I see how much improved the situation is for minorities and women in corporations. There are still many barriers, of course, especially to top management positions, but even more so, in the 1950s and 1960s, it was a constant struggle. I also assume that my situation was made more difficult because I was one of the few women at the time who never left the labor force. I certainly was one of the few Asian women to do so. I am sure that for those women who quit their jobs to raise children and then reentered the labor force in the 1970s, they found a very different situation from what I had faced in the prior two decades. I am surprised now when I talk to young MBA students, both minorities and women, that some of them do not realize how much the social movements of the last few decades have done for them. When I hear young women, for example, say that the women's movement has done nothing for them, I want to tell them how wrong they are.

For example, I was the only professional woman in my department, and frequently, I was treated as if I were a secretary. Most obvious in this respect was that I was continually asked to punch a time clock, although no professional men in the division were asked to do so. At first I was told that it was because I did not deal with outside people. When I informed them that indeed I did, I received a temporary reprieve, but every time I changed positions, I had to go through the same irritation all over again. I was also told when I asked for raises that they had no one with whom to compare me, although surely RCA had other analysts in other divisions. Even so, they always saw me as different from the others.

Another example of the limitations placed upon me occurred when I applied for a David Sarnoff Fellowship. This was an award, which paid salary and tuition to enable the employee to get an MBA, given to promising employees. Although two men from my division were awarded the fellowships and were sent to Harvard to obtain their MBA degrees, I was told that I was ineligible for the fellowship because it was company policy not to include women in the program. I tried to argue that whatever the reasoning behind the policy, it did not apply to me. I told them that I did not intend to have more children, that my husband was not likely to get transferred, and that I had already shown my loyalty by working for the company for over a decade, but all to no avail. It was simply not company policy to invest in the career development of women.

During those years with the International Division, there were frequent layoffs, cutbacks, and reorganizations. I went through at least four of them, as I remember. Probably three of those four times, following the reorganization, I was given a job that had previously been done by a man—or even two men—but I was never given either the title or the salary to go with it. The final straw came for me when I was told that despite my excellent work record, I would probably be let go, because I was the "second breadwinner" in my family. I was angry enough at the time to make a complaint to the personnel department. This was about 1964, the same year I finally became an American citizen. Even though the legislation to protect women was not in place, the company was concerned enough to relent on the decision to lay me off. Again, I do not presume that RCA was any different from any other company in their treatment of women and minorities at the time. As legislation and times changed in the country, I was given opportunities to advance.

Although those were difficult times for me, as I look back, I see an important lesson. I was often angry at the circumstances in which I found myself but never to the point of allowing it to hinder my effectiveness. I feel strongly that people must speak out if they feel they are being treated unfairly, but they must do so in a way that does not upset themselves. Women, especially, cannot afford the luxury of becoming irrational in their anger. One of the things that may help is to remember that what counts is the outcome, namely your success in achieving your goals.

The opportunity I had been waiting for came in 1969 when I was transferred from the International Division to the corporate staff. This is also, of course, when things began to change for working women in the country as a whole. I was made manager of market research, then later promoted to director of international marketing. The really big hurdle, though, was the promotion, which I eventually received, to vice president for international trade relations. At RCA, the difference between a director and a vice president is the difference between middle and upper management. It was then, and still is, an extremely difficult barrier for women and minorities to cross.

One of the things that I am sure made the difference for me in my climb up the corporate ladder is the broad experience I was able to obtain off the job as well as on. It is not enough just to be good at what you do. To reach top management, you need to be a well-rounded person.

Neither women nor minorities, I think, have understood this important aspect to a corporate career. Instead, they often think that doing a good job is all that will be necessary. It is not. No matter what your area, if you are just the best in your field, the most you can hope for is to be the head of your particular department or area. It is not enough, though, to help you reach top management. Too often, women and minorities stay among themselves and do not force themselves to mix. This is a career mistake. The good news, though, is that if you have not done so already, you can start now to develop the kind of experience you need for a top-level position. In my case, I did not become active in community and civic affairs until I was in my mid-40s. It was then that I had both the time and the money to do so.

We often think that we do not have time to do volunteer work on top of our jobs and our family life. But this is what white men do. They are involved with the Junior Chamber of Commerce, with sports, in churches, and so on. It is a way to learn, to build confidence, to gain connections and constituencies, as well as to broaden your horizons. It is a means to constant learning. I also feel that it is a responsibility. Women and minorities must do the same. Although each of us has to choose when we want to be involved, I feel strongly that if we understood how important and worthwhile such involvement is, we would find the time. It cannot be done overnight. It takes time to develop experience and confidence.

In my experience, I first became involved with a local civic club. Then I got involved, both locally and nationally, with the Republican party. I worked on broadening the base of the party and opening doors to new constituents. I spoke with various ethnic groups and women's groups about the need to be involved with politics. I was fortunate enough to have worked with three distinguished men and one woman when they served as Chairman of the Republican National Committee. They are Senator Robert Dole, Vice-President George Bush, Secretary of Labor Bill Brock, and Mary Louise Smith of Iowa. In addition, I was appointed by President Ford as a commissioner for the National Commission on the Observance of the International Women's Year. In addition to my involvement in public affairs and politics, I have also been active in the arts, and I have traveled widely.

I left RCA in 1982 to become New Jersey Governor Thomas H. Kean's special trade representative and director of the Division of International Trade for the State of New Jersey. I now work with different constituencies and have the satisfaction of doing something that may make some impact on people's lives.

As a woman, a nonwhite, and foreign-born, I had few role models. In a sense, I was my own mentor in my career development. The experience I gained, especially off the job, was invaluable, and it translated directly and indirectly to gains on the job. Without the barriers and restrictions that I faced, I feel that I could have accomplished more and more quickly. The important lesson, though, is that even with such barriers, my optimism and sense of purpose led to favorable results, for myself, and hopefully, for others.

11

Corporate Programs for Ensuring Minority Advancement

Since the early 1960s, many organizations have invested a considerable amount of resources in programs to support their equal employment opportunity policies and objectives. As a result of their efforts, many have made progress in hiring minorities. Unfortunately, as the statistics point out, minorities are still sorely underrepresented in the upper ranks of most businesses. In many organizations, the turnover rate is higher for minorities. When exit interviews are conducted, they often cite a lack of opportunity for advancement as the major cause for their leaving. Suits are currently being filed by some minority individuals charging that they have been systematically denied raises, assignments, and promotions because they are minorities. Poor job assignments are often cited as preventing them from getting the opportunities to develop the skills or acquire the experience they will need for higher level management jobs. Others believe that different norms or criteria are used in their performance reviews or that changes are made in the number or variety of positions open when they become eligible for promotion.

Success is always relative, and some companies have made more progress than others. Most of those that have been more successful have launched systematic programs that begin to address their basic human resource policies and corporate culture. This section contains a series of corporate statements describing programs that they believe have contributed to their success in promoting minorities to middle- and upper-level management positions. These programs illustrate the types of interventions that have been associated with more significant progress in integrating women and minorities into higher levels of management.

These companies should be commended for coming forth and allowing their programs to be described in print. Because of potential legal ramifications, many organizations are reluctant to put anything in writing or talk publicly about their organizational policies and programs. What is more important is that they should be commended for their commitment to the issue. The depth and strength of their commitment can be seen in the amount of time and resources they have allocated to ensure that their objectives can be realized. It can also be seen in the fact that many of their programs have begun to challenge the traditional organizational structures and policies that represent hurdles and barriers to advancement. By no means do they represent "the solutions." These companies themselves are the first to point out or emphasize that their program is not the "answer" or the "panacea" or a "final step" in our search for change. But they do represent beginning major steps and foundations on which to build. They have demonstrated a willingness to critically examine what they themselves have been doing to hinder the upward mobility of minorities in their organizations. They have also designed systematic interventions that are company-specific, internal, and in many cases based on an ongoing collection of data that is used as the basis for future planning and implementation of new programs. These subchapters are offered to readers as descriptions of programs in practice and are not intended to be read as research reports.

All of the companies included in this section were asked to provide some background information about their organization, to describe a program, policy, or practice that they felt had been particularly successful and to discuss what their future efforts might be for ensuring the advancement of minorities into their highest levels of management. Each of these contributing organizations chose to respond in their own way with some highlighting one key program and others describing almost all of their organization's past and current efforts to ensure equal employment opportunity. It is surprising that, given the mandate, few, if any, discussed the future in much detail. All, however, saw continuing organizational commitment and support for the types of programs they described. Of the programs described here, those by McNeil Pharmaceutical, Allied-Signal, Exxon, and Xerox were prepared for presentation at the conference.

A summary of these corporate policies and practices in this section can be seen in Table 1. As one can see, the contributing companies are large organizations, representing a wide range of industries. Most of their programs for ensuring the success of minorities in management can be grouped into the five categories of top management support and involvement, management accountability, recruiting, training and other human resource management programs, and external relations. It is important to note that the descriptions detailed here may not represent the total picture of any one organization's programs. As indicated before, each of the companies was asked to discuss some aspect of their organization's efforts that they felt was either unique or had been particularly successful.

In reading these corporate summaries, one is impressed by the uniqueness of their efforts. To illustrate, Johnson & Johnson has a series of programs that all underscore a strong emphasis on education. Merck's program stands out as being one of the most comprehensive training efforts in affirmative action wherein every individual employee participates and is responsible. IBM and Bank of America both have a very impressive array of external

Table 1. Summary of Corporate Programs Discussed in Chapter Eleven

Company	Number of employees	Business	Programs
Allied-Signal, Inc.	144,000	Diversified manufacturer; aerospace, automotive, electronics, instrumentation, & engineered materials	Voluntary internal audits of EEO/Affirmative Action programs Black Orientation Management Seminar Women's Career Conference Accomplishment of equal opportunity goals tied to incentive compensation for senior managers Support and endorsement of chairman & executive committee
AT&T	118,000	Long distance telecommunications	Series of workshops: Managing a Diverse Work Force, Race Issue in the Workplace, Gender Issues in the Workplace Strong commitment from top management
Bank of America	70,000	Financial services and products to consumers, corporations, & institutions	Goal setting and computerized monitoring system Employee development programs Management guidance Accountability; incentives or bonuses tied to the achievement of goals Communication system, internships, college recruitment practices Leader in projects designed to keep and increase a steady flow of minorities in business Top management oversight, interest, involvement, and support BankAmerica Foundation, in-kind services, lending practices, and employee efforts support job-training, child care, community service and other activities.
Exxon Research and Engineering Company (an affiliate of Exxon Corporation)			Affirmative Action Advisory Committee Training Programs: Workshops on Leadership in a Diverse Work Environment for middle- and upper-level managers (each 10 hours in length) Support and personal involvement of top management

(*continued*)

Table 1.   (*Continued*)

Company	Number of employees	Business	Programs
IBM, Inc.	400,000	Information processing system, equipment, and services	Faculty Loan Program Community Service Assignment Program Ongoing involvement in external activities: partnerships with government, education, community-service, and cultural organizations; also assists individual Employee efforts by contributing funds, equipment and sometimes the full-time service of employees themselves Management accountability for support of equal opportunity programs and objectives Specialized education and on-the-job training Support and endorsement of senior management
McNeil Pharmaceutical (an affiliate company of Johnson & Johnson)	77,400	Health care	College recruitment Recruit top-notch blacks for middle management positions Realistic career development plans for high potential blacks from middle management Performance appraisal designed to ensure perceptions of fairness Internship programs for minorities and females; job placement particularly in engineering and the sciences Scholarships, summer training programs for MBA minority students Financial support for qualified black candidates pursuing academic work toward graduate degrees in science Support for other educational programs geared toward accelerating the development of minorities in the business community; strong support from top management
Merck & Company	31,000	Pharmaceutical company,	Comprehensive study of company's climate and needs in af-

Table 1. *(Continued)*

Company	Number of employees	Business	Programs
		develops and manufactures products to improve human health, animal health, and environmental health	firmative action Manager's set goals for affirmative action and are held accountable All employees share in responsibility for affirmative action Training programs designed to assist minorities and women in skill development and provide training for managers in skills related to EEO Personnel policies are designed to provide equal opportunity: recruitment, placement, promotion, training & development, appraisal & counseling and compensation Comprehensive training program for Merck managers, supervisors, union representatives, and all Merck employees in the United States Chairperson a very strong, outspoken advocate of equal opportunity
Xerox	100,000	Office automation, information systems	Black Values in the American Work Force Step-Up program (Blacks recruited, trained, and placed in Xerox jobs) Project Booster (establish relationships between field marketing people and members of the black community for sales, technical, and clerical positions)

relations programs in addition to their systematic and programmatic internal efforts. Xerox has begun to grapple with the difficult implications of stereotypes, beliefs, and value systems. AT&T's workshops recognize the diversity of its work force and the impact good interpersonal relations can have on the bottom line. Exxon recognizes that the issues and problems faced by employees from each of the various minority groups represented in its work force are different and places a strong emphasis on how to deal with this diversity in their training programs for their middle- and upper-level managers. Lastly, Allied-Signal stands out for the compensation system it has designed that links the accomplishment of equal opportunity goals to inventive compensation for its senior managers.

There are also a number of general observations that can be made from these statements that underscore some commonalities among these organizations. First, they share some organizational characteristics, namely size and age. All of the organizations are fairly large and have been around for quite some time. Size has traditionally been associated with greater affirmative action compliance. Older, more established companies often have more systematic human resource programs for their employees. The same can often be said for larger organizations as well. They are also highly visible and open to more scrutiny by both the government and the general public. As a result, they tend to be more concerned about their employees as well as civic or community responsibilities.

A second observation is that these companies operate in rapidly changing environments. In recent years, many of them have undergone rapid growth often by diversifying into new businesses through acquisition and mergers. Operating in such fast-paced, dynamic environments naturally produces changes in the nature of the business itself that in turn raises new and different issues of concern for their minority populations. For example, Johnson & Johnson found that a declining representation of blacks were grossly underrepresented. The job mix in J&J companies has now shifted toward the specialist; it had been dominated by generalists. The company has also found that there is lower black representation in the technical majors that would qualify candidates for the jobs that are currently being generated by these changes. Modernization and other business realities have forced older facilities to be closed that were often located in areas where black candidates were more available.

A third characteristic these organizations share is their philosophy of human resource management. Many of them stressed that their equal employment opportunity programs are embedded in a long-standing commitment on the part of their organization to their employees. That is, people are seen as a valuable resource, critical to the productivity of the organization. Allied-Signal Inc., for example, believes that one of its major assets is its people. Full utilization of all its employees is viewed as the most desirable and economically sound way to manage its businesses. Bank of America cites a 1928 statement by the organization's founder, Amadeo Peter Gianni, that addresses equal employment opportunity: "We have made the road to promotion an open one, along which every employee should seek to advance." Similarly, Johnson & Johnson cites a document, *Our Credo*, written by Robert Wood Johnson during the 1940s that contains phrases emphasizing respect for individual dignity, the importance of recognizing merit, and mentions equal opportunity for employment and development. Exxon Research and Engineering Company states that its most recent affirmative action efforts are based on the business objectives of designing a work environment conducive to maximizing the productivity of its work force. And the newly reorganized AT&T points out that survival and growth during the remainder of the 1980s and into the 1990s requires that companies produce more goods and/or services with less expense—which means fewer people. The company views its human resources as critical to its vitality. Consequently, it places a heavy emphasis on team work and intergroup networks and alliances because people will be depending on each other to produce more in order to achieve business goals in the future.

Another commonality of interest is the fact that many of these companies have used some sort of a participative model in the planning and implementation of their programs. That is, they have sought to *actively involve* their employees. Most of the organizations have used employee surveys or interviews on a continuing basis over the years in order to assess the perceptions of their employee populations with regard to equal employment opportunity, to ascertain what problems exist, to try to understand the causes of problems they may have already identified, or to solicit recommendations for actions that needed to be taken.

Some organizations have chosen to create a more formalized mechanism whereby employees play a critical role in the actual execution of their policies or programs. For example, Exxon Research and Engineering Company established an Affirmative Action Advisory Committee that is made up of senior management of the company. The committee was charged with ensuring the full utilization, retention, and upward mobility of the company's women and minorities as well as the ongoing efforts of the company in compliance, outreach, and recruiting. One of the actions taken by this committee was to develop and institute an ongoing training endeavor for all middle- and upper-level managers that uses eight "resource people" representing Asian, Hispanic, black, and white female employees of the company in each course. Merck saw the active involvement of employees as being critical to its success and used line managers instead of professional trainers in its comprehensive affirmative action training program. AT&T also uses employees as facilitators in their workshops. Johnson & Johnson used a team of senior black managers to help them examine its ability to recruit, promote, and retain black managers.

Sometimes, this emphasis on participation reaches outside the organization. For example, Xerox sponsored a workshop in which 15 Human Resource, Equal Employment Opportunity, Affirmative Action, and Employee Relations managers from *Fortune* 100 corporations addressed the issue of how to integrate blacks into the middle and senior management ranks. Bank of America's numerous programs with the communities it serves underscore a strong commitment toward collective work as do the several projects that involve relationships with a variety of colleges, universities, and other educational organizations. Similarly, through their faculty loan program, IBM employees work with academic faculties to improve the education of disadvantaged students. The company's Community Service Assignment Program also allows some of their employees to serve full time on the staffs of non-profit, community-based organizations.

The types of programs and policies that many of these organizations have launched are very similar. All of them have instituted some type of training program. Most of them have designed programs that use their employees as facilitators or trainers and invest a considerable amount of time and resources in training them for this role. These programs have generally been developed for managers or all employees regardless of their race. In the statements that were prepared for this volume, there were fewer programs directed at the minority individuals themselves. An example of one program is the one conducted annually by Allied-Signal in the 1970s, which was an intensive 3-day conference at which recently hired minority college graduates received a comprehensive orientation to the company. Senior managers participated as guest speakers, and the topics discussed included corporate culture, organizational structure, and the company's business objectives.

The exact nature of the training programs tends to differ as does whether employee participation is voluntary or involuntary. Most of them have been tailored to address the specific needs of their particular organization. Most of them have determined these needs by maintaining ongoing systems for collecting data from their employees and from the organization's performance records in order to determine how well each organization is meeting its equal employment opportunity goals.

Merck's three-phase training program was designed to reach every Merck employee in the United States. Participation in the program is mandatory. The program is designed to elicit active employee involvement. The three workshops developed by AT&T are designed to provide new, positive experiences for their employees that discourage the stereotypes of women, minorities, handicapped individuals, and others, who are perceived to *differ* in some way that is considered to be the norm. Based on the data gathered by their advisory committee, Exxon Research and Engineering Company developed an ongoing training program for their middle- and upper-level managers to increase their knowledge, understanding, and skills for functioning effectively as leaders in a diverse work environment. As in the other companies, the program was tailored specifically to the needs of the company.

The necessity of having top management endorsement and support for their programs was another critical component in all of our participating companies. This was seen as *essential* if equal employment opportunity and affirmative action were to be viewed as an integral part of their company's business philosophy. In some of the organizations this support has led to managers being held accountable for the achievement of their organization's equal employment opportunity goals. For example, at Allied-Signal Inc., the incentive compensation for senior managers is tied to the accomplishment of goals set in the annual action plans of these managers for the hiring and promotion of minorities and women into significant executive-level positions. In other organizations, like Merck, all managers are required to set goals for affirmative action and are formally measured on their results. It is believed that management plays a pivotal role in assuring true affirmative action and that equal employment opportunity policy must be totally integrated into managers' daily decision making and tasks. Bank of America shares this orientation. About 30% of a manager's compensation is based on how well he or she has met goals concerning equal opportunity, affirmative action, and other areas of people management. The incentive system for senior management is also contingent upon their achievements in these areas. The company has developed an institutional support system to aid managers in their attainment of their goals. This support includes a computerized system that provides them with data regarding progress toward the goals that have been set, the availability of minorities and women, and other supporting information to help them achieve their goals.

Taken together, the set of programs, policies, and practices in this section represent a significant step forward in the achievement of corporate goals to ensure the success of minorities in management. All of these organizations should be commended for the commitment they have demonstrated over the years through their continually evolving, systematic programs and efforts. They serve as models for the business community at large, demonstrating the benefits that can accrue when companies treat *all* of their people as invaluable resources. We wish to thank them once again for their openness and willingness to share their efforts in writing. Hopefully, other organizations can learn from their experiences and use their programs as building blocks for future programs.

Shifting Markets, Shifting Structures

Gail Judge

Johnson & Johnson, employing approximately 77,400 people worldwide, is engaged in the manufacture and sale of a broad range of products in the health care and other fields in many countries. The company's primary interest, both historically and currently, has been in products related to health and well-being. Total revenues at year-end 1983 were $6.1 billion.

The company is organized on the principles of decentralized management and conducts its business through operating subsidiaries that are themselves, for the most part, integral, autonomous operations. In the United States, there are 22 operating subsidiaries. Approximately one-half of the 77.4 thousand employees are working in the United States.

The thread that weaves through this multicompanied corporation is a document called *Our Credo*, which was written by Robert Wood Johnson during the 1940s and which contains the principles upon which all of our businesses are based. We are proud that this document includes phrases that mention equal opportunity for employment and development—considering everyone as an individual—respecting dignity and recognizing merit. These words of *Our Credo* establish solidly the fact that equal opportunity and affirmative action are integral parts of our company's business philosophy.

As we move from philosophy to the practical application of these tenents, it is important to state that we are pleased with our affirmative action achievements. By year-end 1983, females constituted 26.3% of the exempt work force and minorities represented 12.7%. Also, 12.8% of management-level positions were held by women and 9.3% of those in management were minority group people.

While our decentralized structure presents the opportunity for each operating company to demonstrate creative and innovative leadership in imple-

Gail Judge • Vice President, Personnel, McNeil Pharmaceutical (an affiliate company of Johnson & Johnson), Springhouse, Pennsylvania 19477.

menting our commitment to equal opportunity, it also creates problems in that there is no corporate or centralized office that promulgates goals and holds the subsidiaries responsible to achieve their fair share. It is up to each subsidiary to set its own goals in keeping with its unique business circumstances, resource availability, employment needs, and competitive environment. In order to understand our successes and disappointments with regard to the integration of minorities into Johnson & Johnson, it is necessary to keep decentralization as a focal point in our considerations.

Having said that we have made significant progress in integrating females and minorities into our organizations, let me state that our present focus is on bringing these people up to the highest levels of management, many of which already have achieved lower and middle management ranks.

During the past 4 years, we have been concerned about our record in retaining and promoting our black managers. Until 1979, we were trending positively, then we plateaued and our growth became static. Our ability to recruit, promote, and retain black exempt employees became the subject of serious management concern.

Approximately 2 years ago a group of senior black managers formed a corporate committee to help the corporation probe the black managerial situation. They made recommendations, the corporation listened, and we have worked hand in hand in the activities that followed.

Two important studies were embarked upon between February and July of 1984:

1. An independent consulting firm was engaged to conduct an interpretive analysis of retention and turnover of black managers. A random sample of current and former black and white managers was selected. Archival data, questionnaires and semistructured interviews were collected and conducted.
2. The second study was a comparative analysis of individual Johnson & Johnson companies from 1976–1983. This study was intended to look carefully at what had happened in each of the Johnson & Johnson companies to contribute to the decline in the growth of black management.

We approached the problem through both perceptual and factual avenues in an effort to thoroughly diagnose and address the issues at work. We knew that we had to deal with not only the empirical data but also with the interpretations or perceptions of that data if we were to make progress.

What follows now is an example of some of our findings:
On the level of *perceptions:*

- Both current and former black and white employees found J & J a good place to work with competent top management and excellent benefits.
- Both black and white managers had some concerns with the career counseling they receive from their supervisors, although J & J received high grades as a place for gaining valuable work experience.

- Black managers, both current and former, felt that they faced greater difficulty in obtaining sponsorship and establishing social contacts because of race.
- Black managers and departed white managers question the fairness of the performance appraisal system.
- A number of former black managers listed favoritism in opportunity as one of the reasons they left the company.

On the level of *factual analysis* of individual companies:

- Corporate statistics, which had been trending positively, became diluted when new high-technology companies were acquired, companies whose representation of blacks was grossly under the traditional level for J & J companies.
- There has been a dramatic change in the job mix of J & J companies. Whereas there was a domination by generalists, there is now a shift toward the specialist.
- This movement, coupled with recent college graduate trends and perhaps the recruitment effort of other companies, has made it more difficult to increase or maintain black exempt involvement. In addition, there is a lower black representation in the technical majors that would support candidacy in the jobs we are generating.
- Modernization and other business neccesities have required the closing of older facilities in geographical areas where historically large numbers of black candidates have been available.

We conclude from both of these studies that the perceptions of our black managers with regard to declining black representation are valid, but the changes that have occurred result from the changing nature of our business rather than from a lessened commitment to equal opportunity for all our employees.

As a result of these studies, several approaches have already been taken to address our black exempt situation. We recognize that the perceptions exist in the minds of our black employees, and we will address those perceptions by communicating what we have learned to be the facts. Additionally, each company has been given a list of recommendations to implement as they see fit to provide better management development practices, two-way communication systems, and whatever conditions that our studies have highlighted as needing improvement—the companies have been given the tools and procedures to put into practice what we have learned.

Several task forces have been formed to address *college recruitment*, including special emphasis on scientists, *mechanisms to ensure implementation of the performance appraisal system* and *addressing the negative perceptions of fairness of the human resource systems*. These task forces will be responsible to probe these topics in an effort to determine how the corporation can utilize these vehicles to better equip our environment to enhance both the hiring and development of black employees with an objective of integrating our top management.

The things that we learned from our studies that need to be done include:

1. Steadfastly to recruit a percentage of top black students off the campuses. No matter what the business circumstances are, we must bring in every year enough blacks to provide a reservoir of talent for development for the future.
2. Identify those high-potential blacks from middle management who could be promoted to affiliate management boards within a short period of time and prepare realistic plans for their career development.
3. In spite of our promotion from-within policy, recruit top-notch blacks for middle manager positions to provide role models for lower level blacks to emulate.
4. Each company would examine its own unique needs and develop goals and programs that make sense for them as opposed to being pressured to behave uniformly regardless of circumstances.
5. Continue to support affirmative action programs such as the following, which have proven to help us attract outstanding minority employees:
   • Intern Programs in cooperation with colleges and universities to help accelerate minority and female job placement particularly in the areas most difficult to find: engineering and the sciences.
   • J & J Leadership Awards Program that provides full scholarships to minority students who are pursuing master's degrees in business administration. This program offers summer training positions in addition to scholarships.
   • Encourage programs to fund qualified black candidates with financial support for academic work toward graduate degrees in the sciences.
   • Continue to support other educational programs geared toward accelerating the development of minorities in the business community.

In conclusion, we recognize the growing challenge we at J&J have in attracting and keeping qualified blacks and other minorities whose availability in the disciplines we need is severely limited. We can put our best recruiters to work and hope that they will be successful in bringing back to us the best that's out there. But, where the real challenge is, industry needs the help of academia. How can we, working together, improve the education of young blacks—very young, in the early grades so that when they become college age they will be able to pursue the kind of higher education that will prepare them for today and tomorrow's industry needs? That's where the real progress needs to be made.

An Affirmation Action Advisory Committee

Robert A. Hofstader

In this paper, I will focus on an upward mobility project undertaken at the Exxon Research and Engineering Company, an affiliate of Exxon Corporation. My comments will include an overview of actions, activities, and programs at the Exxon Research and Engineering Company.

In 1981, the president of Exxon Research and Engineering Company (ER&E) established what is now called the Affirmative Action Advisory Committee (AAAC). This committee is made up of senior management of the company. In addition to ensuring the ongoing efforts of the company in compliance, outreach, and recruiting, this committee assumed the additional responsibility to pay attention to the full utilization, retention, and upward mobility of the company's women and minorities. It is important to note that this endeavor was not due to outside governmental or societal pressures; instead, it was a design based on long-standing business objectives of effecting a work environment conducive to the fullest productivity of the company's human resources.

Critical to this charter was the initiation of a research project to determine the factors that contributed to upward progress at the company. The first step in conducting the research was to survey a representative sample of the entire population of employees by conducting individual interviews with Asian, black, Hispanic, white female, and white male employees. Over 300 employees responded to the following:

1. Questions relating to their expectations, factors that helped and factors that hindered success, performance and career development systems, role models, and informal networks. Although the results from the interviews

Robert A. Hofstader • Manager, Education and Development Unit, Exxon Research and Engineering Company, Florham Park, New Jersey 07932.

were analyzed on a number of dimensions, several common factors became immediately apparent for all ER&E work sites. These factors, along with the overriding elements of professional and technical competence, became the framework and guideline for addressing issues correlating with success and upward mobility in our work culture.

2. The factors perceived by the employees as impacting success were:

- Projects and assignments—particularly relating to their significance, clarity, and timing
- Communication—both written and oral, as well as the opportunity to communicate on important topics
- Visibility and exposure
- Recognition—including the method of performance feedback, promotions, and career development
- Mentorship/sponsorship—including the relationships that provided knowledge of the organization and opportunities
- Social and political interactions—including both formal and informal support groups.

As mentioned before, the factors perceived as impacting success were identified as a result of a survey of all employees; however, various ethnic groups saw some factors as more important than white employees. There was divergence among ethnic groups as well. For example, black employees saw mentorship/sponsorship as a key factor critical to success, whereas the Asian employees were more concerned with communication skills. Also important here is that ethnic groups and women perceived specific bias and barriers in the systems; white males saw few or none. They perceived the environment as neutral and noninhibiting and expressed surprise at the minorities' and women's perception of bias. In addition, they believed that factors identified by the ethnic groups and women as important to success were available to anyone who wished to pursue opportunities for advancement.

Feedback of the data to the Advisory Committee resulted in further action on the part of the committee that took the form of meeting with representatives of each group by racial/ethnic and gender background. The intent of these sessions was to further understand and clarify the data.

Following these sessions, the committee met for the purpose of deepening its knowledge and sensitivity to possible individual and systematic barriers in the ER&E work environments that adversely affect its minority and female employees. The decision was then taken to disseminate the research findings to all employees and to follow this effort with decisions on specific action interventions. With the research and the data feedback to the organization complete, the committee turned its focus to action. One of several actions taken by the AAAC was to develop and institute an ongoing training endeavor for all middle- and upper-level managers tailored specifically to the needs of the company and based firmly on all previous data gathered.

3. The main objectives of a training effort known as Leadership in a Diverse Work Environment (LDWE) were:

- Increase supervisory knowledge and understanding of ER&E's affirmative action efforts and management's committment to those efforts
- Increase understanding of the factors relating to success and careers in ER&R
- Increase the awareness of the dynamics of cultural and gender diversity in ER&E work locations
- Identify supervisory actions that enhance full human resource utilization throughout the ER&E work environment.

4. In addition to these objectives, several other criteria, decisions, and considerations emerged for the development team:

- The workshop would have the personal involvement of ER&E's top management.
- The climate of the workshop would be one of learning and exploration as opposed to either a didactic or punishing event.
- The learning experience would include "resource people" who would dialogue with course participants and would serve as representatives of gender and racial/ethnic groups included in the research.
- Research and findings from the original interviews plus the additional dialogues of specific groups with the Advisory Committee members would be consolidated and presented to participants in the form of ER&E case studies
- Multiple learning methods would be used in the training effort (films, large- and small-group discussions, individual development of learning and possible supervisory actions, and tasks focused on the consideration of systemic organizational change and supports necessary to make it successful).
- The workshops would be ER&E-specific and based on internal data as opposed to external training packages irrelevant to the ER&E corporate culture
- All of the workshops would be focused, concentrated, and 10 hours in length
- The design of the workshop would be structured in a way that provided opportunities for additional data gathering and provided input for additional activities.

Three pilot programs were run for managers. Course size was 17 to 20 participants each and included members of the Advisory Committee and 8 "resource people" representing Asian, Hispanic, black and white, and female employees of the company.

Following the overwhelming success of the pilot programs, LDWE was reviewed for slight design changes, and the decision was made to operationalize the program.

To date, over 90% of ER&E's middle- and upper-level managers have experienced Leadership in a Diverse Work Environment. All participants and resource people have contributed on an ongoing basis to the development of recommendations and actions for future activities for Exxon Research and Engineering Company. These contributions, in the form of organizational actions and supports, have been heard throughout, and in person, by the members of the AAAC.

In conclusion, it would be both misleading and inaccurate to look at LDWE as either a panacea or a final step in ensuring the fuller utilization of all of ER&E's employees through deeper understanding of cultural and gender awareness. It is, however, a beginning major step toward augmenting the possibilities for retention, utilization, and upward mobility of ER&E's minority and female employees through increased awareness on the parts of the managers and the overall ER&E employee body. It provided us with a foundation on which to build.

It is finally essential to reiterate that LDWE and actions beyond are a result of continuing research, diagnosis, and implementation. The willingness of the company to critically examine its own culture and develop actions and activities that are internal, company-specific, and based on ongoing collection of data has been a key to the extension of the company's developmental endeavors.

Executive Accountability

Wilbert S. Crump

Allied-Signal Inc., with its worldwide headquarters in Morris Township, New Jersey, is a diversified manufacturer serving a broad spectrum of industries through more than 40 businesses.

A "blue chip" company, and one of the 30 companies included in the Dow Jones Industrial Average, Allied-Signal is one of the nation's 30 largest industrial organizations. In 1985, sales totaled $9.1 billion, and the corporation had some 144,000 employees in more than 600 locations in over 30 countries.

Although Allied-Signal has always recognized the need to grow and change with the times, no period in the company's history has been as fast-paced or dynamic as the past 6 years. The corporation diversified into new businesses through multimillion-dollar acquisitions, more than tripled its sales, expanded its technological capabilities and became a major multinational organization. (Allied Corporation merged with the Signal Companies in September, 1985).

Today Allied-Signal's businesses are grouped into four principal sectors: Aerospace, Automotive, Electronics and Instrumentation, and Engineered Materials.

The businesses of the Aerospace Sector provide highly specialized, sophisticated systems, subsystems, and components for military and civil aircraft, as well as for air traffic control, missiles and spacecraft, military land vehicles, and antisubmarine warfare.

The Electronics and Instrumentation Sector is a market leader in audio-video recording systems, laser-based typesetting equipment, and electronic and fiber-optic interconnect systems for the computer industry.

The Automotive Sector is one of the world's largest independent sup-

Wilbert S. Crump • Director, Equal Employment Opportunity, Allied-Signal Inc., Morristown, New Jersey 07960-2245.

pliers of automotive components and systems, brakes, filters, and spark plugs.

In Engineered Materials, Allied-Signal is an important manufacturer of circuit board laminates, specialty printing inks, and proprietary catalysts and processes for the petrochemical and other industries. The sector includes high-growth potential businesses in superstrength fibers, engineered plastics, and amorphous metal alloys.

Allied-Signal also has an interest in the oil and gas industry through 50% ownership of Union Texas Petroleum, one of the nation's largest and most successful independent oil and gas companies.

As this brief summary of the corporation's business interests suggests, Allied-Signal is an aggressive manager of its multibillion dollar assets, constantly seeking to maximize the return on its shareholders' investments. It should be stressed, however, that Allied-Signal also recognizes the fact that one of its major assets is its people. Indeed, an integral and driving part of the corporation's management philosophy is the belief that the maximum utilization of the full potential of all its human resources (and that certainly includes the approximately 20% minorities and 30% women in the company's total work force) encompasses more than the "legal" or "morally" right thing to do. Rather, the company believes that full utilization of all its people is quite simply the most desirable and economically sound way to manage its businesses.

Consequently, the subject, ensuring minority success in business, which implicitly suggests the concepts of equal employment opportunity and affirmative action, is not new to the corporation. For example, during the early 1960s, Allied-Signal joined several other companies in subscribing to the government-sponsored Plans for Progress Program. Plans for Progress was initiated by the Kennedy administration and was a voluntary commitment on the part of those corporations who signed the pledge to affirmatively recruit, train, and promote blacks and other minorities. This commitment was made by Allied-Signal and others before the passage of the Civil Rights Act of 1964. Although there was no federal enforcement to the program, the company, nevertheless, implemented an internal auditing system to measure its success in meeting its pledge. The results of these monitoring efforts reflected a steady increase in the hiring of minorities into the various EEO job categories.

Over the years, the corporation has continued its commitment by annually planning and introducing comprehensive and progressive Equal Employment Opportunity programs. Thus, in the early 1970s when minorities and women were first entering industry in significant numbers, the company recognized that to facilitate their full utilization at all levels of management and to give them a chance at success equal to the chances of the traditionally white male-dominated work force, new programs had to be designed. This proved to be a formidable (and at times costly) challenge to many corporations that became the targets of major civil rights suits during the 1970s for their alleged discrimination in the hiring and promoting of minorities and women.

As the testimony in many of these early lawsuits reveals, particularly those alleging failure to promote, employers uniformly maintained that minorities and women were not being discriminated against but rather they were not experienced enough or lacked the overall management skills necessary to successfully compete for higher level positions. At the same time, minorities and women uniformly argued that employers either excluded them from developmental programs that would provide them with the requisite skills, or they did not "affirmatively" go about establishing or implementing programs and support systems that would enhance their chances of competing successfully.

Hence, at Allied-Signal the objective and challenge was not only to hire more, but to capitalize on the existing talent of the many minorities and women already in the company's work force. The first step in this process was a careful review of the affirmative action plans (AAPs) of all the company's facilities. To ensure that the review of these AAPs was done in as thorough and professional a manner as possible, the company attempted to parallel, internally, the kind of rigorous EEO and affirmative action audits that are conducted by the Office of Federal Contract Compliance Programs (OFCCP)—the federal agency mandated to ensure compliance with EEO regulations on the part of government contractor and subcontractor firms. To accomplish this, the corporation took the then rather unique step of requesting technical assistance from OFCCP officials in the form of training four company human resources professionals in the process of conducting full-scale audits of the corporation's EEO and affirmative action programs. Once these personnel were trained, the EEO department began scheduling a series of "mock" compliance audits of select company facilities with 50 or more employees. The company's EEO director, along with one or more of the newly trained human resources professionals, would then proceed to coordinate and conduct a full-scale affirmative action audit of the facility as would be done by the OFCCP. Specifically, these audits included such close scrutiny as reviewing the facility's applicant flow data by race and sex; interviewing employees and supervisory management; examining salary and compensation practices; and, analyzing hiring and promotion rates by job categories. Not only were broad EEO job categories examined to determine if minorities and women were either underrepresented or underutilized, but specific job family groups (e.g., accountants I, accountants II, senior accountants, and accounting managers) were examined as well.

Upon completion of these audits, the appropriate management of the facility was notified of the audit team's findings. This step involved a discussion of any deficiencies that were identified during the audit, along with "recommended remedial actions" to correct them. The facility was then given the choice of either adopting the audit team's recommendations or providing alternative solutions that would serve the same purpose of correcting any cited deficiencies. Although these compliance audits proved to be useful in a number of ways, they were especially invaluable in that they not only afforded the corporation an opportunity to underscore its commitment to EEO by implementing a series of innovative, proactive affirmative action measures but also resulted in ensuring that the company's facilities were in compliance.

Ensuring minority success in corporate management, however, goes beyond conducting audits or having the "right numbers" of minorities and women based upon their availability in each of the government-defined EEO job categories or groupings. It also involves orienting, developing, and providing minorities and women with support systems that will truly enhance their chances to successfully compete with their peers. To this end, in the 1970s, Allied-Signal piloted and annually conducted a Black Orientation Management Seminar, which was fully endorsed and supported by the senior management in the company.

The seminar was an intensive 3-day conference at which recently hired minority college graduates received a comprehensive orientation to the company, including its business objectives, organizational structure, and corporate culture. The conference included case studies in which the participants were required to provide solutions to problems, which were then evaluated by senior managers responsible for the given function or area about which the case was written. Moreover, to accomodate participants who might choose a line (operations) career path versus a staff career path, a special point was made to include hypothetical case studies involving solutions to both line and staff problems. Senior managers also participated as guest speakers to underscore the company's genuine commitment and support of the objectives of the program, and minority managers who had achieved significant managerial level positions within the company participated by sharing experiences and responding to questions, thereby serving both as realistic role models and as informal mentors.

Conference participants were required to prepare an in-depth assessment of their professional qualifications, strengths and weaknesses, and short- and long-range career aspirations. Through the "real world" problem solving required by the conference, combined with an assessment of their own abilities, the participants were confronted with what was required to maximize their full potential in the corporation in terms of what they needed to do to get where they wanted to go.

During the 4 years in which the Black Orientation Seminar was run, it was considered successful. Even today the corporation can see the progress of some of those managers who participated in the seminars as they advance in their careers with the company. The only less than positive comments received from the participants were that some would have liked to have had even more time to work on problem-solving cases and to hear more from line and staff managers working in their particular discipline.

At about the same time the Black Orientation Seminar was inaugurated, the company developed and introduced the Women's Career Conference. This seminar, which was also an intensive 3-day conference, was designed to help secretarial and clerical women assess their growth potential for more responsible professional or managerial positions. Participants were given the opportunity to have an in-depth assessment of their abilities and potential.

They were also made aware of the availability of the company's tuition reimbursement programs for additional education, as well as in-house training programs. Women managers in the company participated in the conference to serve as role models, and members of senior management also demonstrated their support of this program by serving as guest speakers. More importantly, about 30% of the first 120 women to participate in the program were subsequently promoted from nonexempt jobs into professional or managerial positions. Today the program is now available to all nonexempt employees, including men.

Throughout most of the 1970s, both of these programs proved to be extremely valuable. They helped assure the attendees that Allied-Signal was sensitive to their concerns and problems. More importantly, these programs also revealed to the attendees what management expected of them as they moved up the corporate ladder and provided assurance that the company and its resources would be there to assist them along the way.

As the 1980s arrived, it became apparent that the corporation would have to refocus its efforts if it were to continue to provide minorities and women with assistance to ensure their success. The objective now was to accelerate their entry into middle- and more senior-level positions. To accomplish this objective, it was decided that bolder initiatives would be necessary. Consequently, in 1980 the chairman and his executive committee adopted a proposal wherein the hiring and promoting of minorities and women into significant-level executive positions would be incorporated into the annual action plans of senior managers eligible for incentive compensation. In effect, this program ties incentive compensation to the accomplishment of equal opportunity goals. One of the unique features of this program is that it goes beyond the achievement of government-mandated EEO requirements.

One of the major challenges of putting this program together was the need to devise an equitable system of allocating annual EEO goals for each sector and organizational unit. Determination was first made of the overall goal for the company, and then each unit or sector head was assigned specific goals according to the proportion of such positions in that organizational unit. For example, if the company were to decide that its overall goal or objective was to promote an additional 100 minorities and women into higher-level jobs and if a given unit controlled 20% of such jobs in the company, then that unit would be held accountable for hiring or promoting 20 additional women and minorities.

Senior management accountability for meeting affirmative action goals is a dramatic and, to date, successful approach to increasing the utilization of women and minorities in both line and staff positions at senior levels. Since its inception, minorities and women in senior executive positions have increased from slightly more than 30 to an excess of 150. The full endorsement of the chairman and his executive committee has had the desired effect of generating the necessary support from managers at other levels. At this point, the concept of accountability for EEO objectives has been embraced by all levels of the company's management. Moreover, the positive outcome of the program is that not only has the corporation increased its utilization of minorities and women in higher level positions, but those promoted as a result of the program, with very few exceptions, have so far proved to be very effective managers. As conceived, the program, therefore is not just about meeting numerical goals, but rather it is about providing the training and development necessary to make effective managers out of promising minority and women employees.

Allied-Signal is pleased and encouraged by the results of its various EEO programs, convinced that it is the appropriate direction for the 1980s. The corporation, however, equally looks forward to a time when seminars and efforts to ensure minority success in business are no longer needed, a time when all people, regardless of race or sex can truly aspire to and achieve their full potential in corporate America. Given the many changes in any large corporation, however, one of the questions that is currently being addressed is where to go from here. With the acquisitions and divestitures undertaken by the company in the last few years, some modifications will undoubtedly be needed to assure that the company continues to attract and retain human resources talent possessing the skills and expertise needed to effectively manage the new composition and businesses of the company. In any event, Allied-Signal is equally committed that affirmative action goals and objectives will continue to be part of its staffing philosophy.

Black Cultural Orientation
Management Mobility and Productivity

John L. Jones

Xerox is one of the giants in the office information industry, a multinational enterprise of some 100,000 people. With the first plain paper copier, Xerox launched an industry and embarked on growth course unequalled in business history.

Today, Xerox is a leading supplier of equipment to automate the office. The company offers a broad line of office products and systems that create, reproduce, distribute, store, and retrieve information. Xerox high-tech products and services are helping the offices of the world manage their information more easily and effectively.

To achieve business objectives in its rapidly changing environment, Xerox has instituted a process where its people are required to be creative, problem-solving individuals who are willing to work as members of teams. Through recognition and reward schemes, groups of employees are recognized for their ability to collectively solve problems. A challenge Xerox has (as does other companies) is to insure the inclusion of all employees' productive energies into the team framework.

Xerox takes pride in the fact that it is a benchmark company in Affirmative Action. The company has a very high percentage of minorities and females at all levels of the corporation. Over the years, the corporation has continually demonstrated its commitment to hire, retain and develop blacks, other minorities, and females. Xerox began in 1966 with the "Step-Up" Program, which hired 13 "unemployable" blacks into permanent nonmanagement positions. Later, with the collaboration of the National Alliance of Business, the program was expanded, and 250 to 300 blacks were recruited,

John L. Jones • Director, Personnel, Americas Operations, Xerox Corporation, Stamford, Connecticut 06904.

trained, and placed in Xerox jobs. Another expansion effort of the Step-Up Program led to the development of Project Booster, a program that sought to establish a relationship between field marketing people and members of the black community for sales, technical, and clerical positions. Today the percentage representation of minority males at the senior management level is among the highest, if not the highest, of the *Fortune* 100 corporations.

I. THE CHALLENGE

A challenge faced by Xerox and other progressive companies is that of successfully promoting and integrating a larger number of blacks, women, and other minorities into the middle and upper management ranks. Often minorities and women in their movement up the corporate ladder believe they reach an invisible wall that restricts their gaining upper management positions. At this level, movements are not necessarily based on one's technical ability, because it is assumed that he or she is capable of doing the job. Instead, a key criterion is the chemistry factor, that is, one's ability to fit into the team or mold. Being faced with barriers to further upward mobility, many blacks become frustrated and leave the corporate environment.

A workshop sponsored by Xerox in early 1984 brought together 15 Human Resources, Equal Employment Opportunity, Affirmative Action, and Employee Relations managers from *Fortune* 100 corporations to address the issue of how to smoothly integrate blacks (and by implication other minorities and females) into the middle and senior management ranks.

The workshop explored what appeared to be a commonly faced conflict of black managers across America's corporations. In some cases, black managers with excellent backgrounds seemed to effectively adapt and become senior executives, whereas in other cases, apparently well-qualified and motivated blacks appeared to experience difficulties in their career mobility. Evidence for this is suggested by the feedback of some white managers during performance appraisal discussions with black managers subordinate to them. When discussing management style, black managers are often categorized as being "overly aggressive," "not a team player," "confrontive," "tough to manage," and "does not take direction well." Based on recognition that such feedback appears all too common for black managers, some critical questions were raised by the workshop participants aimed at understanding the following questions:

- Are there unique differences in the style, approach, or management behavior of black managers that conflicts with white management norms and expectations?
- Are there value or cultural differences that distinguish the behaviors of black and white managers and generate conflicting situations and experiences?

The interest of the participants focused mainly on the second question regarding cultural and value differences. It was felt that by exploring the nature and scope of apparently culturally based differences that seem to impact the behavior of black managers, maybe we can determine why conflicting situations arise between black and white managers in fulfillment of corporate expectations, and what solutions might alleviate such conflicts.

The concerns of black managers are, in fact, increasingly expressed through management behaviors that when manifested, may negatively impact the assessment of their performance and their career mobility. As a result of the discussions in this workshop, several factors were identified that appeared to the workshop participants to affect the thoughts and behaviors of blacks within the corporate environment. It was concluded that, although these factors could not accurately be termed "black values," they did represent "a shared view of the world" to which most blacks would ascribe. The workshop participants agreed to use these phrases interchangeably.

A major assumption of those in the workshop was that the American workplace is facing and will continue to face a diversity of serious new human resource concerns that must be addressed strategically. Some of these concerns appeared to be based on cultural/value differences that stem from an increasingly diverse work force at both the management and nonmanagement levels. Therefore, a better understanding of culture and values and their impact on differences in management styles and expectations of black and white managers are important to harnessing worker energy and contributing to improving performance of U.S. industry.

Even though the workshop focused on the shared views (cultural orientation) and behaviors of black managers, it was believed the implications applied to other minority groups as well as to females. The following sections will discuss the four significant "shared views" of black managers that were identified during the workshop and some examples of the behaviors they are believed to foster.

Before discussing the shared views, it is important to understand their context. It is probable that some white males will say they share similar views and that the resultant behaviors are not indigenous to blacks. Although some of the shared views and some behaviors might not be exclusive to blacks, blacks believe the reason they share these views and exhibit these behaviors are driven by being black in the American workplace, which they believe does not necessarily attribute similar value to black and white worker input and competence. The point is that blacks tend to experience the American workplace in the context of the shared views, whether or not these views also describe the experience of some whites. The career mobility and productivity implications must be seen from the perspective of blacks. Blacks believe the key issue is that being black in the American workplace makes it inordinately more difficult to be productive and have high career mobility than being white.

II. SHARED VIEWS

A. A Sense of the Lack of Entitlement and Empowerment

Black managers say that the management of U.S. corporations has yet to enfranchise them as managers to the point of their feeling that they really belong and that they have the authority to help establish the rules of the game. Blacks will often say they do not feel entitled or empowered to exercise the full range of authorities and are therefore not able to carry out the pre- rogatives resident in their management positions. If they felt entitled or em- powered, they believe it could significantly enhance the productivity of their organizations.

The following story illustrates this point:

> A group of black managers were choosing sides for their monthly touch football game. Noting that they were one person short of two evenly split teams, one of the managers invited a white youth—about 14 or 15 years old—to come and play with them. The youth, eager to play, accepted the invitation, walked over, picked up the football, and announced he would be the quarterback. His pronouncement was not contested; he was the quarterback for the first set of plays. He was later replaced.

The point is, this young kid, in the company of adults, at their invitation, felt entitled and empowered.

The business analogy is that blacks often observe that the ideas they put forward in meetings are often summarily dismissed, yet many times their ideas become the adopted solutions after being repeated by white colleagues. Seldom is credit given to the originator who happens to be black.

As a result of not feeling entitled or empowered, black managers believe they have to outperform their white peers and that any mistake could be fatal to their career ascendancy. This creates difficulty in maintaining a balanced perspective in the face of severe admonition of the absence of expected crit- icism following a significant performance slip. It also means that constant feedback of how one is doing could be required.

Believing they are not entitled or empowered, blacks spend much (too much) of their creative energy affirming their legitimacy and proving they belong as managers. As a result of this, many find it hard to know whether they are winning or losing.

B. Intensity of Emotion—Controlled Rage

In dealing with many frustrations resulting from a feeling of not being included in the corporate clique, black managers are often pushed to operate on a plane of emotional intensity that borders on controlled rage. Many black managers constantly struggle with stress, incremental to the garden variety of deadlines, quality demands, and competition that all managers share.

This intense build up of emotion often manifests itself in the following behaviors: a tendency to short circuit the thorough thought process when issues focus on blacks, especially if the discussion is not favorable. There is also a tendency to attribute many things to race and racism. For example, when blacks and other minorities are passed over for promotions, negative feelings often arise, resulting in suspicion and distrust. On the other hand, when a minority is promoted, there is a tendency for whites to associate the promotion with race, which further exacerbates the stress quotient of minorities.

C. Heavy Identification with the Oppressed, the Underclass, and the Subordinate

Because of the heavy religious background of many blacks, there is a continuous struggle with what is moral, right, and just. Some corporate practices are often looked upon by minorities as being unfair to minorities. Some blacks believe too close an identification with corporate America could mean a loss of their cultural identity.

There is a tendency to personalize systemic practices that may be totally impersonal, such as applying moral standards to what are essentially amoral or objective management practices. For instance, the objective standards used to determine a layoff may be based on such measurable criteria as performance, tenure, and critical skill needs. These criteria are neither moral nor amoral, but to the black manager, the end result may look like another way to restrict his or her movement in the corporate world; thus such actions are viewed as unfair and "not right," a moral judgment.

Identification with the oppressed, therefore, creates what is characterized as "cultural paranoia." By this, it is meant that there is a lack of trust, formulation of suspicion, and second guessing of the people and actions in the work environment. This then leads to a higher need for black affiliation inside the company as well as outside.

D. Preoccupation with Race and Racism

Too often in corporate America, blacks find that to white managers, they are perceived as "black" managers, who happen to work in a corporation, instead of the other way around. The implication is that as "black" managers, they are perceived to be less productive than if they were simply viewed as managers who happen to be black.

With this preoccupation, black managers cannot devote their total corporate attention to their primary objective, which is to do their job and to do it well. Therefore, for black managers to successfully mold themselves into the corporate structure, they need to change the view others hold of them. Black managers say they first and foremost must be seen as bonafide representatives of the corporation who happen to be black.

The workshop participants identified several behaviors that were believed to be a result of this shared view. We found that black managers felt a need to present a self-image that is both unique and positive. This, in their eyes, proves to others that they are a "super minority." To prove this superiority over others, there is a willingness to share know-how and information with others. Black managers are also constantly struggling over the degree of assimilation and the stress associated with assimilation. This brings to the black manager's mind two very important questions: (1) How far should I go to become like the other managers?, and (2) In order to become like them, does this mean that I must lose my cultural identity?

The major behavioral tendency of a preoccupation with race and racism is for black managers to look for racial components in negative feedback, especially when that feedback is directed toward their particular minority group. Additionally, there is a struggle in balancing the demands of corporate and community expectations driven by race. How do you rightly divide yourself without causing conflict with other groups? In the corporate environment, you do not want to be labeled as a radical, whereas community demands compel you to contribute to your people and their cause whether you want to or not.

There are behaviors resulting from this shared view that should have a positive impact in the workplace as well. Because of the cultural differences, minority managers tend to bring different points of view to decision making, therefore producing a wider range of solutions to problems.

III. IMPLICATIONS FOR CORPORATE AMERICA

A major question arising from the workshop was, what can corporations do to better utilize the creative and problem-solving talents of black managers? The workshop participants identified some actions that can be taken by the *corporation* and by the *individual employee* relative to how to better utilize black managers' talents, and by implications, the talents of other minority groups, such as Hispanic, Native American or female managers.

The participants observed that corporations must realize the American work force is changing. As a result, there is an intense need for companies to identify the productivity impacts and to learn how to effectively manage a more culturally diverse work force. Additionally, corporations need to be more sensitive to and to address the needs of nonwhite male managers who come from different cultural orientations. We can begin to address these needs by identifying issues early and by helping managers understand the implications of working in a multicultural environment and managing a culturally diverse work force. Therefore, operating in a proactive manner rather than reacting to issues as they arise is required.

A. The Employer Level

The workshop participants concluded that corporate actions should take four basic approaches. The first action would be for top management to understand the issues, such as lack of empowerment and entitlement, felt by black managers. Second, corporations should address the issue of subconscious stereotypes (often referred to as institutional racism). Third, corporations should examine corporate policies and their potential effects on a culturally diverse work force. Fourth, through the services of an outside organization, corporations can study multicultural issues and their effects on the corporation as a whole and develop solutions to whatever issues are found.

1. Understanding the Issues and Their Impact

As mentioned in the Shared Views section of this paper, black managers entering middle and senior management positions often feel that they are not easily accepted and that they do not have the same authority associated with their title and position as their white counterparts. In order to counteract differences, top management should be made aware of this issue and its impact on the effectiveness of managers who are black. Corporations should consider more flexibility regarding the use and exchange of power and should provide for more clearly defining success.

2. Subconscious Stereotyping

The workshop participants noted that "all too often many majority managers unwittingly label black managers according to subconscious stereotypes" (often referred to as institutional racism). For example, blacks believe they are very often placed in situations where they have to continually prove themselves as managers, whereas white managers are seen as "managers" without any racial labeling. Corporations need to develop means to help white managers manage the potential negative impact of subconscious stereotyping. Through encouraged involvement with minorities, their causes, or communities, all levels of management can become more comfortable with minorities. Companies can also develop a broader pipeline to minority managers who have effectively dealt with the rage and subconscious stereotyping issue and can identify the different ways of managing various situations.

3. Corporate Policies

A third way companies can begin to address multicultural issues is by consciously examining the value systems on which corporate policies have been based. The workshop participants established that some black managers tend to see the corporation and its practices from a different viewpoint. In many cases, a disjuncture between majority management expectations and minority management behaviors was found to be culturally related. A better understanding of cultural impacts can, in some cases, change the interpretation of behavior and associated assessments.

4. Outside Support

Finally, corporations can commission organizations like the Conference Board or others to study the cultural-type issues raised at the workshop and their impact on corporate cultures and managerial productivity. These organizations can also identify additional actions that can be implemented to eliminate potential conflicts that arise because of management expectations and minority management behaviors arising from cultural orientations and value systems that might differ from that of the majority male manager.

B. The Individual Employee

From the individual black manager's standpoint, the workshop participants identified actions to help address the apparent disjuncture between black managerial behaviors and white management expectations due to different cultural orientations. Three considerations were discussed by the workshop participants: (a) personal relationships with others, (b) coping with daily job pressures, and (c) long-term career mobility. In order to address these levels, the workshop participants noted that black managers must become more aware of the shared views identified, the behaviors often exhibited because of them, and the impact of these behaviors on the black manager's performance as evaluated by his or her white manager.

Networking was seen as a major vehicle through which "shared view" awareness and the behavioral implications that follow from them can be addressed. Through developing networks, black employees can discuss pressing issues and address such things as the behavioral implications of the shared views. One type of network is company caucus groups. Caucus group interactions can play a very important role in the success of minority managers. Caucus groups, sometimes known as special interest groups, are a collaboration of employees of a particular color or ethnicity who come together on their own to exchange information, share experiences. and the like with the purpose of increasing their information base, furthering their job effectiveness, and career potential. In companies like Xerox Corporation, caucus groups have been very successful for individual employees as well as being viable communication links with management.

During the workshop, participants assessed the implications of the behaviors generated by these shared views, in terms of coping with day-to-day responsibilities, personal stress, and the impact on long-term career upward mobility. We found that some behaviors that might be effective in daily activities may negatively affect long-term career mobility. For example: The fear of losing black cultural identity may lead to a high need for black affiliation.

Blacks have a strong need to associate with each other. On a day-to-day basis this might have a positive effect in coping with daily stress, but in the long run it could hinder career mobility. White managers might interpret this as clannishness or lack of sociability, both negative for moving up the career ladder. Because black managers desire to move up in the corporation, it becomes imperative that they associate with many white managers as well. At this point, blacks become concerned with how much of themselves they can let go.

IV. CONCLUSION

American industry is entering a new era. Soon corporations will be made up of a myriad of culturally diverse individuals, with minorities and females as a group making up the majority of the workplace. As a result of such changes in the work force, companies are faced with the challenge of effectively promoting and intergrating the talents of blacks into middle and senior management positions. It is my belief that the corporations that take seriously the need to address the issues and implications of a diverse work force will have a better opportunity of unleashing more of the productive capacities of their people.

The Black Values in the American Work Force Workshop mentioned at the outset examined the apparent conflicts faced by black managers within American corporations and found that cultural orientation has a great influence on how blacks view and negotiate the corporate environment. Before the creative talents of black managers can be maximally utilized in the corporate world, the shared views identified in the workshop must be addressed in a positive way. We should be reminded that, although the workshop focused on the shared views of black managers, these or other shared views can be implied for other minority and female groups as well.

Corporations should continually strive to create an environment where diverse work force management is an explicit objective. I believe that by addressing these issues, corporate America will be better positioned to use all the creative talents that are present in its work force.

Managing Diversity in a Competitive Market

Elizabeth P. Dixon and Roy Stewart

AT&T, in its current form, has existed only since January 1, 1984. Before that date the line of business which came to be known as AT&T Communications was a relatively small and unknown portion of the Bell System. It provided long distance communications services; hence its name, Long Lines. Although Long Lines was a nationwide operation, most of its approximately 42,380 employees were based in the New York/New Jersey area.

At divestiture, this organization changed in two very important ways: It became much more visible and acquired a large increase in the number of its employees. In fact, the employee population has soared to more than 180,000—and it now includes business and residential sales of new products in addition to long-distance services. It is highly visible and open to scrutiny by both the government and the general public, including organizations interested in the progress of minorities in business.

These changes have had a dramatic effect on all aspects of the company's thinking. More managers are managing more individuals of varying ethnic groups and cultural backgrounds. This being the case, the company has found it desirable, and in fact necessary, to provide to its employees information to assist them in living and working successfully in a diverse corporate culture.

In a recent internal publication, Charles Marshall, AT&T Vice Chairman, reaffirmed the company's commitment to affirmative action. He stressed that the best way to achieve the ideals of affirmative action and equal opportunity is to change people's experiences and knock down myths. Providing new,

Elizabeth P. Dixon • Manager, Corporate Equal Opportunity Policy, AT&T, Basking Ridge, New Jersey 07920 and Roy Stewart • Manager, Equal Opportunity/ Affirmative Action, AT&T, Basking Ridge, New Jersey 07920.

positive experiences and discouraging the stereotyping of women, minorities, disabled individuals, and others who are perceived to differ in some way from what is considered the "norm" are the goals of workshops developed over the past 2 years. Three of these workshops, Managing a Diverse Work Force, Race Issues in the Workplace, and Gender Issues in the Workplace, will be briefly discussed here. Their purpose and reception by the employee population will be explained.

I. MANAGING A DIVERSE WORK FORCE

Managing a Diverse Work Force was developed as a joint project of AT&T's corporate training and equal opportunity organizations, utilizing the services of Management Dynamics, a California-based consulting firm. Its purpose is to provide supervisors with the information and tools necessary to deal effectively and fairly in the work environment with subordinates of a different race, color, sex, nationality, religion, and with a physical and/or mental handicap.

The 1-day workshop is led by a trained facilitator, an AT&T employee, who provides direction rather than a single set of concrete answers. The course is offered to all management employees. In some areas of the country most upper-level managers, up to the level of vice president, have attended the course. Class size is kept deliberately small, from 12 to 15 students, to encourage participation and ensure that no one is lost in a large group. The following provides an overview of the workshop.

After welcoming participants to the session, the facilitator presents the assumptions upon which the workshop is based. These include:

- Most managers genuinely want to treat all their subordinates fairly and equitably.
- We all make and operate from assumptions about people who are different than we are.
- We have been socialized not to talk openly about differences in race, sex, and the like.
- There are a great many misconceptions about EEO and its application.
- The effective management of a diverse work force will enhance managers' abilities to accomplish their organizational goals.

The facilitator next presents the workshop objectives that are:

- To provide practical information about the EEO laws and their application
- To provide an opportunity for workshop participants to increase their awareness of behaviors that constitute discrimination and have a chilling effect on employee productivity

- To address the "walking-on-eggshells" style of management so that a manager is better able to exercise appropriate managerial behavior
- To discuss a communications process that can be used when managing a diverse work force

At this point, participants are invited to introduce themselves, and the facilitator sets forth guidelines for workshop participation. Everyone is requested to participate actively, to be open and honest in discussion, to give feedback to peers in a specific manner, and to accept it from others without becoming defensive. Each person is encouraged to examine his or her values from a different perspective and not to reject new information or experience because it does not comport with these values. The facilitator stresses the importance of the confidentiality of remarks made during the workshop.

As a first exercise, the workshop participants are divided into subgroups and asked to list reactions to EEO and affirmative action. They also answer such questions as:

- Why is there an EEO policy in the company and what function does it perform for the company?
- Is the policy internally or externally driven?
- What is the vested interest in the policy for managers and for the company?

The entire group reassembles and the reactions and answers are discussed. The intent is to provide participants with a clearer understanding of EEO and affirmative action and how they differ. They come to an understanding that EEO has a positive effect on employees and is not another name for reverse discrimination. Implementation of an effective EEO policy and affirmative action plans has a positive effect on the company's bottom line.

Participants are provided with an outline of major federal legislation concerning EEO and affirmative action. This is a useful tool, both for the remainder of the workshop and to keep for future reference.

The next section of the workshop involves a film produced especially for AT&T. Viewed in three segments, it presents the scenario of a highly successful manager beginning a new assignment, managing a very diverse group of people, a situation he (a white male) has never encountered before. The film shows the manager, Hal, having many of the stereotypical reactions toward women, minorities, disabled individuals, and those perceived to have a different sexual orientation.

In the first segment, Hal makes all the wrong moves. He patronizes the women and disabled worker. He implies that his minority employees are slackers and asks the white males to help everyone else along.

The second segment shows Hal discovering he has a big problem. The productivity in his organization is dropping, which impacts on other organizations. Now he must find out why. As he discusses his problem with various individuals, the "walking-on-eggshells" syndrome surfaces as a method of supervising minority employees. A manager who has been sued on a charge of race discrimination now handles minorities "with kid gloves" and documents everything. Other managers offer various solutions, including open communication and treating each employee as an individual.

The final segment discusses the assumptions that minorities and women make regarding white males. They (a) are ruthless, (b) are hypocritical, (c) are insensitive, (d) are entitled to whatever they have or can get, and (e) cannot be trusted.

This film stresses that a level of trust must first be established before subordinates feel comfortable and confident enough to bring problems and/or concerns to the attention of their managers. Hal receives a great deal of new information to consider and several suggestions as to how to solve his problems.

After each segment of the film, workshop participants discuss what they have seen and their reactions to it. Although the instances of prejudice and discrimination in the film are blatant, they serve as examples of much more subtle behavior that occurs in the workplace. The participants consider whether they have seen such behaviors in themselves and/or their associates, and if so, what has been and what now will be their responses to them.

The final portion of the workshop involves a discussion of effective communication with subordinates and the development of a management effectiveness plan. Participants are encouraged to open lines of communication with their subordinates and receive some practical ideas on how to accomplish this. They are warned that their efforts may not always meet with success at first, but they must keep the lines of communication open.

The Management Effectiveness Plan contains each manager's:

- Overall objectives for managing a diverse work force
- Vested interest in attaining these objectives
- Action step to be taken toward attainment
- Obstacles, actual or perceived, that stand in the way of attainment
- Plans for overcoming these obstacles

The Management Effectiveness Plan is discussed, and practical suggestions are offered that may make attainment of stated objectives easier.

At the end of the course, participants fill out an evaluation sheet detailing their opinion of the workshop's content, impact, and future usefulness. A sampling of these forms indicates that the majority of those who have attended the workshop found it valuable, even though some of the information was perceived to have been presented in a less than subtle fashion. The evaluations are done by means of a numeric scale, so actual comments are rare. However, most managers feel they have come away with a more positive opinion of EEO and Affirmative Action.

Unlike other workshops which AT&T offers, Managing a Diverse Work Force puts emphasis on the laws and regulations connected with EEO. Managing diversity successfully is a necessity for the high-performance manager. Only when people are treated as individuals and valued for their individuality are they able to contribute effectively to the achievement of organizational goals and attain personal goals within the business environment.

II. THE NEED FOR AWARENESS

As companies chart new and innovative courses for survival and growth during the remainder of the 1980s and into the 1990s, it is clear that they share one common goal, to produce more goods and/or services with less expense. Because the largest expense of most companies is wage and salary costs, less expense may translate to less people. Many factors are involved in producing more with less people, and one of the most important is how well people get along with their fellow workers. Because people will be depending on each other to produce more, they must be more tolerant and sensitive.

We put a strong emphasis on teamwork at AT&T. One of the key components upon which management employees are annually evaluated is interpersonal skills. One of the key elements of this group of skills is "Intergroup Networks and Alliances." This is defined in official company policy guidelines as "informal working relationships and information channels between or among individuals and groups." The following are some of the characteristics of Intergroup Networks and Alliances:

- Open communication, trust, and mutual respect
- Cooperation to achieve business goals
- Resolution of cross-functional conflicts
- Timely responses to changing requirements

The company offers direction in effecting Intergroup Networks and Alliances. There are many ingredients that contribute to the success or failure of people working together. One such ingredient is the awareness needed by all employees who work in a pluralistic environment. How does a company go about making people aware of fellow workers who are different because of race or gender? The answer is training. Two workshops are offered that help people understand people who are different from them. The courses are entitled "Race Issues in the Workplace" and "Gender Issues in the Workplace."

Before launching into a description of the workshops' individual modules and methods of delivery, some common information that addresses both workshops should be mentioned. Although strongly supported by upper management, the workshops are not universally required. They are open to occupational as well as management employees and are offered twice a month. The courses are 1 day in length, and organizations that send participants are not charged any expenses. The workshops are highly interactive, and people learn from one another, not from the course leader. Volunteers deliver the workshops, which is extremely important and will be discussed later. Class size is limited to between 14 and 20 students.

A. Race Issues in the Workplace

The first portion of the course consists of introductions, objectives, and a review of the schedule and agenda. The following are the workshop objectives:

- Develop a working definition of prejudice and racism
- Practice identifying examples of prejudice and racism
- Collaborate to develop approaches toward dealing effectively with aspects of prejudice and racism that may occur in the workplace

The schedule and agenda cover housekeeping details and the structure of the day's activities. The activities consist of group exercises, videotapes, group discussions, case work, and course evaluations.

Participants next develop a list of expectations, concerns, and questions. The purpose of this discussion is to give people the opportunity to address anxieties and questions they may have about the workshop.

Participants then discuss what they have learned from the precourse assignment. Before coming to the course each person is asked to interview a man and a woman with whom he or she works. They ask these people (a) To describe any examples of racist attitudes or behaviors they have seen or heard of recently at work and (b) whether they think people of color are treated fairly at work.

Attendees are also asked to read a minority newspaper, which is provided as part of the precourse package.

Next, the videotape "Eye of the Storm" is viewed and discussed. This high-impact video, which was filmed in Iowa, deals with how an all-white class of third graders learns to be prejudiced toward each other. The learning of prejudice is accomplished by dividing the class in half and giving each group different color-coded collars. With the color differential foremost in the students' minds, one group is given several classroom privileges that are denied to the second group. The privileged children gain a sense of power and superiority that is manifested by taunting the children without privileges. The two groups of children then exchange roles. The hurt and pain that the students inflict upon each other is analyzed in a group discussion.

Participants then develop and write down their definition of prejudice. With the aid of a handout containing some definitions, subgroups write working definitions that are supported by examples. The subgroups each appoint a spokesperson to report their findings to the entire class.

Attendees next view the videotape, "Black History: Lost, Stolen, or Strayed." The tape compares the history of the black American with a history that has been altered. Many examples of the contributions made by blacks are cited. Stereotypes of black people in films, television, literature, and radio are covered. Participants get an opportunity to share what they have learned and talk about how they were impacted when growing up.

Participants now formulate their definition of racism and give examples. After receiving some definitions, subgroups work on combining their own thoughts with textbook definitions. An important element in this exercise is the role of power as it relates to racism.

The next task is to design a racist community. This is done on a large easel pad. People chart the location of banks, the railroad, minority housing, white housing, schools, factories, etc. Through discussion, people become aware that they may be describing Any Town, USA. People learn to understand the racist environment in which they live.

Participants then review several case studies. They divide into groups and go over various situations which may occur at work. Each group then decides how they would respond to the situations. One of the situations deals with a supervisor who overhears some white subordinates making racial remarks about a fellow worker. A discussion then takes place, which includes the question of what the supervisor should do, either as it happens or at a later time. Although there are no correct answers in the case studies, participants start to think about how they can combat racism in the workplace. Additional time is spent on how people can take a more active role in curtailing racism.

After a review of expectations, concerns and questions posed earlier in the day, attendees complete a course evaluation.

B. Gender Issues in the Workplace

The workshop opens with introductions and a review of objectives, course schedule, and the agenda. The workshop objectives are:

- To examine how people are socialized as men and women and how this affects their ability to work together
- To obtain working definitions of prejudice and sexism
- To generate discussion on how men and women are treated in the workplace because of gender
- To determine if there are gender-related problems in the workplace and to develop strategies to solve them.

The format of the course is similar to Race Issues in the Workplace, with group exercises, videotapes, discussions, and course evaluations. Participants develop a list of expectations, concerns, and questions that are then discussed as a mixed-gender group.

Attendees break into small groups and receive cards that contain statistics, attitudes, observations, and the like about male/female behavior. An example of the information that appears on the cards is the following: Females make only $0.67 on the dollar made by males. The subgroups choose two of the cards that surprise or interest them. Everyone reconvenes to discuss the cards.

Participants next select a man or woman as their choice for a series of 20 different occupations. Based on the premise that each person, man or woman, is equally qualified, attendees select using gender as their only criterion. Examples of the occupations cited are airline pilot, police officer, and your boss. The purpose of this exercise is to help participants get in touch with prejudgments they make about gender. Discussion is refocused to the realities and direction of gender-based occupations.

Next, students view the videotape, "To Be a Man," which explores the attitudes, values, and socialization of three men—a southwestern ranch owner/used-car salesman, a northeastern recent divorcee (whose wife is a career woman), and a divorced man who has retained custody of his two children and has become a "house father." Each man deals with the impact of the changing role of women in society in a different way, either by adhering to what early socialization and values taught him or by adapting his life-style to become part of the "changing times." In a fishbowl group exercise, in which the women class members are in an observation role, men share their feelings on the attitudes and behaviors displayed in the film. Men share accounts of their upbringing and current lives in relation to the film.

A videotape entitled "A Woman's Place" is shown next. It explores the feelings of women who are determined to fight for "freedom" and a new life despite the values and socialization they have encountered for many years. These women have come to realize that they have a choice. The film also examines the role the media plays in stereotyping women to demean their role in society. The media stereotyping is also shown to have a significant impact on children with respect to what little girls and boys "should be." As in the previous exercise, students gather in a similar fishbowl format, this time with the men in the observation role. Women discuss their feelings on the attitudes and behaviors displayed in the film. They also share aspects of their personal lives. Women talk about how men's attitudes and behaviors affect their professional and private lives.

The facilitator now delivers a brief talk on sexism and the imposition of values. Definitions are described that are associated with men's and women's issues. Participants are helped to understand that gender, prejudice, and sexism prevent the workplace from being as productive as it ought to be.

Attendees organize into same-gender groups and identify behaviors that men do when working with women that inhibit collaboration and women do when working with men that inhibit collaboration. The groups reconvene to discuss these points.

The final exercise in this workshop has participants list and discuss:

- Something they will continue doing in the workplace that is gender-sensitive
- Something they will stop doing in the workplace that is gender-sensitive
- Something they will start doing in the workplace that is gender-sensitive

The most important aspect in the delivery of race and gender awareness programs is the role of the course deliverer or facilitator. Her or his role is to facilitate and not to lecture. He or she must have the ability to create an environment that promotes the learning process among participants. Students must learn from each other. Facilitators are volunteers from each of the company's departments. They must meet several criteria in order to be accepted into the program. The most important of these is their belief in what they are doing and their commitment to fighting racism and sexism in the workplace. The facilitators must also possess adequate training and platform skills. They must be willing to undergo up to 6 days of rigorous training provided by an outside consultant and commit to doing 4 or 5 workshops per year. They are also responsible for obtaining a substitute in the event they have a schedule conflict with one of their workshops. It is critical that their upper management supports their commitment to the program.

The evaluations of the programs discussed before have been very positive. Between 75% and 80% of the attendees responded favorably that the workshops meet the stated objectives and that they were made more aware of racism and sexism in the workplace. People gain a real understanding that many "everyday" expressions, such as "black ball," "white lie," and "voodoo economics" are inappropriate, may inflict pain on others, and are a detriment to a harmonious work environment. Most people appreciate the opportunity to learn.

III. WORKSHOP EVALUATION

All three workshops are evaluated in the same fashion. Each participant is asked to complete an unsigned evaluation form. Below are some of the questions that appear on this form.

- Do you think the workshop met its objectives?
- Which parts of the workshop did you find most instructive? (Such areas as videotapes, exercises, discussion groups, and casework are listed here.)
- Do you think your understanding of problems associated with this issue has improved as a result of this workshop?
- Do you think the workshop was worth the time involved?
- Did the facilitators demonstrate competence in conducting the workshop?

All of the preceding questions are rated on a sliding scale. The material is used to improve the workshops in areas that are perceived to be weak. As a result of this process, all of the workshops have the potential to change and grow, depending on the needs of the employee population.

IV. CONCLUSION

Awareness programs such as those discussed here are necessary for corporate vitality. Although awareness issues may be in everyone's job description or in company policy statements, employees must take on responsibility and ownership. Upper management support demonstrates the commitment that will pervade the entire organization, regardless of size, in a relatively short time. By recognizing attendees, volunteer facilitators, or instructors and by participating in awareness workshops, executives can make awareness an integral part of a corporation's culture. Otherwise, the corporate culture is incomplete.

When asked about AT&T's commitment to affirmative action, Vice Chairman Marshall has said that it's a way of life in this corporation. It is also what is best for business. "A business cannot be strong if it utilizes only a portion of its population." Using every employee's talents to his or her fullest extent takes awareness of that employee as an individual and what makes him or her unique. That is the function of AT&T's awareness workshops.

A Commitment to Employees and the Society

The Faculty Loan Program

International Business Machines Corporation

IBM is in the business of providing information-processing systems, equipment, and services. The company develops, manufactures, markets, and services computer systems—ranging from the large-scale IBM 3090 to the intermediate-sized System/36 to the IBM Personal System/2—as well as related programming, telecommunication products, storage devices, printers, typewriters, copiers, supplies, and educational materials. About 400,000 IBM employees work in manufacturing plants, laboratories, and sales and administration offices in more than 130 countries. Nearly all those employees are citizens of the countries in which they work.

I. COMMITMENT TO EMPLOYEES

Along with its business goals, IBM has a strong commitment to its employees. One example is its equal opportunity program. IBM is an equal opportunity employer with programs to ensure that all employees have the same chance to succeed. All personnel-related programs are administered without regard to race, color, religion, sex, national origin, handicap, or age. A department of equal opportunity was established by IBM in 1968 to develop guidelines for implementing the company's equal opportunity policy. At the corporate level, a director of equal opportunity and affirmative action programs and a staff of management specialists monitor all aspects of equal opportunity and affirmative action within the corporation. Each IBM operat-

International Business Machines Corporation • Armonk, New York 10504.

ing unit has a manager of equal opportunity and affirmative action, and most programs are monitored at each site location by equal opportunity coordinators and compliance officers.

At all levels, the equal opportunity staff:

- Outlines procedures for affirmative action programs
- Provides advice and guidance to management on all aspects of complying with both government regulations and company policy,
- Develops and monitors training programs to ensure that IBM's equal opportunity commitment is understood by all employees

Each IBM manager is responsible for, and is evaluated on, active support of the program and its objectives. Each IBM employee annually attends a meeting at which the company's equal opportunity and affirmative action programs are reviewed. IBM locations are audited for compliance with company policy and participation in affirmative action programs. The company's policy is carried out through a variety of equal opportunity and affirmative action programs. Most are aimed at recruiting, hiring, training, advancement, and education of minority groups, women, and the handicapped. Disabled veterans and Vietnam-era veterans are also included in these programs. The goal of these programs is to help each individual realize his or her full potential.

The skills of IBM employees are continually expanded through specialized education and on-the-job training. The results are mutually beneficial: Employees improve their chances for advancement, and IBM improves its ability to succeed in a fast-growing and highly competitive industry. As IBM Chairman John F. Akers said:

> IBM's policy of equal opportunity is founded on sound business judgment and our basic belief in respect for the individual. . . . Senior management at each location or operating unit takes the necessary action to comply fully with our equal opportunity policy. However, I expect each manager, at every level, to ensure this commitment is honored in all of our business activities.

II. COMMUNITY SUPPORT

IBM's commitment to responsible corporate citizenship has resulted in the development of programs benefiting people around the globe. In all, the company's contributions of cash, equipment, and other resources to social, cultural, and educational programs worldwide amounted to more than $188 million in 1986. One such program is the Faculty Loan Program, which IBM developed in 1971 to provide support in minority education.

A major frustration for educators is not having the time or the resources to offer their students the courses and the attention that they need. IBM tries to lend them a hand through the Faculty Loan Program, providing extra help where it is most needed. Through the Faculty Loan Program, the company has provided more than 700 IBM employee "loans" to minority colleges, universities, and related projects with high black, Hispanic, Appalachian,

American Indian, handicapped or disadvantaged student enrollments in its 15 years. The aim of the program is to improve the education of disadvantaged students. The program also provides IBMers with an opportunity to contribute to the educational community. It opens important channels of communications among IBM, students, and educators and provides employees with a valuable development experience.

Typical assignments focus on computer science, engineering, and business administration with IBMers serving as adjunct faculty members. However, special assignments have also included planning, curriculum development, student counseling, administrative support, and activities designed to increase the participation of disadvantaged high-school students in engineering and the sciences. Also eligible for consideration are special assignments made to educational agencies, projects, councils, and majority colleges and universities with the basic minority/disadvantaged focus of the program. Leaves are granted with full IBM pay and benefits. Requests are generally initiated by the educational institution and filled with IBMers who have expressed an interest in the program and fit the needs outlined in the requests.

Beginning with academic year 1981–1982, special assignments aimed at the high-school level have been included. Since that time, carefully selected mainstream, predominantly white institutions as well as specially selected educational agencies, consortia, and the like have also been included. In all cases, however, assignments must have the program's minority/disadvantage focus. In 1986, more than 100 IBM employees were "loaned" to 85 schools in 24 states, the District of Columbia, and Puerto Rico.

The program is one of two major community-service leave programs sponsored and funded by IBM. The IBM Community Service Assignment Program has also allowed more than 900 employees to serve full time on the staffs of nonprofit, community-based organizations with salary and benefits paid by IBM. This program also began in 1971.

III. CONCLUSION

In 1962, when IBM joined the federal government's Plan for Progress, the company's U.S. minority employee population was 1,250 or 1.5% of the total employee population. In that same year, the company's women employees numbered 10,000, representing 12.7% of its total population. By year-end of 1986, the percentage of minorities had grown to 16.0%, or 38,000 employees. The percentage of women employees more than doubled: At the close of 1986, IBM's U.S. women employee population had risen to approximately 68,500 or 28.0% of all U.S. IBM employees. Of recent hires, 48.8% were women and 22.5% were minorities. About 5,500 women and more than 3,600 minority employees held management positions at year-end, and of these almost 600 women and more than 500 minorities were in the top 20% of U.S. management jobs.

IBM strives to meet local needs as a responsible corporate citizen in the

132 countries and many communities around the world in which it does business. Frequently, the company joins in partnerships with government, education, community-service, and cultural organizations. IBM also encourages and assists employees in their individual efforts by contributing funds, equipment—and sometimes the full-time services of employees themselves. As the community benefits, so does IBM, its customers, and its people. IBM has always responded to a wide variety of social, civic, and cultural needs in our society. IBM's ongoing involvement in external activities reflects a commitment to responsible citizenship wherever IBM employees live, work, and do business.

Comprehensive Training

Arthur Strohmer

Merck & Co., Inc., develops and manufactures products to improve human health, animal health, and environmental health. Merck is the largest ethical pharmaceutical company in the world. The company is a leader in the research and development of drugs to treat high blood pressure, arthritis, and glaucoma. Merck is important in the field of antibiotics and is a leader in the development and production of vaccines for mumps, measles, and hepatitis. Merck medications for the prevention and eradication of parasites in animals are key contributors to meat production throughout the world. Water treatment systems and specialty chemicals for a wide variety of industrial and food uses round out Merck's product line. Merck is headquartered in Rahway, New Jersey. The company has 26 plants in the United States, 51 plants overseas, 12 experimental farms and research laboratories in 18 locations worldwide. Merck has 31,000 employees, of whom 14,000 are located in the United States. Total sales of the company in 1985 amounted to approximately 3.5 billion dollars.

I. MERCK AFFIRMATIVE ACTION PHILOSOPHY

Merck has a long-standing commitment to equal opportunity and has pledged itself to a continuing program of affirmative action. The company, by policy, has committed itself to provide equal opportunity for all of its employees with regard to recruitment, placement, promotion, training, development, and compensation. Further, the company's management is expected to make thoughtful and equitable efforts to correct imbalances in any areas of the work force where particular groups of employees may not be adequately

Arthur Strohmer • Director, Human Resources, Merck & Co., Inc., Rahway, New Jersey 07065.

represented. Managers in Merck must set goals for affirmative action and are formally measured on their affirmative action results.

In addition to its commitment by stated policy, Merck believes that true affirmative action can be attained only when *all* members of its work force— both management and nonmanagement—understand the company's commitment, are aware of the benefits to be gained by true equal opportunity, and are aware of the role each employee must play in making it a reality.

This belief that all employees share in the responsibility for affirmative action is the basis for one of the most comprehensive affirmative action training efforts in corporate America.

Since 1968, Merck has had a department solely dedicated to equal employment activities. The very early history of that department included the development of training programs that were designed to assist minorities and women in skill development and to provide training for managers in subjects relating to the growing presence of EEO regulations and guidelines.

As affirmative action began to overshadow the less proactive equal employment opportunity, Merck—along with other responsive companies—began to assess what it needed to do to better assure (and accelerate) the effective utilization of minorities and women in its work force. What emerged from this assessment were many actions, the foremost of which was a three-phase training program designed to reach every Merck employee in the United States.

Although each of the training phases represents a major "point-in-time" activity, elements of all three phases are ongoing for new employees to the Merck work force. And, each is periodically updated to reflect changes in societal attitudes and company needs.

II. DEVELOPMENT OF THE PROGRAM

Although the primary intent of this discussion is to describe the programs themselves, it is equally important to take a look at the developmental process which led up to the completion of the training activities. This process, itself, was developmental—both for the company in helping it to strengthen and refine its commitment, and also for the many employees involved in helping them to better understand the nature of both company and societal needs in the area of affirmative action.

A. Phase I

What was to result as Merck's Phase I program began as a comprehensive analysis of the total affirmative action environment in the company. The process began in 1975. That year represented a time period in which few, if any, companies could say they had reached the state where true equal opportunity was a fully developed reality. Even fewer could say that they were taking advantage of every opportunity to promote affirmative action in their work forces. Affirmative action—as a concept—was still relatively new. Definitive regulations for the implementation of affirmative action were not substantially in place before 1972. Merck, like most other companies, was still in the process of defining and formulating its response to these regulations.

As a first step, Merck began the process of data collection and analysis of its affirmative action environment by obtaining input from its employees. Over 300 employees in the company were interviewed during the course of the data-collection phase. These employees represented all levels of the organization, from senior management down. Care was taken to obtain input from each of the company's divisions and a broad cross section of functional areas. In order to assure objective data and confidentiality in handling the data, Merck engaged the consulting firm of Boyle/Kirkman Associates, Inc. Their role was to conduct employee interviews, to engage in a comprehensive study of the company's personnel policies and practices, and, at the conclusion of the study, to present recommendations to the company for improving its affirmative action results.

The study began with a primary emphasis on women in the company. It quickly evolved into a comprehensive environmental analysis that had an equal focus on minorities. Both minorities and women were, at that time, experiencing barriers to organizational advancement in most companies, and both were developing heightened expectations for organizational success.

The interviews focused on a wide range of factors in the company's environment that could potentially affect female and minority success and growth. Of special focus were the company's personnel policies. Employees were asked to comment on the impact these had on the personal growth and development of minorities and women. More important, was the effectiveness of their actual use. Were policies being applied in the manner for which they had been intended? Did managers and supervisors know and understand the policies they were expected to implement? Did managers fully understand their EEO and affirmative action obligations? Employees were asked to enumerate the problems they were encountering in fulfilling their career objectives. They were asked to suggest the things the company might do to manage and motivate minorities and women more effectively.

Not to be excluded was input from managers, themselves. Managers were asked if there were any unique problems in managing minorities and women. They were asked for their assessment of possible reasons for the relative scarcity of women and minorities in upper-level responsible jobs. And, finally they, too, were asked to suggest ways in which the company might better manage and utilize the talent and potential that existed in its growing minority and female population.

Concurrent with the interviewing activity, a comprehensive review was being made of the company's full range of personnel policies and its affirmative action plans and programs. Each was analyzed with respect to its appropriateness, its effect on minorities and women, how well it was being implemented, and the assessment of its adequacy by the company's minorities and women.

Analysis and data collection spanned a period of approximately 6 months. What resulted was a very comprehensive assessment of the company's climate—and its needs—in affirmative action. Recommendations were just as comprehensive and addressed themselves to changes in specific personnel policies, suggestions for improvements in the company's affirmative action plans and the process used to develop them, and a particular emphasis on the need for expanded career development and training programs for women and minorities.

The foremost recommendation, and the recommendation that led to Phase I of Merck's affirmative action training program, was that the company's managers needed to develop far more effective skills—skills that were necessary for managing in an affirmative action environment. It is important to note that the company, for some time, had a clearly stated policy assuring affirmative action. However, the environmental analysis showed clearly that to enunciate a policy of affirmative action will not, in itself, lead to marked change in the utilization of women and minorities in the work force. The policy must be totally integrated into all business decisions and into managers' ongoing daily behavior. Management was viewed as the key component in assuring true affirmative action. And, managers were not viewed as having the understanding or the skills necessary for them to fulfill their critical affirmative action role: hence, Phase I.

The Phase I program titled "Managing in an Affirmative Action Environment" was designed to bring managers' knowledge of affirmative action needs and their skills in implementing it up to date. It was also designed to communicate the company's commitment to equal opportunity for *all* of its employees and a similar commitment to affirmative action where such equality was not yet a reality.

The program was developed cooperatively by Boyle/Kirkman Associates, working together with a team of Merck personnel specialists. The environmental analysis had shown that the first need was one for a heightened awareness of what affirmative action was, what equal employment opportunity really means, and an understanding of their differences. Basic to this awareness and understanding was a fuller comprehension of EEO and affirmative action legislation and judicial measures. But it was realized from the beginning that the management program needed to go well beyond general awareness. It needed to focus on very specific techniques and provide skill development in approaches for managing and motivating women and minorities more effectively.

It was decided that the program take the form of a workshop to provide for maximum discussion and experience-based learning. Goals for the program were very specific. On completion of the program, participants should:

1. Understand Merck's commitment to affirmative action and the difference between it and equal opportunity
2. Understand the recent legislation that supports affirmative action's changing role

3. Understand their own behavior by having had an opportunity to discuss and analyze their own attitudes toward minorities and women in Merck
4. Have a greater expertise in interviewing, in communicating with, and developing women and minorities on a daily basis
5. Be able to develop a strategy for implementing their own affirmative action plans to better utilize minorities and women within each of their own departments

To reach these goals, a workshop of 2 days was developed. To provide experiential learning, maximum use was made of case studies, role plays, and discussion teams. These were supplemented by brief lectures on EEO and affirmative action legislation. Where relevant, Merck's personnel policies were reviewed and discussed in depth along with their implications for affirmative action. Key among these were the company's policies and practices in the areas of interviewing, hiring, performance appraisal, career development, and compensation.

It was decided that the target population for the training needed to be the *total* management team. To bring about significant environmental change, all 2,000 managers in the company needed to be provided the training. And, since the actions and management decisions of managers at lower levels in the company needed to be supported by their senior management, a "top-down" approach was followed. The first training program was given to the company's top-level management. Presidents of each division and senior corporate management attended this first program and participated in the same discussions, the same case study exercises, and the same role play activities that were to be provided to managers in each of their organizations. No manager was exempt from the training activity, as each had an impact on the company's affirmative action results. The program they experienced is outlined next:

I. Merck's EEO and Affirmative Action Commitment
   A. Policy and objectives
   B. Individual manager responsibility
II. EEO/Affirmative Action Laws and Regulations
   A. Key concepts (including burden of proof, job relatedness, systemic discrimination, "good faith" efforts, disparate effect, reasonable accommodation, parity, consistency of treatment, documentation)
   B. Criteria for EEO decisions (including pattern of results related to the job, objectivity, consistent application)
   C. Complaint procedure (management's role, typical investigation requirements)
III. EEO Planning (information relevant to the development of appropriate plans, including work force analysis, areas of utilization, developing goals, exercise of developing a plan for a sample department)

IV. Recruitment, Interviewing, and Promotions
   A. Finding women and minorities
   B. Interviewing (job relatedness, job descriptions, qualified versus best qualified, guidelines for effective interviewing, interview practice)
   C. The job offer
V. Appraisal and Counseling (management techniques, management errors and assumptions, counseling techniques, job relatedness, consistency, EEO concerns, typical problems in appraisal and how to overcome them)
VI. Career Development (management assistance for self-development, company support programs)
VII. Compensation (nondiscrimination in compensation, equal pay provisions, effective salary administration, company and managers' responsibilities)

It is important to note that concurrent with the delivery of the Managing in an Affirmative Action Environment Program, Merck was simultaneously making changes to its Performance Appraisal Program and its approaches to training and development. A major new career development program was implemented, and special effort was made to enroll the company's women and minorities in this program.

B. Phase II

Merck's Managing in an Affirmative Action Environment Program was designed specifically for managers of the company's salaried work force. Domestically, approximately 25% of the Merck population was composed of hourly organized employees. As such, this group was managed by policies determined by a number of different contractual agreements. Some of these policies were different from those affecting salaried employees. What was consistent was the company's commitment to affirmative action at all levels and in all parts of its work force.

Phase II was a 2-day workshop for supervisory personnel of Merck, titled "Managing Affirmative Action for Increased Productivity." Included in the training population were union representatives of each bargaining unit. Both supervisors and union management were viewed as potentially instrumental in assuring that the company's commitment to affirmative action was a *total* commitment and one that included *all* levels of supervision.

The Phase II program took its direction from Phase I. Many of the needs were the same, even though specific policies governing the hourly work force were different from those in use with salaried employees. The methodology used in the program was essentially the same as that used in Phase I. Case studies, role plays, and group discussion were used to enhance the learning experience of the program. The company's policies were reviewed along with a comprehensive review of EEO and affirmative action legislation. As with Phase I, the supervisor's role was the primary focus.

The target population was the 700 supervisors who managed the company's hourly work force. Each supervisor was expected to contribute to the company's total affirmative action effort. The program, similar to Phase I, was designed to provide training in the "how" to do that.

As with Phase I, Merck decided to combine its efforts with those of an external consulting firm, both to add an objective third party to the effort and to get the training job done more quickly than internal resources could accomplish. Terrence R. Simmons Associates was engaged to develop the details of Phase II training. To conduct the training, Terry Simmons had the added advantage of being able to relate well to the supervisors of Merck's hourly employees. He was "down to earth," practical, and familiar with the needs that existed in a company's operating facilities.

The program focused on these areas:

I. EEO and affirmative action legislation

II. Merck's policies and commitment to equal employment opportunity and affirmative action

III. Interviewing and hiring responsibilities of the Merck supervisor

IV. Day-to-day management practices (including employee orientation, performance management, employee development, retention and morale)

V. Informal affirmative action steps (including individual treatment, the potential for disparate treatment, situations with EEO, and affirmative action implications)

Phase II was completed in 1980. Its completion, and the completion of Phase I, laid the groundwork for a training effort that was unique in corporate America.

C. Phase III

With the completion of the Phase I and Phase II programs, Merck's entire management and supervisory force had been provided training designed to improve their effectiveness in supporting the company's affirmative action efforts.

At this point, Merck took a step back to review whether it had done everything possible to assure a supportive climate for affirmative action. Its managers had been trained. New and expanded training programs were in place for women and minorities. A number of policies had been revised based partially on data collected from employees during Phase I interviews. And, the company's Equal Affairs' representatives at each Merck facility had been provided training to increase their effectiveness.

Concurrent with the development of the Phase I training program, Merck conducted a major attitude survey of its domestic population that numbered 16,000 at that time. Data from this survey suggested one last need, a need that had not been addressed by either management or supervisory training. There remained 13,000 nonsupervisory employees who had not been trained in affirmative action awareness, nor had they been provided the opportunity to participate in helping to bring about the major environmental change Merck was seeking. Data from Merck's attitude survey showed rather clearly that affirmative action awareness among its employees varied substantially. More important, employees' assessment of the company's commitment to affirmative action and their assessment of how affirmative action affected them personally also varied.

In response to an attitude survey question that asked, Who receives special treatment in the company?,

24% of males said *females do.*
42% of males said *minorities do.*
33% of females said *males do.*
45% of females said *minorities do.*
12% of blacks said *women do.*
47% of blacks said *whites do.*

On the other hand, few employees in any group felt they were *recipients* of special treatment:

Only 4% of males said *we do.*
Only 4% of females said *we do.*
Only 2% of blacks said *we do.*

Clearly, there were significant differences in the perceptions of employees about how affirmative action affected them and how they perceived it affecting others.

Although a majority of employees indicated in the survey they felt the company's senior management was committed to affirmative action, the majority was not great enough to satisfy then Merck Chairman John J. Horan. Himself a very strong and outspoken advocate of equal opportunity and affirmative action, Mr. Horan directed that steps be taken to improve the awareness of *all* employees regarding the company's commitment and that the widely varying employee perceptions be addressed.

Merck began its development of what was to become the Phase III training program by again interviewing its employees. Close to 400 employees at all levels were interviewed. The objective of the interviews was to identify those affirmative action issues that are of primary importance and that require exposure, explanation, and clarification. Assisting Merck in the data collection were two external consultants: Terrence Simmons Associates, the firm that developed and conducted Merck's Phase II program, and Harbridge House, Inc. Merck's decision to again utilize the expertise of external consultants was based on the desire to move quickly and to assure objectivity in data collection and recommendations. In addition, the development of a program for all 16,000 domestic Merck employees was a task of such magnitude that

Merck's internal Human Resources staff needed to be augmented in order to get the job done. Harbridge House would enlist the services of Allstate's Audio-Visual Communications Division to develop supportive, professionally produced audiovisual materials.

The interviewing activity resulted in the identification of seven goals for the program:

1. Communicate Merck's commitment to equality for all employees.
2. Allow employees to freely express their feelings about affirmative action.
3. Help employees understand why we have equal employment opportunity and affirmative action programs.
4. Provide an open forum for discussion of the issues surrounding affirmative action.
5. Show how affirmative action benefits all employees.
6. Demonstrate that all employees have a role in affirmative action and in their own career development.
7. Reinforce line management's role in the communication process.

The development of a program to meet these goals was no easy task. First, a structure needed to be set up to accomplish the training. Each of the company's divisions selected a member of senior management to serve as the division's coordinator. Division coordinators had the responsibility for seeing that every employee in their organization attended training. Their role included the scheduling of sessions, monitoring of attendance, assuring that program materials were available for each session, and the collecting of evaluative data at the conclusion of each session. Further, they were to monitor sessions to assure that sessions were going well.

Next, divisions were asked to select "master trainers." It was determined that 100 master trainers would be needed to train line managers and supervisors to conduct the program for their departments. Line management, discussion leaders were to number approximately 1,000. The 1,000 would lead sessions for the remaining 15,000 Merck employees. Master trainers were given 3 days of intensive trainer training. During this training, maximum time was devoted to practice teaching. On completion of their training, the 100 master trainers returned to their divisions and began the task of training the 1,000 discussion leaders to conduct the program. After approximately a year, 15,000 Merck employees had attended the 1-day workshop led by a manager in their chain of command.

1. The Program

The Phase III Program, because of the method used for its delivery (i.e., the use of line managers versus professional trainers), needed to be highly structured. Maximum use was made of audiovisual materials and structured discussion. Discussion leader manuals contained detailed outlines and instructions for the use of case studies and exercises that were a part of the session. The completed program package included an introductory film, seven video case studies, brief lecturettes, questionnaires, exercises to promote group discussion, and the outlines, overheads, and flip chart materials needed to conduct the session. Active employee involvement was vital to the success of the program; therefore, program materials were designed to stimulate lively employee dialogue, and discussion leaders were trained in effective questioning techniques.

The program included the following topics of discussion:

I. Introduction and legal aspects

II. Merck's affirmative action program (how the AA plan is developed; how AA objectives are implemented)

III. How affirmative action affects everybody (perceptions of discrimination, selection decisions)

IV. What you can expect from Merck (sexual harassment guidelines, Merck's programs, special treatment)

V. What you can do yourself (fairer appraisals, informal systems and corporate realities, problem resolution)

VI. The future of affirmative action (statistical look at affirmative action, what each of us can do)

The program received very favorable response from Merck employees. A vast majority indicated that their awareness of both the strength and the nature of the company's commitment had significantly improved. Responses to evaluation questionnaires showed a substantial reduction in the "we–they" special treatment perception that had been evident in the company's attitude survey data. Most employees stated they now understood that they, too, had a role to play in assuring affirmative action along with the company's management.

Because of its uniqueness, Merck in conjunction with Harbridge House decided that the program was worthy of marketing to other organizations. Since its development and use in Merck, 75 companies have purchased the program for use in their organizations. The program has been given to approximately 200,000 employees. Merck received the first "Exemplary Voluntary Efforts Award" from the U.S. Department of Labor in 1983 in recognition of the program. Phase III was cited in the February 1, 1984, *Congressional Record* as an exemplary program. The introductory film used in the program received the Silver Screen Award from the Industrial Film Festival for outstanding creativity. Finally, the State of New Jersey purchased the program for all 65,000 state employees. Merck turns all royalties received from program sales over to a variety of affirmative action causes.

III. HAVE THE TRAINING PROGRAMS WORKED?

Response within Merck to the company's affirmative action training has been quite positive. But employee response is not a true measure of the full contribution the training has made to Merck's affirmative action results. A truer measure is the changed demographics of the Merck population. During the decade from 1975 to 1985, the white male population of Merck increased by 21%. During the same time period, white females increased by 49%; minority males by 85%, and minority females by 211%. More important, a substantial part of this growth was movement of protected classes into professional and managerial jobs.

Although this growth cannot be attributed solely to the company's training programs, it is safe to say the growth could not have been so favorable, so orderly, and so generally accepted by employees without the training.

An Overview of Equal Opportunity Programs

Robert N. Beck, William F. Holmes, and Nancy L. Merritt

BankAmerica Corporation is one of the largest diversified financial services corporations in the world, with assets of over $100 billion and deposits of $94 billion. Through its network of branches and subsidiary offices, BankAmerica Corporation provides financial services and products to consumers, corporations, and government institutions. BankAmerica is the parent company of such diverse entities as Bank of America NT & SA and Seafirst Corporation. The corporation's 60,000-plus employees service customers around the world through more than 1,600 branches and offices in the United States and 70 countries.

I. A UNIQUE LEGACY

Bank of America began in San Francisco in 1904 as Bank of Italy, formed by a former produce merchant, 34-year-old Amadeo Peter Giannini. Giannini's goal was to offer financial services to the small depositor and borrower. This was a revolutionary idea at a time when commercial banks would not make a loan to a consumer of average means. He also visualized a statewide system for his bank, and in 1907 introduced the branch system into the banking industry.

Giannini was a believer in the individual. He considered a person's hand-

Robert N. Beck • Executive Vice President, Corporate Human Resources, Bank of America, San Francisco, California 94104; **William F. Holmes** • Vice President/Manager, Equal Opportunity Programs, Bank of America, San Francisco, California 94104; and **Nancy L. Merritt** • Senior Associate, de RECAT & Associates, Inc., San Jose, California 95129 (formerly with Bank of America, San Francisco, California 94104).

shake—not a written contract—to be the basis for doing business. His belief in the dignity and talents of each individual could be seen in the treatment of both customers and those who serve the customers—his "family," the employees of Bank of America. A 1928 Giannini quote sets the tone for our long history in addressing the area of equal employment opportunity: "We have made the road to promotion an open one, along which every employee should seek to advance. Talent is the one thing for which we are most constantly on the lookout."

Prior to the Civil Rights Act of 1964, women comprised 60% and minorities comprised 15% of Bank of America's employees. The Giannini tradition of respect for the individual, progressive employee relations policies, and promotion from within opened opportunities to all employees. Development of talent concentrated on the pool of internal employees drawn from the diverse pool of talent available in California. This internal pool was supplemented, not led, by recruitment from the outside. Our focus was on developing employees for a career in a way to ensure that they could compete on an equal basis. That focus was characterized by top management oversight, interest, involvement, and support for seeing that people had the opportunity to effectively utilize their knowledge, skills, and experience.

Nevertheless, areas remained for improvement. In 1974 a group of women officers sued the bank for failing to assign women to overseas positions. The suit resulted in an innovative consent decree that was aimed at developing individuals' abilities to compete equally. Under the consent decree, Bank of America established a collection of trusts to provide funds for the training and development of women employees. Equity was preserved, as the consent decree provided that no less qualified person should be promoted over a more qualified candidate. The goals set for women in the consent decree were exceeded.

The trusts were funded by, but established independently of, the bank. Closed out in 1985, they are the only programs for designated groups ever directed at Bank of America employees. They were managed by trustees, not the bank itself. Indeed, rather than dividing employees by designing special programs for employee segments, Bank of America has emphasized the integration of employees—stressing their commonalities, not directly sponsored special all-women or all-minority groups.

II. WHERE WE STAND TODAY

The characteristics of our work force show the results of this long history of providing opportunity. Bank of America is comprised of 73% women and 40% minorities. Since 1975, women have advanced from a total representation of 27% to 62% of officials and managers, and 57% of professionals. More importantly, compared with 1975, there are now over four times as many women in the upper levels of management, going from 6% to 26% at levels of vice president (or equivalent) and above.

Minorities have advanced to a total representation of 26% of officials and managers, and 27% of professionals. Currently, 11% of vice president (or equivalent) and above positions are held by minorities.

III. BEHIND THE SUCCESS OF OUR EFFORTS: TOP MANAGEMENT'S ROLE

Top management support and a top-down driven, systematic approach are the cornerstones for our equal opportunity program. A goal-setting and goal-monitoring system, communication, employee development, and other programs are also in place to support our efforts. All parts of our approach are made possible by the continuing strong commitment and involvement of top management, both accountability and resources for managers throughout the company, and communication both to and from our employees.

Top management realizes that it is in our best interests to have an expanded pool of talent at all levels in the organization. Senior management sets the tone for the company and provides the conceptual and operational framework to carry out programs. To keep the focus on this, there are major policymaking bodies within the corporation that annually review our progress and approve our future equal opportunity goals and initiatives. Once we have approval from these groups and directives for any additional initiatives, our equal opportunity plans go to the public policy committee of the corporation's board of directors for final approval. The goal-setting process is interactive, both within the policymaking bodies and between these groups and management. The groups receive suggested goals and have the opportunity to question, discuss, and confirm corporate direction before reaching their decisions.

After these senior management bodies give their approval, all division directors receive goals for their equal opportunity efforts in the coming year. These are driven down through their organizations. Each year our clearly enunciated policy on affirmative action is also sent throughout Bank of America from our CEO.

IV. ACCOUNTABILITY AND RESOURCES

Recognizing that Bank of America has a large, diverse, and widespread work force, the responsibilities for equal employment opportunity and affirmative action have been decentralized throughout the corporation. Each manager is the focal point for turning our equal opportunity policies into realities and is responsible for demonstrating commitment to this area.

A manager is held accountable for the efforts made to foster the equal access and participation of employees for career development and advancement. Managers endeavor to make employment decisions on the basis of merit and ability and encourage employees to develop their full potential. Managers also strive to ensure that the work environment is free from intimidation and harassment. A part of our Performance, Planning, Coaching, and

Evaluation system is a Management Supplement that has specific accountabilities for the manager's performance in equal opportunity, affirmative action, and other areas of people management. A significant percentage of a manager's compensation is based on accomplishments against these management supplement goals. Within the senior management ranks, incentives or bonuses are a large component of their compensation for accomplishment of their business objectives. The amount of the incentive earned by senior managers is also influenced by performance against equal opportunity and affirmative action goals and other people management areas.

Along with accountability comes institutional support. We have developed a computerized system that calculates the availability of minorities and women, the attendant goals, and the progress toward meeting those goals. This monitoring system establishes a valid means of comparison to determine progress made against the objectives we have established. Periodically, each division receives data, broken down by major unit, enabling managers and human resources professionals to sit together to review progress and determine if additional initiatives are needed. The information the manager receives tells him or her not just the progress toward the goal but the trends in employment activity that enable the manager to assess the adequacy of good faith efforts to reach the goal.

This management support system is an integral link in the chain of equal opportunity commitment. It is through this regular review system that line managers can fulfill the other side of their responsibility—to identify and upwardly communicate issues and concerns that become the basis for revision of corporate policy and new program initiatives. In this endeavor, managers have additional resources available to them through the corporate Equal Opportunity Programs, Personnel Relations, and Legal departments. Experts in these areas are available to managers for advice in any area concerning equal employment and affirmative action.

Managers receive guidance through a number of channels other than simple quantitative data. The basic communication comes through a clear statement of our EEO policies in the "Manager's Guide to Managing Human Resources"—a guide for managers on human resource matters. Other chapters in the Manager's Guide deal with practices having an EEO impact, such as staffing, compensation, and personnel relations. They also receive periodic reports, information through management briefings, and specialized guidance designed to address specific issues or situations. Equal opportunity and affirmative action are fundamental modules of early training for every manager. Finally, managers have the full panoply of media available to all of our employees.

V. COMMUNICATION WITH EMPLOYEES

Employees cannot develop trust and believe that we are committed to equal opportunity and affirmative action without understanding our philosophy, being a participant in implementing our strategies, and finally, seeing the results in our organization. Effective communications are pivotal to the success of all facets of our program. A key value we have communicated is the commitment to "encourage and support a diversity of skills, talents, and viewpoints."

Our annual reaffirmation of our policy on equal opportunity and affirmative action comes from our CEO and is widely distributed and posted at work locations throughout the bank. In addition, each year we revise and distribute a booklet that sets out our reaffirmation, describes our equal opportunity and affirmative action programs, and communicates our progress to date. We follow this up for current employees with staff meetings at which EEO and affirmative action are discussed and at which the bank's policies are clearly communicated. New employees receive information on our EEO and affirmative action policies through a formal intake process that includes introduction to our company handbook, a structured orientation session with their manager, and additional orientation activities.

We also periodically inform employees of our policies, progress, and initiatives through widely distributed employee publications, such as *On Your Behalf* (a monthly magazine for BankAmericans). Other internal periodicals are also used to highlight individual success stories, present career-path options, provide role models, and give out other information. Consistent consideration is given to portraying our work force diversity in all internal and external company communication vehicles. This can take the form, for example, of representing senior-level women and minorities within shareholder's communications or having outstanding individuals from these groups as featured speakers at internal functions. Our policies and practices are also communicated to customers and the general public through company ads, annual reports, and word of mouth.

Communication leads both ways. Effective internal channels of communication give employees a way to express their views, request guidance, or make suggestions. We encourage employee feedback through orientation sessions, staff meetings, opinion surveys, conferences, workshops on EEO, and informal talks with managers. Our "Meet Senior Management" and "Coffee With . . ." programs permit employees to meet face-to-face with our senior managers in a relaxed and open way.

But we also have more formal lines of communication. Open Line is a channel for communicating with senior management to ask questions, make comments, and register complaints in a confidential manner. Generally, employees receive a confidential reply mailed to their home address. No one in management will know their identity.

Another channel, designed to resolve work-related problems, is the Let's Talk program. Let's Talk is a process based on the idea that many on-the-job problems can be cleared up by frank and prompt discussions. Through Let's Talk, employees may express their concerns to successive levels of management up to their division's vice chairperson.

Together these programs provide an effective array of ways for employees and managers within Bank of America to know, understand, and make use of our commitment to equal employment opportunity.

VI. OTHER INITIATIVES

So institutionalized and ingrained are equal employment opportunity and affirmative action that it might appear that the "systematized" aspects of our approach are the sole means of implementing equal opportunity. To the contrary, so diverse and large a community presence is Bank of America that equal opportunity assumes a wide range of initiatives apart from traditional EEO and affirmative action. These affect how the bank manages equal opportunity at the top, how we relate to our community, and how we look to the next generation of the business work force.

Succession planning is an important process for our top managers. Our succession planning system searches our middle management and professional work force to identify employees who have a high potential for advancement to senior management. Employees in this group are carefully groomed, guided, and monitored to ensure that they develop the skills to take over successfully the duties of senior management positions when opportunities arise. We take special steps to ensure that a pool of women and minority candidates is contained within our high-potential population and that senior managers are aware of their talents. We have established goals to increase the representation of women and minorities within our senior management group.

Although we are not overly introspective, we periodically study our upward mobility efforts to ensure that they meet the needs of both senior management and candidates for advancement and that they work to include a diverse collection of our most talented employees. Such a study, for example, led to enhancements in our upward mobility program and recognition for Bank of America in 1986 through a national award.

A. Our Relationship with Our Community

Bank of America plays a significant part in the communities it serves in a wide variety of ways. Our financial practices take into account the developmental needs of communities, including areas of high ethnic or minority concentrations having developmental opportunities. We support job training, child care, community service, and other activities through our BankAmerica Foundation, in-kind services, lending practices, and employee efforts. We maintain an active minority purchasing program to assist disadvantaged businesses in getting a start. We work with community organizations to bring employment opportunities to disadvantaged areas. Finally, we share our experiences and expertise with others, including community organizations and other employers, so that our communities may benefit from our collective efforts.

B. Working toward the Work Force of the Future

Our initiatives here encompass both short- and long-term goals. We play a leadership role in internship programs, such as Inroads, to bring the most promising young minority students into early work experiences with Bank of America. In our college recruitment practices, we continue to develop relationships with a variety of colleges and universities, including institutions aimed at serving minority consituencies. We are a leader in projects directed toward keeping and increasing a steady flow of minorities into business. The most notable recent effort is the Project to Increase Minorities in Business (PIMIB), under the sponsorship of major corporations in cooperation with the American Assembly of Collegiate Schools of Business (AACSB), the accrediting body for business schools. One of our executives was chairman of the PIMIB committee to look at ways of enhancing upward mobility. We also work with PIMIB in addressing longer-range problems, such as preparatory schooling for minority children.

Bank of America's many endeavors in equal opportunity are an integral part of its business strategies, its employment philosophies, and its relationship with the communities it serves. Our endeavors are not an attempt to be "all things to all people," but rather, a collection of individual initiatives designed to achieve specific needs that we all share.

12

An Overview of Corporate Policies and Practices

Donna E. Thompson, Nancy DiTomaso, and David H. Blake

The progress of minorities into top-level management positions has been very slow. As a result, many black managers leave the corporate world and start their own businesses (e.g., Hymowitz, 1984). In his discussion of these low-advancement prospects, Carnevale (1985) suggested that a two-track career system exists for blacks with a relatively small group of "haves" and a larger group of "have-nots."

Unfortunately, although much has been written in the popular press, little, if any systematic research has been done on the career development and advancement of minority managers into top-level management positions. This has been due, in part, to the fact that there are few minority managers in the top executive ranks of American corporations. It is also a reflection of the more general state of the managerial career development literature. As Schein (1986) points out in his critique of the field, the general area of careers often suffers from fractionation with subfields ignoring one other because it is interdisciplinary. He further emphasizes the need for more integrative constructs and theory and the need to consider process so that a more complete understanding of career dynamics can be gained. The scarcity of research is also a function of the fact that what we are really talking about here is succession planning or the process by which top management identifies and prepares the next generation of leaders. Although Carnazza (1982) surveyed corporations about their practices in this area and suggested a useful conceptual framework, little research has really been done looking at succession planning for nonminority or minority managers. This may be due to both the

Donna E. Thompson, Nancy DiTomaso, and David H. Blake • Rutgers Graduate School of Management, Newark, New Jersey 07102.

difficulties encountered when attempting to conduct this type of research and the highly sensitive nature of the topic.

One of the critical findings suggested by the success stories of minority managers that were described in Chapter 10 was that individual career planning and preparation is important. That is, people need to take more active roles in their own career management. Minority managers must plan for their own development so that they can respond to opportunities. This finding is consistent with current research in the career area (Hall, 1986). However, no amount of individual career planning and preparation can be effective if organizational opportunities for career movement are not available. Organizations need to have some type of career management system for preparing, implementing, and monitoring individual career plans.

Research in recent years has demonstrated the impact that an organization can have on the career motivation and development of its managers. Campbell and Moses (1986) described the fundamental shifts in careers occurring at AT&T since the late 1950s that resulted from technological, marketplace, and governmental developments. Their discussion focused on the impact of deregulation in the telecommunications industry and the divestiture of AT&T on career continuity. Changes in the way an organization does business often result in a change in the composition of its managerial work force and the difficult issue of how managers trained in one organizational culture often have difficulty adapting to another must be grappled with. Similarly, Schein's (1985) work demonstrates how the history, assumption, and philosophies of an organization's founders and leaders shape its culture and in turn, how this culture socializes its managers.

In a study of the development of young managers' career motivation, London and Bray (1984) also found evidence of the effects of organizational culture on managerial careers. Managers in a high-potential development program were more motivated to advance in the corporate hierarchy than were managers in another company that did not provide special treatment or concern for development and in which there were few opportunities for advancement and movement to more challenging job assignments. In the development-oriented company, managers were viewed as an important resource for the future, whereas in the latter, managers were seen as necessary to meeting business needs. Finding no company differences in the backgrounds of the participants, the researchers proposed that the motivation levels of the managers from the nondevelopment-oriented company would increase if they were transferred to the development-oriented company. In his book, *Developing Managers: A Guide to Motivating and Preparing People for Successful Managerial Careers,* London (1985) underscores the critical role that organizational policies, practices, and conditions can play in influencing the individual characteristics of career motivation of career resilience, career insights, and career identity. His research suggests that organizational career development programs need to extend beyond goal setting and career planning to include the nature of supervision (e.g., feedback). the nature of the job (e.g., the level of challenge), and organizational conditions (e.g.. opportunities for advancement).

It appears therefore, that although a great deal is not known at the present time about succession planning, more general research in the careers area has found that organizational culture, policies, and practices are related to managerial development. In addition to the findings described before, we know for example, that early job experiences can be critical to later managerial career success (e.g., Berlew and Hall, 1966; Bray, Campbell, and Grant, 1974; Stumpf and Hartman, 1984). For example, in a major longitudinal study of the development of managers at AT&T, Bray, Campbell, and Grant (1974) found that giving recruits challenging jobs early in their careers provided a potent stimulant to development. Recent work by McCall, Lombardo, and Morrison (1988) further demonstrate the critical role job experience plays in later executive success. In their study, these researchers found that successful executives were much more likely to have experienced different types of job assignments throughout their careers, whereas those who were not successful were more likely to have remained in one functional area.

Another general conclusion that can be drawn from the literature is the importance of early career experiences. Hall and Nougaim (1968) found that more capable managers tended to get more challenging jobs, which, in turn led to more rapid development. On the basis of these and other findings, Hall and associates (1986) suggested that experiencing psychological success early in one's career leads to further job and career involvement and future success. In other words, success breeds success. The process through which work goals lead to good performance, psychological success, heightened self-esteem, involvement, and higher future goals is a self-reinforcing cycle.

Given this growing body of evidence for the increasing importance for an organization to play an active role in the career management of its employees and the current status of minority advancement into the executive ranks, we felt that it would be useful to examine what companies are currently doing in the area of career development for their minority and nonminority managers. This chapter will provide an overview of corporate policies and programs. It is based on the results from a mail survey to the 808 firms in the *Forbes* combined list of the top, publicly owned U.S. companies in sales, profits, assets, and market value for 1983 that was described in Chapter 7. As you may recall, the surveys were mailed to the CEO of each company. A total of 218 questionnaires were returned for a response rate of 27%. Responses were well-distributed across industry type, with the primary concentration in durable and nondurable goods manufacturing; transportation, communications, and other public utilities; and finance, insurance, and real estate. See Tables 1 and 2 in Chapter 7 for a distribution of the sample and a summary of the respondent characteristics.

Chapter 7 discussed corporate perspectives on factors hindering minority success in management. The focus here will be on the practices and policies these corporations have developed to facilitate the progress of minority managers into upper middle- and top-level management positions. The questions upon which this discussion will be based are provided in Table 1. As one can see, there are three different types of questions. The first section asks respondents to rate the success of their company's performance on a series of

Table 1.   Questionnaire Items

Section A

Each item listed below refers to one step that a company may take to make more certain that minorities will successfully gain positions in middle and top management. For each item, please indicate how successful your company has been by circling the number, from 1 to 7, that best represents your company in your opinion. Please give a response that indicates what you consider to be your company's recent performance, on the average, for each item. No answer is right or wrong for each company's circumstances are different so please be frank.

1. The *hiring* of minority managers
2. The *promotion* of minority employees to management positions
3. The assignment of new minority managers to *challenging first-job assignments*
4. The *development* of minority managers to prepare them for promotions
5. The promotion of minority managers to *middle-level management positions*
6. The promotion of minority managers to *upper-level management positions*
7. The *retention* of minority managers after 5 years from hire
8. The *education of nonminority managers* in your company so that they make better decisions about minority managers

Section B

Below is a list of programs that many companies use to improve the success of their managers. For each item, please indicate how much this item is available for all managers in your company by circling the number from 1 to 7, which best represents your company in your opinion. (When we indicate a "specialized" or "formalized" program, we mean one that is written policy, takes place at specified times, for example, twice a year, and is or should be known as part of the company's development procedures by all managers.)

1. A formalized *mentor* system.
2. *In-house training* programs
3. *External training* programs
4. A formalized program to place new managers in a *variety of jobs* during their first few years so they can learn about critical activities in the organization
5. Systematic *goal setting* for job performance
6. Special counselors assigned to each manager to answer questions or give advice about career choices
7. Clear *career-path planning*
8. A formalized system of *feedback* on job performance
9. Considering all of the above management development items, which would you consider to be of *special importance*, if any, for the development and eventual success of minority managers in your company? Please mark all that you consider of special importance for minority managers.
10. Are there any special *programs or policies in addition to the above* that your company has found to be particularly successful in assisting the development of minority managers? If so, please briefly describe them.

Section C

In the following questions, we are asking you to briefly give your opinion about different kinds of problems or issues that may help or hinder the success of minority managers in business.

1. In your opinion, what is the most important *organizational policy or practice* that your company needs to use to ensure the success of minorities in management positions in your company?
2. In your opinion, what is the most important thing that needs to be done with *nonminority managers* in your company to ensure the success of minorities in management positions in your company?

Table 1. (*Continued*)

Section C (*continued*)

3. In your opinion, what is the most important thing that minority *managers* need to do themselves in order to ensure their own success in management positions in your company?
4. In your opinion, what is the most important *resource constraint* in your company that may impede the successful advancement of minorities into management positions in your company?
5. In your opinion, what is the most important thing that schools of *management* should be doing, differently or better, to make sure that minority managers are ready for success when they enter your company?
6. In your opinion, what issues, if any, are of particular importance for *minority women*, compared to minority men, which you think will have to be addressed before their success in business is ensured?

steps that impact on minority progress into the upper ranks of management. The second asks them to rate the availability of a number of human resource programs and practices that research has identified as being related to effective management development, to indicate which of these they feel is of special importance to minority managers, and to describe any additional programs that they have found to be particularly successful. Lastly, the corporations are asked to give their opinion about different issues that may either hinder or facilitate the future advancement of minority managers.

As this chapter is read, it is important to keep several things in mind. This is only a preliminary study that was launched to gain some insight into corporate experiences and plans for enhancing the success of minority managers in top- and middle-level positions in management across the country. In order to maximize chances of an adequate return, the questionnaire was necessarily short. As such, it provides a somewhat brief and "sketchy" overview of corporate perspectives on policies and programs needed to ensure success. Like most surveys, it lacks detail. For example, it does not contain questions concerning the specific characteristics of the types of training programs these companies may use to develop both their minority and nonminority managers or questions about what special programs may exist for each type of minority. It is also trying to assess corporate perceptions or judgments about what has and needs to be done to further minority advancement. Respondents were asked to make a judgment about the experiences of their company as a whole. The responses we received represent general perceptions and, as such, may not reflect the diversity of experiences in any organization. In line with this, it is also important to remember that the questionnaire was designed for response by the CEO or the vice president of human resources and that most of the respondents were white males.

The questionnaire does accomplish what it was originally designed to do. That is, it does provide a "snapshot" of the broader picture of what many companies are doing to ensure minority success in their organizations. In the section that follows, we will describe that picture. Our description will be based on the findings from the total sample of participating companies because there were very few differences by industry and respondent characteristics. Where they do exist, such differences will be noted.

I. HOW COMPANIES ARE DOING

Companies were asked to rate their recent performance on a series of steps that, if taken, make it more likely that minorities will successfully gain positions in middle and top management. As one can see in Table 2, in general, the companies reported that they were only *somewhat successful* in their efforts to accomplish each of these steps. It is noteworthy that the majority of companies did *not* report being either successful or very successful on any of these steps. The two steps where they felt they had had somewhat more success were in the *retention* of minority managers after 5 years from hire (23% successful; 36% very successful) and in the education of non-minority managers so that they could make better decisions about minority managers (22% successful; 33% very successful).

Our findings are consistent with the statistics reported elsewhere in this book regarding the slow progress minorities have made in the executive ranks of most American corporations. The companies participating in our survey reported having the *least success in promoting minorities to upper-level management positions and in hiring minority managers.* In fact, 64% of our sample reported that they were not at all successful in their efforts to promote minorities to top management positions. This is in spite of the fact that at least 90% report having some success in promoting minority employees to management positions in general and 44% successful in their efforts to promote them to middle-level management positions. In other analyses of the data, we found

Table 2. Self-Rated Company Performance on Steps to Ensure Minority Success[a]

	Not at all successful	Somewhat successful	Quite successful	Very successful	Mean response
Hiring	32	41	12	14	2.907
Promotion	12	40	24	23	3.463
Challenging first job assignments	17	30	24	25	3.523
Developing	12	37	32	18	3.427
Promoting to middle level	23	31	22	23	3.420
Promoting to upper level	63	16	13	5	2.297
Retaining	13	27	23	36	3.903
Educating nonminority managers	20	24	22	33	3.561

[a]Percentages do not necessarily equal 100% because of rounding errors and missing data. The original seven categories were combined to arrive at the four categories listed above.

that relatively greater success in promoting minorities was related to the percentage of total employees in management positions. Generally speaking, the greater the number of total managers in the company, the greater the number of minorities in management positions. There was also a tendency for larger organizations to be somewhat more successful in promoting minorities to upper-level management positions.

Also of interest are the findings related to hiring. Thirty-two percent of our sample felt that they were not at all successful in their efforts to hire minority managers, and only 41% felt they were somewhat successful. Clearly, these organizations believe that they still have a problem with the recruitment and selection of competent minority individuals for their management positions and not as much with their development. This finding is consistent with the data reported in Chapter 7 that indicated that the problem identified as being of most importance to the successful advancement of minority managers from the view of these corporations was the *lack of qualified minority candidates.* Yet, 87% of them do report some success with developing their minority managers to prepare them for promotions. Taken together, these results imply that these companies perceive that they have the types of policies and programs already in place to develop minority managers so that they can succeed in advancing to their top management positions.

They also suggest that these organizations do not feel they can develop and promote the minority managers who currently fill their middle-level management positions into upper-level management positions and that they need to go outside of the organization to find qualified candidates. This interpretation raises additional questions regarding selection and promotion policies and practices. Have these companies been successful in their selection of minority candidates in the past? The response patterns from this survey would seem to suggest that they believe they have not because they perceive that they have the necessary development programs. Unfortunately, we do not have objective data to answer this question at the present time. Or, do these companies prefer to fill such top management positions from the outside and not to promote from within? Again, we did not gather factual information concerning company promotional policies and practices or succession planning in this study.

II. WHAT COMPANIES ARE DOING TO DEVELOP THEIR MANAGERS

In order to better understand what may be contributing to these reported success rates, it is useful to take a look at the types of human resource programs the companies provide for all of their managers. Such programs represent the mechanism that companies use to develop, promote, and retain their managerial resources. They also communicate something about the climate for development within an organization. The companies in our sample reported providing a substantial amount of *feedback, goal setting,* and *training* for all of their managers. More than 90% of them reported providing at least a moderate amount of feedback on job performance, 89% used systematic goal setting for job performance, 94% made in-house training programs at least moderately available, and 87% used external training programs. As Table 3 indicates, they did not report using any of the development programs to the maximum amount possible.

A formalized mentor system was the *least* available. Eighty-two percent of the sample reported only providing a minimum amount of mentoring to all of their managers. Special counselors, career path planning, and placing new managers in a variety of jobs during their first few years so they can learn about critical activities in the organization were also all less available. The presence of in-house training, external training, career path planning, and feedback programs were related to a higher percentage of total employees in management positions.

In analyzing the data from the survey, we looked at what programs or policies might be related to success in the promotion of minorities to management positions. The results indicated that *different* programs were related to success in promoting minorities to middle-level and upper-level management positions. As can be seen in Table 4, companies who were more successful at promoting their minority employees to middle-level management positions had in-house training programs, external training programs, used systematic goal setting for job performance, and had a formalized system of feedback on job performance. In contrast, although *goal setting* and *feedback* programs were also found to be related to greater success in promoting minority managers to upper-level management positions, in-house and external training programs were not. Having a formalized program to place new managers in a *variety of jobs* during their first few years so that they could learn about critical activities in the organization and clear *career-path planning* were found to be related to

Table 3. Mean Responses of Questionnaire Items Concerning the Availability of Programs for All Managers[a]

	Mean	Standard deviation
Mentor system	1.667	1.138
In-house training	4.793	1.430
External training	4.070	1.332
Variety of jobs	2.690	1.466
Goal setting	4.808	1.481
Special counselors	2.071	1.345
Career-path planning	2.714	1.430
Feedback	5.060	1.520

[a]The scale for each item ranges from 1 to 7; 1 refers to a minimum amount of availability; 7 refers to a maximum amount of availability.

Table 4. Programs Related to the Promotion
of Minorities to Management Positions

Middle level positions	Upper level positions
In-house training	Variety of jobs
External training	Career-path planning
Goal setting	Goal setting
Feedback	Feedback

minorities gaining positions in *top management* but not middle management. Unfortunately, as indicated, these latter two programs were among those that were the least available to all managers in these companies.

III. PROGRAMS OF SPECIAL IMPORTANCE FOR MINORITY MANAGERS

The respondents were also asked which of these management development programs they considered to be of special importance for minority managers in their companies. The importance ranking of these programs are shown in Table 5. As one can see, the response pattern is consistent with the reported availability of these management development programs as described in the preceding section. A formalized system of feedback on job performance is considered to be of special importance by 80% of the corporate participants, followed by 66% considering in-house training and 63% goal setting for job performance to be of importance. Approximately half of our sample (49%) did indicate that clear career-path planning would be of special importance for the development and eventual success of minority managers in their companies. This is in spite of the fact that 44% reported having only a

Table 5. Ranking of Programs Considered To Be of
Special Importance for Minority Managers

1. Formalized system of *feedback* on job performance (80%)
2. *In-house training* programs (66%)
3. Systematic *goal setting* for job performance (63%)
4. Clear *career-path planning* (49%)
5. Early placement in a *variety of jobs* (47%)
6. Formalized *mentor* system (46%)
7. *External training* programs (38%)
8. Special *counselors* assigned to each manager (23%)

[a]Numbers in parentheses refer to the percentage of the companies considering a program to be of special importance for the development and eventual success of minority managers in their companies.

minimal amount of such planning available to all of their managers. Similarly, almost half of the sample (47%) considered a formalized program of early placement in a variety of jobs and a formalized mentor system (47%) to be of special importance to the successful advancement of minority managers despite the relative lack of availability of such programs for all of their managers. Only 23% indicated that special counselors assigned to each manager to answer questions or give advice about career choices would be of special importance for minority managers.

Respondents were also asked to describe any special programs or policies in addition to those already described that their company has found to be particularly successful in assisting the development of minority managers. These responses are summarized in Table 6. Forty-one percent of the 37 companies who responded to this question indicated that special training or management development programs for minority managers had been particularly successful in their organizations. The other programs or policies included management accountability, multicultural management or awareness programs, programs to identify individuals ready for promotion, role models and networking, job announcements, and race relations advisory committees.

Last, the data were analyzed to see if there was any relationship between the success a company has had in promoting minorities to either middle or top management positions and the types of programs they *say* they would emphasize to further ensure the advancement of their minority managers. Companies who were more successful promoting minorities to middle-level management positions reported that they would emphasize in-house training and external training. Similarly, those companies who were more successful in promoting minorities to upper-level management positions also reported that they would emphasize in-house training and external training. These findings are somewhat inconsistent with the data relating existing human resource programs to success in promoting minorities to middle- and upper-level management positions that were already discussed and shown in Table

Table 6. Additional Programs or Policies Companies Have Found To Be Particularly Successful (*N* = 37)[a]

Program or policy	Percentage
Special training or management development programs	41
Holding managers responsible	14
Multicultural management or awareness programs	14
Programs to identify individuals ready for promotion	14
Role models and networking	12
Job announcements	5
Race relations advisory committee	3

[a]Organizations in some cases listed more than one response so percentages do not necessarily equal 100%.

4. As one will recall, different programs were found to be related to success at these two different levels of management positions. Also training, both in-house and external, was only related to greater success in promoting minorities to middle-level, not upper level management positions. Thus, although our respondents believe that both in-house and external training is what is needed to ensure the success of their minority managers into their top-management-level positions, a closer look at the types of programs they actually have in place yields a different picture.

IV. CORPORATE PERSPECTIVES ON FUTURE ISSUES

The last section of the questionnaire consisted of a series of open-ended questions that asked respondents to give their opinions about problems and issues that will need to be addressed in future efforts to ensure the success of minorities in top management. These future expectations are important because they are likely to shape future policy and program decisions. Approximately half of our sample responded to these questions.

A. Organizational Policies or Practices

Table 7 summarizes the opinions regarding the most important organizational policies and practices that companies believed they needed to use in the future. Twenty-six percent of the companies responding to this question mentioned a firm commitment of top management as being critical to the success of their future efforts to ensure the success of minorities. Fifteen percent felt that more systematic affirmative action programs were needed. It is noteworthy that only 2% expected that their success depended on their ability to strengthen the financial condition of their organizations. The re-

Table 7. Most Important Organizational Policies and Practices Mentioned by Companies ($N = 106$)[a]

Program or policy	Percentage
Firm commitment of top management	26
Affirmative action	15
More formalized management development programs	12
Improve performance evaluation systems	8
Improve communication/awareness training	8
Improve career planning/goal setting	8
Increase promotional opportunities	8
Improve selection/placement	7
Mentors and role models	5
Strengthen financial condition	2

[a]Organizations in some cases listed more than one response so percentages do not necessarily equal 100%.

maining responses reflected the need to improve a variety of internal, human resource programs, ranging from more formalized management development programs to using mentors and role models.

B. Nonminority Managers

Table 8 reflects the respondents' opinions regarding what the most important things that need to be done with nonminority managers in their companies to ensure the success of minorities in management positions. Almost one-third (30%) of the sample felt that nonminority managers needed to increase their awareness of the issues related to working in a multicultural work environment. Fifteen percent believed that these managers needed to see the company strengthen its commitment to equal employment opportunity and affirmative action. Also of interest was the finding that 12% believed that nonminority managers needed to be held accountable for their achievement of their goals in this area with some type of reward or their compensation tied to their performance in this area.

C. Minority Managers

Almost one-quarter of the sample (22%) expressed the opinion that the most important thing that minority managers need to do in the future to ensure their own success is to perform and do the job. The other responses to this question are shown in Table 9.

Fifteen percent felt that they needed to be more patient and to minimize

Table 8. Most Important Things Needing To Be Done with Nonminority Managers (N = 117)[a]

Response	Percentage
Awareness	30
Company commitment to EEO /AA	15
Hold them accountable/reward	12
Enforce colorblindness (both ways)	8
Availability/selection	7
More exposure, work-related	6
Train them better	6
Nothing need be done	5
Mentoring	3
Time	2
Replace them/change them	2
Better train subordinates	2
Unofficial, informal training	2
Career planning	2
Create opportunities	1

[a]Organizations in some cases listed more than one response so percentages do not necessarily equal 100%.

Table 9. Most Important Things Minority
Managers Need To Do Themselves (N = 119)[a]

Response	Percentage
Perform/do the job	22%
Patience/minimize differences	15
Active career planning	13
Politics/mentors/culture	13
Better education	8
Continual/extra training	5
Confidence/assertiveness	5
Be better	4
Mainstream/get right training	4
Get feedback	4
Writing & communication skills	4
No difference	2
Support need for EEO/AA	1

[a]Organizations in some cases, listed more than one response so
percentages do not necessarily equal 100%.

their differences from nonminority managers. Thirteen percent responded
that minority managers need to take on a more active role themselves in
planning their own careers. Thirteen percent also felt that minority managers
needed to better understand the culture and politics of their organizations
and suggested that finding a mentor might facilitate this learning process.
Only 8% believed that minority managers needed a better education to ensure
their success in the future.

D. Resource Constraints

Organizational efforts to improve the successful advancement of minorities have often been hampered by the lack of resources to support or maintain their programs and policies. We asked the companies participating in the
survey to give their opinions on what the most important resource constraint
was in their organizations that might impede future minority progress. Almost forty percent (39%) of those who responded to this question felt that
limited promotional opportunities represented the largest barrier to minority
advancement. Also of interest was the finding that 25% of them felt that the
lack of qualified minority candidates themselves was the biggest problem.
The other responses to this question can be seen in Table 10.

E. Graduate Schools of Management

Opinions regarding what the most important thing that schools of management should be doing differently or better to make sure that minority
managers are ready for success when they enter their companies are shown in

Table 10. Most Important Resource Constraints
(N = 97)[a]

Constraint	Percentage
Listed promotional opportunities	39
Lack of qualified minority candidates	26
None	16
Inadequate training programs	6
Managerial attitudes and stereotypes	5
Other	7

[a]Organizations in some cases listed more than one response so percentages do not necessarily equal 100%.

Table 11. Almost half of the sample (43) believed that the curriculum should be changed so that more emphasis is placed on communication skills, interpersonal skills, and affirmative action. Consistent with their recommendations that minority managers themselves need to perform, 15% of our respondents felt that graduate schools of management need to maintain the same set of high standards for minorities and nonminorities. Only 6% felt that graduate schools of management need to focus on the recruitment of more minority students. Likewise, only 6% mentioned that business schools should create internships or work–study programs so that minority graduate students can interface with company staffs.

F. Minority Women

The last question asked company respondents to give their opinions regarding what issues, if any, are of particular importance for minority women that

Table 11. What Schools of Management Should Be Doing Differently or Better
(N = 99)[a]

Response	Percentage
Change curriculum so more emphasis is placed on communication skills, interpersonal skills, affirmative action	43
Maintain same set of high standards for minorities and minorities	15
Greater emphasis on confidence building, strong self-image, need for upward mobility and corporate politics	13
Tougher standards	7
Recruit more minority students	6
Internships, work–study programs to interface with company staff	6
Increase technical competence	5
Invite minority managers from "real world" to share experiences	3
Improve job search skills	1

[a]Organizations in some cases listed more than one response so percentages do not necessarily equal 100%.

will need to be addressed before their success in business is ensured. The results are found in Table 12. More than one-third of the companies who responded to this question (36%) believed that there were *no issues* of particular importance to minority women as compared to minority men. Twenty-four percent reported that women needed to be more concerned with how they presented themselves in the business world. Only 1% of the companies reported any problem with the availability of competent minority women.

V. SUMMARY AND IMPLICATIONS

This overview of corporate policies and practices indicates that the companies who participated in our survey reported experiencing the greatest difficulties in the hiring of minority managers and in their promotion into top management positions. This finding is consistent with the frequently cited statistics regarding the slow progress minorities have made in the executive ranks of most major corporations. It is also consistent with the corporate perspectives on factors that may hinder the success of minorities in management that were reported in Chapter 7 of this volume.

Clearly, these findings suggest that we need to probe further into both selection and promotional policies and practices. Many questions remain unanswered. Future research needs to be conducted to determine what the specific issues and problems are with these human resource programs and policies. For example, is there really a problem with the availability of qualified candidates as these companies suggest? Or, is this a perception that helps rationalize the slow progress minorities have made in many companies? A similar rationalization was often made in the past when organizations were being held accountable for their failure to achieve affirmative action goals. The companies who responded to our survey reported some success in their

Table 12.   Important Issues for
Minority Women (N = 84)[a]

Issue	Percentage
None	36
Presentation of self	24
Women have to be better	8
Stereotypes/attitudes	7
Politics/connections	7
Need wider exposure	7
Need to work harder	2
Just a matter of time	2
Availability	1

[a]Organizations in some cases listed more than one response so percentages do not necessarily equal 100%.

promotion of minorities to middle-level management positions. What is happening to these individuals? As indicated in the preceding discussion, these companies also report being more successful in their programs and practices designed to develop minority managers in order to prepare them for promotions.

There are some obvious inconsistencies in these data. If these development programs are successful, why are the middle-level minority managers these companies have succeeded in promoting not considered to be an adequate pool of qualified candidates for top management positions? In order to answer this question, we need to look more closely at the promotional policies in these companies. Is it not the case that whenever possible, companies do try to promote from within, particularly for openings in the executive ranks? Moreover, as Schein (1986) has suggested, although most organizations claim that they use state-of-the-art human resource programs such as performance appraisal or management development systems, the ways these programs are actually administered may be quite different. Understanding how such programs are actually implemented or put into practice will help one better understand their impact on the development of minority managers.

From a policy standpoint, our findings suggest that companies need to adopt programs that place new minority managers in a variety of jobs during their first few years so they can learn about critical activities in the organization and to institute clear career-path planning. These two types of programs were found to be related to the successful promotion of minority managers into top-level management positions. Approximately half of the companies considered these management development programs to be of special importance to the development and eventual success of minority managers despite the fact that relatively few of them had such programs. Additional support for this suggestion can be found in the research cited earlier demonstrating the critical role that early job experiences play in later managerial success (e.g., Berlew and Hall, 1966) also underscore the need for organizations to have some systematic way of preparing, implementing, or monitoring individual career plans (e.g., Storey, 1976).

Our results also indicate that both in-house and external training programs can be useful in facilitating the promotion of minority managers to middle-level management positions but not to top management positions. Future efforts will need to be directed, however, toward discovering what types of training programs are more effective in ensuring minority success. Our findings further suggest that companies should implement both systematic goal setting for job performance and a formalized system of feedback on job performance for the development and eventually successful advancement of their minority managers to both middle-level and upper-level management positions. However, although these steps are both necessary and important, organizations must move beyond them as London (1985) has suggested and also address the quality of supervision, the nature of the jobs they provide for their managers and general organizational conditions if they are going to succeed in motivating and developing their minority and nonminority managers. The culture of the organization must be examined to determine if it is conducive to the development of managers. Some acknowledgment of this need is seen in the preceding discussion wherein our responding companies indicated that the firm commitment of top management was the most important organizational policy or practice needing to be addressed in the future. As Schein's (1985) work has demonstrated, the assumptions and philosophies of a company's leaders shape its culture and the subsequent socialization of its managers.

In looking at the types of programs considered to be of special importance for minority managers, one is struck by the fact that most of the suggestions or recommendations do not relate to selection, hiring, or promotional opportunities even though these areas were identified as key problem areas that need to be addressed. On a positive note, however, we do see less of an emphasis being placed on the need for minority individuals to acquire more education in future recommendations. Greater emphasis is being placed on management accountability that suggests a move toward structural or institutional changes rather than personal blame or inadequacies.

VI. REFERENCES

Berlew, D. E., and D. T. Hall. 1966. The socialization of managers: Effects of expectations on performance. *Administrative Science Quarterly* 11:207–223.

Bray, D. W., R. J. Campbell, and D. E. Grant. 1974. *Formative Years in Business*. New York: Wiley.

Campbell, R. J., and J. L. Moses. 1986. Careers from an organizational perspective. In D. T. Hall (Ed.), *Career development in organizations* (pp. 274–309). San Francisco: Jossey-Bass.

Carnevale, A. P. 1985. *Jobs for the nation: Challenges for a society based on work*. Alexandria, VA: American Society for Training and Development.

Carnazza, J. 1982. *Succession/replacement planning: Programs and practices*. New York: Center for Research in Career Development, Columbia University Graduate School of Business.

Hall, D. T., and Associates. 1986. Career development in organizations. San Francisco: Jossey-Bass.

Hall, D. T., and K. Nougaim. 1968. An examination of Maslow's need hierarchy in an organizational setting. *Organizational Behavior and Human Performance* 3:12–35.

Hymowitz, C. 1984. Taking a chance: Many blacks jump off the corporate ladder to be entrepreneurs. *Wall Street Journal*, August 21, pp. 1, 16.

London, M. 1985. *Developing managers: A guide to motivating and preparing people for successful managerial careers*. San Francisco: Jossey-Bass.

London, M., and D. W. Bray. 1984. Measuring and developing young managers' career motivation. *Journal of Management Development* 3(3):3–25.

McCall, M. W., M. M. Lombardo, and A. M. Morrison. (1988). *The lessons of experience*. New York: Harper & Row.

Schein, E. H. 1985. *Organizational culture and leadership: A dynamic view*. San Francisco: Jossey-Bass.

Schein, E. H. 1986. A critical look at current career development theory and research. In D. T. Hall (Ed.), *Career development in organizations*. San Francisco: Jossey-Bass.

Storey, W. D. 1976. *Career dimensions I, II, III, and IV*. Croton-on-Hudson, NY: General Electric.

Stumpf, S. A., and K. Hartman. 1984. Individual exploration to organizational commitment or withdrawal. *Academy of Management Journal* 27:308–329.

V

Plans for Action
Where Do We Go from Here?

The final step in the problem-solving process is to decide what needs to be done, and this is the purpose of Part V. For minority and other managers, for corporations, and for schools of management, we summarize what we feel we have learned about how to ensure minority success in management careers. We intend our recommendations for actors at various levels, because social change is a social—not an individual—process. And, we make our recommendations in several different ways, because different audiences will hear the message from different vantage points. To this end, we begin with a challenge to top-level nonminority managers.

David Clare, president of one of the largest and most respected corporations, Johnson & Johnson, tells us again that we all share the responsibility of relieving the next generation of the problems we have faced in our own. Clare tells us that unlike many other business problems, where experience can be the guide, we do not have a precedent for finding a solution to the upward mobility of minority managers. Progress has been made, but it is limited, and there is a perception that it may be coming to an end. An important implication, says Clare, is that minority managers currently at midcareer, if they themselves feel blocked, can discourage new entrants, thereby negatively affecting their performance as well. At the same time, the perceptions of nonminority managers are often that minorities are being favored over them. For Clare, therefore, overcoming the misperceptions by all actors is a key to making future progress. He argues that management development, however it is structured, should contribute to the solution, but corporations must also find a way to deal with the informal life of the corporate world. Finally, he also says that commitment from the top backed by accountability must lead the corporate challenge to provide access to top corporate positions for minority managers.

What corporations can do to facilitate minority success is also a subject of the Kanter paper, which underlines another major focus of this book, namely that changes must be strucutral—that is, organizational—as well as individual. Kanter applies the theory that she developed in her earlier work to

321

understanding minority advancement in management. She discusses the role of opportunity, power, and numbers, as characteristics of organizational positions as much as of the people who hold them and shows that minority managers may frequently be found in positions with low opportunity, low power, and in isolation from other minority managers. Opportunity breeds motivation and ambition, whereas lack of opportunity leads to reticence. People with opportunity develop traits associated with success, whereas people who are stuck turn off, according to Kanter. Similarly, people with power hold corporate positions with high discretion, visibility, and relevance; as such, they are able to get things done. People in organizations without power are more likely to play it close and are unable to help the careers of others around them. Whether one is part of the majority or the minority and if the latter, how large the minority is, also has an effect on how one is able to function in his or her corporate roles. All of these aspects of structure, according to Kanter, are often interpreted as if they had to do with personal characteristics, rather than being created by the design of the corporation itself and derived from one's place within.

In addition to providing the structural analysis discussed before, Kanter also summarizes what she feels are the key issues today. She bases her conclusions on the result of focus groups asked about minority advancement in management, as well as drawing from the literature and from her own previous work, which compares the management practices of corporations that are progressive with those that are not so progressive in people management. Among other things, she concludes that ensuring minority success is a good business practice.

Her analysis leads her to six conclusions that confirm the need for structural changes on the part of corporations to ensure minority success. First, old-fashioned, inflexible, and difficult-to-change assumptions of who is eligible for top-level jobs are often combined with very slow movement for change. Kanter labels these the dinosaurs and the snails. Second, she says that there appears to be verbal fatigue about the whole issue, meaning that people are just tired of talking about it. Third, she concludes that there is an implementation gap between the desire corporations are often assumed to have to make change and their actual accomplishment of it. Fourth, Kanter finds that structural barriers described before still exist in most corporations, and they continue to adversely affect the careers of minority managers. Fifth, she argues that a tendency toward segmentalism inhibits positive change in many corporations. Finally, she concludes that there is hope to the extent that some corporations are being more integrative, rather than segmentalist in their structures. Being better at managing change and removing structural barriers works well for all participants, including minorities in these firms.

In a subsequent chapter, Blake, DiTomaso, and Thompson summarize the conclusions from the Rutgers Graduate School of Management conference, Ensuring Minority Success in Business. This chapter serves as a summary of the recommendations for this book as well, because this volume incorporates much of the material from the conference and what has been added beyond the conference follows its logic. Blake *et al.* make recommendations for both corporations and for schools of management. For corporations, they stress the importance of commitment from the CEO; accountability for all levels of management, and suggest a systematic program to facilitate the use of coaches, mentors, and networks, for minority, as well as for other, managers. In addition, Blake *et al.* emphasize the need for greater effort in career planning for minority and other managers. Many corporations have career planning as part of their performance appraisal system, according to Blake *et al.*, but often more must be done to make sure it is realistic and effective. In addition, Blake *et al.* outline ways that corporations can monitor their success in the advancement of minority managers. They also discuss the role that human resource departments may take to enhance minority advancement, and they caution that it is individuals, not groups, that should be the focus of corporate attention and assistance.

Blake *et al.* also have recommendations for schools of management. They say they must be attentive to increasing the numbers of minority students and retaining them to graduation; enhancing the curricula to include training in multicultural management; and provide a forum for teaching students about the soft side of corporate life. They also discuss the role that schools of management can play in management development for midcareer executives, and they comment on the importance of published research for disseminating new ideas and new understandings of issues related to the advancement of minority managers. Corporations can also assist schools of management in these efforts, for example, by providing tuition reimbursement to their own employees or even paid leaves of absence and opportunities for internships. Due to the difficulties with revising curricula in most university programs, Blake *et al.* recommend an innovative way to introduce topics regarding the management of diversity in an MBA curriculum. They also speak to the need for group work that helps students from different backgrounds to learn how to work with each other. And, they recommend an elective (perhaps a noncredit) course on career strategies and self-development. Extracurricular actions are suggested to help minority students especially gain knowledge about how corporations work before they have to accept the first full-time job. Blake *et al.* also argue that schools of management need to be responsible for postgraduation follow-up to facilitate the career progress of minority and other alumni.

Finally, we remind our readers that enhancing minority success contributes to the productivity of the corporation and benefits the whole society. In keeping with the problem-solving framework around which this book is organized, we remind readers that the benefits of diversity in problem solving is that better decisions are made. At the same time that corporations are increasingly facing the need for more creativity, innovation, and resourcefulness, they are also becoming more diverse in terms of race, ethnicity, sex, and many other dimensions to the human experience. As these changes become more evident, effective management will become a key strategy for corporate, as well as minority manager success.

In this book, we have emphasized the need for structural change, that is, changes in organizational policies and practices and not just in individuals. But the need for systematic, programmatic change involves change at different levels, including among individuals. To successfully implement such change, we have also argued that we need to be cognizant of the differences among minority groups and between minority groups and nonminority women, as well as between both and majority men. Systematic change involves reexamining corporate culture, operationalizing the steps to success, and assessing the barriers to change. The result is an integration of business and human resource objectives. The benefits occur on many levels: more effective and efficient use of human resources, innovative and creative decision making, satisfying work environments, and ultimately, better products and the marketing of them. But there are no quick fixes.

Changes must be systematic and they must embrace diversity. To do so facilitates cooperation and can offset the unproductive competition that is the bottom line in many corporations. Effective multicultural management can also confront and minimize the competition for disadvantage that so often has been the result of recent efforts to solve social problems (i.e., the "they-get-it-all, what-do-we-get" attitude). Using the analogy to cross-cultural management, which most international companies have recognized is essential for their successful operation in foreign countries, we outline the need for managing the increasing diversity of domestic operations. All the multicultural evidence suggests that managing diversity effectively is well worth it for all involved.

13

The Corporate Challenge

David R. Clare

I appreciate the opportunity to share some thoughts on a very vexing problem. There are some things that I know a fair amount about. I am not reluctant, for example, to express opinions about production and manufacturing. That's because I spent many years working with machinery and with the people who design, operate, and maintain it. It is with a rather different attitude, however, that I comment on increasing minorities in top management positions. I don't pretend to be an expert. But I am somewhat comforted by the fact that everything I have seen and heard on the topic suggests that no one thinks he or she has all the answers on this question.

By most standards, Johnson & Johnson's role in promoting equal opportunity is excellent. At the end of last year, more than 9% of those in management were minority persons and more than 13% of our combined U.S. sales forces were minorities. Intern programs established by several of our affiliates in conjunction with colleges have helped accelerate minority and female job placement.

Our affiliates support our MBA leadership award program in which 28 minority students currently participate. It provides full scholarships for those pursuing master's degrees in business administration and offers summer training positions at our companies. One of our affiliates recently designed, funded, and implemented a program to assist qualified black candidates with financial support for academic work toward graduate degrees in the sciences.

There are a number of other programs I might cite, including one to expose minority high-school students to the business world during the summer. But after all has been said, the fact remains that minority executives have not attained a substantial role in our upper management ranks.

We are not alone. IBM—which has unquestionably been a leader in the endeavor to facilitate the upward mobility of minorities in business—ac-

David R. Clare • President, Johnson & Johnson, New Brunswick, New Jersey 08903.

knowledges that it too has fallen short of its objectives. That company's EEO director was quoted in a recent company publication as saying, "The company's number one goal is to improve the rate of growth of both women and minorities at the senior management and executive positions."

Articles within the past year in *Business Week,* the *New York Times, Fortune,* and a number of other publications conclude that American business has done a reasonably good job of attracting minority candidates for management positions but has so far failed in helping them attain a significant number of positions in upper management.

As with any problem, acknowledging that it exists is a big part of the solution. A review of what is being said and written on this topic makes it crystal clear that many people agree that concern with improving the positions of minorities in business is neither an illusion nor a passing fad. The concensus is that many minorities in business feel that they have little mobility, and they are tired of waiting for advancement.

Most of the problems that all of us face in business seem to have solutions that often arise from our experience. We know, for example, that new consumer products—no matter how good they look in test markets—fail at a rate exceeding 75%. We know that economics of scale in manufacturing are sometimes an illusion because you can't always economically manufacture the same product the same way in big markets and small markets. We know that research efforts must be directed toward useful products, or they will often be an unaffordable luxury that drain resources in the rest of your businesses.

We know these things because of our experience. We and other managers can learn from that experience and apply those often hard-earned lessons to today's problems. In doing so, we can compress the amount of time we spend on a problem, and we greatly increase the probability of success. In short, there is often an analogy between one business problem and another.

In the challenging question of minority management development, I would suggest to you that one of our difficulties is that there is no analogy, there is no clear precedent, and there is no base of experience on which we can confidently lean. All of us remember when it was hard being an Italian or a Jew trying to make his or her way in corporate America. Lee Iaccoca at Chrysler and Irving Shapiro at DuPont come quickly to mind as examples of how far we have come in that regard. Those difficulties—it seems to me—are largely behind us, but, even at their height, they were relatively modest barriers compared to what blacks. for example, are facing today.

As with any business problem, we will have a better chance of solving it if we can agree on how to define it. First let's look at some numbers from the federal Equal Opportunity Employment Commission. The number of blacks holding jobs classified as "managers and officials" increased more than 135% between 1972 and 1982. This substantial increase in the number of blacks working at our companies doesn't match what whites have achieved. Still, we have come a fair distance compared to our past experience.

What is worrisome, however, is that these black managers increasingly feel that they are trapped in lower or middle-level jobs with no chance of attaining senior executive status. The past president of the Black MBA Association was quoted as saying, "You would be lucky to find two dozen black senior executives who are heads of divisions or subsidiaries in all the *Fortune* 1,000 companies."

The problem is not unique to American business, of course. Neither government nor educational institutions have done a better job than business corporations. Indeed, there is, I think, consensus that business has done better than those institutions. Yet, we know that achievement has been limited and has lost momentum and a sense of progress over the last several years.

The ill effects of the situation are exacerbated by the contrast between expectation and reality. In the 1960s and 1970s, American business went out and recruited the best minority candidates it could find. They were often courted, wooed, and even raided to help achieve corporate objectives. Now that generation of people finds itself in a position that rightly or wrongly—it thinks is a dead end. Many blacks, for example, apparently feel they were shunted into staff functions such as personnel and public and government relations that effectively keep them out of line management jobs that would lead to top positions.

That attitude can breed its own negative result. It can hurt their performance in the positions they hold. Perhaps more important, disillusioned older minority employees can convey a sense of futility to newer recruits.

We recently completed a study among black and white managers within our own company. We were happy to find that they rate Johnson & Johnson as a good place to work. They think management is competent and the benefits exceptionally good. But they also have specific complaints that we take to be typical of the situation at a number of companies—dissatisfaction at career progress and a perceived lack of fairness in career development.

Gail Judge discusses the results of this study in more detail in another chapter in this book. We believe the findings from the study will help our affiliate companies to develop strategies to rectify and improve the situation for minority managers.

The problem in industry in general was expressed by Eleanor Holmes Norton, former EEOC Commissioner: "If the first generation of blacks has inordinate difficulties, it will act as a discouragement to others. Corporate personnel directors must be sensitive to the mid-corporate life problems of blacks who could form a whole subgroup of disheartened workers within corporations."

One of the most disturbing aspects of the problem to me is the one of perception. In instance after instance, people see the same situations and draw different conclusions. In an IBM survey printed earlier this year, the question was put: "Is the company doing too much or too little?" Twenty-nine percent of the white males and females said "too much," whereas 36% of the minority employees said "too little." Our own surveys bear out that same point. A significant number of white managers feel that black managers, by virtue of their race, receive more favorable treatment than white managers.

At the same time, a significant number of blacks who left the company indicate that they feel they were forced out because they were black. It seems to me that such perceptions are the heart of the problem.

If there is such a gulf of misunderstanding between blacks and whites in business, little progress can be made. Maybe we should all keep that foremost in our minds as we seek ways to improve the situation.

I won't offer answers to this problem here, but I will pose some questions that many people think are either completely true or completely false: Are minorities penalized by their experience so that they are unable to absorb a corporate culture as easily as others? Is there additional pressure on minorities, artifical barriers that they have to surmount? Is more expected of managers because they are black, and do they have to do better than a comparable person of another background? Or is it the reverse, and minorities are favored and treated with kid gloves so that they are never truly tested?

These are hard questions. They bring out people's emotions, and the answers can be painful. But perhaps only by raising the questions openly more often can we be confident of getting the right answers. And only with those answers can we properly define attitudes and change them if need be.

Attitudes are critical, but we mustn't lose sight of the fact that we are also talking here about a larger question of management development. It is possible that some of the difficulties with the advancement of minorities spring from larger difficulties in industry in general.

Is it fair to put a minority manager into a sink or swim situation without proper guidance, and is that why some of them are sinking? It seems to me that, before you can answer that question, you have to ask whether it is fair to put *any* person into such a situation. If your company has a carefully structured management development program with clearly defined patterns of advancement, precisely stipulated tenures in certain positions leading to other positions, and well-conceived and regular personnel evaluations, then such standards must apply to everyone equally.

If, on the other hand, your company tends to treat management development more by the seat of its pants—putting people into spots they are almost ready for on the theory that they will achieve more than they think they can—then everyone should be put on that basis, too.

Or your company may not have a clear bent in either direction but assumes the role of the individual manager is to keep the personal development of his or her subordinate clearly in mind. Such a policy must be pursued with particular care in the case of minority managers.

Several years ago, the book entitled *Black Life in Corporate America* was widely hailed for alerting us that minorities were unhappy with the progress they had made in business and skeptical if not despairing of their hopes for the future. This was a revelation to many corporate managers. But some minorities who read the book with care were concerned that it did not contain a strategy for individuals to attain success. Even so, in their view, the book properly stressed informal considerations that are often more important than formal ones in the progress of minorities within a corporation.

It is easy for some of us to dismiss the emphasis on informal contact, on life-style, or on how comfortable one person feels with another, but we should listen carefully to minorities themselves before we dismiss this concern. Consider for a moment this quote from the sole black partner of one of the nation's largest executive search firms: "By and large, it is a matter of chemistry. Most companies want a guy who is six foot two, blue-eyed and blond." Whether that is true or false, some people obviously believe it, and it affects their confidence and their self-esteem. This is a more subtle thing than prejudice. It is an attitude and view of the world that can cripple a person's ability to function effectively.

Greater exposure between minorities and white corporate management will help improve informal understanding. Our chairman last year participated in such a program when he went to Florida A & M University as one of a series of executives who talked to students at weekly forums there. Whatever you call that—acculturation, socialization, or whatever—it makes those students aware that someone takes them seriously and closes, ever so slightly, the gap between them and white corporate management.

One of the most obvious ways to help break this pattern is to create viable role models for aspiring minorities. One successful minority manager in a responsible position—providing a clear demonstration every day of unquestioned competence—is probably worth scores of other efforts.

Let me end by mentioning some other ways that top management can communicate its support for a commitment to equal opportunity in executive ranks:

1. Upper management can set the example at the top. Appointing minorities to key positions on boards of directors sets a good example.
2. Support for EEO must become part of the company's climate through expressed concern and help.
3. Tangible support must be provided for managers at all levels, including backing up their decisions and supporting policies.
4. Training programs for both white managers and the minority managers reporting to them can provide, simultaneously, an expression of top management concern and a means of improving attitudes and skills. Some people have recommended special training assignments. These would help young managers get some exposure through different career opportunities to assist minorities in developing skills necessary to move into top management positions.

There are, I am sure, a number of other things that should be carefully considered, many of which are discussed in other chapters in this book.

Most important, however, in my opinion is one word—*accountability*. We all know that management development takes place best in our companies when individual managers know that they are regularly measured and evaluated on their ability to select and develop good executives. They know, and we know, that the best way to get to the top is to rise on a foundation of talented and aggressive managers pushing from below.

When managers know that their ability to develop people is being looked at almost as closely as their ability to deliver profits, they will pay attention and work hard at it. It seems to me the same thing must be true to make minority executive development work. We must get our best managers to understand that their ability to solve this toughest of management development problems has a direct bearing on their individual success. To do otherwise is to ignore a pool of potential executive talent that cannot and must not be overlooked.

If we fail, it would send a message to still another generation of minority young people that opportunity doesn't exist for them. If too much time passes without more minorities emerging into top management, we may permanently see many more youngsters who believe that great success can only be attained in sports or entertainment. If business cannot meet that challenge, who can?

14

Ensuring Minority Achievement in Corporations

The Importance of Structural Theory and Structural Change

Rosabeth Moss Kanter

In 1977, I proposed a theory to account for the differential success of some groups (e.g., white males) compared to others (e.g., women and minorities) in the management and upper professional ranks of corporations (Kanter 1977a). This theory shifted the focus of attention away from individual characteristics of the members of the group and toward aspects of organizational position. It shifted the "credit" or the "blame" for job achievement away from personality or learned propensity and toward the position or structural location as a determinant of work behavior and occupational achievement. Therefore, action steps to change *structures,* not individuals, are the natural extension of the theory.

In this chapter, I revisit this model to examine its relevance today. How much change has there been from the perspective of this theory, and what other kinds of changes need to be made?

I. THE STRUCTURAL THEORY

The theory has three essential elements: opportunity, power, and numbers. Each of them has a profound effect on who succeeds and who fails in organizations. And affecting or changing these structural variables makes a

Rosabeth Moss Kanter • Class of 1960 Professor of Business Administration, Harvard Business School, Boston, Massachusetts 02163.

difference in the degree to which people can move ahead, especially in large corporations.

Opportunity, first, is a critical aspect of work motivation, accounting for the persistence of negative stereotypes about groups who have been outside of the mainstream.

Opportunity is defined in terms of the developmental potential of jobs. From any particular position, how possible is it to move into other positions; how much access is open to other activities?

Opportunity concerns career growth, and that growth can happen broadly, through new learning opportunities. new challenge, or new responsibilities as well as through promotion. But in the major American corporations that I was preoccupied with as I developed this theory a decade ago, opportunity tended to converge on only one process—upward mobility. So all of the other ways in which people could be developed or could grow into higher positions tended to be inaccessible without career promotions up a ladder. Furthermore, the presence or absence of this kind of opportunity tended to divide people into two different groups that can be called the "moving" and the "stuck."

The "moving" are very well known; so much so that like the large numbers of words the Eskimos have for snow because of its salience, the corporate world has a large number of colorful names and labels to refer to people who are moving. (One way to learn about any culture is by simply seeing how many words proliferate around a phenomenon.) In American corporations, I have counted at least 20 different pseudonyms for people who are in that moving position, including "high-flyers," "superstars," "fast-trackers," "giants," "one-performers," "high pots," "golden boys," and "water-walkers."

In contrast to the "water-walkers" and the "fast-trackers" who are given developmental opportunities and moved along the ladder because of their location in the jobs with growth potential are the people that can be called the "stuck." Their informal names and labels are also revealing: "deadwood," "over-the-hill," "paycheck-oriented, not career-oriented," "just nine-to-fivers." The images are all of people who cannot be counted on or expected to do any more than today's job. But even though the label gets attached to a person, it is really a description of a stuck situation.

There are systematic differences between the moving and the stuck in work behavior and motivation.

The moving, not surprisingly, show higher aspirations. If the doors were opened, the movers wanted to move right in them. The stuck, in contrast, tended to lower their aspirations even if they started out very ambitious. Second, the moving tend to be more goal-oriented and set higher achievement standards. The stuck set lower standards because of their limited opportunity—why bother to try to do better if the job will not change? Third, the moving tend to exhibit greater work commitment and engagement—even to the extent of becoming "workaholics"—because they were given so many opportunities to move along and up the corporate ladder. But the stuck tended to disengage and dream of escape. In fact the dreams of escape for people in various sections of the corporation, minority or majority, tended to be remarkably the same regardless of the part of the corporation they were in: for men in blue-collar jobs, to run a small business, such as a gas station; for women in clerical jobs, to run a family; for men in management and professional jobs, to run a consulting firm. Despite the superficial differences in arena, the underlying issue was similar.

The people who felt that they were deprived of opportunities within an organization wanted another realm where they could be in charge, be important, grow through watching the business or family grow.

This theory helped account for why the development and persistence of certain stereotypes about minority groups: "They're not as ambitious," or "maybe a little lazy," or "they don't have the same kinds of achievement aspirations," or "you can't count on them for that 150% effort." All of those stereotypes tended to reflect stuckness. The people with high opportunity, who were moving, developed all of the traits associated with success. The people who were stuck responded to their situations, turned off. So the first factor in ensuring minority success is to ensure true opportunity: placement in the jobs with advancement and development potential.

The second element in the theory is power, an important and sometimes provocative concept. The structure of power influences behavior and success chances because of the amount of power available to particular positions and organizational locations. Job level or title is not enough to determine success prospects without examining in detail how much power a job really made available. People who are powerful are known to be able to get things done. It is an active rather than a passive concept. Power in organizations does not necessarily correlate with height on the organization chart or closeness of reporting to central (corporate) authority—indeed, in some major American corporations the closer a job is to corporate staff, the less power may be available.

Instead, power concerns the ability to get things done, to mobilize resources, to gather the information resources and support it takes to have an impact, to make a difference. Some people, by virtue of position in power structures, are more able than others to gather those kinds of power tools.

Like opportunity, access to power is a matter of the design of the organization and the location of certain people in the structure. The first aspect of power, is a job with high discretion—where occupants can make their own decisions about what to do, and routines, rules, precedents, or detailed orders are relatively uncommon. Second, gathering power is easier in jobs with high visibility, where achievements can be easily known, permitting the person in the job to develop a track record. A track record is essential in getting others to lend the tools of power—for example, to give support when they have ideas, to give information, or to allow budget extensions. Third, people also have more power if they are in jobs with "relevance," jobs controlling uncertainty or involved with solving the critical problems of the organization.

Finally, power stems from forming certain kinds of powerful alliances, because nobody gets things done alone in organizations. Effective power-holders always work through and with other people.

The first power-conferring alliance is upward, with backers and supporters at higher levels, often called sponsors who would confer reflected power—some of their own aura—that would convey legitimacy as well as open doors. Real power, as opposed to the ability to just do the job, requires the endorsement of others with power who say, in effect, "You're not taking a chance by betting on this person."

In addition to sponsors, power alliances come from peers and below—peer support and the ability to build a team below, who can back up the person, reinforce his or her leadership, and help him or her with accomplishments.

Data show that minorities are not only disproportionately found in stuck positions in organizations, but they are also disproportionately missing from the positions with high discretion, high visibility, and high relevance. Furthermore, they are less often in a position to build the kinds of alliances necessary to have power.

The absence of access to power helps account for other familiar stereotypes persisting around minorities in organizations. The sentence proposing that "nobody wants to work for one" can be ended with the name of nearly any group that has been excluded in organizations. My research shows that when people have preferences for bosses, they want bosses with power. Therefore, in resisting minorities or women, they are not so much describing whether or not they wanted to work for a particular kind of person, as they are guessing about who is likely to be well-positioned enough in the corporate structure to help their own careers. The stereotype about *people* turns out to be a conclusion about *power*. A second stereotype holds that people in the out groups do not make good leaders. But research shows that, almost inevitably, people seen as having power are also seen as being good leaders. They are given more latitude, liked better, viewed as more attractive, and forgiven for their excesses.

Thus all the things that give people advantages in leadership roles seem to be available to people well-positioned in the corporate structure to gain power. The second action step from this theory, then, involves change in who gets access to power—not power in the sense of necessarily being the dominant party but the simple power of being able to get things done, to be potent in the organization.

The third building block of the theory is the phenomenon of numbers or the difference effect—the sheer effects of being the only one of a kind in a group of another kind.

This experience can be conveyed in the form of a fable or a parable (Kanter, 1980) about the fate of one "O" in a group composed of nothing but Xs.

This is another important building block of the theory explaining organizational achievement, because opportunity and power alone do not necessarily guarantee that people who are "different" can easily succeed in a large organization. (And "difference" also affects access to opportunity and power.)

The only "O" (or those who are few in numbers because they are in nontraditional roles) faces distinctive pressures influencing his or her organizational performance. They live in a fishbowl and seem to operate on a tightrope. They are scrutinized more carefully, their achievements evaluated more. They were asked to be a representative of their group rather than to be themselves. They felt they must overachieve in order to simply hold their place. And therefore, they felt there was undue pressure on them—as accounts of stress among black executives indicate (see Campbell, 1982; Davis and Watson, 1982). In some cases, they feel they must turn their back on the group they came from in order to be accepted by their new group—the X group or the majority group.

People in this position also face what economists have termed "statistical discrimination"—that is the assumption that the Os, the *unusual* member of their group (because they are pioneers in a nontraditional role) must be exactly like all the other members of their group that play the traditional roles. So when Xs see an "O," they make an assumption that that singular O must fit all the stereotypes of the others who are not achieving members of the corporation.

Thus, minorities and women in new corporate jobs are constantly battling old images. There are a set of very familiar and often contradictory stereotypes that to be applied to out-groups almost regardless of who the out-group is. For example, stereotypes proclaim that the right role for an O is to be nurturant, or more effective in a helper role, a mother or servant; sexy or athletic; a figure for fun, an entertainer, or cheerleader. These three all reflect classic positions for the immigrant, the former slave, or the woman who chooses to enter men's worlds; many prominent blacks, Jews, and Irish rose through sports or show business—when they could move out of servant or caretaker roles. But if the O rejects fitting into classic stereotypes, he or she is then labeled too militant, too aggressive.

The very commonness of those sorts of stereotypes assigned to different groups and the commonness of the situation that occurred when people were isolated reinforced the importance of *numbers* along with opportunity and power. Letting in just a few of a group or spreading them one by one throughout the organization is not good enough (Martin and Pettigrew, 1983). Because numbers count, organizations need to avoid creating isolates—Os in a sea of Xs—simply to make it easier for both Os and Xs to play normal parts rather than the exaggerated drama of tokenism (see Kanter, 1980).

II. THE SITUATION TODAY

To advance minorities and women, then, change needs to occur in the structures of opportunity, power, and numbers. But since public attention has focused on these issues, what sorts of changes have actually occurred? I looked at three different sources of data about change or lack of change. One was my own work for *The Change Masters*, an account of the kind of corporation that is more innovative, more entrepreneurial, and that will have to be the model for the future (Kanter, 1983). I also reviewed the research of schol-ars studying minorities in the corporation, such as John Fernandez, George Davis and Glegg Watson, and others. Then I reviewed data from a field study that Goodmeasure, Inc. had recently conducted for a major American corpo-ration concerned with careers for minorities. The study involved interviews with 16 groups of male and female majority and minority (black and Hispanic) managers, composed according to sex and race so that they were in homoge-nous groups (Goodmeasure, 1983).

I drew six conclusions from these data that confirm the importance of affecting the three key structural aspects of the organizations: the opportunity structure, the power structure, and the structure of numbers. Without changes in structure, little will improve. But with changes in structure, the prospects for minorities in management are brighter.

A. The Dinosaurs and the Snails

My first conclusion is that American corporations seem populated by snails and dinosaurs. The dinosaurs are those corporations that do not see the need for change, are not necessarily ready for change, and are hoping that the forces of the market will somehow solve the problems for them—once overt discrimination is eliminated and doors open, then extraordinary action is no longer necessary. The snails refer to the snail's pace with which progress seems to be occurring.

Clearly, there has been some progress for minorities in corporations over the last decade. The number of blacks in management has doubled, for exam-ple, but the numbers have gone up between 1970 and 1980 from about 2.4% to 5.2% in the managerial ranks overall (and from 6.8% to 7.2% of public sector managers between 1972 and 1982) (U.S. Bureau of the Census, 1982). So the magnitude is still very small. There does tend to be agreement by the experts, by the corporations, and by the groups of minority managers that my firm interviewed that there is some progress. The beast is alive and moving, albeit very, very slowly.

Active discrimination is considered extremely rare today. One recent study of business students is typical in finding much less negative stereotyp-ing of blacks than in earlier studies (Stevens, 1984). And Fernandez's recent surveys reflect changing values and a gradual opening of doors (Fernandez, 1981). Yet, there are still concerns about how long further progress is going to take and whether, in fact, corporations have really addressed the heart of the issue.

I feel that business has moved from an *era of exclusion* to an *era of token-ism*—which is the necessary first step. They have moved in a few directions, generally toward the obviously talented, the already educated, and the al-ready suitable. So the problem has shifted from opening closed doors, to worrying about whether people get up the escalator—or whether progress will continue.

Attaining high level positions is a very different matter from moving into entry positions and the rung or two above. There are special issues at higher levels in organizations that are more difficult to address through the kinds of equity-oriented hiring programs firms put in. It is easier to open doors than to ensure upward mobility. One of the reasons for that is that higher level (or more powerful) jobs tend to be ever riskier and ever more difficult to evaluate in terms of the track record of previous work—the uncertainty quotient goes up (Kanter, 1977a, Chapter 3).

It is much more difficult to write good job descriptions or to do competency tests for the high-power, high-risk, general managership kinds of jobs in organizations. So in areas where jobs are high in uncertainty, decision makers have to guess about who has the character or the competence to do things that have not yet been done, are not clearly specifiable, and involve risk.

Whenever there is uncertainty about evaluating people's future performance potential because there is no past record to assess, no clear competency tests that people can take, and a long time before results of actions will be demonstrated, then what do managers do? They do the rational thing, they fall back on "trust": Who can be trusted to carry out a high uncertainty responsibility, carrying the firm into the future. And how do decision makers know whom they trust? Studies show that they are more likely to trust somebody who will make the kinds of decisions they would make because of social similarity. Thus does power reproduce itself in kind: people with power preferring others like them for the more powerful jobs. In short, the difference factor gets to be more and more important as a barrier as one rises on the ladder because it becomes (even unconsciously) a cue to the assumed competence of the people in jobs with high uncertainty—certainty of "character" or "response" or "values" or social type in place of certainty about job behavior.

Thus, without access to power jobs, mere entrance into the corporation will not produce change. People at higher levels need experience and comfort with minorities, and minorities need to get jobs that are sufficiently high risk and high visibility so that they have a chance to develop a track record that makes them "trustworthy" for the most serious and significant positions in the corporation.

A related concern about the rate of progress for minorities is the sheer time it would take if corporations let minority career mobility happen "naturally" without intervention. In a number of extremely sobering research reports, researchers have used mathematical models to project the time required to reach various forms of equality if there were no interventions such as affirmative action or change in corporate structures. One projection involved the time to gain black and white occupational equality, assuming equal occupational mobility on the part of each generation: It found that it would take eight generations before there would be equal occupational attainment. Another researcher found that the black and white earnings gap could be closed, the researcher said, if employers eliminated hiring discrimination immediately and did nothing else, in *50 years*. And more recently, a researcher studied one steel plant and varied the conditions and the assumptions of the mathematical model, concluding that even under a variety of favorable conditions (though not involving major structural changes), it would take from 24 to 56 years to hire 50% blacks in that steel plant (Feinberg, 1984).

Thus, the combination of snails and dinosaurs (old-fashioned, for high-level jobs, along with the snail's pace of progress for minorities as it occurs "naturally") confirms that it will take changes in corporate structure to create equity.

B. Verbal Fatigue

The second conclusion from revisiting my structural theory and reviewing recent evidence about the corporate world is the prevalence of what can be called "verbal fatigue"—that is, the impatience that affected parties manifest with simply discussing the issue anymore. Minorities want action, not talk. Majorities do not want action, but they also do not want to talk about EEO and AA issues. In the Goodmeasure study (1983), most interviewees did not want to speak with the consultants, let alone talk to each other about these matters.

The white, male managers often claimed reverse discrimination; they were concerned about the "lowering of standards" they thought was going on in their organization; or they felt they faced the same career roadblocks as minorities, without getting help or support. (Of course, on the latter issue they may be right. That is another good argument for structural changes. They do benefit everybody in the organization and not just specific groups.)

In short, the majority of managers denied the problem of race. But however they put the issue, they said consistently: "No more programs"; "let's not talk about this anymore"; "I can't go to another session where we open up the same issues." That disinterest is sobering—especially in the light of findings that the very successes corporations have in bringing minorities in sets the stage for new intergroup conflicts that do deserve attention (Alderfer, Tucker, Morgan, and Drasgow, 1983).

The minorities in the study also expressed verbal fatigue. They wanted no more talk, but for the opposite reason. They were cynical about their own corporation's efforts or were ambivalent about affirmative action. On the part of Hispanic managers, especially, there was concern about being labeled minorities in the first place. There was high variability in whether they considered themselves minorities at all (see also de Forest, 1984). In general, there was ambivalence about affirmative action because of anger at an assumption that minorities got their jobs at the company only because of affirmative action, not because of competence. So interviewees said, in effect, "If we keep talking about AA/EEO, it's going to look like I'm no good, and the only reason I'm here is because the corporation had to find people like me." Verbal fatigue, then, was another reason to seek underlying structural change rather than continue merely to discuss the issues and exhort managers to change their attitudes.

C. The Implementation Gap

A third conclusion centered around the implementation gap. This is a familiar problem in organizational change, even around positive issues like productivity improvement and innovation-improving programs, so it is not surprising that it occurs around minority career progress. There is a gap between corporate intent and results, between the desire to make change and the actual accomplishment of it.

In the Goodmeasure study, as well as in the research literature, there is a common perception that goodwill and positive intent with respect to minority advancement exists at the top. Even in companies where minorities are very concerned about progress and very cynical, they still tend to believe that top management's heart is in the right place. (Fernandez, 1981, is an exception. His survey respondents perceived better racial attitudes at the middle than at the top.)

Although good will was assumed at the top, a lack of change or implementation was perceived below the top. Rhetoric was not translated into concrete actions. Thus, managers were not measured on EEO (or even people development in general); there was uncertainty about appraisal and careers for minorities, and there was seen to be variability in the application of standards. People felt even when there was a formal complaint system, they did not dare use it because they would get labeled one of those "militants" again. Even when companies expressed good intent, then, there was a gap between the existence of a value and its manifestation in practice.

A study just conducted of 85 major corporations and their use of 40 progressive personnel programs confirms the implementation gap (Kanter and Summers, 1984). The most common programs were not hands-on ones that changed the way line managers operated; rather, they tended to be programs that could be put on from the top by corporate staff, like job postings—which was hiring-oriented rather than structural anyway. By far the *most common* of any equity-related program in the 85 corporations were career planning and EEO awareness—the former asking individuals to take responsibility for their careers, and the latter talk-oriented. The things that were *least common* were mentor–sponsor programs that attempted to influence underlying power dynamics of the organization. Despite goodwill at the top, respondents felt that the implementation of change was missing because things had not happened yet to change the structure to affect people on a daily basis.

D. Structural Barriers Remain

Furthermore, those structural barriers that I had identified a decade ago seemed to remain. With respect to opportunity, minorities in the Good-measure study felt there was cap on advancement. One manager said, "When I talk about being a vice-president, my managers say 'now let's be realistic.'" Minorities and women felt they were repeating jobs or remaining too long in jobs. Although this perception may or may not reflect fact—sometimes only statistical comparisons can show—still frustration was evident whether or not the facts were.

There are three principal ways people can get stuck in their organizational careers (Kanter, 1977a), with implications for the degree of expressed frustration. The first way to get stuck is to be in a dead-end job. Everybody knows this is a dead-end job, and everybody else in that job is in a dead-end too, which is the situation in some clerical jobs and some factory jobs. But this was not the case in the managerial jobs that the Goodmeasure study looked at. They were not dead-end jobs to begin with—quite the contrary. Thus, without more opportunity for them, minorities felt frustrated in watching majority managers advance.

The second reason that people can get stuck in organizations involves taking a nontraditional route to an otherwise high-opportunity job—a situation often confronting minorities. Whereas everybody else in this job is going to move on because they went through the right steps to get there, anyone who came in from a different door, through a different route—promoted off the plant floor to be a personnel manager or brought in because of a special hiring program—is often seen as lacking some essential background characteristic necessary for the job two or three levels above despite competence in the current job. And therefore, they start to get stuck regardless of current performance. This phenomenon may occur also because of the tendency of corporate programs to take majority blue-collar workers and give them opportunities in management; minorities are not the only ones to get stuck this way. It is ironic that people get stuck because of special programs supposed to give them opportunity.

Opportunity for minorities has also been affected by the state of the economy for the last few years, until somewhat recently. Because of this, many large corporations were certainly not high in opportunity, but were characterized instead by layoffs, freezes, and forced attribution, sometimes known by euphemisms like "de-hiring." Thus the third reason people get stuck is the pyramid squeeze: lack of open positions at higher levels and too many qualified candidates at lower levels. Under these conditions, if opportunity is equated only with upward career progress, then it is inevitable that some minorities will find themselves stuck, regardless of promise, and majority group members will feel more threatened by the increased competition and attention to EEO.

If minorities in the Goodmeasure study often felt there was a ceiling on their advancement (perhaps as a function of structural forces such as those outlined before), they also shared with the respondents in other studies concern about being barred from the power jobs (America and Anderson, 1978; Campbell, 1982; Davis and Watson, 1982; Fernandez, 1975, 1981; Jacobs, 1984). Even popular articles offering advice about the best job opportunities for minorities do not suggest that high-power jobs are readily available (Gayle and Lovett, 1982; Martin, 1984).

Limited access to power, like limited opportunity, has a structural component. Instead of the high-discretion/low-routine, high-visibility, and high-relevance jobs that constitute positions with potential power, minorities tend to be concentrated in staff jobs, especially in personnel and public relations.

Lack of sponsorship is also a problem for minorities. They find it difficult to get connected with people who will pull them along. But working for a powerful boss can be essential to get considered for important promotions in systems that scrutinize not only what the objective performance rating is but also which manager generated the rating.

And with respect to numbers, the third structural variable, minorities still feel very isolated, very alone in a world populated by another kind. Because corporations have let in just a few, those few experience the stress of isolation, of being in a fishbowl and being the brunt of jokes, having to develop "a good sense of humor" to survive (Campbell, 1982a; Davis and Watson, 1982). Such structural solutions as clustering (Kanter, 1977; Martin and Pettigrew, 1983) or support groups and networks (McNatt, 1984) are still rare.

So my fourth conclusion is that structural barriers do remain. Career structures or the provision of opportunity have not been affected. Alternatives for personnel development to lockstep ladder careers have not been considered enough. Access to power has been underexamined—for example, not just ensuring that minorities get into certain levels but that the jobs they do get are designed to be empowering. And finally, the issue of peer support or not being alone or finding at least a few more of the same group in the organization—this has not tended to inform personnel policy.

E. "Segmentalism" as a Structure Preventing Change

The fifth conclusion is that bureaucracy, or what I have come to call "segmentalism," inhibits productive change in these areas (Kanter, 1983).

Segmentalism is an approach to organization that involves dividing organization into tiny territories or tiny boxes and setting up fences between territories. There is, as a result, limited communication or mobility from department to department, level to level. Under this system, few incentives exist for collaboration or for moving outside of one's box. People are given very specific instructions and are expected to carry them out unvaryingly and with very little change.

As I show in the research reported in *The Change Masters*, it is almost impossible to get any change when segmentalism prevails—not only change to ensure progress for minorities but also change in terms of productive new ideas. Segmentalism stifles innovation.

The consequences of segmentalism tend to inhibit career advancement for nontraditional employees: for example, the kind of lock-step careers that occur—the limiting of opportunity to only moves up the job ladder. Growth and challenge occur only if promoted: otherwise, the person is stuck. Opportunity exists only through the hierarchy, so that if the person is unfortunate enough to have a boss that does not provide challenge, there is no way to learn anything more or contribute more. The job is ultimately confining because segmented organizations make very little use of task forces, special assignments, or other ways to help people move out of their boxes and learn how to do more.

There was very little power under segmentalist circumstances. Limited communication across levels and departments was matched by a dependence on a single manager for getting information from the system and to the system. This means that the achievements of minorities are not automatically visible, and they are dependent on the message their own manager—just one person—carried about them to the system. And, in turn, they are dependent on what their own managers—single manager—chose to tell them about what else was going on in the organization, as system barriers militated against stepping out to learn it for themselves. It is difficult to communicate directly—a level above, a level below, outside the department. Thus, under segmentalism, minorities, like others, feel bound and fenced in and limited by the structure.

Furthermore, in segmentalist organizations, there is limited networking and collaboration. The only networks that existed tended to be social and perhaps exclusionary—not task-related. In fact, in one case, an attempt on the part of minorities themselves to create networks to build a base of power and opportunity and growth and learning was undercut when the organizers of a black professional association were all transferred, thereby breaking up the network. This was done perhaps because of an unconscious desire on the part of this corporation to keep things under control and manageable with people in their boxes, in their departments, only focusing on the immediate job at hand. Segmentalism, remember, is a change-prevention strategy.

But under such conditions, it is difficult for *anybody* to feel he or she has much opportunity and power—and this accounts for some of the white backlash alongside of the limited chances for minorities. White males in these organizations feel that they, too, are deprived. The scarcity mentality that tightly segmented systems produce sets up competition between levels, between departments, and between groups. For example, in one classic instance of these kinds of competitions, there was a company in which department-to-department warfare was quite clear. Staff departments hurled epithets at each other that were like racial slurs: the finance people were called the "bean counters," whereas the personnel people were "the happiness boys" or "the giveaway artists." The warfare between departments was just as strong as the mentality of arguing and competing and feeling resentful across groups.

Thus, it becomes clear that the sorts of structural barriers that remain are found disproportionately in certain kinds of organizations whose culture and structure (in every respect, in terms of the way all work is performed and not just in terms of minorities or out-groups) inhibit progress for minorities—as well as inhibiting productive change resulting in business growth.

F. Rays of Hope: The Integrative Corporation

My sixth conclusion is more positive. There is a different kind of corporation offering a different kind of model, one called "integrative." Such companies are good at managing change, are highly productive, and also tend to be better at removing the structural barriers to minority advancement. In one very powerful analysis, colleagues and I compared "progressive" (by reputation) and less progressive companies in the same industries. The ones with the propeople bias, the integrative culture, were more successful financially over a 20-year period using any one of five measures of financial success (Kanter, 1983; Kanter and Summers, 1984). The new model, then is not only good for people, it is good for business. It makes a difference for all people in those organizations, enabling them to be more productive, and it certainly paves the way for greater future success for minorities, even if current numbers do not yet show it. The structural changes reflected in the new model have the potential to speed up the snail's pace of progress while avoiding problems of backlash because they do not produce the scarcity mentality.

The features of such Change Master (Kanter, 1983) companies can be outlined (although it is misleading to characterize whole companies because they often differ dramatically from division to division). They tend to be characterized by much more open opportunity and empowerment. Their job assignments are broad rather than narrow. They focus less on dividing up the territory (giving everybody their box) and focus more on getting people oriented toward results and doing whatever they need to do to get those results, including reorganizing the department, pulling together their own teams, using procedures or methods of their choosing, going outside the area, or taking on new responsibilities. The focus is on results, rather than doing just the narrowly specified job.

They tend to emphasize people development and communication across levels, across boundaries, and across sectors. They tend to be less category conscious in every sense. Not only had they eliminated the four levels of cafeterias that existed in the segmented kinds of organizations, but they were often on a first-name basis across every area or level.

One leading bank that is very innovation-conscious even considered the elimination of titles in order to remove barriers between people—barriers to anybody getting the opportunity to work with anybody else based on skills and competences, on contribution to a project or to getting results, rather than being limited by status, by level, by department, by function, by category.

Change Master companies also invest heavily in education and training. They have many more people-oriented practices and programs, and they have had them longer, as the comparison of 47 progressive companies shows (Kanter and Summer, 1984).

Power is also more open in these kinds of organizations. They are more decentralized. There are more power positions. There are more general managers who can approve things. There are more opportunities to take on significant line management roles for a piece of the business. Managers have a whole program or business to manage earlier in their careers. Such companies tend to use more teams, and they tend to formalize multiple relationships, whether via matrix situations, or simply the complexity of project teams that allow people to group across areas. Therefore, they are more empowering. encouraging more support, more collaboration, and more networking (Kanter, 1983, Chapter 6). And they share more information. which gives people one of the key tools to get things done.

Opportunity and power, therefore, seem vastly improved in these kinds of organizations. And also their "mix-and-match" kinds of philosophies, their networks and lateral trees, help somewhat with the problems of limited numbers. That is, minorities tend to feel less isolated and to feel there is more chance to show their competence because they can easily cross boundaries, work with people in other departments, get together and network across vast areas of the company.

But, of course, even an integrative structure is not enough, and opportunity and power will never fully equalize without special attention to increasing numbers. Problems of numbers still remain even in the integrative Change Master companies. The problems stem from the downside of this environment. Such companies substitute for bureaucracy a great deal of ambiguity, uncertainty, informality, leaving people to their own devices to get things done. A common job description in high-technology firms for example is: "Do the right thing." In other words, figure it out and make it happen yourself, without inhibiting rules but also without useful guidelines. Under those circumstances, people who are already feeling isolated and that they do not know the rules of the game sometimes flounder.

Thus the new integrative company reflected in leading-edge progressive companies is definitely the model for structural change, but it does not solve all of the problems. Increasing the numbers of minorities, reducing the difference effect, and providing the comfort of numbers are still extremely important.

III. CONCLUSION

Clearly the rethinking of organization structure is good for people and their careers. It is certainly good for minorities. Furthermore, it must be done if minorities are going to make progress, unless the society wants to wait the estimated 24 to 50 years, or eight generations, to see change resulting from the so-called "natural forces." At the same time, rethinking structure and culture is also good for business. The progressive companies are systematically more profitable, and high-innovation companies are the ones now producing dramatic market place successes.

The issue of minority and female progress belongs alongside the other major issue currently preoccupying management: changing corporate culture and structure toward the models of excellence and the models of change that have received national attention. If a people emphasis contributes to organizational success, that emphasis has to include *all* the people.

The organizations that will flourish in the times ahead, the organizations that can create sufficient innovation, will have to be, by definition, comfortable with diversity and comfortable with integration. The new model for management needs to be less category conscious and more team-centered. That model is the way not only to help integrate people who have been out of the mainstream, but it is also the route to business success in a time that demands high innovation.

IV. REFERENCES

Alderfer, Clayton P., Robert C. Tucker, David R. Morgan, and Fritz Drasgow. 1983. Black and white cognitions of changing race relations in management. *Journal of Occupational Behavior 4*, April:105–136.

America, Richard F., and Bernard F. Anderson. 1978. *Moving ahead: Black managers in American business*. New York: McGraw-Hill.

Campbell, Bebe Moore. 1982a. Black executives and corporate stress. *New York Times Magazine*, December 12.

Campbell, Bebe Moore. 1982b. Blacks who live in a white world. *Ebony*, March:141–145.

Davis, George, and Glegg Watson. 1982. *Black life in corporate America*. New York: Anchor Press.

de Forest, Mariah E. 1984. Spanish-speaking employees in American industry. *Business Horizons*, January–February:14–17.

Feinberg, William E. 1984. At a snail's pace: Time to equality in simple models of affirmative action programs. *American Journal of Sociology 90*:168–181.

Fernandez, John P. 1975. *Black managers in white corporate corporations*. New York: Wiley.

Fernandez, John P. 1981. *Racism and sexism in corporate life: Changing Values in American Business*. Lexington, MA: D.C. Heath.

Gayle, Stephen, and Lovett Gray. 1982. Ten best places to work. *Black Enterprise*, February:37–48.

Goodmeasure, Inc. 1983. *Confidential report to (anonymous) corporation on minority focus groups*.

Jacobs, Sally. 1984. In the mainstream, an uncertain victory. *New England Business*, April:13–19.

Kanter, Rosabeth Moss. 1977a. *Men and women of the corporation*. New York: Basic.

Kanter, Rosabeth Moss. 1977b. Some effects of proportions on group life. *American Journal of Sociology*.

Kanter, Rosabeth Moss. 1980. *A tale of "O": On being different in an organization*. New York: Harper & Row.

Kanter, Rosabeth Moss. 1983. *The change masters*. New York: Simon & Schuster.

Kanter, Rosabeth Moss, and David Summers. 1984. *The roots of corporate progressivism*. Unpublished report to the Russell Sage Foundation.

Martin, Joanne, and Thomas F. Pettigrew. 1983. "Overcoming resistance to minority inclusion: Shaping the organizational context." Mimeo.

Martin, Thad. 1984. "The best jobs for blacks." *Ebony*, September:35–38.

McNatt, Robert J. 1984. "Pride and prejudice: The story of black employee associations." *Black Enterprise*, April:63–65.

Stevens, George E. 1984. "Attitudes toward blacks in management are changing." *Personnel Administrator 29*, June:163–171.

U.S. Bureau of the Census. 1982. *1980 Census of Population, Supplementary Report*. Washington, DC: U.S. Government Printing Office.

15

Action Steps for Corporations and Graduate Schools of Business

David H. Blake, Nancy DiTomaso, and Donna E. Thompson

The previous chapters of this volume have presented the results of academic research, described specific efforts of various corporations, and related personal observations of minority managers. Part I of this chapter discusses recommendations for specific action steps to be taken by corporations. Part II outlines ideas that the nation's graduate schools of business might consider in order to address the issues raised previously. Our purpose is to be suggestive, though not exhaustive, and perhaps somewhat challenging. The reader should not look for exact blueprints, and thus be disappointed, but will instead find ideas that should be revised and built upon to improve the corporation's or school's efforts. Of course, any program of action will have to be shaped to fit the particular circumstances, current practices, tradition, culture, and objectives of a specific organization.

I. CORPORATE ACTION STEPS

A. CEO's Commitment

There is widespread agreement that the personal and vigorous commitment of the CEO is important to efforts to ensure the success of minority managers. Without his or her visible involvement, it is likely that the rest of the organization will not take seriously the pronouncements of support for efforts to improve the opportunities for minorities as managers. The CEO's potential for impact is based on the ability to use the symbols of the office, the

David H. Blake, Nancy DiTomaso, and Donna E. Thompson • Rutgers Graduate School of Management, Newark, New Jersey 07102.

management of the CEO's own office and staff, the role of the board of directors, and the willingness and power to set into motion policies that will advance the corporation toward its goals. A failure to exercise these opportunities will often be viewed by minority and majority managers alike as indicative of a less than strong concern. More positively, the full and systematic use of these opportunities will reinforce the efforts of others and will constantly remind people that the CEO means business on this issue.

There are numerous opportunities to communicate with corporate managers. Speeches, written messages that go to employees and others, award dinners, annual reports, internal and external communication pieces, promotional material, and formal meetings are just a few of the mechanisms by which the CEO can set the tone for the company. Many CEOs have periodic meetings with lower-level managers to take the temperature of the organization, and there are scores of brief and informal meetings during which others will be guided by what they see as the CEO's concerns, style, and image. All of these encounters provide an opportunity for the CEO to reinforce his or her personal commitment to the success of minorities in the CEO's corporation.

The composition and management of the CEO's office can also convey important signals to others in the firm. Although the size of the CEO's immediate staff varies from company to company, the staff itself is often perceived to be an extension of the CEO. Therefore, the conduct of the staff and the messages that they convey regarding the upward mobility of managers are an important way to reinforce the CEO's commitment. Equally as important is whether minorities are represented on the CEO's staff. Working for or close to the CEO is seen as a real plum and an important step in one's career. If this staff is obviously open to minorities, the message will be received throughout the corporation. If the opposite, the message is even clearer. The implications for appointments to the CEO's staff are obvious.

The board of directors can similarly reinforce their views on this issue. Whether through the establishment of a formal committee or the constant asking for relevant data about the progress of minority managers, the board, too, can make its views very clear. However, the board also should be aware of its ability to manage symbols on behalf of its goals. In its meetings or interactions with lower levels of management, with whom and how they interact will provide clues to what is deemed to be important.

Finally, but what is very important, the CEO will need to get involved in the process by which this commitment to minority success is institutionalized throughout the corporation. A strong personal commitment and the issuing of many statements on behalf of minority upward mobility in managerial ranks will mean very little unless the CEO ensures that there are policies and procedures in place to help make this happen. There are too many stories of well-meaning presidents and CEOs who find out that their personal support has not been sufficient to achieve desired goals if it was not backed up by organizational practices.

All the usual means of ensuring full implementation of any program, such as quality or cost containment, are usefully applied to the issue of minority manager mobility. Some of the more important steps are: incorporating the issue into the planning processes of the company at all levels, establishing clear goals for which managers are held accountable, helping managers to achieve those goals, measuring performance, and acknowledging and rewarding for good performance. In short, to do something about this issue, its importance must be articulated, and its implementation must be integrated into the full range of corporate procedures and practices. Anything less will produce less than satisfactory results. Consequently, the CEO must make sure that his or her commitment is supported by the full weight of the organization.

The CEO's role is crucial but so also is that of the many managers at all levels who are in positions where they can assist or hinder the progress of minorities. Unfortunately, in many companies, insufficient care has been taken to help these managers achieve successfully the corporate goals in this area. First, too often, specific goals for upward mobility of minorities are not established, and second, even more frequently, successful performance is not rewarded, and unsatisfactory performance is ignored. The failure to establish precise targets often means that managers will respond to the more traditional quantified goals but will neglect the unquantified goals that do not offer targets of performance. Similarly, the failure to tie reward to performance in the development and promotion of minority managers undermines the credibility of the entire effort. Minority managers are particularly unsettled about the continued reward and success of managers who are indifferent or who themselves do not make an effort to achieve corporate goals for the advancement of minority managers. Failure to link reward to performance in this area refutes the CEO's statements and fails to distinguish between those who work hard on behalf of the goals and those who do not.

B. Coaching and Mentoring

Another area for corporate action to assist minority managers is the development of a culture that will provide them with the direction and guidance that helps their careers. Unfortunately, in general, many managers are poorly prepared to fill the training or coaching function that is essential to the growth and development of more junior managers. The ability to coach a more junior person is rarely taught in business schools and not likely to be part of the corporation's management development offerings. Nonetheless, its absence harms the junior colleague in developing the skills and knowledge to make a successful career.[1] Although a problem when an unprepared senior manager coaches any subordinate, it is even more problematic when the subordinate is a minority manager because it is often one of the first or few times that the

---

[1] The inability to be a good coach and to prepare subordinates for future career moves can limit the growth opportunities for the more senior person, too. The senior manager's own career progress often depends upon whether he or she has groomed a successor, thus freeing the supervisor to move up.

senior manager has worked closely with a minority. The trepidations, the unknown, and the fears of doing something insensitive or foolish often result in little or ineffective coaching.

On the other hand, effective coaching can help the minority manager to understand and work with the work practices, managerial abilities, company politics, career growth patterns, and formal and informal customs and networks that are so important to success. But the minority manager must be told of the shoals and the opportunities just as a nonminority employee would be. Recently, a white executive on his first day at the east coast headquarters of a company that had just acquired his previous employer was pleasantly but directly told that in headquarters it was customary to wear one's suitcoat at lunch in the cafeteria. This friendly advice saved the new manager from making a highly visible gaffe and avoided embarrassment. In a somewhat similar situation with a different company, a black manager was not told of a particular custom in which the most junior person was to serve coffee because his boss was afraid that he would appear to be patronizing or interfering. As a result, there was awkwardness and embarrassment, both of which could have been easily avoided.[2] The point is that for a minority manager to succeed, he or she must be coached in exactly what it takes to get ahead, and the information conveyed must be extensive, subtle, and yet very direct.

An important variant of this relationship is that of the mentor.[3] Many executives recall with fondness and gratitude their mentors, the more senior executive who took a real interest in the junior person's success. Personal coaching, positioning the younger protege to get good experience and exposure, and forcefully advancing the cause of the younger person have all been instrumental in the careers of successful executives. This advocacy for a younger manager is thought to be a necessary ingredient for upward mobility, especially in getting beyond some of the hurdle positions in the management hierarchy. Some managers do not know how to be a good mentor; others do not have the confidence to be an effective mentor with minorities. Yet the lack of sufficient minority role models with mentoring ability and internal clout requires that mentors for minorities be found among nonminority executives.

Coaches and mentors can be particularly valuable in pointing out, explaining, and introducing the minority manager to important formal and informal networks that help advance a career through the making of contacts and the exchange of information. These are the formal and informal networks that exist in all companies. In addition, there are networks outside the company that may be important but largely hidden unless one is introduced. Networking is important, and minorities have a particularly difficult time

[2]Sandra Day O'Connor as a new justice of the Supreme Court faced a similar situation.
[3]In my terminology, a mentor differs somewhat from a coach, for the former becomes an active advocate of the more junior manager's career in addition to being a counselor. Of course, both roles may be performed by the same person, though that is not necessary.

identifying and participating in these social structures. Unfortunately, there are still some vestiges of discriminatory practices, for example, there are the exclusionary practices of formal clubs and informal groups. But even more frequent are the barriers raised through patterns of behavior that unintentionally or out of ignorance exclude minorities, a real possibility because they are so underrepresented in managerial ranks. The coach, the mentor, and the company as an institution can help to get minorities included in these activities.

Along with a systematic mentoring program, companies might consider the establishment of an executive resource system to which minorities (and others) may turn for advice on specific matters. Members of this resource system may have different specialities, for example, career choices, interpersonal skills, written communication, and others, on which they are willing to counsel rising managers. The formalization of such a system for minorities may enable them to obtain advice and guidance more readily than if it were left to chance. Any organization has a wealth of knowledge and skills among its managers. It is wasteful not to tap the storehouse of information and managerial savvy to benefit the ranks of future executives, minority or not.

Some companies have successfully established a minority network/support system. Where there are sufficient minority managers, a network of this sort may have many positive results, though a minority managerial ghetto will be counterproductive for all. Some companies are concerned about the establishment of a "minority caucus," because of the potential for segmentation and for problems being escalated in intensity. Much depends upon how a company handles its relations with such groups, for they are likely to be formed anyway, officially or unofficially.

To provide these related roles of coach and mentor for minorities, companies may want to identify specific managers who will provide guidance to the upwardly mobile minority manager. Of course, personal chemistry cannot be forced, but the opportunity for sensitive and tough-minded coaching should be made available in a rather deliberate fashion. Early in a minority manager's career, perhaps a coach and/or mentor should be assigned to him or her to help initiate the process. A more laissez-faire approach probably means that it will not happen. Because the mentor or coach may or may not be the minority manager's immediate manager, the coaching or mentoring role should not be perceived as undermining the traditional relationship between boss and subordinate. Instead, the "assignment" of a coach or mentor recognizes the importance of these functions and, in a sense, ensures its occurrence through specific managerial policies.

As mentioned earlier, coaching, mentoring, or counseling are skills that not all managers possess, but the skills can frequently be developed. A company that is introducing a coaching and mentoring system to assist in the retention and promotion of minority managers may find it useful to "instruct" the coaches in how to coach, both in general terms and for minorities in particular. We are not referring to massive and expensive programs, but we are suggesting that effective coaching and mentoring can be learned, identified, and used on behalf of the development of a company's managerial future. A modest effort can reap significant benefits.

C. Career Planning

Along with the coaching received, minority managers should be encouraged to develop a realistic career strategy and then to gain the knowledge and job experience that will advance those goals. It has been noted that minorities often think in terms of jobs, not in terms of careers. The latter perspective is long-term, developmental, and constantly in need of updating; the former has a more limited time horizon.

However, to identify the need is not the same as its implementation. Consequently, companies will want to work with minority managers to develop a career strategy, to identify possible career moves, and to recommend experiences, exposures, and knowledge needed to reach these more advanced positions. A number of companies have instituted career planning as a formal part of the management review or management development process. This is especially important for minority managers for a number of reasons. First, it identifies future steps and explicitly states the kinds of attributes and experiences required. From this, a developmental plan can be established that will enable the minority manager to see clearly what has to be done to prepare him or her for future growth. If formally developed and explicitly stated, the document can be a road map for which the minority manager and others (boss, coach, mentor, human resources person) can work to ensure that personal development does indeed occur. The corporation should make sure that this career planning is undertaken and understood and periodically updated to review progress and reflect changes.

As part of this process and based on career objectives, an inventory of strengths and weaknesses should be drawn up with specific plans for expanding the strengths and correcting the weaknesses. Although painful, such a self-assessment with the participation of others is an important step in formulating a plan for career growth.

There is some concern that managers generally find it difficult to talk openly and directly with their subordinates about areas where improvement is needed. This is especially a problem when the constructive criticism is directed at work habits, interpersonal skill, or style. The problem is often far more difficult when a nonminority boss needs to be candid with a minority subordinate.[4] Because of a fear of offending the minority or a reluctance to appear confrontational, there is a tendency to avoid such situations and perhaps gloss over some of the more difficult issues. In an attempt to be pleasant or supportive, candor and directness are replaced by indirection, subtlety, and inadequate communication. The result is that the essential feedback and guidance so necessary for self-improvement and growth is not provided.

---

[4]The reverse, a minority boss and a nonminority subordinate, can also present difficulties but for different reasons.

Obviously, each individual is different, but pleasantness is no substitute for constructive feedback and direction.

As a corollary, minorities should be counseled to move into jobs where there is high visibility and where their successes (and failures) will be noticed. Minority managers express a strong desire to be able to succeed, but the opportunity should come only after sofficient training and preparation has been received. Showcase or dead-end jobs should not be assigned to minorities with a good future in the company, for the short-term need of the company is likely to be a disadvantage to long-term career prospects. Some people have raised cautions about the ". . . tions" jobs, such as public relations, community relations, human relations, and others, for they tend not to be line, mainstream, or stepping-stone jobs. Obviously, this differs by company, but the general point is an important one.

D. Keeping Track of What Happens

Much can be learned about the success of a company's efforts to promote and retain minority managers through the collection and analysis of various kinds of performance data. Monitoring the individual career steps of minority managers may reveal problem areas that can be addressed or successes upon which other efforts can be founded. Here follows a brief list of trouble signals:

- Departments or units from which there seems to be only lateral not upward movement for minorities.
- High rates of voluntary turnover of minorities from certain departments or at a consistent period of career growth.
- Appropriate next-step or springboard positions rarely occupied by minorities.
- Disproportionate numbers of minorities in certain departments.
- Minorities frequently lose out for promotions to specific jobs.
- Relative to the number in the company or unit, too few minorities are identified as possible promotion candidates.
- Reasons given for turn down of minorities for promotion is frequently lack of experience or qualifications.

The thinking behind each item is clear, but special note should be made of the evidence that some jobs have attached to them criteria that are not related to the ability to perform the job. Consequently, instead of criteria, they become barriers to entry that screen out people who do not meet these irrelevant criteria. Although these job criteria are rarely designed to impede the progress of minorities, this indeed may be the result. For example, in one high-technology company where sales experience is thought to be crucial for any general management job, sales positions are only fitted with people who have already had experience selling similar products in other companies. Such a practice makes it difficult for minorities elsewhere in the company to gain needed experience, and it also precludes hiring minorities for sales positions from undergraduate or graduate schools.

Periodic analyses to ensure that the criteria for promotion to various managerial positions are well-defined, job-related, and consistently applied should be undertaken. The job criteria should be related explicitly to the ability to perform the job, not to a set of extraneous factors that may have been established years ago for some now-forgotten purpose. Many managers, minority and majority, agree that this is a problem that reduces the opportunities for minorities to move ahead. Periodic reviews or quick checks could be put into motion whenever a managerial opening occurs that has not been filled since the system of reviews was implemented.

Exit interviews are a useful mechanism for gathering data about the reasons for minority manager turnover. Much can be learned about possible improvements from candid discussions in these sessions. Similarly, companies may want to delve into the specific reasons why seemingly qualified minorities were not chosen after having been identified as possible candidates for a position. Perhaps the criteria are unnecessary to the job. On the other hand, there may be some experiences and exposure needed for the position that the minority manager does not have. If so, is this a failure of the career planning or management development process? The general point is that data can be gathered both in the aggregate and at certain decision points that can help a company understand what needs to be done to assist in the upward mobility of its minority managers.

E. Role of the Human Resources Department

The role of the human resources department is a critical but difficult one. Although it needs to ensure that various mechanisms are in place to assist the career development of minority managers, it should not be so active and interventionist that the operating managers have an excuse to avoid their own personal involvement and responsibility. Similarly, whenever possible, the posture of the human resources department should be that of helping others to be more effective, not that of telling others what to do or doing it themselves. At the same time, the human resources department has the responsibility to make certain that the talent of minority managers is being developed to benefit the company and individuals. Thus the human resources department performs several functions: It is an advocate for the development and promotion of minority managers, a consultant to assist corporate units and their managers to develop the systems, procedures, and personal skills to foster the upward mobility of minority managers, a counselor to individual minority managers to help them develop, and finally an operating unit to establish action steps that will help the corporation achieve its goals.

F. Focus on Individuals, Not on Groups

In attempting to deal with the general issue of the upward mobility of minority managers, there is a danger that a company's perspective may become skewed toward dealing with the problem in the aggregate. Minority managers are concerned about this tendency, for it is individuals who are promoted, not classes of people. Therefore, corporate action plans should be developed that maximize the opportunities for and the potential of the individual. Each manager, minority or majority, has different skills, experiences, weaknesses, and objectives. Therefore, plans that are implemented should deal with the individual and his or her repertoire of skills, not with a group of employees as if they were all alike and undistinguishable.

Of course, data gathered and programs established will benefit more than one individual, but, nonetheless, the purpose of the programs should be to enhance the mobility of individuals. It is an individual who has the opportunity for advancement, and it is on the individual that major corporate attention should be paid.

II. RECOMMENDATIONS FOR GRADUATE SCHOOLS OF BUSINESS

The country's undergraduate and graduate business schools have an essential role to play in increasing the likelihood of success for minority managers. These schools sit astride the crucial educational, research, and information transmission processes that shape the values, objectives, and practices of American corporations and their managers. Concepts such as participative management, competitive strategy, corporate culture, and many others have frequently been developed or refined by business school faculty and transmitted to the corporate world through books, articles, speeches, consulting assignments. and thousands of classroom lectures and discussions.

Although certainly not the only source, business schools are a major breeding ground for future minority and nonminority managers. In 1985, more than 230,000 bachelor's degrees in business were awarded, and nearly 70,000 MBAs were earned. Thus, these schools help to educate many of the minority men and women who turn to corporate America for employment, challenge, and success. Equally as important is the opportunity to shape the attitudes, skills, and behavior patterns of generations of nonminority managers who as subordinates, peers, and bosses have much to say about the upward mobility of minorities. The influence of the schools may be overestimated, but at the same time it is a mistake not to recognize and do something about the potential of the schools for having a positive impact.

However, the positive impact is not limited to the classroom alone, and management schools should be aware of the other ways in which they can affect this issue. Many schools and their faculty are actively engaged in continuing management education. Each year, thousands of managers receive midcareer, noncredit training provided by their companies. Some are sent to programs at schools of business; others are instructed by business school faculty who are teaching in-house programs designed and managed by the companies themselves. In either case these are ready-made and not very costly ways for a company to address the issues of upward mobility of minority managers.

The more research-active and knowledge-producing schools occupy a particularly important role in the generation and transmission of knowledge about management issues and practices. Their faculty conduct the research and publish the articles that set the trends for managerial thought and action. Whether through original research or more applications-oriented articles, new ideas and new concepts are often introduced and popularized through the prestige of pathbreaking books and articles. The resulting visibility gives some faculty and their schools an impact that is national in scope, a position of influence and leadership that can be used to shape the agenda for addressing these issues.

Business school deans and faculty are often accorded leadership roles in professional, business, or civic organizations, giving them the opportunity not only to speak to the issue but also to attempt to do something that will enhance the attention given to these matters. Moreover, many business schools have a program to develop mutually beneficial corporate relationships. Although these relationships serve many purposes, they also represent an opportunity for focusing discussion and developing an agenda that may help the schools and companies to be more effective in addressing the issue of upward mobility of minorities.

However, pointing out both the opportunity and the responsibility is not sufficient, and thus the remainder of this chapter discusses what business schools can do to help increase the chances for the success of minority managers. Although the focus is on graduate schools, there is much that is applicable to undergraduate schools as well.

A. Student Recruitment and Admissions

Racial, ethnic, and gender diversity is and will be increasingly characteristic of American corporations. Thus, our graduate schools of management should provide the opportunity for all their students to attend school, work in study groups, socialize, and generally function in an environment that is purposefully diverse. Much personal experimentation, observation, and learning can take place within the relatively benign environment of the business school but only if the student body provides these opportunities. Minority students can test their intellectual and social skills and thereby gain confidence in such a setting. Similarly, majority students will be able to learn about and gain respect for cultural differences, make mistakes of insensitivity and learn from them, and develop experience in working in groups to analyze a case or prepare a report. This intensely personal kind of learning cannot occur in a student body where there is no exposure to diversity.

As a result, the student recruiting and admissions policies of graduate schools should, and for the most part do, seek to obtain this diversity. However, the task is difficult. The number of blacks, for example, completing undergraduate school is declining. Some minorities are ill prepared for the quantitative nature of the Graduate Management Admissions Test and MBA programs. Still others never even consider that a career in business is an available option until it is too late in their college careers to take helpful preparatory courses. Other minorities succumb to the offers from corporations to begin careers following undergraduate school, postponing graduate management study for a while or often forever and thereby possibly limiting their career prospects. Finally, graduate school is costly, particularly on top of 4 years of undergraduate expenses.

Career and academic counseling early in the undergraduate experience is imperative, and these efforts may have to reach out into the social, religious, and other support networks for minority students. The process may benefit from corporate and graduate school collaboration with undergraduate schools to introduce early on the possibilities and the requirements for graduate work in business. Some companies have instituted highly successful intern programs for undergraduates and graduate students to attract them to the world of business. However, with a few exceptions, the efforts of graduate schools to build up the pool of qualified and interested minority undergraduates seem to have reached a plateau of effectiveness.

Some graduate schools have instituted summer programs for undergraduates or even high-school students, but there is a potential contradiction inherent in some of these programs. Many graduate schools prefer that their students have several years of experience before attending an MBA program. If minority students are encouraged to attend right out of undergraduate school, they may be at a disadvantage with their classmates who have had some corporate experience, experience that is useful in the classroom. On the other hand, some minorities will find it difficult to leave a lucrative job to return to graduate school at great expense, particularly when their employer is encouraging them to stay. In this situation, the short-term needs of the company may be working against the interests of the graduate schools, their own long-term needs, and the minority employee.

Financial aid is a big factor in attempting to increase the numbers of minorities in graduate schools. However, the issue should be viewed in the broader context of expensive undergraduate costs incurred (average college expenses per year are $10,199 for private schools and $5,604 for state schools) and the substantially lower family income base of many minorities. Their families are less able to afford 4 years of undergraduate college and then graduate MBA work in addition. It is not surprising that many minority students find it difficult to ask their families to help assume graduate school costs while they defer current income possibilities. Thus the financial aid issue is large and more extensive than the costs associated with attendance at graduate school.

In addition to increased financial aid for tuition and living expenses, consideration should be given to work/study and internship programs in which corporations sponsor minority students in graduate school and provide summer and/or part-time employment. Some accounting firms have established variations of this model for accounting students (not just minorities) with some schools. Of course, there is no guarantee that the supported students will join or be asked to join the company upon graduation. However, such a program, if widely adopted, could make graduate school more feasible by alleviating some of the financial burdens, providing on-the-job learning experiences in the corporation and assisting in the corporate recruiting process. By working with corporate sponsors, the graduate schools would be able to extend their recruiting efforts much earlier in the undergraduate years.

Recognizing that many minorities are not able to continue on in graduate school after 4 years of college expenses, companies should be particularly eager to assist current minority employees to obtain master's degrees. Tuition reimbursement programs for part-time study are widespread. However, special programs to assist minorities to return to graduate school on a full-time basis and with company support would be highly desirable. Again, there would be no guarantees that the employee would return to the sponsoring company, but the contribution made to that person's development and to the upward mobility of minorities in general would be substantial.

Perhaps a system could be worked out among corporations whereby a sponsoring company would be partially reimbursed for expenses incurred by the company that hired the erstwhile employee. Thus a kind of cost-sharing approach could be developed under the aegis of business groups like the Business Roundtable, the National Association of Manufacturers, the U.S. Chamber of Commerce, industry associations, and regional business associations.

The financial aid approaches briefly outlined are costly. However, the evidence suggests that the cost to individuals, the corporate community, and American society of not tackling these issues is far greater indeed.

B. Curricular Innovations

The MBA curricula at most graduate schools of business fail to provide the understandings and tools that will assist minority *and* majority managers to be effective in organizations characterized by racial and cultural diversity. There are two types of curricular innovations that can address the issue of minority success. First, the theory and practice that will enable *all* managers to be more effective in working with a work force (at all levels) and a consumer clientele that will be increasingly diverse; second, the training and development that will specifically assist minority managers to succeed in business. Both efforts should proceed simultaneously, for the macro- and microdimensions are of equal importance.

All students and managers need to develop skills appropriate to management in and of diversity. It is unlikely that a required course in this subject would be acceptable given the already crowded curricula, but at the very least, the traditionally required courses in behavioral science, organization theory, management of human resources, marketing, the environment of business, and business policy should tackle these issues in the context of their own disciplines and traditions. To avoid dysfunctional fragmentation, glaring gaps, and unnecessary redundancies, faculty teaching in each of these areas could develop a "course plan" that would identify specific topics that would be covered as part of the more traditional and broader course. The result would be a "matrix course" that would ensure that all students were exposed systematically to these issues but in a number of different courses. It would be useful to hand out to all students an outline and syllabus for this matrix course so that they would become aware of its special and well-constructed nature, its component subject areas, and the importance attached to the material by the school.

There are many topics that should/could be covered, but several stand out and are discussed briefly. Given the growing social and ethnic diversity of American society and the globalization of business, MBA students should be helped to understand and be able to deal with cultural diversity. Cultural awareness and sensitivity are going to aid managers whether they are whites working with blacks, Americans working with South Koreans, or whatever. These topics can and should be taught in ways that enable graduates to operate effectively in different environments and with different people and to identify cultural differences and similarities. In a similar vein, the development of an individualized set of interpersonal skills for dealing with diversity should be approached directly in the curriculum, not just assumed as something that happens along the way to an MBA degree.

Research and anecdotal evidence have suggested that mentoring and coaching are crucial to the successful climb up the corporate ladder. Effective coaching and mentoring are particularly important for the progress of minorities, and nonminority women, too, who are often excluded from the informal learning process that occurs in any corporation. Coaching is an important managerial function, but it receives little attention in most graduate schools. Consequently, a modest portion of the curriculum should be devoted to the coaching skills and the mentoring relationship, especially why and how to be a good coach and mentor in general and for minorities in particular.

The required introduction to marketing course should address the differing patterns of consumption of various ethnic groups and regions in the United States. The objective is not to point out differences but rather to emphasize that an understanding of the diversity of the markets will enable a company to develop strategies that may increase sales.

Of course, there are many topics that might be covered in such a course, and each faculty will design a course that is based on their strengths, needs, and particular context. A few of the topics that might be included in the proposed matrix course are:

- Income growth and distribution in the United States
- The growing diversity of the United States and its work force
- Discrimination in the workplace: Its causes and costs
- Understanding cultural patterns and behavior
- Managing diversity
- "Coaching" or how to develop subordinates
- Joys and rewards of mentoring

- Diagnosing the real corporate culture
- Career-path planning
- Ethnic, racial, and regional markets and marketing
- Government regulations and corporate practice in equal employment opportunity programs

Regardless of the specific topics, a deliberate introduction to management of and in diversity is appropriate for both majority and minority students.

Similarly, faculty can contribute to the effectiveness of their students by providing opportunities to undertake group work that has the by-product of mixing races and ethnic groups in a simulated work situation. No doubt some learning about diversity will take place by osmosis, but in some situations it may be helpful to address formally some of the explicit and implicit experiences and concerns generated by this group work. For some students, majority and minority, such projects may be the first time that they have worked in a culturally and racially mixed group toward specific goals. Both group and individual concerns or reactions may be profitably discussed by the interventions of a skilled instructor. Most of all, the concerns and reactions of the students, majority and minority, should be addressed and confronted directly, not swept under the rug to avoid dealing with sensitive or unpleasant matters.

Any school's curriculum will include a number of electives that can contribute to student learning. Whether as part of a more traditional course (e.g., marketing research and the need to differentiate between consumers of different ethnic or racial backgrounds) or as a separate course (e.g., managing organization diversity), opportunities can be provided for students to become more knowledgeable about and skilled in managing in a multicultural environment. Faculty should be encouraged to review their existing courses to see whether relevant material on managing diversity could be included.

In addition to the effort to expose all students to these issues, an elective course specifically designed to prepare minority students for the business world might be established. These courses could address some of the problems that minority managers may face, discuss career strategies and self-development plans that will enhance their careers, and help the students to be more effective managers in the predominantly white corporate world. A combination of rigorous cognitive material about managing along with noncognitive attitude and skills development may help minority students to effect a better transition from the student-level to junior-level manager and eventually to senior executive. Again, faculties will and should develop their own courses, but collaboration among faculty at different schools may stimulate ideas, concepts, and teaching materials that can enrich the offerings at a number of schools.

C. Extracurricular Programs

Much learning can take place outside of the formal curriculum in graduate business schools. For minority students it is especially important to create opportunities that will help them in their corporate careers. For example, many minority students lack experience in or even second-hand knowledge of large corporations. Internships arranged by the school can introduce minorities to the corporate world in a relatively nonthreatening fashion. However, the school's staff along with corporate counterparts should monitor each internship experience and provide immediate, comprehensive, and continuing feedback to the student about his or her performance and what has been experienced during the internship. Both in the school and at the corporation, specific people, with whom the student can discuss various issues, observations, and questions should be identified in addition to the immediate manager. The corporate world is complex, and learning can only take place when questions can be asked with confidence that the response will be candid and yet supportive and constructive.

In addition to a tightly managed internship program, schools can establish career strategy seminars and workshops designed especially for minority students. Staff members, alumni and alummnae, and corporate executives can provide instruction and guidance on what is involved in managing one's career, including the necessity of taking charge of a career, diagnosing the corporate culture, creating a network of corporate contacts, career pitfalls, dead ends, opportunities, and other topics designed to help minorities overcome the personal and institutional barriers that impede their upward mobility. Similarly, students should be confronted with the need to make personal choices in the pursuit of a career. Like it or not, trade-offs most likely will have to be made between the expectations of the company (and individual supervisors and colleagues) and personal life-style considerations. The potential for conflict between different values and the realistic implications for career success ought not to be downplayed. Candor and realism are essential.

Minority managers often mention the need to build up the confidence of minorities so that they feel that they can and will be able to succeed given the requisite ability, hard work, constant learning, and good fortune. This point is critical, for too often in the minority experience, there is the sense that the "system" is loaded against full and equal involvement by minorities. It is difficult to strive for success if one feels that it will be denied no matter how persevering or effective a person is. Therefore, bringing successful minority managers to campus as role models will help in instilling the conviction that it is possible for a minority man or woman to achieve significant responsibility and success in the corporate community. Other efforts to build a sense of personal ability and empowerment along with the knowledge to work effectively in the system should be pursued.

D. Postgraduation Follow-Up

Many graduate schools of business assist their alumni with career or job changes, networking events, and professional update sessions. In addition to these, schools could make important contributions to the success of their minority graduates by the establishment of an ongoing career counseling service. The formal assistance and personal linkages created in school could still be made available to recent graduates who confront a professional situation or a personal reaction where guidance would be helpful. The ability to get some advice or talk out a problem in a noncorporate setting may be of great benefit in the early stages of a career, and a school-sponsored service could either provide the assistance directly or act as a transmitter putting the recent graduate in touch with an alumnus who has volunteered to help. Certainly, an employee must learn to seek advice from within his or her company, but the existence of a colleague, a former instructor, or a counselor at school might ease the transition problems that may occur in the early stages of a career.

In a different vein, a graduate school of business should seek feedback from the employers of its minority graduates. The purpose is not to keep tabs on individual careers but to obtain information about how the school can improve the educational experience of its minority graduates. No doubt relevant corporate executives would be willing to participate in a process that identifies strengths and weaknesses and develops programs to improve upon both.

III. CONCLUSION

Ensuring the upward mobility of minority managers is an issue that requires the involvement of individual managers (minority *and* majority), corporations and their executives, and schools of business. Efforts to increase the opportunities for and the successes of minority managers can benefit by cooperation and collaboration among schools of business and corporations. There are no easy answers, and a proprietary approach to the issue is counterproductive. This chapter has identified some strategies for action that should be considered, adapted, and replaced by better ideas. But action must be taken, for the problem is significant and cannot be resolved by one sector alone.

16

Toward the Benefits of
Multicultural Management

Donna E. Thompson and Nancy DiTomaso

Minorities are not making the same progress as nonminorities in the executive ranks. As we have discussed throughout the book, the organizing framework we have used to explore this fact has been the problem-solving process. We hope this volume has provided the reader with some ideas about what can and should be done, rather than what has not been done. Much of the previous work on the topic has documented the problems faced by minorities rather than their progress. This book has taken a proactive approach to the topic. It has attempted to provide the background for a better understanding of why minority managers have not yet reached top management positions in proportionate numbers in most corporations as well as what has been done to ensure their success. In this final chapter, we would like to conclude with some thoughts on the future.

I. WHERE DO WE GO FROM HERE?

Clearly, we are dealing with a multifaceted, complex problem that has a number of critical issues that need to be addressed. An initial reaction that some readers might have at the conclusion of the book is that the search for solutions in the preceding chapters really did not come up with anything novel. Others may believe that organizations have done everything they can do with regard to affirmative action and equal employment opportunity, that it is just a matter of time before women and minorities advance into higher managerial ranks. But, as we have seen in the preceding discussions, that

Donna E. Thompson and Nancy DiTomaso • Rutgers Graduate School of Management, Newark, New Jersey 07102.

could take anywhere from 50 to 80 years (e.g., see Kanter, Chapter 14) and even then, there is no guarantee. Moreover, as the examples in Chapter 5 by Fernandez illustrate, although some progress has been made, the unfortunate fact is that prejudice and discrimination are "alive and well" in American corporations.

What is novel about the solutions that have been proposed throughout this volume is the emphasis that has been placed on the need for organizational policies, practices and structures to change, not just the individual. That is, what we have seen is a *need for structural changes* within American corporations and less "blaming of the victim" or the individual minority employee. In addition, our findings underscore the fact that *each minority group has a unique set of problems* or faces a different set of hurdles in their efforts to successfully advance to upper-level management positions. Moreover, they also suggest that the problems experienced by minority women may differ in many respects from those experienced by minority men (and for nonminority women may differ from those of various minority groups. It follows therefore, that the solutions to these problems and issues must be different as well. What we as authors would like to suggest is that organizations take somewhat of a new, "fresh," approach to this "old problem" that they have been grappling with. Systematic, programmatic organizational intervention is needed that includes the individual employee and the system-wide properties of the organization.

The first and perhaps most critical step in this approach requires that organizations *reexamine their culture* before launching any such changes. Numerous examples abound in the organizational change literature that underscore the need to examine and change organizational culture in order to bring about any successful and long-lasting organizational change. This reexamination of an organization's culture involves not only the identification of actual norms, values, customs, or rituals that may exist within a company but of desired ones as well. It entails the operationalization of what is currently needed for success in a particular organization as well as what is likely to be needed in the future. The discrepancies between the current culture and the desired culture should be identified along with what is needed to bring the organization closer to the desired state. This systematic approach must move beyond evaluating the company's culture and include a careful assessment of other potential barriers to organizational success such as the context within which the organization operates (e.g., the complexity or stability of the environment); the strategy, structure, and reward system of the organization; and the communication system and the human resource systems (e.g., career development systems, performance evaluation, and training and development).

The findings from this evaluation process form the basis for the strategic planning, setting, and *integration* of clear business and human resource objectives. Thus the management of human resources becomes an integral part of the business and not just a "nice thing" to do for their employees. The "payoff" to companies that have achieved this integration are many and have been well-documented in such popular books as *In Search of Excellence* (Peters and Waterman, 1982), *The Change Masters* (Kanter, 1983), and *High Output Management* (Grove, 1983). As a consequence of this integration of business and human resource objectives, there will be a strong top management commitment to human resource programs because they are serving important business objectives. As we saw in our discussion of corporate programs for ensuring minority advancement in Chapter 11, top management endorsement and support was a critical component to success in all of the participating companies. Moreover, equal employment opportunity, affirmative action, and other human resource programs were viewed as an integral part of each company's business philosophy.

Organizations have found that their ability to adapt to the massive corporate restructuring, turbulent external environments, increased foreign competition, political, economic, and demographic changes depends at least in part on how skillfully they have been able to manage their resources, including human resources. In short, organizations need to acknowledge that their culture and the accompanying organizational structures that maintain that culture needs to be changed to include good strategic human resource systems. Managerial resources, in particular, especially at the higher levels, are the most critical resource in most organizations. The odds are that in many American companies, the makeup of their employee population has changed over the years. Just as it is likely that they have had to adapt the way they manage their business in response to the economy, technology, or competition, they now must respond to the changing nature of their work force. In many cases, they will find that they have become *multicultural*. A diversity of values, perspectives, and sometimes language exists within their company. Such diversity needs to be reflected in their top management team so that the organization can capitalize on the wealth of diverse talents, skills, and resources it provides. And managing these differences may require a new corporate culture, complementary organizational structures, policies, and practices that support that culture and special managerial talents.

It is not unusual for organizations to acknowledge the impact that culture can have on the effectiveness of their overseas operations. In fact, many of them spend a considerable amount of money improving the way they handle the operations of their divisions and subsidiaries abroad, training their employees to adapt to the host country's culture. Indeed a "buzz word" in recent times has been the phrase *multicultural management*. For the most part, however, this phrase has been restricted to overseas operations. What we are proposing, here, is that organizations acknowledge the changes that have taken place within the walls of their organizations and adopt a multicultural perspective in the management of their home locations.

Parallels can be drawn between the "culture shock" that minority or nonminority female managers may experience in their attempts to advance further up the corporate ladder into higher levels of management and the "culture shock" often experienced when Americans begin working in a foreign country. For example, they may encounter different norms of behavior and values. Their new colleagues and bosses at these higher levels may be very different from them (e.g., family and educational backgrounds, recreational interests). Business may be conducted by a different set of rules that requires them to develop or acquire a new set of skills. The language may be different with unfamiliar professional jargon, or cliches. Behavior patterns, operational procedures, and performance standards may differ as well.

Almost inevitably, many Americans working overseas initially respond to this "new" business environment with some feeling of discomfort. If intensified, this discomfort can lead to changes in job attitudes (e.g., lower job satisfaction, organizational commitment, or job involvement). Moreover, they may rely on their original culture even more because of the discomfort and frustration experienced. The psychological consequences of such an adaptation or accommodation process may result in considerable stress being experienced and an increased use of defense mechanisms. Consequently, work performance may suffer. What we are suggesting here is that the movement into the higher levels of management by minority managers may have a similar devastating impact on the individual and in turn, organizational productivity, because of the nature of the corporate cultures that characterize so many American businesses. Changing these cultures so that diversity and heterogeneity are viewed as valued assets will enhance their own organizational effectiveness as well as that of their minority managers.

II. WHY ADOPT A MULTICULTURAL MANAGEMENT PERSPECTIVE?

The likelihood that organizations will succeed in their efforts to promote women and minorities into highly visible upper-middle- and top-level positions will be increased substantially with the adoption of a multicultural management perspective. That means a more effective and efficient use of human resources that can be important in the fast-paced, dynamic environments most companies are operating within at the present time. But it means much more than that. The premise on which this book has been based is that discrimination is a cost not only to those who are excluded but also to those who do the excluding. Ensuring minority success in corporate management through the adoption of a multicultural management perspective can result in a number of positive outcomes for corporations, society, and minority managers themselves. Such a culture fosters more innovative and creative decision making, satisfying work environments, and better products because all people who have a contribution to make are encouraged to be involved in a meaningful way. In our complex and ever-changing world, more information, more points of view, more ideas and reservations are better than fewer. Furthermore, in the interdependent world we live in, the more people who buy into the process, the more likely it will succeed.

Without such a multicultural management perspective that values diversity, organizational efforts to increase the representation of minorities in their top executive ranks are likely to fail. As has been well-documented within this volume and elsewhere, to date, many attempts to ensure the advancement of minorities into upper-level management positions have not been very successful. Some of the interventions they have used have been "band-aids," treating symptoms but failing because they have not really addressed the underlying problems caused by the organizational culture, structure, reward, or other management systems. Often, interventions have taken the form of "special training" programs. As we have seen in far too many organizations, you cannot attempt to "open up" critical and controversial issues in a one-shot sensitivity training session where you encourage managers to change and get results. As Ralph H. Killman points out in his book, *Beyond the Quick Fix: Managing Five Tracks to Organizational Success* (1984), organizational change requires a comprehensive diagnosis, which in turn, must include an assessment and integration of culture, strategy, structure, and management skills. The action plan for the change that results from this diagnosis must include systematic steps with sufficient time for their execution if long-lasting improvements in morale and performance are to result.

In other words, what we have learned from our past efforts to ensure the success of minorities in management is that you *cannot* just take a program or intervention and "plug it in" and expect it to be successful without changing the supporting organizational culture in any way. The companies represented in Chapter 11 that have been more successful in launching programs for ensuring minority advancement have begun to address their basic human resource policies and corporate culture in a systematic fashion. Moreover, each of their interventions has also been somewhat unique, tailored to "fit" the needs of their particular organization. Kram's work (1985a,b) on corporate mentoring programs also serves as a useful illustration of how critical certain organizational conditions, including the corporate culture, can be to the success of this type of career development program. She found, for example, that opportunities for frequent and open communication between individuals and across hierarchical and departmental boundaries must be established. In addition, organizational members themselves must have the necessary interpersonal skills and desire to build such mentoring relationships. Last, the corporate culture, reward systems, job design, and other human resource management systems must support such relationships. If not met, conditions such as these can pose serious obstacles to the success of a mentoring program. Kram's work further underscores the need to use systematic principles of planned change (e.g., systematic data collection, diagnosis, action planning, intervention, and evaluation) when designing and implementing an effective mentoring system so that it can be tailored to meet the demands of a particular organizational context.

The history of organizational efforts to establish successful affirmative action and equal employment opportunity programs that was described in Chapter 1 also necessitates the use of a systematic and programmatic organizational intervention approach. As Kanter pointed out in her discussion of the importance of structural theory and structural change for ensuring minority achievement in corporations (see Chapter 14), many employees in American corporations suffer from "verbal fatigue." That is, people are, quite frankly, tired of talking about affirmative action. If, however, organizations adopt a multicultural management perspective and implement the complementary organizational changes that are consistent with such a perspective, they are more apt to succeed in their efforts. Unfortunately, the history of affirmative action and equal employment opportunity programs in this country has left most people (i.e., minorities and nonminorities, men and women) feeling that they have not been fairly treated or that they have themselves been victims of discrimination. A multicultural management perspective promotes a perception of equity. Equity, in turn, is a powerful mediating variable impacting on employee morale, goal setting, effort, and performance and therefore, organizational productivity (e.g., Katzell and Thompson, n.d.).

Adopting a multicultural management perspective does require that organizations learn to place a positive value on *diversity*. Indeed, if one were to study the top management teams in many American corporations one would undoubtedly describe them as being homogeneous. Very often, they are characterized by individuals who come from similar backgrounds, sharing alma maters, extracurricular interests, and even religion. The barriers this can create have been underscored in several of the papers in this book (see, for example, the discussion of such obstacles to management mobility and productivity by John L. Jones in Chapter 11). In many companies, the selection of such a homogeneous top management team has been an integral part of the overall strategy of the organization. For example, John Fernandez (Chapter 5) quotes Chester Bernard that a "culturally homogeneous (all the same) group of managers was necessary for the smooth, efficient functioning of a corporation." However, as we have already suggested, it is likely that the rest of the work force in many organizations can best be described as heterogeneous. A wide variety of different types of people comprise the lower ranks of many American corporations: women, minorities, people of different ethnicities, citizenship, age, class, regions of the country, high tech and low tech, old school and new school. In effect, they bring to their organizations a variety of different subcultures—different value orientations, patterns of socialization. problem-solving styles, means of communication and language, custom, and habits. By adopting a multicultural perspective, companies will be able to capitalize on the variety of perspectives that this diversity of people brings to their organizations.

At the present time, most organizations have not placed a positive value on this diversity. Consequently, they have not capitalized on this important resource. This is a strange phenomenon, particularly in light of the fact that organizations frequently resort to going outside the organization when filling higher-level management jobs (often in spite of promotion-from-within policies) because they need a "new" perspective or a "different" viewpoint. Despite this acknowledgment of the value of different orientations to the management of their organization, they fail to realize, develop, and utilize the wealth of talent that lies within their own corporate walls. This resource has the potential capacity for better problem solving, creative, innovative thinking, development of new ideas, and better ways of doing things that will become increasingly important for organizations over the next several decades. Research studies from the group problem-solving and decision-making literatures provide evidence demonstrating how better quality, more creative solutions, new ideas or products can come from having people work together who have different perspectives, knowledge, abilities, skills, or cognitive styles (for reviews of research in these areas, see Goodman, 1986; Guzzo, 1982; Hoffman, 1979; McGrath, 1984).

In short, adopting a multicultural perspective and creating a culture (and establishing supporting organizational structures and policies) that values diversity will enhance organizational productivity. With such a perspective, organizations will begin to confront the conflict that often exists within their organizations as a result of the diversity of their work force and the improper way it has been handled. Most organizations tend to avoid it or deny that such conflict exists. In dealing with it, organizations will have to recognize the sensitivity and the uncomfortableness that may exist on both sides and that it is better to deal with sensitive issues than to sweep them aside. Dealing with this conflict and working toward successful resolution strategies will lead to a more efficient and effective use of human resources. People will not use up all of their energy in conflict, withholding of information, and diverting their attention from the most critical problems of the organization.

Addressing this need to reevaluate corporate culture and adopting one that values diversity and conflict resolution will also help organizations adapt better to changes in environment, technology, and culture. The kinds of changes that we foresee over the next several decades—more decentralization, more emphasis on entrepreneuralism within large companies, and stress on creativity, innovation, and sophisticated technologies will likely lead to even more conflict, misunderstanding, and diversity. Organizations must learn to deal with such diversity in order to survive well.

III. WHAT FACTORS CONTRIBUTE TO SUCCESSFUL MULTICULTURAL MANAGEMENT?

Some factors are found in organizational issues. Some relate to the skill of the manager in the organization. And still others relate to the diverse subgroups within the organization. Most of these have been discussed elsewhere in this volume. What we will attempt to do here is to highlight and integrate them.

A. Organizational Issues

First and *foremost*, corporations need to address structural and other organizational level issues if they are going to succeed in creating a culture that values diversity. Thomas Pettigrew's research on the social psychology of race relations (1971, 1984) that has been conducted over a 30-year period has documented the need to change society's institutions in order to improve race relations or to achieve racial equality. His research and that of other social scientists have long challenged the dominant recommendations that have focused primarily on changing the attitudes of white people toward blacks. Pettigrew believed that institutional components of prejudice were as important as individual ones in the development and maintenance of racial attitudes. Throughout his career, he has maintained that institutionalized prejudices require institutional change (see Pettigrew, 1971, 1984, for a more detailed description of his beliefs and research). According to Pettigrew (as cited by Kimmel, 1986), modern forms of racism are "more subtle, indirect, procedural and ostensibly nonracial." If the structure of institutions such as the workplace are changed to facilitate and encourage optimal black–white contact, racial attitudes will improve.

Changing the structure of an American corporation requires that it view its human resources and their diversity as critical components of their own organizational effectiveness and productivity. This value, in turn, should be an integral part of the organizational mission statement along with the organizational structure, goals, policies, and practices that are designed to carry out that mission.

Strong and visible support, endorsement, and implementation of this organizational mission statement by top management must occur. The critical role that strong endorsement by top management played in the success of corporate policies and practices was well documented in Chapter 11. Moreover, the more general literature on organizational change underscores the important role that top management must play for any organizational change or intervention to succeed.

Every employee at every level of the organization needs to feel ownership of those objectives that will lead to the attainment of the organizational mission. Goal setting should be practiced throughout the organization. Accountability for the attainment of those goals is also required. If appropriate, some form of participation should be used in the setting of these goals or to help manage the organizational change process. The valuable role that participation by employees can have (e.g., the use of employees as facilitators at Merck or as role models in an AT&T program) was evident in the successful corporate programs discussed in Chapter 11. Similarly, the need for accountability was discussed in several chapters of this book (see, for example, Chapters 8, 11, and 15).

Human resource policies and practices need to be evaluated and appropriate changes made to make them more consistent with the organizational mission. High performance standards are needed along with good feedback and performance appraisal systems. Pay needs to be based on performance, differentiating poor from good performers. Systematic programs such as these are critical factors to creating an environment that people will perceive as being fair and equitable. Quality human resource programs can also increase employee commitment to the organization that means they will be more likely to identify, accept, and work toward the achievement of the organization's goals. If they are more satisfied, more involved in their jobs, and more committed to the organization, they are also less likely to leave the organization. Consequently, such systems may be useful in preventing the high turnover rates among top-performing women and minorities. Last, recent research showing that such policies can affect people's performance and therefore, the organization's productivity will be enhanced (for research demonstrating the impact of human resource programs on employee morale, turnover, and productivity, see Guzzo, Jette, and Katzell, 1985; Katzell and Guzzo, 1983; Katzell and Thompson, 1985; Peters and O'Connor, 1982).

Human resource programs also need to be integrated so that they are consistent with systematic career development. For example, Spilerman suggests in Chapter 2 that companies may improve their success rates in promoting minorities to middle- and upper-level management positions if they institute early recruitment programs for them and offer rewards for completing college. Some of the current "popular" trends in human resource management programs may facilitate the attainment of successful multicultural management as well. For example, the current emphasis on teamwork, whether it be in the context of project teams, gainsharing, employee stock ownership, or quality of work-life groups holds promise for combating discrimination and prejudice within our corporate walls if certain conditions are met. Direct intergroup contact can result in reduced racial stereotyping and increased liking for members of the other race (e.g., Cook, 1984, 1985; Riordan, 1978).

Organizations must also deal with the conflict that is an inherent part of their diversity and not adopt a pattern of smoothing or avoidance. As Kanter suggests in her discussion of the "pyramid squeeze" in Chapter 14, the conflict that exists because of the lack of positive management of diversity is likely to intensify in the future. Also, the climate of the country in general is also likely to intensify the perceptions of differences among subgroups of the population and intensify conflict. As we saw in the discussion of company programs in Chapter 11, programs and policies related to minorities and women have been affected by factors external to the organization or by major changes in the business such as mergers, acquisitions, and divestitures. Corporate programs that not only train their employees in conflict resolution but provide mechanisms and time procedures for dealing with the conflict within the organization need to be developed. Such programs would demonstrate the value of adopting a win–win orientation toward conflict resolution and not a win–lose orientation (i.e., just because a minority gets promoted, does *not* mean that a white loses).

B. Managerial Skills

Managers need to be trained to be less ethnocentric. That is, they need to be trained so that they do not judge others by using their own personal or cultural standards. A manager cannot successfully communicate if he or she views another's subculture and its customs as foolish, ridiculous, or simply not quite as good as his or her own.

Managers also need to realize that there is no single way of doing anything and that others may view a situation from a totally different perspective. The fact is that most managers feel comfortable in a predictable environment. Homogeneous environments are more predictable. Moreover, we tend to like and prefer to associate with people who are similar to us. Managers must learn to deal with the discomfort that they may experience when interacting with a minority or nonminority female employee who is different from them. If not managed properly, this discomfort may lead to frustration and negative feelings that not only discourage positive and effective work relations but may impact on the decisions they make about the individuals working for them. Such decisions, in turn, affect their career advancement.

Competent multicultural managers are able to develop solutions to problems faced by using this cultural diversity as a resource rather than as a barrier to overcome. This is not an easy task, particularly in light of the time pressures and turbulent environment that most managers operate within. This will require many managers to change the way that they think about and perceive people. It requires them to become aware of the implications their behavior has for male and female employees from different cultural backgrounds. There is some evidence that teaching people to think actively about others, rather than to go along with previously established categories of distinction can be a useful strategy for overcoming prejudice (e.g., Langer and Imber, 1980; Langer, Bashner, and Chanowitz, 1985).

However, awareness itself is not enough. Such awareness must be put into "practice." The productivity, growth, and even continued existence of any organization depends to a large extent on its ability to motivate all employees. Managers or supervisors play a key role in employee motivation (e.g., Katzell and Thompson, 1987). When all employees are from the same culture, this is not as difficult as in a multicultural organization. The manager must learn how to motivate employees and individuals, to help them see how their own personal goals can be achieved at the same time that they are working toward the organization's goals.

Managers must also accept and learn how to administer and implement the human resource programs and systems that were described in the preceding discussion of organizational issues. The effectiveness and impact that any one of these programs can have on any individual employee is largely a function of how well a manager can implement it. Above all, the manager must take an active role in the career development of his or her subordinates and learn how to give meaningful and timely performance-based feedback. With regard to minorities and women, he or she must be aware of the unique barriers and problems each one of them may have to deal with in order to succeed. By taking this active role, the manager can help alleviate some of the discomfort and frustration that these employees experience that lead them to either leave the organization or demonstrate poorer performance than they might otherwise. As suggested earlier, the manager must be held accountable for the development of his or her people and rewarded accordingly.

How do we develop these necessary skills? This is not an easy question to answer. Although we do not propose to have all of the answers, we do believe that creating an organizational culture that values diversity, along with the supporting organizational structure and human resource programs and policies that have been discussed, will result in an environment that will facilitate the acquisition of such skills. The fact that human resource objectives would be integrated with the business objectives should help substantially. Intensive, systematic training will be critical as well. Such training should be mandatory and *ongoing*. That is, a certain amount of training should be mandated annually. Managers should also receive feedback from their employees (in an anonymous way) at regular intervals. Such training would encompass the areas described before as well as multicultural team building and the management of conflict and communication skills in general.

C. Issues for Minorities and Nonminority Women

The chapters in this volume have also highlighted a number of things that minorities and nonminority women themselves need to do to ensure their successful advancement (e.g., hard work, perseverance, determination, self-confidence, positive attitude, and sense of oneself). For example, we know that educational attainment and fields of specialization play a crucial role in expanding employment opportunities prior to labor-market entry (see Spilerman, Chapter 2). The unique issues relevant to each specific minority group or women have also been discussed (see, for example, Smith and Tienda, Chapter 3; or the minority perspectives on success in business presented in Chapter 10).

In addition to those things that have already been discussed, a workshop preparing them for the "culture shock" they are likely to experience as they move up the corporate ladder might prove useful as well. Consistent with this, a training program could also be developed that helps them address the internal barriers that may often hinder or prevent them from advancing that John L. Jones discusses in Chapter 11. Such a program might address the effects that expectations can have on behavior, for example. Expectations often have a self-fulfilling impact. That is, when people expect others to reject them, they may act in ways that confirm these predictions (Snyder and Ickes, 1985). Last and perhaps most important, these training programs should place a particularly *strong* emphasis on career development so that minorities can take responsibility for their own careers.

IV. WHAT DIRECTIONS SHOULD FUTURE RESEARCH PURSUE?

We cannot leave this discussion of the benefits of multicultural management or what can be done to ensure the successful advancement of minorities into higher level management positions without discussing the need for research. There seem to be an almost overwhelming number of research questions that need to be explored. Many of our contributing authors have ended their chapters with suggested research directions. This is due in part to the fact that what we are really talking about in this book is career development that at the present time is still a very young science. We are also dealing with a very sensitive subject. Consequently, there are some very real methodological issues and constraints that have presented barriers and blocks to conducting research in this area in the past that will need to be addressed in the future.

Future research needs to *systematically* explore the critical organizational, individual, and interpersonal factors facilitating and hindering the successful advancement of nonminority women and minorities in management. The development of successful managers and key decision makers is a complex process. Research and experience have led to the development of a number of theories, hypotheses, and programs designed to increase the numbers of minorities and women in higher-level management positions. Unfortunately, as the statistics show, these programs often fail to produce the desired results. The fact is that many of these have only focused on a single factor such as individual abilities or skills necessary for managerial success. The key to finding out what leads to successful advancement of women and minorities requires a carefully thought-out process that takes into consideration such factors as organizational characteristics, human resource policies and practices, the nature of the business, career development patterns within the organization, and individual needs, preferences, and attitudes. At the present time, we simply do not know what leads to the successful advancement of nonminority women and minorities. Do similar or different profiles characterize the career paths for minority, nonminority, male, and female managers? Does the same profile of factors predict successful advancement into top-level management positions for different types of organizations or even different functional business areas (e.g., marketing, finance, or administration)? The key to successful multicultural management and the implementation of a successful advancement program may be to tailor the program to the specific needs and characteristics of an organization and its members.

Future research also needs to be *programmatic* in order to systematically study a wide range of individual and organizational factors that may be related to the successful development of minority, nonminority, male, and female managers. These factors should be selected on the basis of findings from prior theory and research suggesting that they may influence successful managerial development and advancement. Examples of these factors include organizational design characteristics, human resource policies and practices, career development patterns, organizational culture, motivation, communication patterns, and managerial style. Series of studies need to be designed to examine these critical individual, social, and organizational factors.

In order to address some of the methodological problems encountered in the past, whenever possible, future studies should employ *multiple types of measurement* (e.g., survey, interview, and objective statistics) at *multiple levels of management* within the organizations (e.g., top, middle, and lower management levels) across a number of organizations. In addition, they should include a sample consisting of minority, nonminority, male, and female managers. Objective measures of selection, development, promotion, and turnover rates for minority, nonminority, male, and female managers need to be gathered as well. The information from these sources should be integrated to provide a more comprehensive understanding of how the specific variables under study relate to one another in either the facilitation or hindrance of male or female minority or nonminority success in business. Moreover, because the findings from each of these studies will be related to selection, development, promotion, and turnover rates for various groups of employees, their impact on the bottom line could be estimated as well.

Examples of the kinds of topics and research questions that future research needs to address are:

I. Career Development

  A. Are the career development profiles for minorities, nonminorities, female, and male managers similar?
  B. If not, how do they differ?
  C. Do they differ within the same organization, or across industries, for example?
  D. What do the profiles look like at lower, middle, and upper levels of management?

II. Human Resource Policies and Practices

  A. What human resource programs and policies are related to successful advancement?
  B. What are the characteristics of these programs? For example, does a specific type of performance appraisal and feedback system appear to be related to successful advancement across various organizations?
  C. Are programs that have been specifically designed to facilitate the advancement of women and/or minority managers effective? Or are companies more successful if they do not have such special programs and include women and minorities in their regular programs designed to develop managerial talent?

III. Communication and Information Flow

  A. What informal social networks exist within the organization? Are minority and nonminority women managers integral members of these networks?
  B. Who talks to whom? Where do they get information? How easy or difficult is it to get information?
  C. What kind of information is provided from supervising managers? Does the type of information provided differ for nonminority women and minorities compared to white men?
  D. When is miscommunication most likely to occur? Are there consistent

misinterpretations of verbal and/or nonverbal communication behaviors characteristic of minority, nonminority, male, and female managers?

IV. Motivation: Productivity and Turnover

A. How does the organization's motivational climate (e.g., allocation of rewards, goal setting, and feedback) hinder selection, advancement, and retention?
B. What things are turning people on and off about their jobs and the organization?
C. Do the same things motivate minority, nonminority, male and, female managers?

V. Management Style

A. Do minority, nonminority, male, and female managers have similar management or work styles?
B. Is a similar pattern of management styles found at lower, middle, and upper levels of management for each of these groups? If not, how do they differ? How do these styles compare with those characterizing the members of the top management of the organization?
C. How are managers from each of these groups perceived by other members of the organization, namely their subordinates, peers, and supervisors?

VI. Organizational Culture

A. How does organizational culture (e.g., values, general attitudes, specific attitudes toward EEO and AA) relate to successful advancement?
B. Is one culture more conducive than another?
C. Do subcultures exist within an organization?
D. How is the culture perceived by top, middle, and lower management and rank-and-file workers?
E. Do subcultures differ for minorities and nonminority women? If so, in what ways? Does this help or hinder?

VII. Organizational Design Characteristics

A. Why are some organizations more successful than others in hiring, developing, promoting, and retaining female and minority managers?
B. What organizational characteristics (e.g., size, industry) are related to success?

V. SUMMARY AND CONCLUSIONS

The results of future research such as this should provide a number of benefits to the business community, minority, and nonminority men and women pursuing careers in management, and the growing body of knowledge on managerial development and effectiveness.

Organizations spend a large proportion of their budgets on wages and salaries. Therefore, it is important to use human resources wisely. By creating an environment—a culture—that says that people matter, that all members of the organization are an important asset, organizations can increase their effectiveness and efficiency. When people feel that they can make a contribution to an organization and feel that the organization is acting in their interests, they put forth more effort and are more committed workers. In concrete terms, this means better problem solving; creative, innovative thinking; the development of new ideas; and better ways of doing business.

VI. REFERENCES

Cook, Stuart W. 1984. Cooperative interaction in multiethnic contexts. In N. Miller and M. Brewer (Eds.), *Groups in contact: The psychology of desegregation* (pp. 155–185). New York: Academic Press.

Cook, Stuart W. 1985. Experimenting on social issues: The case of school desegregation. *American Psychologist* 40:452–460.

Goodman, Paul S. 1986. *Designing effective work groups*. San Francisco: Jossey-Bass.

Grove, Andrew, S. 1983. *High output management*. New York: Random House.

Guzzo, Richard A. 1982. *Improving group decision making in organizations*. New York: Academic Press.

Guzzo, Richard A., Richard Jette, and Raymond A. Katzell. 1985. The effects of psychologically based intervention programs on worker productivity: A meta-analysis. *Personnel Psychology* 38:275–291.

Hare, A. Paul. 1976. *Handbook of small group research*. New York: The Free Press.

Hoffman, L. Richard. 1979. *The group problem-solving process*. New York: Praeger.

Kanter, Rosabeth Moss. 1983. *The change masters*. New York: Simon and Schuster.

Katzell, Raymond A., and Richard A. Guzzo. 1983. Psychological approaches to productivity improvement. *American Psychologist* 38:468–472.

Katzell, Raymond A., and Donna E. Thompson. n.d. *An integrative theory of work attitudes and motivation*. Unpublished manuscript.

Katzell, Raymond A., and Donna E. Thompson. 1985. *The motivation audit*. Paper presented at the meetings of the American Psychological Association, Los Angeles.

Katzell, Raymond A., and Donna E. Thompson. 1986. *Empirical research on a comprehensive theory of work motivation*. Paper presented at the 21st International Congress of Applied Psychology, Jerusalem, Israel.

Katzell, Raymond A., and Donna E. Thompson. 1987. *How leadership works*. Paper presented at the Conference on Military Leadership: Traditions and Future Trends, Annapolis.

Killman, R. H. 1984. *Beyond the quick fix: Managing five tracks to organizational success*. San Francisco: Jossey-Bass.

Kimmel, Michael S. 1986. A prejudice against prejudice. *Psychology Today* 20:52.

Kram, Kathy, E. 1985a. *Mentoring at work*. Glenview, IL: Scott, Foresman.

Kram, Kathy E. 1985b. Mentoring in the workplace. In Douglass T. Hall and associates (Eds.), *Career development in organizations* (pp. 160–201). San Francisco: Jossey-Bass.

Langer, E. J., and L. Imber. 1980. The role of mindfulness in the perception of deviance. *Journal of Personality and Social Psychology* 39:360–367.

Langer, E. J., R. S. Bashner, and B. Chanowitz. 1985. Decreasing prejudice by increasing discrimination. *Journal of Personality and Social Psychology* 49:113–120.

McGrath, Joseph E. 1984. *Groups, intereaction, and performance*. Englewood Cliffs, NJ: Prentice-Hall.

Peters, Thomas J., and Robert H. Waterman, Jr. 1982. *In search of excellence*. New York: Harper & Row.

Pettigrew, Thomas F. 1971. *Racially separate or together?* New York: McGraw-Hill.

Pettigrew, Thomas F. 1984. *A profile of the Negro American*. Princeton, NJ: Van Nostrand..

Riordan, C. 1978. Equal-status interracial contact: A review and revision of a concept. *International Journal of Intercultural Relations* 2:161–185.

Synder, Mark, and William Ickes. 1985. Personality and social behavior. In G. Lindsey and E. Aronson (Eds.), *The handbook of social psychology* (3rd ed., Vol. I, pp. 883–947). New York: Random House.

Index